Legal Fundamentals
FOR CANADIAN BUSINESS

RICHARD A. YATES *Simon Fraser University*

PEARSON
Prentice Hall

Toronto

Library and Archives Canada Cataloguing in Publication

Yates, Richard
Legal fundamentals for Canadian business / Richard A. Yates.

Includes index.
ISBN 0-13-127378-7

1. Commercial law—Canada. I. Title.

KE919.Y38 2006 346.7107 C2005-901992-1
KF889.Y38 2006

ISBN 0-13-127378-7

Vice President, Editorial Director: Michael J. Young
Editor in Chief, Business & Economics: Gary Bennett
Director of Marketing, Business & Economics: Bill Todd
Associate Editor: Stephen Broadbent
Production Editor: Jen Handel
Copy Editor: Nancy Carroll
Proofreader: Kelli Howey
Senior Production Coordinator: Patricia Ciardullo
Composition: Phyllis Seto
Art Director: Mary Opper
Interior and Cover Design: Michelle Bellemare
Cover Image: Getty Images

2 3 4 5 10 09 08 07 06

Printed and bound in the United States of America.

PEARSON
Prentice Hall

BRIEF CONTENTS

CONTENTS

PREFACE

Approach

Although some may raise their eyebrows at yet another business law text in an already crowded field, I have observed that most of the texts currently used are too extensive or detailed for some courses. I have attempted in this text to create a shorter book (only 10 chapters) without sacrificing essential content. I have found that the text usually drives the course, and many instructors complain that they don't have enough time in a 14-week term to deal with all of the subjects they would like to cover. Sometimes instructors teach a course that must be delivered in an even more condensed time frame. Some teach specialized courses in marketing, computers, finance, and the like and find that they have to spend so much time on a general introduction to business law that they don't have time to focus on the law that affects the specialized topic that is the primary objective of the course. This text gives business law instructors the flexibility to deal with all of the topics, to customize their course by supplementing it with additional material, and/or to concentrate on an area of specialization.

Many instructors feel a pressing need to deliver the introductory and foundation material efficiently so that there is enough time left to cover more advanced material. Hence, in this text there is only one introductory chapter setting out the history, institutions, and litigation processes used in Canada, only one chapter on torts, and three chapters on contracts. A great deal of effort has gone into making these chapters as efficient as possible, while still covering the essential concepts and rules. The remaining five chapters deal with more advanced and technical information—everything from the legal issues regarding agency and employment to the timely issues of intellectual property—and have not been simplified to the same extent as the first five. Although somewhat condensed here, these topics don't really lend themselves to abbreviation.

Features

I've incorporated several features in the text to engage students. Visuals are used to help students grasp concepts quickly.

Throughout the text there are **Case Summaries** designed to illustrate the legal concepts being discussed. Such case studies are the heart of any business law course and create a dynamic practical environment for a subject that, without them, would be dry and uninspiring at best.

For some I have also included **diagrams** that illustrate the legal relationships in the case. There are also a number of **figures** and **tables** included throughout the text; these are designed to clarify and summarize information so that it's easily accessible to students.

The **Cases for Discussion** at the end of each chapter are based on actual court reports. I have not included the decisions so that the cases can be used in assign-

CASE SUMMARY 6.7

Simpson v. Consumers' Association of Canada[9]

Inappropriate Sexual Comments and Conduct Can Constitute Just Cause for Termination

Mr. Simpson was the executive director of the Consumers' Association of Canada and over the years had been involved in many sexually inappropriate situations with several different female employees. After several complaints, he was dismissed from his employment for cause. He sued for wrongful dismissal, claiming he should have been given reasonable notice. At trial it was held that since these activities took place outside the workplace, they were not just cause for dismissal and he was awarded damages equivalent to 18 months' notice. On appeal, the court rejected this position finding that the various incidents did take place at job-related activities and constituted just cause. His conduct could not be justified as part of a sexually charged atmosphere at work since he was the cause of that situation. Nor could he rely on the fact that there was no sexual harassment policy in place, since it was his obligation as manager to prevent this sort of thing from happening. Even long-term senior employees can be terminated without notice if they sexually harass other employees.

ments or for classroom discussions. Instructors have access to the actual outcomes in the Instructor's Manual, or students can follow the reference to discover the outcome for themselves.

Also at the end of each chapter, **Questions for Further Discussion** can be used in class or group discussions. They raise issues with respect to the topics discussed. There are no solutions provided as they are intended to point out the dilemmas often faced by those who make or enforce these legal principles.

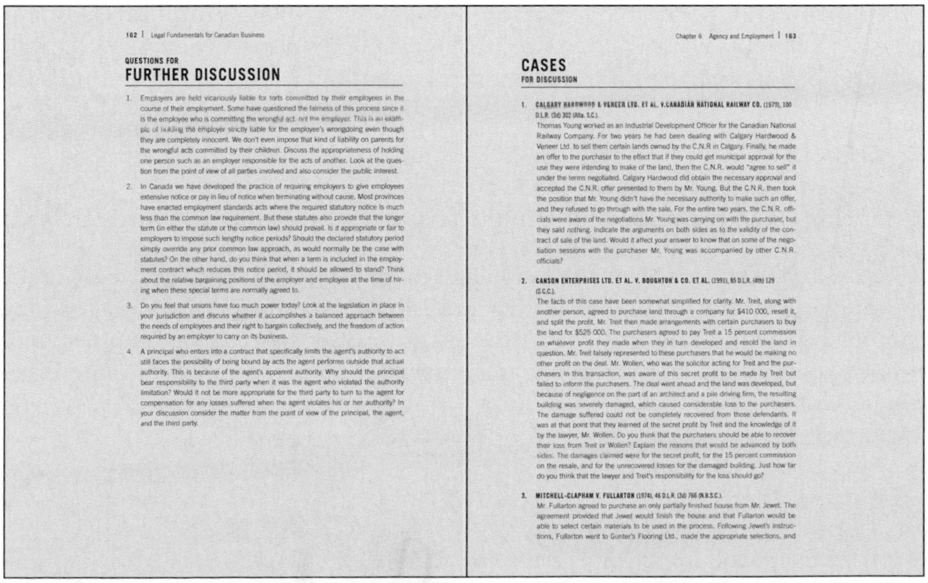

162 | Legal Fundamentals for Canadian Business

QUESTIONS FOR
FURTHER DISCUSSION

1. Employers are held vicariously liable for torts committed by their employees in the course of their employment. Some have questioned the fairness of this process since it is the employee who is committing the wrongful act, not the employer. This is an example of holding the employer strictly liable for the employee's wrongdoing even though they are completely innocent. We don't even impose that kind of liability on parents for the wrongful acts committed by their children. Discuss the appropriateness of holding one person such as an employer responsible for the acts of another. Look at the question from the point of view of all parties involved and also consider the public interest.
2. In Canada we have developed the practice of requiring employers to give employees extensive notice or pay in lieu of notice when terminating without cause. Most provinces have enacted employment standards acts where the required statutory notice is much less than the common law requirement. But these statutes also provide that the longer term (in either the statute or the common law) should prevail. Is it appropriate or fair to employers to impose such lengthy notice periods? Should the declared statutory period simply override any prior common law approach, as would normally be the case with statutes? On the other hand, do you think that when a term is included in the employment contract which reduces this notice period, it should be allowed to stand? Think about the relative bargaining positions of the employer and employee at the time of hiring when these special terms are normally agreed to.
3. Do you feel that unions have too much power today? Look at the legislation in place in your jurisdiction and discuss whether it accomplishes a balanced approach between the needs of employees and their right to bargain collectively, and the freedom of action required by an employer to carry on its business.
4. A principal who enters into a contract that specifically limits the agent's authority to act still faces the possibility of being bound by acts the agent performs outside that actual authority. This is because of the agent's apparent authority. Why should the principal bear responsibility to the third party when it was the agent who violated the authority limitation? Would it not be more appropriate for the third party to turn to the agent for compensation for any losses suffered when the agent violates his or her authority? In your discussion consider the matter from the point of view of the principal, the agent, and the third party.

Chapter 6 Agency and Employment | 163

CASES
FOR DISCUSSION

1. **CALGARY HARDWOOD & VENEER LTD. ET AL. V. CANADIAN NATIONAL RAILWAY CO.** (1979), 100 D.L.R. (3d) 302 (Alta. S.C.).
Thomas Young worked as an Industrial Development Officer for the Canadian National Railway Company. For two years he had been dealing with Calgary Hardwood & Veneer Ltd. to sell them certain lands owned by the C.N.R in Calgary. Finally, he made an offer to the purchaser to the effect that if they could get municipal approval for the use they were intending to make of the land, then the C.N.R. would "agree to sell" it under the terms negotiated. Calgary Hardwood did obtain the necessary approval and accepted the C.N.R. offer presented to them by Mr. Young. But the C.N.R. then took the position that Mr. Young didn't have the necessary authority to make such an offer, and they refused to go through with the sale. For the entire two years, the C.N.R. officials were aware of the negotiations Mr. Young was carrying on with the purchaser, but they said nothing. Indicate the arguments on both sides as to the validity of the contract of sale of the land. Would it affect your answer to know that on some of the negotiation sessions with the purchaser Mr. Young was accompanied by other C.N.R. officials?
2. **CANSON ENTERPRISES LTD. ET AL. V. BOUGHTON & CO. ET AL.** (1991), 85 D.L.R. (4th) 129 (S.C.C.).
The facts of this case have been somewhat simplified for clarity. Mr. Treit, along with another person, agreed to purchase land through a company for $410 000, resell it, and split the profit. Mr. Treit then made arrangements with certain purchasers to buy the land for $525 000. The purchasers agreed to pay Treit a 15 percent commission on whatever profit they made when they in turn developed and resold the land in question. Mr. Treit falsely represented to these purchasers that he would be making no other profit on the deal. Mr. Wollen, who was the solicitor acting for Treit and the purchasers in this transaction, was aware of this secret profit to be made by Treit but failed to inform the purchasers. The deal went ahead and the land was developed, but because of negligence on the part of an architect and a pile driving firm, the resulting building was severely damaged, which caused considerable loss to the purchasers. The damage suffered could not be completely recovered from those defendants. It was at that point that they learned of the secret profit by Treit and the knowledge of it by the lawyer, Mr. Wollen. Do you think that the purchasers should be able to recover their loss from Treit or Wollen? Explain the reasons that would be advanced by both sides. The damages claimed were for the secret profit, for the 15 percent commission on the resale, and for the unrecovered losses for the damaged building. Just how far do you think that the lawyer and Treit's responsibility for the loss should go?
3. **MITCHELL-CLAPHAM V. FULLARTON** (1974), 46 D.L.R. (3d) 766 (N.B.S.C.).
Mr. Fullarton agreed to purchase an only partially finished house from Mr. Jewet. The agreement provided that Jewet would finish the house and that Fullarton would be able to select certain materials to be used in the process. Following Jewet's instructions, Fullarton went to Gunter's Flooring Ltd., made the appropriate selections, and

Finally, the **Questions for Review** are designed to help students review the chapter material. As they respond to the questions, referring back to the content of the chapter, students should develop a good grasp of the concepts and principles contained in the chapter.

Supplements

Legal Fundamentals for Canadian Business is accompanied by a comprehensive supplements package on the **Instructor's Resource CD-ROM** (0-13-201826-8). This resource CD includes the following instructor supplements:

Instructor's Manual: This manual includes a number of aids, including outlines of how lectures might be developed, chapter summaries, answers to review questions, and suggestions for conducting classroom discussions. The court decisions for the end-of-chapter cases are also provided, and sample examination questions are included for each chapter.

TestGen: This supplement contains a comprehensive selection of multiple-choice, true/false, and short essay questions with answers. Each question has been checked for accuracy and is available in TestGen format. This testing software permits instructors to view and edit the existing questions, add questions, generate tests, and distribute the tests in a variety of formats. Powerful search and sort functions make it easy to locate questions and arrange them in any order desired. TestGen also enables instructors to administer tests on a local area network, have the tests graded electronically, and have the results prepared in electronic or printed reports. TestGen is compatible with Windows and Macintosh operating systems.

PowerPoint® Slides: This supplement provides a comprehensive selection of slides highlighting key concepts featured in the text to assist instructors and students.

These instructor supplements are also available for download from a password protected section of Pearson Education Canada's online catalogue (**vig.pearsoned.ca**). Navigate to the book's catalogue page to view a list of available supplements. See your local sales representative for details and access.

Acknowledgments

I would like to acknowledge the help of all those who have assisted in making the production of this work possible. My wife, Ruth, has helped, encouraged, and supported me in more ways than I can list. I wish to thank as well the reviewers whose suggestions and criticisms were invaluable as the text was honed and shaped into its final form, including:

Craig Dyer, *Red River College*
Gerry Lindley, *Seneca College*
David Mair, *Georgian College*
Greg Marshall, *Nova Scotia Community College*

Gail McKay, *University College of the Cariboo*
David Purvis, *Sir Sandford Fleming College*
Martha Spence, *Confederation College*
Don Valeri, *Douglas College*

Also, my thanks to the firm, guiding hands of all those at Pearson, who supported me throughout the long gestation period of this text, including Gary Bennett, Editor in Chief, Business and Economics; Laura Forbes, Acquisitions Editor; Stephen Broadbent, Associate Editor; Jennifer Handel, Production Editor; and Patricia Ciardullo, Senior Production Coordinator.

CHAPTER 1

The Canadian Legal System

An understanding of law and the legal system in Canada is essential for the business person. Business activities, like other forms of human endeavour, involve significant human interaction. Whether you are a manager, a consultant, a professional, or a consumer, you must deal with suppliers, employees, creditors, lawyers, insurance agents, landlords, accountants, shareholders, senior managers, as well as government agencies. All of these relationships carry with them important rights, responsibilities, and obligations. If you think of business as a game, the rules of the game are embodied in the law and you must know those rules in order to play. As with other aspects of business, it is not good enough to simply leave legal matters in the hands of the professionals. A basic understanding of the law is necessary to manage the legal affairs of a business and to be a knowledgeable client.

Knowledge of law is vital for business

Even lawyers sometimes forget the basics. For example, a lawyer in Vancouver recently forgot about his duty not to compete with a former client (called a fiduciary duty). He was sued and had to pay the profits he earned from that competing business. The judgment against him was in excess of $30 million.[1] This text reviews both the structure of the Canadian legal system and the principles that most impact people in their business dealings. The first chapter examines the underpinnings of the legal system and some basic Canadian institutions upon which the commercial legal environment is built.

What Is Law?

Most people think they understand what law is, but, in fact, an accurate definition is difficult to come by. For the purposes of this text, law is defined as **the body of rules that can be enforced by the courts or by other government agencies**. There

Definition: Law consists of rules enforceable in court

1. *3464920 Canada Inc. v. Strother*, 2005 BCCA 35, [2005] B.C.J. No. 80 (B.C.C.A.).

are serious problems even with this simple definition, but from a practical standpoint and for the purposes of this book, which is primarily about business law, law consists of rules with penalties that are likely to be enforced. We will focus on those rules that have an impact on commercial activity and business people. It is also important to realize that the rules are not enforced just by the courts, but that rules, having the status of laws, are also enforced by other government institutions (boards and agencies) that are intricately involved with the regulation of business. These include workers' compensation, employment insurance, taxation, and the like. A definition of law varies with an individual's philosophical position; consequently, the definition used here is simplistic at best.

It is important, especially for business people, not to confuse law and morality. The impetus for any given legal rule can vary from economic efficiency to political expediency. It may well be that the only justification for a law is historical, as in "it has always been that way." Hopefully, legal rules express some moral content, but no one should assume that because they are obeying the law, they are acting morally. Ethics has become an important aspect of any business education and with recent, high-profile incidents of corporate abuses, the topic of ethics has become a major area of discussion both at the academic and the practical levels. Law should play an important role in this discussion, if only to point out that law does not define ethical behaviour, and that business people should rise above the minimal requirements of the law.

While we are most concerned with **substantive law** in this text (the rules determining behaviour), we must also be aware of that other great body of law that is concerned with how legal process works (**procedural law**). While there will be some examination of public law, where the dispute involves the government (including criminal law and government regulation), the main thrust of the text relates to a study of the rules that govern business interactions. **Private**, or civil, **law** refers to the rules governing personal interactions where an individual enforces his or her rights by suing another who has injured them. While only a small portion of disputes ever get to court, legal rules are developed in the cases that do. Knowing that those principles will be enforced in subsequent judicial decisions enables parties to resolve their disputes without actually going to trial.

Sources

Each province has been given the right to determine its own law with respect to matters falling under its jurisdiction. Since private law is a provincial matter, it is not surprising that Quebec adopted the French legal system based on the Napoleonic Code. In fact, the French **Civil Code** traces its origins to the Romans and a unique characteristic is that it is a codified body of rules stating general principles that are applied by the courts to the problem before them. In this system the judge is not bound by precedent (following prior decided cases), but must apply the provisions of the Code. For example, when faced with the problem of determining liability in a personal injury case, the judge would apply section 1457 of the *Quebec Civil Code,* which states:

Quebec uses the *Civil Code*

> Every person has a duty to abide by the rules of conduct which lie upon him, according to the circumstances, usage or law, so as not to cause injury to another. Where he is endowed with reason and fails in this duty, he is responsible for any

injury he causes to another person and is liable to reparation for the injury, whether it be bodily, moral or material in nature.

When a person drives carelessly and injures another in Quebec, the judge would apply this provision and order that the driver pay compensation. The decisions of other judges might be interesting and persuasive, but the judge in Quebec is only required to apply the *Code.* Most other countries in the world use a variant of this codified approach to law, and it is this codification that makes the law predictable in those countries.

Other provinces use common law

Common law is based on cases

The other Canadian provinces and the territories adopted a system of law derived from England, referred to as the **common law**. The unique aspect of the common law system is that instead of following a code, the judge looks to prior case law. When faced with a particular problem, such as the personal injury situation described above, a common law judge would look at prior cases (normally brought to the judge's attention by the lawyers arguing the case), and choose the particular case that most closely resembles the one at hand. The judge will determine the obligations of the parties on the basis of that precedent. Of course, there is a complex body of rules to determine which **precedent** the judge must follow. Essentially, a case involving the same issue decided in a court higher in the judicial hierarchy is a binding precedent and must be followed. Thus a judge in the Provincial Court of British Columbia is bound to follow the decision of the Court of Appeal of that province but not the decision of a Court of Appeal in Ontario, which is in a different judicial hierarchy. That decision may be persuasive but is not binding. A considerable portion of a case report is usually devoted to an explanation of why the judge chose to follow one precedent rather than another. This process is referred to as **distinguishing cases**. Determining law through following precedent in our legal system is referred to as ***stare decisis***.

CASE SUMMARY 1.1

R. v. Clough[2]

Provincial Supreme Court Judge Must Follow Appeal Court Decision

Although this is a criminal case, not a business one, it illustrates how a lower court must follow the decision of a higher court. Ms. Clough was sentenced by a British Columbia Supreme Court judge to a nine-month jail term for possession of cocaine for the purposes of trafficking. That judge refused to follow a Court of Appeal case in a similar matter where a conditional sentence had been imposed (no prison time), claiming that case had been "wrongly decided." The British Columbia Court of Appeal overturned his decision and imposed a conditional sentence stating that the trial judge " . . . was bound by the rule of *stare decisis* to accept the decisions of this court to the extent that they may apply to the case before him." Judges who are lower in the hierarchy are bound to follow the decisions of the courts above them, even when they think those above them are wrong.

Common law developed by common law courts

The common law evolved from cases first decided in three common law courts set up under the king's authority during the Middle Ages in England. This body of

2. 2001 BCCA 613, [2001] B.C.J. 2336 (B.C.C.A.).

judges' decisions continued to develop in England and then in Canada. English-speaking provinces adopted the common law by declaration at different times in their history. British Columbia, for example, declared that the law of England would become the law of that province as of 1857 and Manitoba in 1870. Since adopting the common law of England, the courts of each province have added their own decisions, creating a unique body of case law particular to each province (see Figure 1.1).

Equity developed by Court of Chancery

A complicating factor in the development of the common law in England was the creation of the law of equity by the Courts of Chancery. For both political and institutional reasons the common law courts of England became harsh and inflexible, often not providing a right to sue or adequate remedies to satisfy the basic demands of justice. To provide relief from these inadequacies, the practice developed of petitioning the king to overcome these problems. Since, in theory, the king was the source of power for these courts, he also had the power to make orders overcoming individual injustices caused by their shortcomings. This task was soon assigned to others and eventually developed into the Court of Chancery. The common law courts and the Courts of Chancery were merged in the 19th century, but the body of rules developed by the Courts of Chancery (known as **equity**) remained separate. Today, when we talk about judge-made law in our legal system, we must differentiate between common law and the law of equity. For example, if someone erected a sign that encroached on your property, you could claim trespass and ask a court to have it removed. Monetary compensation is the normal common law remedy to trespass. An order to remove the sign would require an injunction, which is an equitable remedy. Equity then is a list of rules or principles from which a judge can draw to supplement the more restrictive provisions of the common law.

Statutes are passed by Parliament or legislatures

Our law is based on common law, equity, and statutes

The third body of law used in our courts is derived from government statutes. As a result of the English Civil War, the principle of **parliamentary supremacy** was firmly established with the consequence that any legislation passed by Parliament overrides judge-made law, whether in the form of common law or equity. Today in Canada most new law takes the form of statutes enacted by either the federal or the provincial legislatures. Since statutes override prior judge-made law, the judges will only follow them when the wording is very clear and specific, which goes some way toward explaining their complicated legalistic form. In any given case today, a judge may be required to follow common law, equity, or statutes in reaching a decision.

FIGURE 1.1 Sources of Law

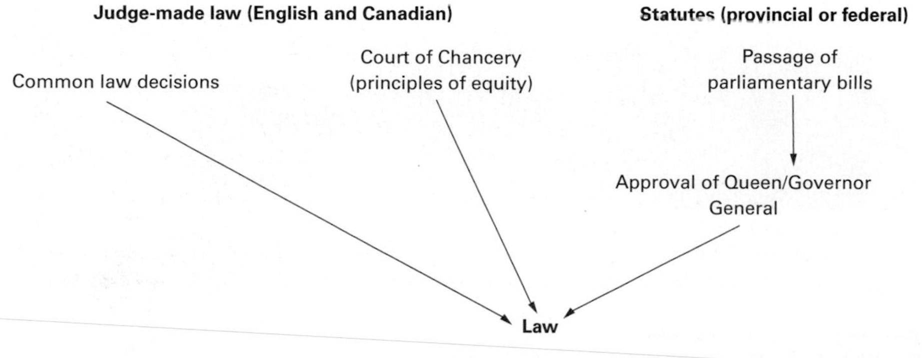

The Law in Canada

Canada was created with the passage of the *British North America Act*, which, in 1867, united several English colonies into one confederation. The *BNA Act* declared that Canada would have a constitution "similar in principle to that of the United Kingdom." In contrast to the United States, which has one constitutional instrument, England has an unwritten constitution in the sense that it is found in various proclamations, statutes, traditions, and judicially proclaimed principles. Thus the **rule of law** (the principle that all are subject to the law and legal process), the Magna Carta (the first proclamation of basic human rights), and parliamentary supremacy are all part of the constitutional tradition inherited by Canada. The *BNA Act* itself—now called the *Constitution Act (1867)*—has constitutional status in Canada. This means its provisions cannot be changed through a simple parliamentary enactment; they can only be altered through the more involved and onerous process of constitutional amendment.

***BNA Act* creates Canada with constitution like Britain's**

Today the main function of the *Constitution Act (1867)* is to divide powers between the federal and provincial governments. The principle of parliamentary supremacy was established in England where there is only one parliament, but in Canada, where there are 11 governing bodies (10 provincial legislative assemblies and one federal Parliament), how is it determined which body is supreme? The answer is that each governs in its assigned area. Thus the *Constitution Act (1867)*, primarily in sections 91 and 92, assigns powers to the federal and the provincial governments. Section 91 gives the federal government the power to make laws with respect to money and banking, the military, criminal law, and weights and measures, whereas health, education, and matters of local commerce are assigned to the provinces under section 92. These categories should not be thought of as watertight compartments. Rather they are sources of power, and so there can be the occasional overlap. For example, one province may prohibit the production and sale of a particular drug from a health point of view, and the federal government may make production and sale of that same drug illegal using its criminal law power. Both laws would be valid. There is no actual conflict here, since it would be possible to obey both laws. However, where it is impossible to

***Constitution Act (1867) (BNA Act)* divides powerzs between federal and provincial governments**

CASE SUMMARY 1.2

Mercier v. Alberta (Attorney General)[3]

Overlapping Provincial and Federal Powers

After a parachuting accident that resulted in a death, both the federal and provincial governments initiated inquiries. The provincial government acted under its power to investigate fatal accidents under the provincial *Fatality Inquiries Act*. The federal government exercised its power over aviation matters derived from the "Peace, Order, and Good Government" clause in the *Constitution Act (1867)*. An application was brought to stop the provincial inquiry, claiming this was a matter of exclusive federal jurisdiction.

(continued)

3. (1996), 134 D.L.R. (4th) 266 (Alta. Q.B.).

The Court of Appeal held that the inquiries of both levels of government were valid and that the provincial inquiry under the *Fatality Inquiries Act* could proceed. This was one of those instances where the legislative power of the provincial and federal governments overlapped and both had jurisdiction.

It is important to remember that the various heads of power listed in sections 91 and 92 of the *Constitution Act (1867)* do not create watertight compartments of federal and provincial control. Rather, they are sources of power authorizing the level of government to make laws of a particular nature and those powers may overlap in some cases as they did here.

Federal law followed where provincial and federal laws conflict

obey both the federal and the provincial law and both are valid, the principle of **paramountcy** requires that the federal law be obeyed. Sections 91 and 92 of *The Constitution Act (1867)* appear in Appendix A on page 307 of this text. You can also access the Act at **www.canlii.org**.

Statute created by first, second, and third reading, and royal assent

Both the federal and provincial governments make law by enacting legislation (see Figure 1.2). The elected representatives form Parliament. The prime minister and cabinet are chosen from these elected members and form the government of the province or Canada, as the case may be. The governments of the territories function in the same way, but they don't have the same status as the provinces; they are subject to federal control. Legislative bodies begin the law-making process when an elected member—usually a cabinet minister—presents a bill for the consideration of the House of Commons. This bill goes through a process of introduction, debate, amendment, and approval, known as first, second, and third readings. Eventually the bill is presented to the Governor General at the federal level and the Lieutenant Governor at the provincial level to receive royal assent. With that assent the bill becomes law, and is then referred to as an act or statute. At the federal level the bill must also go through the same process in the Senate before receiving royal assent.

FIGURE 1.2 The Making of Statutory Law

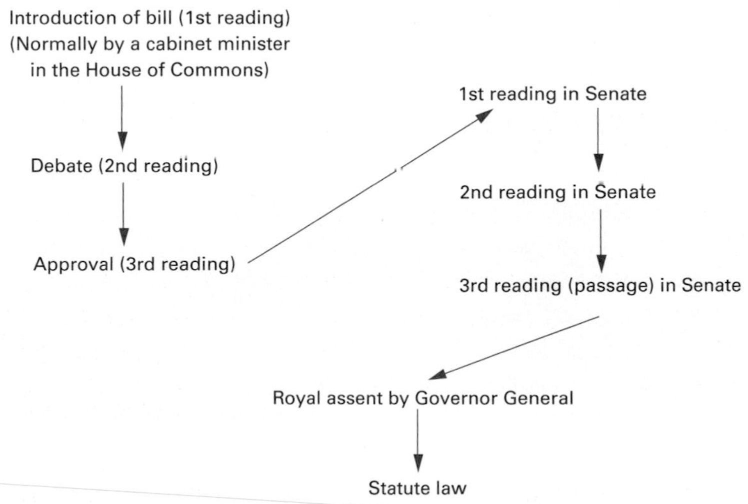

Government enactments are published each year and are made available to the public in volumes referred to as the Statutes of Canada (S.C.), Statutes of Alberta (S.A.), Statutes of Ontario (S.O.), and so on. Every few years the statutes are summarized and are referred to as the Revised Statutes of Canada [R.S.C. 1985], Revised Statutes of B.C. [R.S.B.C. 1996], etc. Today most jurisdictions have made unofficial versions of their current consolidated legislation available on the internet. You can access these statutes at **www.canlii.org**.

Statutes published in print and online

Statutes often authorize a cabinet minister or other official to create sub-legislation or **regulations** to accomplish the objectives of the statute. These regulations are often as voluminous as their authorizing statutes and are published and made available to the public in the same way. If the regulations have been properly passed within the authority as specified in the statute, they have the same legal standing as the statute. Thus, a motor vehicle act in a particular province might set out the requirement to register a vehicle, particular offences, or the right to appeal. The regulations would be more concerned with setting out specific penalties for violations or the fees to be charged for different services.

Regulations have status as law

The Constitution Act (1982) and the *Canadian Charter of Rights and Freedoms*

Canada cut its last ties to England with the simultaneous passage of the *Canada Act* in England and the *Constitution Act (1982)* in Canada. The English Parliament can no longer pass legislation that affects Canada. Although our ties with the English government have been severed, our ties to the monarchy remain intact, and Queen Elizabeth II remains the Queen of Canada. The *Constitution Act (1982)* also included the *Canadian Charter of Rights and Freedoms.*

***Constitution Act (1982)* gives Canada independence**

The beginning of the latter half of the 20th century saw an upsurge of interest in basic human rights. Most jurisdictions enacted legislation prohibiting discrimi-

CASE SUMMARY 1.3

Shirley v. Eecol Electric (Sask.) Ltd.[4]

An Employer's Obligation to Accommodate a Disabled Worker

Mrs. Shirley had a good work record until she suffered a serious whiplash injury in an automobile accident. As she recovered, she wanted to take advantage of a government-funded graduated work program where she would work an increasing number of hours each week until she was able to resume her full-time employment. Her employer, however, insisted on a firm date when she would return to full-time employment, and when she couldn't give such a commitment, her employment was terminated.

(continued)

4. Zakreski J., (Sask. Human Rights Board of Inquiry), February 16, 2001, as reported in *Lawyers Weekly Consolidated Digest*, Vol. 21.

She challenged that decision before the Saskatchewan Human Rights Board of Inquiry, which determined that she had been discriminated against because of her disability. The employer was required to pay her compensation because of their failure to accommodate a disabled worker in contravention of the province's *Human Rights Act*. This case shows that a decision that may make sense from a business point of view may still contravene important human rights provisions, thus exposing the business to significant liability. You should always be aware of your obligations under human rights and other legislation.

nation on the basis of race, religion, ethnic origin, gender, and disability in areas such as accommodation, public service, and employment. All Canadian provinces and the federal government enacted statutes and established regulatory bodies to ensure that these basic human rights are protected.

Federal and provincial statutes guarantee human rights

The problem was that none of these federal or provincial bodies had the power to remedy discrimination when it took place at the hands of government. The doctrine of parliamentary supremacy provided that in England, and later in Canada, the supreme law-making body was Parliament. Thus Parliament or the legislative assemblies in the provinces could simply pass legislation overriding the rights protected in these human rights statutes.

The *Charter of Rights and Freedoms*, which is part of the constitution of Canada, overcomes this problem. All constitutional provisions, including the *Charter*, are declared to be the "supreme law of Canada." Neither the federal nor the provincial governments can change the provisions of the *Charter of Rights and Freedoms* without going through the constitution amending process. Any statute by any level of government inconsistent with the provisions of the *Charter* is void, and any action by a government official violating the provisions of the *Charter* is actionable under the *Charter*.

***Charter* protects from rights abuses by government**

We have to be careful here, because there are limitations built into the *Charter* that give back to government some of the power that the *Charter* takes away. Section 1 allows for reasonable exceptions to the rights and freedoms set out in the *Charter*. This is only common sense and prevents prisoners in jail from claiming their mobility rights, or allows a person to be held liable for his or her fraud or defamation despite the guarantee of free speech. These are simple examples, but the problem can be quite complex, and when dealing with *Charter* questions today, much of the effort of the courts is directed at determining the extent of these reasonable exceptions.

Section 1 limitation allows for reasonable exceptions

Section 33 limitation allows opting out

Another limitation is found in section 33; it is known as the "notwithstanding clause." This provision allows both provincial and federal governments to pass legislation directly in contravention of specified sections of the *Charter* (section 2 and sections 7–15). While this clause seems to undo much that the *Charter* sets out to accomplish, a government choosing to exercise this overriding power must do so clearly, by declaring that a particular provision will be in force "notwithstanding" the offended section of the *Charter*. Those advocating for the inclusion of the clause knew that its use would come at a high political cost, and as a result section 33 would rarely be used. In fact, this has proven to be the case, and very few legislators have had the political will to use the notwithstanding provision of the *Charter*. The Quebec law requiring business signs to be in French only is one notable example of its use. The political consequence of that action was the defeat of the Meech Lake and Charlottetown Accords, which in turn led to an upsurge in the separatist feelings in Quebec and the referendum that almost led to the breakup of Canada. Excerpts from *The Constitution Act (1982)* appear in Appendix B on page 310 of this text. You can also access the Act at **www.canlii.org**.

Charter **protects:**
- Fundamental freedoms
- Democratic rights
- Mobility rights
- Legal rights
- Equality rights
- Language rights

The provisions of the *Charter* protect basic or **fundamental freedoms** (section 2) such as freedoms of speech, religion, the press, and association. Next, it protects **democratic rights** (sections 3–5) at both the federal and provincial levels such as the right to vote, to run in an election, the requirement that an election will be held at least every five years, and that the elected government will sit every year. **Mobility rights** (section 6) include the rights to live and work in any part of Canada, as well as to enter and leave Canada. The most extensive provisions relate to **legal rights** (sections 7–14), which include the right to life, liberty, and the security of person; the right to be told why you are being arrested and to have a lawyer; the right not to incriminate yourself; the right to be tried within a reasonable time; the right to a jury trial; and the right not to be exposed to any unreasonable search and seizure or cruel or unusual treatment. Perhaps the best known provisions of the *Charter* relate to **equality rights** (section 15), where it states that everyone is equal under the law and discrimination is prohibited, specifically discrimination based on race, national or ethnic origin, colour, religion, sex, age, or mental or physical disability. Note that this list does not exhaust equality rights. It only lists some of them. Others are protected through the general provision prohibiting discrimination in the first part of section 15. For example, there is no protection of "sexual orientation" rights, but the Supreme Court of Canada has found that they are protected under this general prohibition. Finally, **minority language education rights** (section 23) are protected. Both the *Charter* and a separate part of the *Constitution Act (1982)* make it clear that aboriginal rights inconsistent with *Charter* provisions are not affected by it and are preserved. These treaty rights predate the *Charter*, and in many cases, predate Confederation itself. They include rights yet to be determined in the native land claims process.

Charter **limited to government actions**

It must be emphasized that the *Charter* and its provisions only apply to our relations with government. Thus, legislation passed by all levels of government and the conduct of government officials must comply with the provisions of the *Charter*. If we experience discrimination in our employment, housing, or public

CASE SUMMARY 1.4

Ramsden v. Peterborough (City)[5]

Are Posters on Public Property Protected by Freedom of Expression?

This is a classic case dealing with freedom of expression. The City of Peterborough had passed a bylaw prohibiting the posting of any material on city property. The bylaw prohibited the posting of "any bill, poster or other advertisement of any nature," on any "tree . . . pole, post stanchion or other object . . . " within the city limits. Ramsden put up advertising posters on several hydro poles to advertise an upcoming concert for his band. He did this twice and was charged with committing an offence under the bylaw. There was no dispute that he posted the advertisements

(continued)

5. [1993] 2 S.C.R. 1094, 106 D.L.R. (4th) 233 (S.C.C.).

in question, but he took the position that the bylaw violated his right to freedom of expression as protected by section 2(b) of the *Charter of Rights and Freedoms*. This case went to the Supreme Court of Canada, which agreed that Ramsden's right to freedom of expression had been infringed by the bylaw.

First the court had to deal with whether such postering was a means of expression protected under the *Charter*. It was clear that postering is an inexpensive and historically accepted way to convey information whether it is advertising or political, social, or cultural commentary. As such, the court found that it was protected under section 2(b) of the *Charter*. The court then had to decide whether the bylaw prohibition was a reasonable limit under section 1. The purpose of the bylaw was not to curtail public expression in any particular area, but to control littering, considered a positive objective. The problem was that the bylaw went too far. It prohibited all postering. The Supreme Court decision quoted from the Ontario Court of Appeal judgment "as between a total restriction of this important right and some litter, surely some litter must be tolerated." The court concluded that the bylaw imposed a limit on freedom of expression as protected in section 2(b) of the *Charter* and that the limitation could not be justified under section 1 as it "is overly broad and its impact on freedom of expression is disproportionate to its objectives."

services such as hotels, restaurants, and places of entertainment, we can make a claim to a human rights tribunal rather than the courts. Such tribunals act under separate provincial or federal human rights legislation.

The Courts

Court structure varies between provinces

- Provincial court

- Small claims

- Family

- Criminal

The traditional vehicle for resolving disputes in our culture is in a court of law. Under the *Constitution Act (1867)*, the actual structure of the courts is left to the provinces, resulting in some variety from province to province, although they are generally similar in nature and function. The lower level courts (provincial courts) are divided into different divisions and functions. The small claims court deals with civil actions where one person sues another for relatively small amounts of money (up to $10 000 depending on the province). Other specialized divisions of the lower level provincial courts include family courts that deal with family law matters, including awarding maintenance and custody of children (but generally not divorce, which must be handled by the superior trial court of the province); youth courts dealing with young offenders; and criminal courts dealing with the less serious criminal offences. Note that Ontario's small claims courts and family courts are a division of the Superior Court of Justice, leaving the Ontario Court of Justice (formerly the Provincial Division) to deal with criminal matters, provincial offences, and some family matters.

Superior court highest trial court

The superior trial courts of the province are variously referred to as the Supreme Court, Court of Queen's Bench—or in Ontario, the Court of Ontario—and Superior Court of Justice Division. They are the highest level trial courts of the province and deal with all serious civil and criminal matters. In the case of

Ontario, the Superior Court of Justice is divided into a Divisional Court, Small Claims Court, and Family Court. Note that some jurisdictions still retain a separate probate or surrogate court to handle estate matters.

Superior appeal court

In all provinces the highest court is a Court of Appeal. This is usually a separate court, but in some provinces it is a division of the superior court. In all cases this court only deals with appeals from lower courts and some government regulatory bodies. A matter tried in any of the provincial courts can be taken to the appeal court of that province, which may be the final appeal for the case. The Supreme Court of Canada may or may not choose to hear cases appealed from provincial courts of appeal. Whereas at the trial level there is a single judge who is sometimes assisted by a jury, at the appeal level several judges hear the case. Usually three judges hear an appeal. Juries are limited to the trial level and are rare in civil cases, with the exception being personal injury cases under tort law. But in criminal matters, where the potential penalty is over five years, trial by jury is guaranteed under the *Charter of Rights and Freedoms.* Where a jury is involved, its function is to hear the evidence and decide issues of fact (what happened and who did what?), whereas the questions of law (what are the legal obligations of the parties?) are left to the judge, who gives instructions to the jury on such matters before they retire to make their decision.

Jury guaranteed by *Charter*

Supreme Court of Canada highest court

The federal government has established the Supreme Court of Canada, located in Ottawa, as a court of last resort for Canadians. Nine judges appointed by the prime minister and cabinet are chosen from the various regions of the country. The Supreme Court hears appeals from all of the appeal courts, including Quebec's. There is no longer a right to appeal to the Supreme Court of Canada. The court selects the cases to hear on the basis of what it thinks is most important for the country. If it refuses to hear a particular case, it is not a comment on the validity of the arguments or the lower court decision. It means only that it has other more important cases to deal with. Usually seven or nine judges will sit to hear a case. The Supreme Court of Canada will also hear references (questions involving serious legal issues normally involving some urgency), directed to the court by the Prime Minister. The most recent was put to the court in 2004 on the question of same-sex marriage.[6] The federal government also has established a Federal Court with a Trial Division and an Appeal Division. These courts handle matters that fall within the federal jurisdiction, such as copyrights, patents, and trademarks as well as matters brought from the federal Tax Court and other federal government regulatory bodies.

Federal Court deals with disputes in federal arena

Regulatory bodies, sometimes called administrative tribunals, are found at both the federal and the provincial levels and may consist of a board comprised of several people or simply one government bureaucrat. Their positions are created by statute, and they make decisions that affect individuals and companies with respect to statutes or regulations. Tribunals often take on the appearance of a court, but they are not. They are part of the bureaucracy of government and are designed to accomplish government purposes. A person adversely affected by a decision and feeling that he or she has been improperly dealt with should first ask whether the decision-maker had the jurisdiction to act. This is determined by looking at both the statute and regulations under which the regulatory body was created and functions. The *Charter of Rights and Freedoms* and the *Constitution Act (1867)* must also be examined to determine whether the legislation relied on was valid. The question can then be asked whether the decision itself and the process

Administrative tribunals are not courts

6. *Reference re Same-Sex Marriage*, 2004 SCC 79 (S.C.C.).

FIGURE 1.3 **Court Structure***

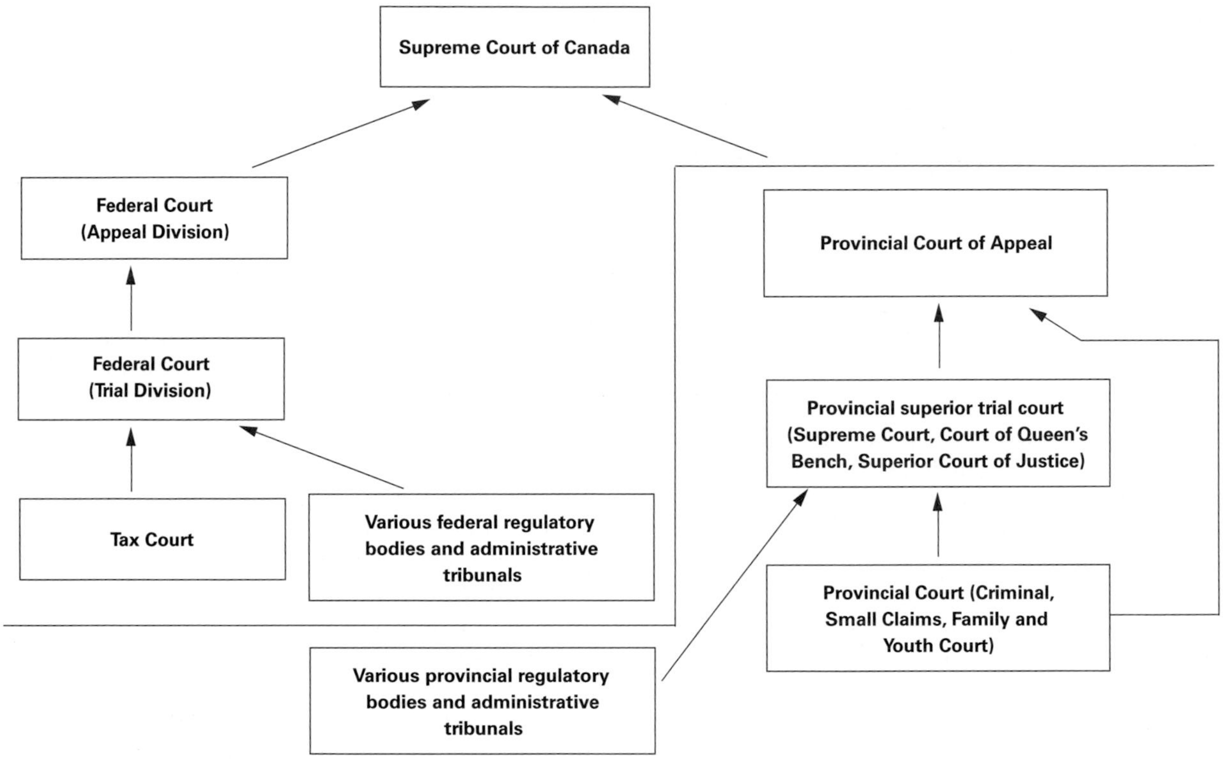

**Provincial structure will vary.*

Regulatory bodies' decisions can be reviewed by a court

were proper. There are certain standards of fairness that must be adhered to; they require a decision to be made without bias or bad faith and only after a fair hearing. Decisions of these regulatory bodies can be challenged in a court when these standards have not been met. It must be emphasized, however, that the wisdom of proceeding with such a challenge must be weighed against the normally significant costs involved, the likelihood of success, and the questionable value of even a favourable outcome. Labour relations boards and human rights tribunals at both the federal and provincial levels are good examples of such administrative tribunals that look like courts but are not. These regulatory bodies and a person's rights before them are discussed in much more detail in Chapter 10. See Figure 1.3 for an illustration of the federal and provincial court structures.

The Litigation Process

A civil action involves one person (called the plaintiff) suing another (the defendant), and the process is quite different from a criminal prosecution. The process of suing another person is involved and lengthy, but each step is designed to

FIGURE 1.4 Pre-Trial Litigation Process (Usually after Negotiation)

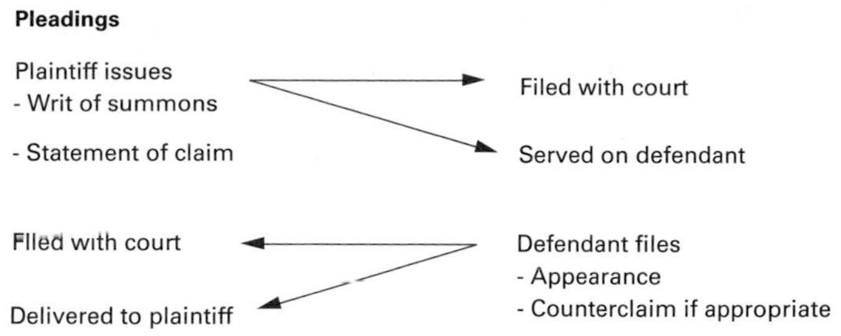

reveal more information, so that the parties will be encouraged to settle without going to trial. If a trial cannot be avoided, this pre-trial process ensures that the actual issues to be determined by the court will be narrowed and refined, so that a decision can be reached more efficiently. The following describes the process in place in a civil action in a superior court. It should be noted that in small claims court many of these steps have been eliminated altogether. There is also considerable provincial variation. See Figure 1.4 for an outline of the litigation process.

Service of writ of summons commences process

The **plaintiff** (the person bringing the action) normally commences a civil action with the issuance of a **writ of summons**. The plaintiff files a document at the court registry and pays a fee; the writ is then served on the defendant. The writ contains a brief description of the nature of the complaint and the address where future documents related to the case can be served. The defendant responds by filing an **appearance** at that same court registry. This is simply an indication that the matter will be disputed. It is dangerous to ignore a writ of summons. If the defendant fails to file an appearance, the plaintiff can normally proceed to judgment without any further notification to the defendant.

Statement of claim identifies issues

The plaintiff then issues a **statement of claim**, which contains a summary of the allegations that support the **cause of action** (this term refers to what the plaintiff is suing for, such as a claim of negligence or breach of contract). This summary is not an argument of the case and no evidence is presented. Rather, it is the plaintiff's allegations or claims as to what happened, and what must be established in order to succeed in the action. Often the statement of claim is included with the writ of summons. In Ontario, the action is in fact commenced with the issuance of a notice of action, including the statement of claim.

Statement of defence defines area of contention

Upon receiving the statement of claim, the defendant must respond with a **statement of defence**. This document indicates which of the allegations in the statement of claim are agreed to and the defendant's version of what happened. The defendant can also issue a **counterclaim** that, in effect, initiates a counter action on the defendant's behalf. It is similar to the plaintiff's statement of claim. These documents are referred to as the **pleadings**, and there can be further communications between the plaintiff and defendant to clarify any uncertainty arising from them.

Discovery: Discloses documents

Next comes the two-stage discovery process (see Table 1.1). First, each party has the right to look at and copy documents in the possession of the other side, such as receipts, reports, and the like, that might later be used as evidence in the trial. The second stage involves the examination under oath of each party by the other side's lawyer. Where companies are involved, an officer or other employee who has knowledge of the matter must be made available to answer these questions. This is done before a court reporter, who puts the party to be examined under oath and records the process, making a transcript available to the parties for a fee. Transcripts can later be used as evidence at the trial. It should be noted that, in an attempt to increase efficiency, many jurisdictions have reduced or eliminated this discovery process, at least in matters involving smaller claims.

Discovery: Produces statements under oath

Payment into court and offers to settle encourage settlement

To further encourage the parties to settle, the defendant can make a **payment into court**. The defendant may agree on liability, but dispute the amount. If so, he or she can pay a lesser amount to the court and notify the plaintiff. The plaintiff then must accept the lower amount or run the risk of paying the court costs, including the costs of the defendant's lawyer, if the eventual judgment is for an amount less than what the defendant paid into court. Similarly, where the plaintiff is willing to accept less than originally demanded, he or she can make an **offer to settle** for a lower amount. If the defendant fails to accept the offer, he or she runs the risk of paying double the plaintiff's legal costs, if the amount of the judgment is more than the settlement offer.

Although these pre-trial proceedings create efficiencies at the time of trial and encourage settlement, they also cause considerable delays and become frustrating for the parties. The courts have taken steps to simplify or reduce the process, and in some jurisdictions the parties are required to go through a process of mediation before they can resort to a trial.

CASE SUMMARY 1.5

Lawton's Drug Stores Ltd. v. Mifflin[7]

Discovery Requires the Production of Customer Lists

When Mifflin sold their business to Lawton's Drug store, the contract included a clause restricting them from opening a similar business in competition. Lawton's had paid extra for customer goodwill which would be lost if Mifflin were to start up a business in competition and recapture that customer loyalty. Six months later Mifflin did open up a business in competition and Lawton's sued for breach of contract. As part of the pre-trial discovery process, Lawton's demanded a copy of Mifflin's customer list. Such lists are extremely confidential and must be kept out of the hands of competitors at all costs, and so Mifflin refused. Upon application to the court, the judge ordered that the customer list be produced. It was relevant to the proceeding in that it could disclose information about whether the restrictive covenant was breached and to what extent. To prevent its misuse by Lawton's, the judge ordered that the list be kept in the possession of Lawton's lawyer, not be shown to Lawton, and only be used for trial purposes. This case shows us just how extensive the discovery process is in requiring the disclosure of all information that has potential relevance.

7. (1995), 402 A.P.R. 33, 38 C.P.C. (3d) 135, 129 Nfld. & P.E.I. R. 33 (Nfld. T.D.).

It should also be noted that in some unique situations instead of just one plaintiff there are many. These are called class action suits and usually involve product liability cases or a situation where a number of individuals have suffered the same loss as a result of the conduct of a particular defendant. It makes no sense for each injured party to bring a separate action; consequently, many jurisdictions have enacted statutes allowing the actions to be brought all at the same time, with one plaintiff chosen to represent all of the injured parties. The result is that one action will be applicable to all those represented in the class, and the decision will be binding on all of them. The process is essentially the same, with the exception that an application must first be made to the court to have the matter certified as a class action. The court may also be asked to decide whether a given individual is entitled to be a member of that class or whether his or her particular situation is different enough to merit initiating a separate action in his or her own right. Class actions are becoming much more common. Some examples include product liability cases and disputes involving complaints against money lenders, franchisers, financial advisers, and employee benefit and pension plans. Class actions have even included claims against government by veterans for improper compensation and a claim of systemic negligence leading to sexual abuse experienced by military cadets.

Class actions involve many plaintiffs represented by one procedure

TABLE 1.1 Discovery Process

- Plaintiff inspects documents in possession of defendant.
- Defendant inspects documents in possession of plaintiff.
- Plaintiff examines defendant under oath.
- Defendant examines plaintiff under oath.

Payment into Court

- Defendant may pay money to the court.
- Defendant informs plaintiff, who may then accept payment.
- Plaintiff may make an offer to settle.
- Offer to settle is filed with the court. Defendant is informed of the offer and may or may not accept.

The Trial and Judgment

Most people are familiar with the trial itself, the first stage of which involves the plaintiff giving evidence to establish his or her claim. After an optional opening statement, witnesses called by the plaintiff testify by responding to questions asked by the plaintiff's lawyer. This is called **direct examination**. As each witness testifies, the defendant's lawyer is given an opportunity to cross-examine. The types of questions that can be asked are broader on **cross-examination** than on direct examination. For instance, leading questions, where the answer is suggested in the question, are permitted on cross-examination but not on direct examination. After the plaintiff has presented his or her evidence, the defendant responds by calling his or her witnesses. Now it is the plaintiff's lawyer's turn to cross-examine. Finally, the lawyers for both the plaintiff and defendant have an opportunity to summarize their cases and make their arguments.

At trial, the plaintiff goes first . . .

Then the defendant

FIGURE 1.5 Standard of Proof

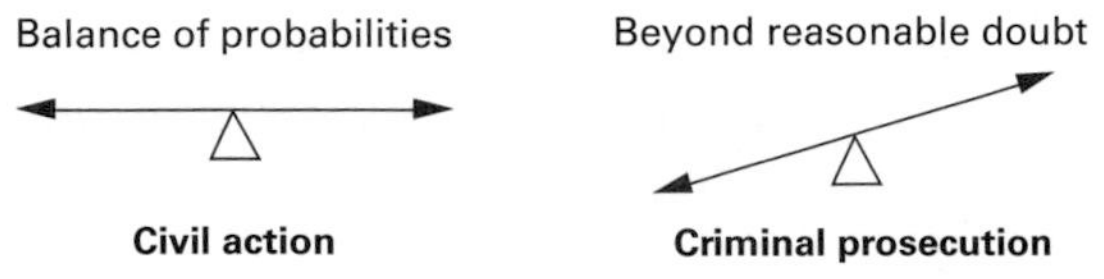

The case must be proved "upon balance of probabilities"

In civil actions plaintiffs have an obligation to establish their claim on the "balance of probabilities." This means that the decision-maker need only be more satisfied that the plaintiff's position is more correct than that of the defendant's. In a criminal matter the standard is much higher, where the prosecution must establish, to the satisfaction of the decision-maker, that the accused is guilty "beyond a reasonable doubt" (see Figure 1.5).

Judge instructs the jury in law, but the jury decides facts

If the matter is heard before a judge alone, he or she will determine both questions of law and questions of fact and render a decision, often at a later date. If a jury is involved, after hearing the evidence the jury must decide exactly what happened. These are called questions of fact. The judge gives his or her direction to the jury, setting out the law to be applied to the matter before them (questions of law), and the jury retires to consider the matter and then renders a decision. Criminal juries consist of 12 people and all must be in agreement with respect to the verdict. In civil cases juries are much less common, and when used, they typically consist of a lesser number (seven in Nova Scotia), and the decision does not have to be unanimous.

Damages and other remedies awarded

Once a judgment is obtained in a civil action, payment is not guaranteed. Although there are other types of remedies that may be sought, the standard judgment is of a monetary award called **damages**. The court orders the defendant to pay the plaintiff a certain sum of money.

Damages are usually designed to compensate the victim for his or her loss. In rare circumstances where the conduct complained of was deliberate, **punitive damages** may also be granted where the object is to punish the wrongdoer rather than simply to compensate the victim. A recent decision of the Supreme Court of Canada[8] made it clear that the award of such punitive damages would be rare and only in circumstances

> . . . where the misconduct would otherwise be unpunished or where other penalties are or are likely to be inadequate to achieve the objectives of retribution, deterrence and denunciation.

The court went on to state that the purpose of such punitive damages

> . . . is not to compensate the plaintiff, but to give a defendant his or her just desert (retribution), to deter the defendant and others from similar misconduct in the future (deterrence), and to mark the community's collective condemnation (denunciation) of what has happened.

Where a monetary award will not be appropriate the court may order an **injunction** (an order to stop the offending conduct); **specific performance** (an order that one contracting party actually fulfill the terms of an agreement, for

8. *Whiten v. Pilot Insurance Co.*, [2002] 1 S.C.R. 595, 2002 SCC 18 (S.C.C.).

FIGURE 1.6 Enforcing Judgment

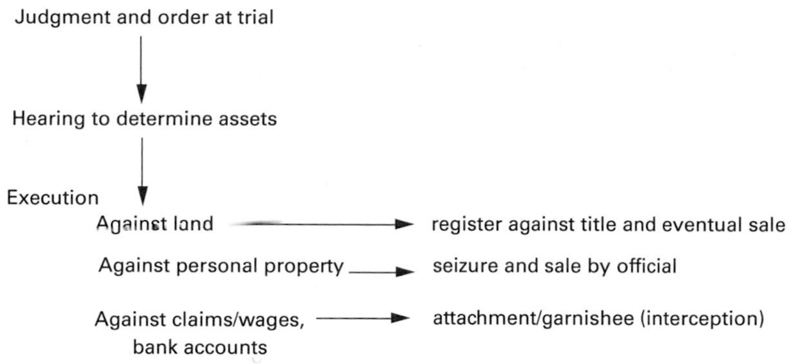

example, transfer title to his or her house); an **accounting**, where the defendant must pay over any profits he or she has made because of his or her misdeed (as opposed to compensating the victim for any loss); or other unique remedies associated with particular kinds of action.

The plaintiff (now judgment creditor) must enforce judgment

Where damages are awarded and the defendant, now referred to as the **judgment debtor**, fails to pay, the **judgment creditor** (plaintiff) must take steps to collect that money (see Figure 1.6). This may include a post-trial hearing to identify the judgment debtor's assets and what steps can be taken to execute against those assets. Bank accounts or wages may be intercepted (garnisheed) by court order. Assets such as cars, boats, and other types of valuable equipment can be seized pursuant to the court order and sold to satisfy the judgment. Similarly, real property in the form of land and buildings can be sold, and title transferred to satisfy the judgment. Of course, if the judgment debtor has no assets, or is bankrupt, trying to collect may be a fruitless exercise. This risk must be taken into consideration when deciding to sue in the first place. Where specific conduct has been ordered under an injunction or specific performance, for example, and the defendant fails to comply, his or her conduct may amount to contempt of court and the defendant can face stiff fines and even imprisonment as a result.

Alternate Dispute Resolution

Alternatives to litigation provide advantages

Negotiation avoids conflict

This topic should not be left without considering some alternatives to the litigation process—referred to as alternate dispute resolution or ADR. The object of turning to alternative methods is to avoid the delay, expense, lost productivity, and public notoriety normally associated with the litigation process. In the majority of cases the parties simply negotiate with each other either directly, or indirectly through their lawyers, until they reach a settlement of the dispute. Where there is some degree of goodwill and the parties are willing to cooperate and compromise, negotiation should be the method of choice in resolving disputes. Sometimes it is necessary to turn to the more structured methods of ADR that have been gaining prominence in recent times (see Figure 1.7).

FIGURE 1.7 Alternate Dispute Resolution (ADR) Methods

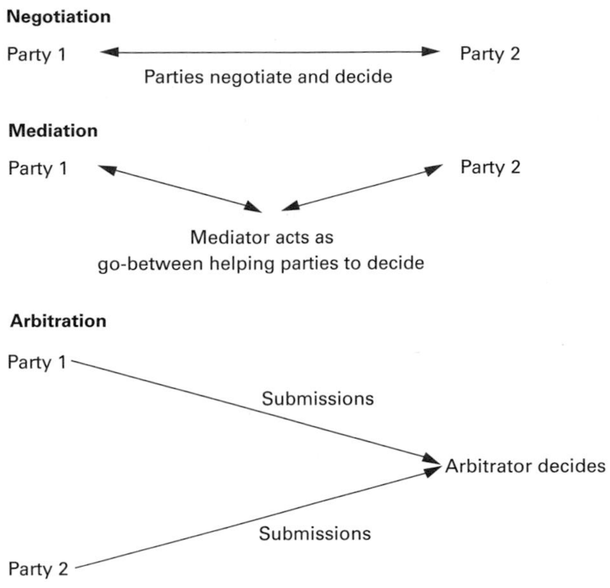

Mediator helps parties to reach a decision

Mediation is the process whereby some trusted third party acts as a go-between or facilitator and assists the parties to resolve their dispute. The job of the mediator is to talk to both parties and try to find some area of common ground between them. This may include making suggestions to the parties, but it is important to remember that it is up to the parties themselves to make the final decision, not the mediator. Mediation is required in some situations, such as collective bargaining, before any further action, for instance, a strike or lockout, can be taken. Mandatory mediation is also now required in many jurisdictions as part of the litigation of civil disputes. Both the small claims and superior court levels may require mediation as part of the process to reduce the number of cases that go to trial and to simplify and more efficiently deal with those that do.

Arbitrators make binding decisions

Arbitration is where the decision-making process is actually surrendered to a mutually acceptable third party. Both of the disputing parties make their case to the arbitrator, who then acts like a judge deciding the matter between them. This is similar to a court process, without all of the formal trappings. The parties themselves not only can agree who the arbitrator will be, but also can place limitations on the scope of his or her decision and what remedies can be imposed. When an arbitrator who has particular expertise in the area of the dispute is chosen, the process can be handled much more efficiently. Arbitration is mandated in some areas, such as collective bargaining. Once a collective agreement is in place, it must include some mechanism where any dispute arising under the contract will ultimately be arbitrated rather than made the subject of litigation in the courts. Another good example is the Canadian Motor Vehicle Arbitration Plan (CAMVAP). Contracts between customers and dealers require disputes arising in that industry to be arbitrated before that body, rather than through litigation. It is

TABLE 1.2 Pros and Cons of Alternate Dispute Resolution (ADR)

Advantages	Disadvantages
Lower cost	Does not deal with legal complexities
Flexible	Not appropriate when power imbalance
Less time-consuming	No precedent set
Private	No pressure to satisfy public demands
Win-win resolution	Limited powers of enforcement

now a much more common practice to include contract provisions requiring arbitration of disputes in all sorts of business transactions and relationships.

There are many variations of negotiation, mediation, and arbitration, making flexibility one of the most attractive features of ADR (see Table 1.2). The parties are free, either at the beginning of their relationship or after the dispute arises, to individually tailor a dispute resolution process to best suit their particular business needs. Litigation is an expensive, time-consuming, relationship-destroying process. Although it is central to our legal system, a business person should turn to the litigation process only as a last resort. Still, the court cases that have been decided determine the law. If we understand that law, we should be able to use those standards to help us as we negotiate, mediate, or arbitrate disputes.

ADR provides flexibility

Criminal Law

Although this text concentrates primarily on civil law, the topic of criminal law has become much more important for businesses in recent years. Corporations are commonly the victims of criminal activities such as shoplifting, employee theft, and fraud in its various forms. Increasingly, senior employees, directors, and executives are finding themselves running afoul of criminal law. It is therefore important to make some reference to the criminal process.

First, it is important to define criminal law and distinguish it from the discussion of civil law that forms the main substance of this text. In a civil action, one individual, the injured party (the plaintiff), sues another (the defendant), usually seeking compensation or other remedy for an injury or wrong suffered. In a criminal matter the state prosecutes the accused. The victim in this process has the status of a witness only. In some cases the accused can actually be the corporation, which can be held criminally liable for offences committed by senior executives or those acting under their direction. Sometimes those senior executives themselves can be charged. It is not uncommon for both criminal charges and a civil action to arise from the same incident. For example, in a serious motor vehicle accident the driver might be charged and tried for the criminal offence of driving while intoxicated, and later the injured victim may sue civilly for compensation for those injuries.

In a criminal action the state prosecutes the accused

The power to make criminal law is given exclusively to the federal government under the *Constitution Act (1867)*, but it is important to understand that there is an entire body of quasi-criminal law enacted by both federal and provincial levels of government. It is designed to enforce statutes passed by their respec-

Power to make criminal law resides exclusively with federal government

tive governments, and although technically not criminal law, it can impose serious penalties, including significant jail terms, for violations. At the provincial level these are called provincial offences. From a business point of view there is little difference between these provincial offences and criminal law, since both impose fines and/or imprisonment.

Provinces have power to enforce statutes creating provincial offences or quasi-criminal law

> The provinces cannot create criminal offences in their provincial statutes, but companies are now exposed to massive fines and individuals can and have gone to jail for public welfare statute violations. The difference between the criminal law and provincial offences is rapidly becoming the sole concern of constitutional lawyers.[9]

The discussion in this text will consider these quasi-criminal offences, sometimes called regulatory or provincial offences, as another form of criminal law that corporations must deal with, although it should be noted that the procedures involved might be somewhat different when governed by a separate statute such as Ontario's *Provincial Offences Act.*[10]

Provincial offences and criminal law very similar

Federal criminal law found in *Criminal Code* and other federal statutes

Federally, the criminal law is found mainly in the Canadian *Criminal Code,* but other federal statutes such as the *Competition Act,* the *Controlled Drugs and Substances Act,* and the copyright and patents acts also contain true criminal provisions. In this chapter a few important criminal law principles will be set out, and in subsequent chapters other criminal rules and principles will be discussed as they relate to those chapter topics.

As has already been explained, the standard of proof in a criminal matter is quite different from the standard required in a civil case. In a civil matter the case must be proved only "upon the balance of probabilities," but in a criminal case the prosecutor must establish "beyond a reasonable doubt" that the accused is guilty of the offence.

Criminal standard beyond a reasonable doubt

Prosecution must prove intent as well as the act

Criminal law not only requires proof that the prohibited conduct took place (the ***actus reus***), but also that there was intent (***mens rea***) to do the act. Note that this doesn't require that the accused must intend harm, only that the act was wilful and not accidental, nor based on some mistake of fact. Usually, once the physical facts of the case have been established (*actus reus*) there is enough circumstantial evidence to establish *mens rea,* so it is then up to the accused to bring evidence to rebut that presumption if that is to be a defence. Of course, insanity, to the extent that a person is not capable of understanding the nature and quality of his or her actions or that those actions are wrong, will also excuse the conduct. Note, however, that intoxication is not a defence for most criminal charges. Nor is ignorance of the law normally an excuse.

The standards of proof, as discussed here, apply to any offence where there is the possibility of imprisonment. In the case of provincial or federal offences that are regulatory in nature, where only a monetary fine can be imposed, the standard is sometimes modified by statute. Some of these offences are called **strict liability offences**, and in these circumstances, once the facts of the offence have been established, the accused can only avoid conviction if he or she can show he or she has acted with **due diligence**. This will be discussed in more detail in other chapters. Essentially, due diligence can be established where the manager or executive involved can be shown to have taken reasonable steps to ensure that the

Due diligence is the only defence to strict liability offence

9. Cassidy, Paul. "Federal proposals for expanded corporate environmental liability need more thought." *Lawyers Weekly*, Vol. 14 No. 40 (March 3, 1995).

10. R.S.O. 1990, c. P. 33.

offensive conduct would not take place, including proper training of the employees involved. Remember that the protections set out in the *Charter of Rights and Freedoms,* especially sections 7–15, apply to all matters where imprisonment may result, whether they are federal or provincial offences. Where the evidence has been improperly obtained, section 24 of the *Charter* gives the judge the right to exclude that evidence if hearing it would "bring the administration of justice into disrepute."

Note *Charter of Rights* protections

Where a person is caught committing a crime, such as theft or shoplifting, he or she can be arrested on the spot, by either a police officer or an ordinary citizen. For instance, the arrest can be made by a store owner, manager, security guard, or other employee. Care must be exercised here, for the power of a police officer to arrest is broader than that of a private citizen. Private citizens can only arrest where they have reasonable grounds and in fact a crime has taken place. In contrast police officers can arrest where they have reasonable grounds whether or not a crime has actually been committed. If a private citizen makes a mistake, he or she is more likely than a police officer to be sued for false imprisonment. Consequently, employers should take great care in training employees to avoid making wrongful arrests.

Private citizen has less power to arrest than a police officer

Often there is no immediate arrest. Sometimes there must first be an investigation to determine the nature of the crime, if any, or to find the offender. Under these circumstances the police often go before a judicial official called a justice of the peace or a judge to obtain a warrant to search a business or residential premises. Once evidence is obtained, the police officer or a private individual who has knowledge of the matter can go before that judicial official and lay an **information**. On the basis of that information, the judicial officer can issue an **arrest warrant** that is then executed by the police. Alternatively, the judicial official can issue a **summons to appear**. This is also served on the accused, usually by the police, but there is no arrest. Rather, the notice requires the accused to appear before a judge at a specified time. In fact, when a police officer witnesses an offence taking place, he or she doesn't always arrest, but often just issues an **appearance notice**, which has a similar effect as a summons to appear. If a person is arrested, he or she must be brought before a judge within 24 hours in most situations. The judge will decide to keep the person in jail, release the accused on his or her own recognizance with a promise to appear later, or require the posting of some sort of security, such as bail or a surety, to ensure a later appearance.

Justice can issue a search warrant, arrest warrant, and summons to appear

Police can arrest or issue an appearance notice

Accused must be brought to judge within 24 hours of arrest

Crimes fall into two different categories. **Summary conviction offences** are minor offences and usually involve lesser penalties with a jail term limited to two years. An **indictable offence** is more serious, with penalties involving heavy fines and up to life in prison, depending on the offence. These terms refer to the judicial process. A summary conviction involves little more than the exchange of information and negotiation by the prosecutor and the defence between the appearance and the trial. An indictment is a more involved and lengthy process, which includes a preliminary hearing before a provincial court judge to determine whether there is enough evidence to proceed before the trial actually takes place. There are some **hybrid offences** where the prosecutor has a choice to proceed by way of indictment or summary conviction. For example, where a person is charged with operating a motor vehicle in a manner dangerous to the public or while impaired, the prosecutor can proceed by way of summary conviction or indictment. Of course, the decision will likely depend on how serious the infraction was, including whether anyone was injured or property was destroyed. Where an indictable offence is involved, the accused also has choices. Usually,

Summary conviction for minor offences

Indictment for serious offences

Prosecutor has choice with hybrid offences

after the lawyers have exchanged information, the accused will plead guilty or innocent and at that time will also make an election as to the nature of the trial. The accused can choose a summary trial before a provincial judge but still face the more serious penalties, or he or she can choose to be tried before a superior court judge, either acting alone or with a jury. If the accused chooses trial by superior court judge alone or before a judge and jury, there is also a preliminary hearing. Often **plea-bargaining**, where the accused is given the opportunity to plead guilty to a lesser offence, takes place. For example, when a person is charged with robbery, a very serious charge, he or she may be given the opportunity to plead guilty to the less serious charge of theft. This process offends some people, but it has advantages from the point of view of serving justice, ensuring a conviction, and avoiding the costs and uncertainty of a trial.

Accused can choose trial before provincial court judge, superior court judge, or judge and jury

Plea-bargaining can avoid trial

Criminal trial similar to civil trial

Where the matter does proceed to trial, it is similar to a civil trial where the prosecutor presents witnesses and evidence to prove the accused has committed the offence. If the defence feels enough evidence has been presented to support a conviction, it will then respond by calling witnesses and presenting evidence favouring its position. The defence then makes arguments to the judge, or the judge and jury. If a jury is involved, the judge instructs the jury with respect to the law, and the jury retires to consider a verdict. Juries in criminal cases consist of 12 people, who must reach a unanimous decision. If they can't agree on their decision, the judge can discharge the jury, empanel a new jury, and start again. If either side feels an error of law has taken place, they have the right to appeal the decision.

Sentences may include fines or imprisonment. Where a summary conviction offence is involved, the fine will normally be limited to a few hundred dollars and the sentence to no more than two years in prison. Where an indictable offence has been committed, the fines and prison sentences can be much greater, with fines up to several million dollars and life in prison reserved for the most serious of crimes. It should be noted that while many American states still impose capital punishment, the death penalty has been abolished in Canada.

Of course, the length of sentence will vary with the seriousness of the criminal conduct. For example, when an Alberta lawyer improperly misappropriated trust funds in his care, he was convicted of criminal breach of trust and sentenced to three and one-half years' imprisonment. He was also required to repay the Alberta Law Society $349 505.98, the amount misappropriated and which the Law Society had paid back to his clients.[11] In another example of criminal breach of trust, a travel agent was sentenced to two years less a day and fined $200 000 for cheating the government out of $750 000 in GST payments.[12]

A judge may also have the discretion to impose a suspended sentence. This is still a conviction but with no penalty. Sometimes conditions are attached, such as community service or a conviction with probation, rather than a fine or imprisonment. The judge also may order an absolute discharge, which does not involve a conviction.

Alternative sentences

Finally, it should be noted that there are a number of offences that don't involve the direct commission of the actual crime. For example, it is an offence for someone to aid or abet another in the commission of a crime, to be an acces-

11. *R. v. Manolescu,* Alta. Prov. Ct., as reported in *Lawyers Weekly*, Vol. 17 No. 17 (September 12, 1997).

12. *R. v. Onkar Travels Inc.*, [2003] O.J. No. 2939, as reported in *Lawyers Weekly*, Vol. 23 No. 20 (September 26, 2003).

sory before or after the crime, or to counsel the commission of a crime. A particular danger from a business point of view is conspiracy. Where several people together plan the commission of a crime, this constitutes a conspiracy and all are guilty even though they may not have directly participated.

Aiding, acting as an accessory, counselling, and conspiracy are also crimes

QUESTIONS FOR REVIEW

1. Why is it important for a business student to understand the law?
2. Define law and distinguish between substantive and procedural law.
3. Explain the most significant differences between the civil law system as used in Quebec and the common law system used in other provinces.
4. Explain what is meant by *stare decisis* and the role it plays in our legal system.
5. Describe the origin of the common law and equity, and explain how they are related.
6. Explain the role played by statutes in our legal system.
7. Explain the origin and the role played by the *British North America Act* in our legal system.
8. Describe the powers given to the federal and provincial governments under the *Constitution Act (1867).*
9. Explain the origin of a statute and its relationship to judge-made law.
10. Explain how the public can gain access to such legislation.
11. Explain the nature of regulations and their legal status.
12. Indicate the importance of the *Constitution Act (1982),* and explain why it was important to the development of Canada.
13. How are individual human rights protected in Canada?
14. Explain the significance of the *Charter of Rights and Freedoms* and also any limitations on its application.
15. Describe the basic rights and freedoms protected in the *Charter.*
16. Describe the court structure in place in your province, and explain how it differs from other provinces.
17. Contrast the nature and function of the provincial court and superior trial court in your province.
18. Distinguish between the types of matters dealt with by a court of appeal and a trial court.
19. Under what circumstances are litigants entitled to a jury trial?
20. Explain the role of the Supreme Court of Canada and its relationship to other courts.

21. Explain the nature of the Federal Court, its function, and the role it plays in the Canadian judicial process.
22. Explain the nature of administrative tribunals and their relationship to our legal system.
23. How is a civil action commenced?
24. Explain the nature and role of a statement of defence, a counterclaim, and the discovery process.
25. Explain what is meant by payment into court and offers to settle.
26. Contrast the process and the requirements of proof required in a civil as opposed to a criminal action.
27. Contrast the roles played by a judge and a jury in a trial.
28. Explain how a judgment can be enforced.
29. Distinguish between negotiation, mediation, and arbitration.
30. Indicate the advantages and disadvantages of alternate dispute resolution over litigation.
31. Distinguish between criminal and regulatory provisions.
32. Distinguish between the powers to arrest of a private citizen compared to those of a police officer.
33. Explain the difference between a criminal and a strict liability offence.
34. Explain the rights of the accused in a criminal process once arrested.
35. Distinguish between summary conviction and indictable offences and the various options of the parties involved.

QUESTIONS FOR FURTHER DISCUSSION

1. Discuss the relationship between law, morality, and ethics.
2. Canada has a tradition of parliamentary supremacy inherited from Great Britain. But that has been modified somewhat by the passage of the *Charter of Rights and Freedoms*. Explain how parliamentary supremacy has been limited by the *Charter*, how that affects the role of the courts, and whether these changes enhance or are detrimental to Canada as a democracy.
3. The process leading to trial is long, involved, and costly. What are the benefits derived from this system? Do they outweigh the disadvantages? In your answer consider how the process may be improved as well as the advantages and disadvantages of alternate dispute resolution methods.
4. One area where the litigation process has been simplified in some jurisdictions is with the modification or elimination of the discovery process. Discuss the reasons for this change and the resulting gains and losses.

5. Describe the essential difference between a criminal prosecution and a civil action, and discuss the advantages and challenges associated with each process. Consider when a business person might have to choose between them and what factors would affect that decision.

CASES
FOR DISCUSSION

1. **BRITISH COLUMBIA GOVERNMENT AND SERVICE EMPLOYEES' UNION V. BRITISH COLUMBIA (PUBLIC SERVICE EMPLOYEE RELATIONS COMMISSION),** [1999] 3 S.C.R. 3, 176 D.L.R. (4th) 1 (S.C.C).
A female forest firefighter in British Columbia lost her job because she couldn't run 2.5 kilometres while carrying a 35 kilogram pack, to satisfy a government imposed standard of fitness required for her job. She showed that this requirement clearly disadvantaged women, who don't have the same aerobic capacity as men. She also argued that there was nothing in her job that required this kind of performance. She made a complaint to the Human Rights Commission of British Columbia. Consider the arguments on both sides. What do you think should be the decision?

2. **R. V. SAPLYS,** Ont. Gen. Div., February 18, 1999, as reported in Lawyers Weekly Consolidated Digest, Vol. 18.
The special investigations unit of the RCMP suspected that a corporation was being used for a fraudulent purpose, but had to close the investigation for lack of evidence. They approached Revenue Canada to do an audit. This was done and the information was handed over to the police. This information was used to obtain a search warrant, and charges were subsequently laid. Indicate what complaint the principals of the corporation had and what should be done with the evidence.

3. **VANCOUVER (CITY) V. JAMINER,** B.C.S.C., December 13, 1999, as reported in *Lawyers Weekly Consolidated Digest*, Vol. 19.
A city by-law was enacted without notice to those affected. The by-law prohibited rooftop signs extending above the roofline of a building to enhance the aesthetics of the urban environment. Jaminer erected such a sign, leased it out for advertising purposes, and was subsequently ordered to remove it by the city. He refused and the city applied to the Supreme Court of British Columbia for an injunction ordering the removal of the sign. Indicate both *Charter* and procedural arguments that might be available to both sides and the likely outcome.

4. **BANK OF BRITISH COLUMBIA V. CANADIAN BROADCASTING CORP.** (1995), 126 D.L.R. (4th) 644 (B.C.C.A.).
The Bank of British Columbia sued the CBC for libel arising from a TV broadcast. The journalist raised the defence that the challenged statements were true. At the discovery of documents stage, the Bank demanded the production of unbroadcasted excerpts of videotape, draft script, internal post-production memos, and journalists' notes. The CBC refused to produce them. This action was brought to force the surrender of those documents. Consider why the Bank thought they were entitled to see these documents and the reasons for the resistance of the CBC. Do you think that proper discovery required their production? Explain.

CHAPTER 2

Torts and Professional Liability

A tort is a civil wrong

Wrongful conduct may be both a crime and a tort

Personal liability involves one person being held accountable when their wrongful conduct causes injury or loss to another. A tort action is a private or civil action where the injured party sues the one whose wrongful conduct caused that loss or injury. Examples of wrongful conduct, or torts, that may be found in business situations are assault and battery, false imprisonment, trespass, defamation, deceit, nuisance, and negligence, with negligence being by far the most important. A tort is committed when the conduct complained of is inherently wrong. When a contract is breached (contracts are discussed below) the conduct, or lack thereof, is unacceptable only because of the agreement. But where someone drives carelessly or defames another, the conduct itself is unacceptable. Criminal conduct also must be distinguished. As discussed in Chapter 1, a crime is offensive conduct considered serious enough for the state to get involved and prosecute the offender. A tort is a civil wrong in the sense that it is the injured party, not the state, that is bringing the action, and the penalties, procedures, and standards of proof are different. Note, however, that specific conduct may be both a crime and a tort, and result in two court procedures, one civil and one criminal (see Figure 2.1).

The reason that a business person has more than a passing interest in tort law is because of **vicarious liability**. An employer is responsible (vicariously liable) for all torts committed

FIGURE 2.1 Crime v. Tort

by employees in the course of their employment. The employer, usually a company, is responsible for any injuries caused by their employees while doing what they have been employed to do, even where the employees were doing it badly or improperly. The employee is liable as well, but it is usually only the employer who has the resources to pay.

Employer can be vicariously liable

Intentional Torts

The listing of torts by categories, as we are about to do, is somewhat misleading. It is only possible to list a few of the recognized categories of torts, and even where conduct does not fit into a well-defined category, the courts will provide a remedy where rights have been violated. These categories are used because it makes the concept easier to understand and because the courts apply different rules and award different remedies depending on the type of tort involved. This first section deals with intentional torts involving deliberate conduct. Note that it is not that the injury was intended, only that the conduct leading to it involves a deliberate act. If the conduct leading to the interference was inadvertent, the appropriate cause of action is negligence, which will be discussed below. (For a summary of the categories of intentional torts, see Table 2.1 on p. 34.)

Intentional torts involve deliberate acts

When one person physically interferes with another, it might be done for the best of motives, and yet it still might qualify as a trespass to person. For example, a medical doctor applying treatment might be doing so in order to help the patient, but if that treatment is unwanted and consent has been denied, a battery has taken place.

CASE SUMMARY 2.1

Swanson v. Mallow[1]

Spraying of Pam Is Battery

During a labour dispute at a Safeway store in Regina, three striking workers on two occasions sprayed Pam (cooking oil) on Monica Swanson who was working as a security guard. As a result she suffered laryngitis, headaches, and nausea, and was unable to go back to work for a year. They were charged criminally, but at a preliminary hearing it was decided there was not enough evidence to proceed. Ms. Swanson also sued in a civil action. At that trial the striking workers were found liable and were assessed damages in the amount of $33 869 for lost income, trauma, and punitive damages. This illustrates the difference between a criminal and civil action. The criminal action required a higher standard of proof and was dismissed, but the civil action was decided on the balance of probabilities and that standard was met. Labour disputes often involve high emotions on both sides, but when the conduct steps over the line and a tort or crime is committed, the perpetrators are liable for their actions. All concerned should take great care to avoid this kind of physical confrontation.

---

1. [1991] 5 W.W.R. 454, 94 Sask. R. 217 (Sask. Q.B.).

ASSAULT AND BATTERY

Battery involves physical contact

Assault involves apprehended physical contact

Threatened contact must be immediate, possible, and unwanted

Assault and battery, a form of trespass to person, involves intentional physical interference with another. A **battery** takes place where there is actual physical contact. An **assault** is a threatened battery in the perception of the victim. If someone points a gun at another, an assault has taken place because of the victim's fear or apprehension of that contact. Even when the person pointing the gun knows there are no bullets, it is still an assault if the victim thinks the gun is loaded. In order to qualify as an assault, the threat of physical contact must be immediate and physically possible to carry out. If someone threatens to beat you up later, or shakes a fist while you drive off in your car, there is no assault. But if someone steps out in front of you shaking his or her fist, the threat of violence is immediate and possible, and so an actionable assault has taken place. The threatened interference need not be harmful, just unwanted. Medical practitioners are sometimes sued for trespass to person (battery) because they failed to obtain proper consent before a surgical procedure. Even where that procedure is beneficial and the motive is to help, people have the right to decide what happens to their bodies, and a doctor cannot proceed without approval. Such consent can be implied where conditions are life threatening, the patient is unable to give instructions to the doctor, and no guardian is available. But no consent can be implied where there is a clear refusal from the victim.

CASE SUMMARY 2.2

Malette v. Shulman[2]

Blood Transfusion to Save Life Still Battery

Mrs. Malette was seriously injured in an automobile accident, and at the hospital Dr. Shulman determined she was in need of a blood transfusion to save her life. The nurse, however, discovered a card in the patient's purse indicating she was a Jehovah's Witness. The card gave instruction that under no circumstances should blood or blood products be administered to Mrs. Malette. Dr. Shulman ignored the card and proceeded to administer the transfusion. When the family arrived they repeated the instruction, which Dr. Shulman also overruled. There is no question that the blood transfusion was needed to preserve her life, but upon her recovery Mrs. Malette sued Dr. Shulman for trespass to person (battery). The judge held that Mrs. Malette had withheld her consent to treatment, that the administration of the blood transfusion against her wishes amounted to a battery by the doctor, and awarded $20 000 in damages. The decision was upheld on appeal. Despite the doctor's clearly good intentions, a person has a right to decide what will happen to his or her own body and this doctor's conduct violated that right.

DEFENCES **Consent** then is a valid defence to a claim of assault and battery. Kissing would be a trespass to the person, but is considered innocent where the two parties consent. Medical treatment is appropriate and not actionable when the patient consents to the procedure—even where unexpected damage results.

2. (1990), 67 D.L.R. (4th) 321 (Ont. C.A.).

In all cases practitioners must take care to ensure that the medical treatment or other conduct goes no farther than the informed consent allows. A hockey player might be protected from being sued by the principle of consent even for a hard check, but if a player were to charge that the other player intentionally speared him with his stick, the consent defence might well be lost. Another important defence for assault and battery is **self-defence**. When attacked, a victim can use reasonable force in response. Such an attack cannot be viewed as an invitation to respond with unrestrained violence. The victim can only use reasonable force or as much force as is necessary to fend off the attack. And that reasonable force must be in response to an immediate threat, not one that has passed. Then the response becomes revenge rather than self-defence.

Informed consent effective defence

Self-defence using reasonable force effective defence

Conduct that amounts to assault and battery in tort law can also constitute several different criminal offences under the *Criminal Code* of Canada. These charges range from the actual use of force to the uttering of threats, intimidation, and making harassing phone calls. As in tort law, self-defence and consent will excuse the use of physical force but that force must be reasonable, and consent will not justify assisting a suicide or other specified types of prohibited conduct. Reasonable force can also be used to accomplish a justified arrest or to defend property. A number of other offences such as robbery and homicide also include the prohibited use of physical force or the threat of such force.

There are a number of criminal offences that correspond to assault and battery

Consent or self-defence will not always justify the use of physical force

FALSE IMPRISONMENT

Another type of intentional tort, also amounting to trespass to the person, is **false imprisonment**. Business people dealing with the public will sometimes get into trouble when they suspect someone of shoplifting, or some other inappropriate conduct, and then restrain the person until the police arrive. This amounts to an imprisonment, and when it is done improperly or without authority, it is an actionable false imprisonment. Most people think of an imprisonment as involving a cell, handcuffs, or some other physical restraint. But an imprisonment may take place even where no physical restraint is present. When someone demands that another person accompany her, or even remain in a certain location, and that person complies thinking she has no choice, that person is submitting to the other, and an imprisonment has taken place. Of course, not all such imprisonments are actionable. If the person really has committed a crime for which he can be arrested, even a private citizen has the authority to arrest. But where no crime has taken place, the imprisonment is false and the victim can sue. Shoplifting, or failing to pay for services, is a serious problem facing people in businesses such as retail stores, hotels, or restaurants. Managers of such businesses are sometimes driven to take decisive action. But they must take great care in doing so, as the potential loss from a false imprisonment allegation can far outweigh the actual losses. The classic example, of a restaurant manager detaining a customer who refuses to pay his bill because he is dissatisfied with the quality of the meal served, is a graphic illustration of employee overreaction and unawareness of the limits of the employee's authority. One such incident cost Marwest Hotel $3500 in damages plus legal expenses over a dispute involving an $8 bottle of wine.[3]

Complete restraint without authority is an actionable tort

Restraint can be physical or submission

No false imprisonment where authority to arrest

3. *Bahner v. Marwest Hotel Co.* (1969), 6 D.L.R. (3d) 322 (B.C.S.C.).

CASE SUMMARY 2.3

Snow v. Brettons Inc.[4]

Clerk's Error Results in Actionable False Imprisonment

Ms. Snow purchased an item at the defendant's store and upon leaving set off the security alarm. A sales clerk took her by the arm and escorted her back into the store where her bag was searched; it was determined that a tag inadvertently left on an item, which Ms. Snow had properly purchased and had gift wrapped, set off the alarm. Upon leaving, her embarrassment was made worse when she met a co-worker from her own place of employment. She sued the store for false imprisonment. The court held that when she returned with the store clerk to the store, it was reasonable for her to think she had no choice and so an imprisonment had taken place. It was false because no offence had occurred. Rather, an employee of the store had neglected to remove the tag. Although the incident only lasted five minutes, it caused great embarrassment and the judge awarded damages of $1000 for the false imprisonment. Four walls or physical restraint are not required to constitute an imprisonment. When a person surrenders his or her will to another, thinking he or she has no choice but to go with that person, it is still an imprisonment and actionable if done without authority. This case illustrates how careful a business dealing with the public has to be when dealing with apparent shoplifters.

TRESPASS

Trespass involves voluntary conduct without authority

The tort of **trespass to land** involves someone coming on to another's land without permission or authority. A person can be a trespasser without even realizing he is on someone else's property. Someone wandering onto another's property, not realizing she had crossed the boundary line, would be a trespasser. By contrast, a person hit by a car and knocked on to another's property is not. Of course, someone with authority, such as a postal employee delivering mail or an official reading a meter, is not a trespasser. This is true even when that person is acting without permission, provided he doesn't go beyond that authority. The entrance of a meter reader would be authorized, but if the meter reader cut through the back yard to get to the next street, such an unauthorized shortcut would be a trespass. A trespass can also take place indirectly when someone throws something onto the land or where a permanent incursion takes place, as when a structure is built that encroaches on another's property. Customers can become trespassers when they overstay their welcome, cause destruction, or otherwise break the rules associated with the premises. In this case the proprietor has the right to eject them using reasonable force (no more force than is necessary). This requires that the proprietor first tell the person to leave and give him or her enough time to vacate the premises before having the individual forcefully ejected.

Trespassers may be ejected using reasonable force

There is also a *Criminal Code* offence of trespassing, where a person loitering on another's property at night by a dwelling house is liable to summary conviction. The *Criminal Code* also permits reasonable force to be used to eject a tres-

4. Ont. Prov. Ct., as reported in *Lawyers Weekly Consolidated Digest,* Vol. 8.

passer and to defend real or personal property. Where the trespasser resists, his or her conduct will constitute an assault against the property owner.

Trespass may also be criminal

Trespassers are responsible for any damage they cause on the property. But no damage is actually necessary for the trespass to be actionable by the landowner. When the trespasser is injured on the property, traditionally the occupier of the land was not responsible unless that damage was caused intentionally or recklessly. Many jurisdictions have passed legislation modifying the duty owed by occupiers to those using their land, but even then the duty owed to trespassers is significantly less than the duty owed to others using the property. When a building encroaches on another's land, this is called a continuing trespass and like other forms of trespass the remedy might be damages or an injunction. An injunction would pose a huge problem, requiring the building to be removed at great expense unless a settlement could be negotiated.

Responsibility to trespasser modified by statute

Injunctions used to stop trespassers

CASE SUMMARY 2.4

Epstein v. Cressey Development Corp.[5]

Necessary Incursion Is Still Trespass

Cressey Development Corporation excavated a lot next to property owned by Mr. Epstein and asked permission to drive supports under Epstein's property to support that excavation. Epstein refused. After unsuccessfully trying other methods to shore up the excavation, Cressey drove the supports under the property anyway. When Epstein found out, he sued for trespass. Cressey claimed the trespass was done out of necessity and that there had been no interference with Epstein's use of his property.

The court held that a trespass had taken place, that damage was caused since future development was now restricted, and that Cressey Development Corporation had been warned by their own engineer that this would amount to trespass. Even so, they went ahead with little concern for Epstein's rights. Punitive damages were justified in this situation. In this case significant damages were awarded, but the award of an injunction to remove the supports would have been much worse since Cressey had completed the construction of the building. Great care should be taken to avoid these situations, and one should never assume that just because such an incursion or other activity is necessary to facilitate your business affairs it justifies interference with another person's property. Your business problems are not the problems of your neighbour.

NUISANCE

Private nuisance involves one person using their property in such a way as to interfere with a neighbour's use of their property. This might involve fumes, odours, water, noise, or other substances escaping from one property so as to interfere with a neighbour's enjoyment of his or her property. Remedies may include damages or an injunction. But the activity complained of must be an

5. B.C.C.A., as reported in *Lawyers Weekly Consolidated Digest,* Vol. 11.

inappropriate use of that property. A person moving into an industrial area can't complain about the noise from a factory next door, and someone in a farming area can't complain about normal barnyard smells. But a person in an urban area could complain about smoke from a neighbour's smokehouse drifting onto his property and making it impossible to use the backyard. Also the interference with the use of the neighbour's property must have been reasonably foreseeable; the offender should have anticipated the result. Reasonable foreseeability will be discussed in greater depth under "Negligence" in this chapter.

Nuisance involves unusual use of property interfering with neighbour

DEFAMATION

Defamation can also be a serious problem for the business person. It involves a false statement about someone to his or her detriment. The statement must not only reflect badly on the victim, but also clearly refer to the person suing. If you said the workers in a particular office were slackers, an individual in that group could not claim defamation since that person could not prove that the statement referred particularly to him or her. It is also possible to defame a product or business. Thus, circulating a false statement that a competitor's brand of beer is contaminated would qualify as defamation. The derogatory statement must also be **published** to be actionable, which means it must be heard or read by someone other than the two parties involved. This might take the form of a newspaper article, a letter to the editor, or a radio or TV broadcast, but it also could be a letter to the other person's employer, or simply a conversation overheard at a restaurant. Sometimes a statement might appear innocent, but because of some special knowledge held by the hearer, it becomes derogatory. The statement in a financial paper about a couple at a business convention might appear perfectly innocent, until it's combined with the knowledge of some readers that both are married to other people. This is called an **innuendo** and even where the statement is made in error, it is actionable as defamation. **Mistake** is no defence. **Libel** is written defamation whereas spoken defamation is **slander**. Libel is treated much more seriously, on the theory that it takes a more permanent form and thus can do more damage. Essentially, libel is easier to prove. With slander, except for a few exceptions, actual monetary loss must be shown, whereas with libel it is enough to show that the defamatory statement was made. Legislation has been passed in most jurisdictions declaring broadcasted (over the radio or TV) defamation to be libel rather than slander. Communications over the internet are becoming an increasing problem, but there is no question that emails now pose the greatest danger. It is so easy to thoughtlessly compose emails and send them to many different destinations that they have become an important cause of defamation actions today.

Defamation involves derogatory false statement

Defamation may involve innuendo

Slander is verbal; libel is written and easier to prove

Broadcasted defamation is libel by statute

DEFENCES There are several important defences available to a defamation action, not the least of which is **justification**. So long as the statement is substantially true this represents an effective defence. However, it is important to note that the defendant must prove the statement true rather than the plaintiff having to prove it false. Remember that it is the actual message being communicated (even if it is an innuendo) that must be true, not simply the bare words or the idea that was intended by the communication. Statements made on the floor of the legislature or Parliament, in senior government committees, and as part of trial proceedings are considered **absolutely privileged**, and cannot form the basis of a defamation action. The free flow of information and the encouragement of debate and free speech are considered to be too important in these circum-

Derogatory statements made in Parliament or court are protected

stances to be hindered by the threat of litigation. Statements made in the context of employment such as the evaluation of another employee's work habits or reports made to the police investigating a case are protected to a lesser extent. This lesser protection is also given to statements made with respect to some matter of mutual interest as with members of professional bodies such as lawyers', accountants', doctors', or dentists' associations. This is called **qualified privilege** and so long as the person made the statement thinking it was true, without malice, and did not communicate it to anyone other than those who needed to know, the victim cannot successfully sue, even if the communication was false and damaging. One of the dangers of using the internet or email is that the message may be communicated too broadly and thus qualified privilege may be lost.

Derogatory comments made pursuant to duty are protected

Fair comment is another important defence used mostly by the media. People are entitled to have and express opinions on matters of public interest, and so commentaries on plays, exhibitions, sports, or even comments on the actions of politicians and other public figures are protected. As long as the expression of opinion is commentary based on true facts known to the public—even where the opinion is unpopular and most of the public disagrees—and as long as it is a possible conclusion based on the public facts and stated without malice, it is protected. For these reasons harsh or derisive reviews of restaurants, plays, sporting competitions, and the like are not actionable. Politicians are also fair game, but great care must be taken to keep the statement an expression of opinion based on known facts. If the commentary involves statements of fact that are not true, they are actionable as defamations. You can conclude that a politician's actions were incompetent, but your statement of what happened to lead you to that conclusion had better be accurate. It is interesting that fair comment also protects political cartoons that get their messages across by exaggeration. The legislation in place also limits the exposure of newspapers and other communications media by limiting the amount of damages that can be claimed by the victim if an appropriate apology is published. Still, it must be remembered that defamatory remarks can be extremely dangerous and cause serious damage to the victim. The courts have awarded significant damages. In *Hill v. Church of Scientology of Toronto*,[6] for example, the total damages awarded were $1.6 million, and in *Leenen v. C.B.C.* and *Myers v. C.B.C.*[7] the damages resulting from the defamation of two medical doctors on the CBC's *Fifth Estate* program came to $1.15 million, plus legal costs of close to $1 million.

Derogatory comments made as fair comment on public matter are protected

Defamatory libel can also constitute a criminal offence under the *Criminal Code* of Canada, where the published words will injure a person's reputation by "exposing him to hatred, contempt, or ridicule." The usual defences discussed above apply, but the truth of the defamation will only justify its publication if it is also in the public interest. Note also that extortion by defamatory libel, or the threat of it, is also an offence. Publishers can also be liable unless they can show they had no knowledge of the inclusion of the offending words. In *R. v. Lucas*[8] a husband and wife were charged with criminal libel when they picketed a provincial court building. Their signs suggested that a police officer investigating the sexual abuse of children failed in his duty and contributed to or participated in sexually abusive conduct himself. The Supreme Court of Canada found that

Libel may also be criminal

6. [1995] 2 S.C.R. 1130 (S.C.C.).

7. *Leenen v. Canadian Broadcasting Corp.*, 2001 CanLII 4997 (Ont. C.A.); and *Myers v. Canadian Broadcasting Corp.*, 2001 CanLII 4874 (Ont. C.A.).

8. [1998] 1 S.C.R. 439 (S.C.C.).

TABLE 2.1 Intentional Torts

Intentional Torts	Nature	Defences
Assault and Battery	Assault: threatened battery Battery: intentional hitting	Consent: must be informed and complete Self-defence: must be reasonable force Accident but not a mistake
False Imprisonment	Complete physical or mental restraint without authority	No actual confinement or submission Had authority to imprison
Trespass	Coming on to or putting something on another's land without authority	Had authority to do so Had consent Accident but not a mistake
Nuisance	Use of property so that it interferes with neighbour's	Appropriate use of property for area Interference was not reasonably foreseeable
Defamation	A published false and derogatory statement: spoken (slander) or written (libel)	Truth, absolute privilege, qualified privilege, and fair comment

although the sections of the *Criminal Code* did interfere with freedom of expression, they were justified under section 1 of the *Charter of Rights and Freedoms* to protect the reputation of individuals so defamed. The original sentences imposed at trial were two years less a day for Mr. Lucus and 22 months for his wife, but these were reduced to 18 months and 12 months on appeal. These convictions were upheld by the Supreme Court of Canada.

Negligence

Negligence involves inadvertent conduct causing loss

Of all the different ways that liability can be incurred in tort, negligence is by far the most important for the business person. Negligence involves inadvertent or careless conduct causing injury or loss to another. At the outset, it must be made clear that negligence is not a state of mind. We are not talking about someone being silly or stupid. Negligence involves the failure of one person to live up to a standard of care required in his or her dealings with others. The term "careless," as it is used in this discussion, refers to the failure to live up to that required standard of care. When suing someone for negligence, several things must be established. First, that there was a **duty of care** in the first place. We don't owe a duty to be careful to everyone in the world or even to everybody in our community—only to limited classes or groups of people determined by legal test and social policy, as explained below. Once it is determined that a duty is owed, the next problem is to determine the nature of that duty. Just how careful does a person have to be? To succeed, the plaintiff must show that the conduct fell below a **standard of care**. Also it must be determined that there was some sort of injury or loss caused by the alleged conduct.

At the outset it is vital to understand the concept of the reasonable person in law. While the conduct of average people might be more important in other disciplines, in law we set a standard of required behaviour somewhat higher than what would be expected of an average person. In effect, the court asks what a reasonable, objective bystander would have done in the same circumstances. This **reasonable person test** requires behaviour that is higher than average but less than perfect. A helpful comparison is the concept of par in a game of golf. Each hole on a golf course has a standard number of strokes associated with it called "par." An average golfer will require more strokes than this number to sink the ball, even though it is possible for a good golfer (or a lucky one) to do it in less. Par, then, is a higher standard or goal, designed to challenge the golfer. It reflects what a good golfer having a good day would likely be able to accomplish. The reasonable person standard in law is similar. It reflects a standard of behaviour we would expect from a prudent person being careful, and while it need not reach perfection, it is clear that average is not good enough.

Reasonable person: better than average but less than perfect

DUTY OF CARE

One of the most significant civil cases in the 20th century is the famous "snail in the ginger beer bottle" case, *Donoghue v. Stevenson,*[9] which took place in Scotland in the 1930s. The decision made by the House of Lords is followed in most common law jurisdictions. Mrs. Donoghue went to a café with a friend, who bought her a ginger beer float. The ginger beer was served in an opaque bottle, so it was not until the second serving that Mrs. Donoghue discovered it contained a decomposed snail. Mrs. Donoghue became violently ill, but she couldn't successfully sue the café for breach of contract, since her friend bought the ginger beer for her. Contract law is a major area of discussion in the following chapters. Instead, she sued the bottler of the product, Stevenson, in tort for negligence. The case turned upon whether the bottler, Stevenson, owed a duty to be careful to Mrs. Donoghue, the ultimate consumer of the product he produced. The case is famous because it established the test to be used when determining whether a duty of care is owed to another. This is the **reasonable foreseeability test**. Thus, we owe a duty to be careful to anyone we can reasonably foresee (anticipate) might be harmed by our conduct. In this case it was clear that Mr. Stevenson should have anticipated that if he was careless in the production of the ginger beer, an ultimate consumer, Mrs. Donoghue, might be injured. Therefore, a duty to be careful was owed to her. This reasonable foreseeability test has become extremely important in the development of the law of negligence and personal liability, although it has been modified in some circumstances. See the discussion of the *Anns* case under the heading "Professional Liability" below.

Negligence requires duty of care

Existence of duty determined by reasonable foreseeability

CASE SUMMARY 2.5

Hunt (Guardian of) v. Sutton Group Incentive Realty Inc.[10]

Duty to Protect Worker from Herself

Linda Hunt was a receptionist working part-time for the Sutton Group Inc. when she attended a Christmas party where she had a considerable amount to drink. At 4:00 p.m. she still had responsibilities to clean up after the party, but her employer, see-

(continued)

9. [1932] A.C. 562 (H.L.).

10. 2002 CanLII 45019 (Ont. C.A.).

ing she was inebriated, offered to call her husband to come pick her up. Instead, she remained for two or more hours at the party before she left with several other people and went to a pub. She then set out to drive home in freezing rain and snow. She was seriously injured when her car slid into the path of another vehicle.

The damages were over one million dollars. She sued her employer for putting her into an environment where she was at risk, and she sued the pub for failing to protect her as a patron. Although the court found that her behaviour had contributed to her loss, the employer and the pub were jointly and severally liable for 25 percent of that loss. Joint and several liability means that if one of the defendants can't pay his or her share, the liability assigned to him or her can be collected from the other defendant. Judicial decisions in Canada have made it clear that employers and commercial establishments serving liquor can be held responsible for injury and loss suffered as a result of serving liquor to the point of intoxication. Care should be taken to ensure that people don't drink to excess and that alternate transportation be arranged when they do. While such liability has not yet been extended to private individuals in this country, it would seem prudent for private hosts to make sure people don't drink to excess. It would also be wise to provide taxis or other means for guests to get home when they do drink too much or to provide some other form of accommodation to ensure they don't drink and drive.

STANDARD OF CARE

In most negligence cases the existence of a duty of care is self-evident, and the problem is to determine whether there was a failure to live up to the appropriate standard of care. As a general rule our law does not impose a duty to act and so omission (nonfeasance) is not generally actionable unless there is some special relationship imposing a duty. These would include roles such as a lifeguard or guardian, or situations where there is a duty to warn of some danger, as is the case with the occupier of property or the manufacturer of a dangerous product. In most examples of actionable negligence, inappropriate conduct or misfeasance is involved. The question remains, therefore, how careful does a person have to be? The general answer in Canadian law is that a person is required to live up to what would be expected of a reasonable person in the same circumstances. So long as that standard is maintained or surpassed, there has been no negligence even where serious harm has taken place. This is the second major application of the reasonable person test as used in the law of negligence, and is, perhaps, the most significant application of this test in our legal system. Remember that reasonable care is not average but is what is expected of a prudent person being careful. In determining reasonable conduct, the courts will look at several factors. The risk of potential damage will be taken into account. Thus, in a desert where torrential rains are rare, extensive waterproofing of a building would not be expected, especially where the costs of avoiding such an unlikely occurrence would be high. Risk, cost, and potential loss, therefore, are important factors to be taken into consideration in determining reasonable conduct.

The standard of conduct required is determined by reasonable person test

Reasonable care is determined by risk, cost, and potential of loss

In situations where high risk is involved with great potential for damage, the duty to be careful is extremely high. When food handlers and motor vehicle operators cause injury, for example, negligence is easier to prove since the required standard of care is extremely high.[11]

Another important factor is the expertise claimed by the person being held to a standard. Doctors, accountants, engineers, and other professionals are expected to have the skills and abilities associated with their profession and to exercise those skills in a reasonable manner. And so the standard expected is that of a reasonable doctor or a reasonable engineer. While it would likely not be negligent for an average person to misdiagnose a person having a stroke or a heart attack, it could well be negligence for an attending physician to make such an error.

Expertise claimed affects reasonableness of conduct

It is often difficult to determine just what caused the loss or injury. Some situations, however, such as a snail in a soft drink, a falling piano, or contaminated food leads one to the conclusion that someone must have been careless. Canadian courts can look at such circumstantial evidence, and, if strong enough, conclude that a presumption of negligence has been established. Then it is up to the defendant to produce evidence that he or she was not negligent. If the defendant cannot, the presumption is confirmed and liability for negligence determined. Until recently this was treated under the principle of *res ipsa loquitur,* but the Supreme Court of Canada has decided that these matters are better dealt with by applying the more flexible principle of circumstantial evidence.[12]

CASE SUMMARY 2.6

Kripps v. Touche Ross and Co.[13]

Accountant Negligent Despite Following Rules

The defendants were a firm of accountants that audited the books of Victoria Mortgage and Housing from 1980 to 1983. These audited statements were used to issue a prospectus and sell debentures to the public. The auditors' refusal to approve the 1984 statements of the company led to its collapse. The debenture holders, who had relied on the previous statements, lost considerably in the collapse and sued the defendant auditors. The debenture holders claimed the auditors had been negligent in providing a favourable audit for the prior years. The problem related to a number of mortgages held by Victoria Mortgage that were in default. They amounted to one-third of the mortgages held by that company. The bad mortgages had been capitalized as valuable assets along with the unpaid interest, instead of being treated as uncollectible losses.

The auditors defended their actions by stating that this was consistent with the rules that they followed (GAAP, Generally Accepted Accounting Principles and GAAS, Generally Accepted Audit Standards), and so long as they acted within those rules, they could not be acting negligently. The trial judge agreed, but on appeal the court found the auditors negligent. Professionals cannot hide behind the rules they make

(continued)

11. In rare circumstances where someone brings something dangerous on his or her property which escapes causing injury to a neighbour, liability may be imposed, even where the owner of the property has not caused the escape. This is called strict liability or the rule in *Rylands v. Fletcher* (1868), L.R. 3 (H.L.) 330.
12. *Fontaine v. British Columbia (Official Administrator),* [1998] 1 S.C.R. 424 (S.C.C.).
13. (1997), 33 B.C.L.R. (3d) 254, [1997] 6 W.W.R. 421 (B.C.C.A.).

themselves and claim that they are following the appropriate standard, no matter what the consequences. "GAAP may be their guide to forming this opinion, but auditors are retained to form an opinion on the fairness of the financial statements, not merely on their conformity to GAAP." The auditors knew the mortgages were in default at the time, thus making their audited statements clearly misleading.

This case illustrates the high standard of care required of professionals and the fact that simply adhering to standard practice or rules of conduct set by a professional association may not always be good enough to escape liability.

Special statutory standards override common law

Historically, special rules were applied to some unique situations. For example, occupiers (the people in possession of property as opposed to the landlord) had a particular responsibility to people using the land, depending on their status. The occupier had to protect an invitee from any unusual danger. Invitees were people on the land for some business purpose. Licensees, who were there out of sufferance or with permission, had to be warned of any hidden danger, but the only duty owed to a trespasser was not to intentionally or recklessly harm him or her. Most jurisdictions have enacted occupier's liability acts, which modify these traditional obligations. Typically, the distinction between invitees and licensees has been abolished requiring the occupier to take reasonable steps to protect all visitors and their property. The obligations to trespassers remain minimal.

CASE SUMMARY 2.7

Malinoski v. 2727677 Manitoba Inc.[14]

Duty of Occupier to Protect Visitor

Mrs. Malinoski was 73 years old when she caught her shoe and fell down a flight of stairs into a parking area. She claimed that the area around the top of the stairs had not been properly maintained or constructed. After the accident her shoe was found caught in a gap between some patio blocks and the plywood where the stairway started. The defendants argued that she wasn't careful, and also that they had only purchased the company six days earlier and couldn't be held responsible. In finding for the plaintiff, the judge made it clear that under the *Occupier's Liability Act* they were responsible for ensuring that the property was in a safe condition, even though they had just recently purchased it. Mrs. Malinoski was held 20 percent responsible because of her contributory negligence. All provinces have similar statutes imposing an obligation on occupiers to make sure their property is safe for those using it.

There are other examples where legislation has been used to change the standard of care required of certain classes. The unique obligations owed by innkeepers to their guests and common carriers to their customers have been modified by statute in most jurisdictions. But it is important to realize that not every time a statute imposes a duty on someone is a new category of tort created. For example,

14. (1995), 105 Man. R. (2d) 145 (Man. Q.B).

human rights legislation and privacy legislation both impose duties and rights, but they are not tort obligations, and the remedies available are limited to those set out in the legislation that creates them. It should also be noted that insurance is a method of avoiding the risks associated with tort liability, and some jurisdictions require insurance. For example, by law all drivers must carry auto insurance as a method of spreading that risk. In business, of course, insurance becomes a very important aspect of risk avoidance, and the cost of acquiring the various forms of insurance required to operate a business successfully must be factored into the overall cost of doing business.

CAUSATION AND DAMAGE

Breach of duty must have led to loss or damage

Finally, to succeed in a negligence action, the plaintiff must demonstrate that the conduct complained of was the cause of the injury or damage (see Table 2.2 on p. 41). With intentional torts such as assault and battery, false imprisonment, or trespass, it is not necessary that actual damage be shown. The commission of the tort is enough to warrant payment of damages, although compensation for losses will also be included in any judgment. But with negligence there must be some sort of injury or damage resulting before compensation can be sought from the defendant. Almost getting hurt is not good enough. It follows that the damages must be the direct result of the negligent conduct complained of. If it were established that the driver involved in an accident knew his or her brake lights weren't working, the plaintiff would still have to demonstrate that the lack of brake lights caused the accident. If the accident involved a head-on collision, it would be very unlikely that this failure contributed to the collision. The defendant may have been careless for driving without brake lights, but that failure did not cause the accident. In some situations it can be a very difficult and complex problem for the court to determine just how much of a causal connection is needed for liability for negligence to be imposed. This will be discussed below under the heading "Remoteness."

FIGURE 2.2 Negligence

Loss → causation → duty owed → duty breached → no defences

Defences

CONTRIBUTORY NEGLIGENCE

Traditionally, if it could be shown that the person who was suing had also contributed to the loss, he or she would receive no compensation from the defendant. This was first modified to a limited extent in common law and, subsequently, by legislation. Statutes such as Ontario's *Negligence Act* allow the court to assign proportional liability, making both parties responsible for the loss (see Figure 2.3). For example, in an automobile accident Jones suffered $100 000 damage because of personal injury and Smith only suffered $10 000 damage to his car. If the court determined Smith to be 25 percent at fault and Jones 75 per-

FIGURE 2.3 Negligence Action

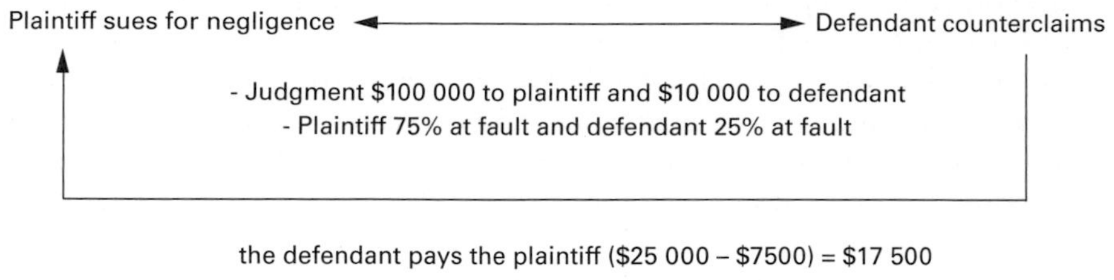
Plaintiff sues for negligence
Defendant counterclaims
- Judgment $100 000 to plaintiff and $10 000 to defendant
- Plaintiff 75% at fault and defendant 25% at fault
the defendant pays the plaintiff ($25 000 – $7500) = $17 500

Where the victim is also negligent, loss is now apportioned

cent, Smith would have to pay Jones $17 500 and legal costs. With contributory negligence, the court is reducing the amount of compensation paid to a victim of negligence because the victim's own carelessness contributed to the loss.

VOLUNTARY ASSUMPTION OF RISK

Where victim voluntarily assumed the legal risk, there is no remedy

People who deliberately put themselves in harm's way are disqualified from suing for the injury or loss that results. Unlike contributory negligence, this is a complete bar to recovery of loss. This used to be a much more important aspect of negligence law, but to raise this defence today, the defendant must show not only that the injured party voluntarily put himself or herself in danger, but also that he or she did it in such as way as to absolve the defendant of any legal responsibility for the consequences. It must be established that not only did the victim assume the physical risk, but the legal risk as well. This is difficult to prove; consequently, when people act foolishly—taking risks that they shouldn't—the courts usually deal with it as contributory negligence. The courts can then apportion the loss between the parties based on their percentage of fault. This is a much more satisfactory result. Still, in extreme cases where people knowingly put themselves in harm's way, the court may find voluntary assumption of risk and completely bar recovery. Thus, when a drunken individual participated in a tubing race at a winter resort and was seriously injured, contributory negligence was applied rather than voluntary assumption of risk, because it could not be established that he had assumed both the legal risk and the physical risk. This was the case even though he had signed a waiver form before commencing the activity.[15]

Rescuers who put themselves into dangerous situations are treated differently. If a person is negligent, putting another at risk, he or she also owes a duty to be careful to someone coming to the rescue of that person. If a bystander pushes a child out of the path of a speeding car, and is injured in the process, she can sue the negligent driver without fear that a claim of voluntary assumption of risk or contributory negligence will bar the action.

REMOTENESS

Another argument that is sometimes raised in defence of a negligence action is that the injury or loss was too remote. In the past, difficulties arose when the connection between the conduct that caused the injury and the injury itself was indi-

15. *Crocker v. Sundance Northwest Resorts Ltd.*, [1988] 1 S.C.R. 1186 (S.C.C.).

rect, convoluted, or the actual injury or damage took some unexpected form. Problems also arose when only economic loss was involved, usually caused by careless words rather than conduct. Courts tended to deal with such cases by making policy decisions but wording them in terms of a legal principle with uncomfortable and confusing results. Today this is partially solved in Canada by an application of the *Anns* case test. It is discussed in more detail under the heading "Professional Liability" below. Essentially, this test allows a court, after determining whether the injury or loss was reasonably foreseeable, to simply ask whether there is any good policy reason to reduce or modify that duty. This is clearly an application of social policy to the situation and is a much more straightforward approach to this kind of problem. Thus, where the events involved are strange, unusual, or involve incidents that cause the courts to question the appropriateness of the application of the normal rules of negligence law, they can now simply make a policy decision. This only partially solves the problem, however, because it still remains a question of fact to determine whether there was sufficient causal connection between the conduct complained of and the resulting injury. If that connection is considered to be too remote or too indirect, the requirement of causation will not be met and there will be no liability imposed.

Where connection is tenuous or the results unexpected, social policy may be applied to reduce or modify duty

Note that when personal injury is involved, we take our victims the way we find them. If the person whose hand I negligently injure is a concert pianist, I will be responsible to pay much greater compensation than if the person is a lawyer or accountant. I will not normally be able to claim that because of the unusual occupation of the victim his loss is too remote or that the damages should be limited only to what a normal person would lose. I must take my victim as I find him and pay the greater compensation.

Responsibility imposed even where unusual occupation or condition causes victim greater loss than normal

TABLE 2.2 Requirements of Negligence Action Plaintiff Must Establish

Duty to Take Care	That injury or loss was reasonably foreseeable (sometimes limited by social policy based on the *Anns* case)
Failure to Take Care	That the conduct complained of fell below the reasonable person standard (or other standard imposed by statute)
Causation and Damage	That the conduct complained of caused loss or injury to the plaintiff

TABLE 2.3 Defences That the Defendant Can Raise to Eliminate or Reduce Liability

Contributory Negligence	Where the plaintiff is also negligent, the court will apportion the damages.
Voluntary Assumption of Risk	Where the plaintiff has voluntarily put him- or herself in danger—and assumed the legal as well as physical risk—this will be a complete bar to recovery.
Remoteness	Where the causal connection is indirect or consequences out of proportion to expectations, liability may be reduced.

Product Liability

A few additional words should be said about product liability. As discussed in *Donoghue v. Stevenson,* when use of a particular product injures a person, there is normally a choice. The purchaser can sue the seller of the product for breach of contract and/or sue the manufacturer for negligence. Contracts will be discussed in the following chapters, but it is important to note at this stage that an action in contract has the distinct advantage of imposing strict liability where the product was defective and caused the injury. There is no need to prove fault on the part of the defendant. However, such a breach of contract action may not be available to the injured party either because he or she was not the person who purchased the product, or because the contract was with the retailer who sold the item, not the manufacturer. The principle that only the parties to a contract have obligations under it is referred to as **privity of contract**. When there is no contractual relation between the parties, the only option is to sue for negligence. The problem is that in a tort action fault must be demonstrated, in addition to showing that the defective product caused the injury. The plaintiff must show that the defendant failed to live up to the standard of a reasonable manufacturer in the circumstances. This can be very difficult to do and is one of the situations where the courts are willing to look at the surrounding events and find that a *prima facie* (clear on the face of it) case of negligence has been established from circumstantial evidence. For example, finding a decomposed snail in a can of soda speaks loudly that someone must have been careless. Either the production process has not been properly designed to avoid this type of thing from happening, or someone made a silly mistake. Then the shoe would be on the other foot, and the manufacturer would face the daunting task of showing that they did everything reasonable to ensure that this type of injury would not happen. Once it is established that some aspect of the product was defective and caused the injury complained of and that the manufacturer was careless, liability to compensate for that injury will be imposed.

When a manufacturer is sued, negligence must be established.

But note the use of circumstantial evidence

The product liability area is where class action suits are particularly important. Whether defective automobiles or tires, ruptured breast implants, or drugs that cause deformities or heart attacks are involved, when many people are injured as a result of the same complaint against the same manufacturer, a class action approach to the problem is an attractive way to proceed.

CASE SUMMARY 2.8

LeBlanc v. Marson Canada Inc.[16]

Duty to Ensure That Product Is Safe

In this case Mr. LeBlanc was seriously injured when using the defendant manufacturer's product. He was repairing the floor of his van, using a kit produced by Marson Canada Inc., when a tube of hardener burst at the wrong end, spraying into his face and causing temporary blindness. Although he recovered his eyesight, his

16. (1995), 397 A.P.R. 309, 139 N.S.R. (2d) 309 (N.S.S.C).

eyes remained so sensitive to fumes that he had to quit his job and sell his furniture refinishing business. There was no question that a duty was owed to the user of the product under the principles set out in *Donoghue v. Stevenson,* but the defendant claimed that they had met the required standard of care and were not negligent.

The court found that although they had done some testing on the tube, the testing was inadequate with respect to how much pressure could be exerted before bursting the tube. They also had failed to warn the user of the danger or to recommend the use of protective gloves, goggles, or clothing. This lack of warning and inadequate instructions with respect to the tube was, "a recipe for disaster which was clearly foreseeable to Marson." The damages awarded were in excess of $75 000. Mr. LeBlanc's wife was also awarded $2500 for the trouble, time, and energy she had taken to care for her husband and their family affairs. This case not only indicates that great care must be taken by manufacturers and resellers to anticipate and control for how their products are to be used and what can go wrong, but also that proper instructions and warnings must accompany the products.

In the United States if a person can show that the product was defective and it caused his or her injury, usually that is enough to establish liability. Some jurisdictions in Canada have moved away from the traditional approach of requiring the demonstration of negligence in product liability cases. Other provinces have moved in that same direction by imposing contractual warranties on a manufacturer guaranteeing fitness and quality, and extending those rights to anyone who uses the product. This, in effect, wipes out the requirement that the victim be the purchaser of the product as discussed above. Courts in other jurisdictions have found that because of advertising, specifications, and other literature, including manufacturers' warranties, a subsidiary contract exists between the manufacturer and purchaser, making the manufacturer directly liable to the purchaser (see Figure 2.4).

In some jurisdictions manufacturers may be sued in contract

FIGURE 2.4 Product Liability

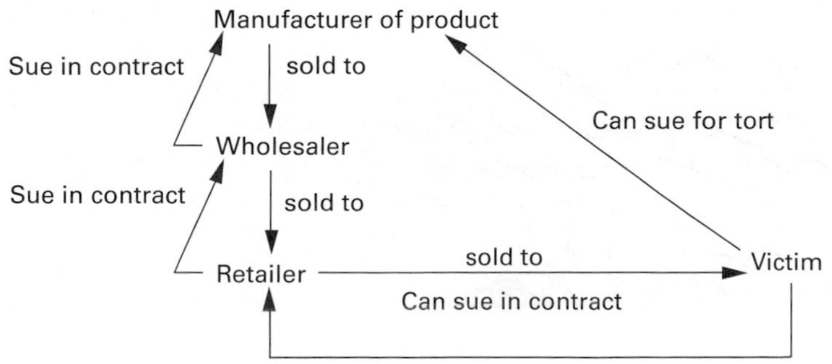

Professional Liability

Professional liability to clients based on contract

A similar situation exists when professionals are involved. They have a direct contractual liability to their clients, and are liable, even without showing fault, when they make errors that cause loss to those clients. However, as they carry out their professional duties, the damage incurred often goes beyond their direct relation to their clients and causes economic or even physical loss or injury to third parties. Those injured claimants then must sue in tort for negligence, and the question for the court to determine is just how far they want to extend such **professional liability** in these circumstances. Historically, the courts refused to provide a remedy where the loss was purely economic, especially where it was caused by words rather than conduct. This changed in Canada in 1965 with the case of *Haig v. Bamford*.[17] In this case an accountant made a mistake on audited financial statements causing loss to a third party investor who had relied on those erroneous reports. Loss in this case was clearly reasonably foreseeable, but if the court applied that test, it would open up the liability of such auditors in an unlimited way for unlimited losses. The Supreme Court held that liability for such careless words could be imposed. However, the court avoided applying the reasonable foreseeability test, imposing instead a more restricted one. For the next 25 years there was some confusion as to when a duty would exist and when it would not. The eventual solution was to supplement the reasonable foreseeability test developed in *Donoghue v. Stevenson* with a Canadian application of the *Anns* case[18] (an English case adopted in a unique way by the Supreme Court of Canada to meet Canadian requirements), which resulted in a much more straightforward and simple approach.

Professional liability to others based on tort and *Anns* case test

While in normal negligence cases the reasonable foreseeability test still applies, the Supreme Court of Canada has made it clear that, today, when faced with new or unique problems, the courts are to apply the two-stage *Anns* case test. The first stage is to determine whether there is a degree of proximity or neighbourhood between the parties, such that one person should have realized that his or her conduct placed the victim at risk. This is essentially another way of expressing the reasonable foreseeability test developed in *Donoghue v. Stevenson*. The second question must then be asked: Is there any reason not to impose the duty, to reduce the scope of that duty, to limit the class to whom the duty is owed, or should the damages awarded be reduced? This second part of the *Anns* test allows the courts to modify the nature of the duty where circumstances warrant on the basis of social policy.

Duty may now be modified or eliminated on policy considerations

The *Hercules* case[19] is a good example of the Supreme Court of Canada applying the *Anns* case. Auditors prepared financial reports for a company as part of the normal annual auditing process. These reports were prepared for the shareholders to use in their evaluation of the performance of management. Instead, the shareholders invested further funds in the company on the strength of the audited reports. The invested funds were lost because of errors in the reports, and the investors/shareholders sued the auditors for negligence. The Supreme Court of Canada held that while damage to the shareholders was clearly reasonably foreseeable, there was a good policy reason to deny the existence of a duty in

17. (1976), 72 D.L.R. (3d) 68 (S.C.C.).

18. *Anns v. Merton, London Borough Council*, [1977] 2 All E.R. 492 (H.L.).

19. *Hercules Management Ltd. v. Ernst & Young* (1997), 146 D.L.R. (4th) 577 (S.C.C.).

this case. The Supreme Court made it clear that they were reluctant to expose accountants and other professionals to open-ended liability where they would be liable for an "indeterminate amount for an indeterminate time to an indeterminate class." Applying this policy, the Supreme Court decided that because the erroneous reports were used for a purpose other than intended, there was no duty and no liability.

Court unwilling to expose professionals to unlimited liability

Today this approach will be used in any new or unusual situation where duty of care must be determined. This applies even when the careless conduct results in physical injury such as a bridge falling because of a design mistake, and people are injured or suffer loss because of the failure. Just how extensive should the liability be to the people using the bridge? What about those who suffer a loss because they can no longer use the bridge? Once reasonable foreseeability has been determined, the court can then apply the second half of the *Anns* case test and impose limits on the basis of social policy considerations. But even with this limited approach towards duty of care, professionals must always remember that they not only are required to be careful in their dealings with their clients, but also may be held responsible for damages their conduct causes to others with whom they are not directly dealing.

Where professionals are involved, there are also some unique problems in determining just how careful the professional is required to be. The general principle is that the professional, like anyone else, must live up to the standard of a reasonable person in the circumstances. Thus, the standard imposed becomes what is expected of a reasonable lawyer, doctor, accountant, engineer, architect, teacher, or consultant. Wherever a degree of expertise is claimed, that expert or professional is required to have the level of skill and expertise expected of a normal person in that profession. Inexperience is no excuse. Further, the professional is required to exercise that expertise and skill in a reasonable manner. Showing that an expert adhered to the standard practice in a particular profession is usually good enough. The rationale is that professionals will generally act reasonably as they practise their profession. Even this may not always be sufficient. If the court can be convinced that standard practice in a particular instance is shoddy or inappropriate, liability for negligence will still be imposed. For example, the Court of Appeal in British Columbia in *Kripps v. Touche Ross*,[20] described above, found that strict adherence to GAAP (Generally Accepted Accounting Principles) and GAAS (Generally Accepted Auditing Standards) was not sufficient to avoid liability for negligence on the part of the defendant accountants when the resulting financial statements misrepresented the condition of the company. If the victim can establish that a duty was owed by the professional, satisfying both parts of the *Anns* case test—that there was a failure to live up to the appropriate standard and that failure caused the injury complained about—liability for negligence will be imposed.

Higher standard of conduct required of experts

Standard practice of profession may not be good enough

Professionals and other experts also have a **fiduciary duty** to their clients. This means they have a duty to act in the best interests of their clients, even to the point of putting their clients' interests ahead of their own. Fiduciary duty will be discussed extensively in this text, especially with respect to agency, partnership, and corporations. It is sufficient to say at this point that the nature of a fiduciary duty involves loyalty and good faith. All information that comes to the professional that relates to what is being done for that client is the property of the client. The professional must not disclose it to others or make use of it for any

Fiduciary duty requires good faith and clients' interests to be put first

20. (1997), 33 B.C.L.R. (3d) 254, [1997] 6 W.W.R. 421.

personal gain. Similarly, if the other interests of the professional are in conflict with those of the client (where the professional could serve his own interests at the expense of the client) those conflicting interests must be disclosed, and the professional must step back from any decision-making process where that conflict exists.

Often the professional will have in his or her possession funds from various transactions involving clients. These are trust funds and must be kept scrupulously separate from the professional's other moneys and must never be used for any other purpose than the client's business. A breach of trust action is a very serious matter, and it will usually result in the professional being disqualified from practising his or her profession. This is a particular problem for lawyers, accountants, financial planners, and real estate and insurance agents. Often criminal penalties are also imposed.

Professionals are also answerable to various professional organizations that authorize them to practise their professions. This may be law societies, medical associations, teachers' associations, various accounting organizations, and others, depending on the profession involved. Their powers vary but often these bodies have the authority to determine who can practise the profession and to set the standard of education, ethics, and skills required. Most bodies can also discipline members and disqualify or limit a member's right to practise in the profession if the complaint against the member is serious enough. It must always be remembered that these bodies are subject to law and must adhere to basic human rights legislation; where their decisions violate basic rules of due process, human rights, or other valid regulations, those decisions can be challenged in the courts.

Disciplinary bodies subject to rules of "due process"

Finally, it should be noted that the risks associated with tort liability can be avoided or significantly reduced for the professional and non-professional as well, simply through the acquisition of appropriate insurance. Insurance has become an essential aspect of doing business. Liability insurance (sometimes called errors and omissions insurance) will protect professionals and others when they make mistakes that cause loss to clients and other people. The insurer not only will compensate the victim for the injury but also will provide appropriate legal representation to cover the insured during the process of the claim. Insurance, however, will not usually protect the insured where the wrongful act was deliberate or fraud was involved. The victim may, in fact, be entitled to compensation in these circumstances, but the insurance company will normally demand repayment from the insured, including any legal expenses incurred. One serious problem with insurance today is the ever increasing cost of premiums. With the huge awards that are being ordered by the courts for malpractice in all professions, the premiums are generally increasing to the point of becoming unbearable. Consequently, many professionals and business people are simply taking their chances and, where possible, not carrying insurance at all. Some professional bodies, however, require insurance coverage as a condition of practice. They sometimes provide that insurance, often at a high cost, as one of the services provided to their members. It is a shame that CEOs, senior managers, and directors of large corporations are not required to belong to a similar professional organization with similar standards relating to skills, competence, and ethics. Perhaps then we would be spared from such recent spectacular failures as experienced by Enron, WorldCom, and Nortel.

Professional risk is reduced by insurance

Negligence may also be criminal

Negligence can also constitute a crime under the *Criminal Code* of Canada, where a person in the performance of a duty does or omits to do something that "shows wanton or reckless disregard for the lives or safety of other persons." If the negligent conduct causes bodily harm the accused is liable to imprisonment up to 14 years, and to life where a death results. There are many other provisions of the *Criminal Code* relating to specific conduct that also provide a penalty for negligence. It should be further noted that organizations, including companies, can also be convicted under these provisions, usually with the imposition of significant fines. An example of a typical sentence imposed for criminal negligence is found in *R. v. Jeffery*.[21] The accused was a truck driver who, while intoxicated, caused an accident that resulted in two deaths. The court sentenced the driver to three and a half years, and extended a driving suspension for over 10 years. This case indicates that the primary consideration in such alcohol-related cases should be deterrence.

Other Business Torts

Negligence is by far the most important tort for the business person or professional. But there are several other related torts of which they should be aware. When a person intentionally misleads another, cheating him or her out of money or obtaining some other advantage, this is a **fraud or deceit**. For more detail, see Chapter 4, where fraudulent misrepresentation is discussed as part of the discussion on contract law. Also, defamation has many different forms, and one way it can take place is where false information is intentionally spread to harm the sales of a particular product. This is called **injurious falsehood or product defamation**.

Other business torts include:

- Fraud

- Product defamation

When one person persuades another to breach a contract with a third person, this may constitute **inducing breach of contract**. Often, one employer "steals" an employee from another employer, persuading that employee to breach his or her employment contract in the process. Whether it is done to obtain the unique skills of that employee, or just to weaken a competitor, the employer usually thinks that the only one that has committed a wrong is the employee. In fact, there is considerable danger for the one inducing the breach. This is because the value of that employee to the business may be much greater than reflected by the salary and consequently the person inducing the breach can be held liable for the loss. This tort can also take place when one person persuades a potential client or customer to breach his contract with a competitor and to deal with his business instead.

- Inducing breach of contract

In the area of intellectual property there is nothing so valuable as a good name and reputation. Sometimes, by using a similar name, logo, or other identifying characteristic of a brand, one business will try to take advantage of another by misleading people into thinking they are associated with or are part of that reputable business, when in fact they are not. This is an attempt to mislead and is actionable as a **passing-off** action. For example, where a fast food restaurant puts golden arches in front of its business or uses a similar name to lead people into believing they are dealing with a business associated with the McDonald's chain, it is passing itself off as something it is not; the owners can be sued. This passing-off action is in addition to the remedies provided under the *Trade-marks Act* and may even be available where the requirements of a trademark are not met.

- Passing-off

21. Ont. Dist. Ct. 1987, as reported in *Lawyers Weekly Consolidated Digest*, Vol. 7.

- Trespass to chattels and conversion

Trespass to chattels takes place when someone damages or otherwise interferes with some item of personal property such as a vehicle or other equipment. Slashing a tire would be an example. Taking a car without authority may be a crime, but it is also a tort called **conversion** and is an actionable wrong even where the person taking the vehicle did not know it belonged to someone else.

The normal remedy where a tort has taken place is damages, which is the awarding of a monetary payment, usually designed to compensate the victim for his or her loss. In rare circumstances, where the conduct was deliberate, punitive damages may also be granted when the object is to punish the wrongdoer rather than simply to compensate. Where a monetary award will not be appropriate, as is usually the case where a passing-off action is involved, the court will sometimes award an injunction ordering the offending conduct to stop. Sometimes an accounting, requiring that a wrongdoer disclose any profits made and pay them over to the victim, will also be ordered.

Note that there are some other non-tort areas where the business person has a duty to maintain a certain standard of conduct in relation to others. These are statutory obligations but do not create tort liability unless clearly so stated in the statute. Thus while discrimination in employment may resemble an actionable tort, because it is set out in federal and provincial codes as a violation or human rights it is not a tort. Such a complaint can only be enforced by the board of commission set up for that purpose and is not actionable in the courts. There is also privacy legislation at both the federal and provincial levels, which imposes obligations on businesses with respect to the information they deal with, especially where it relates to individuals. Where businesses fail to adhere to those regulations, they are subject to serious statutory penalties. And in some provinces (British Columbia, Saskatchewan, Manitoba, and Newfoundland and Labrador) the wilful violation of another's privacy has actually been made an actionable tort by statute.

Note increased emphasis on privacy rights

QUESTIONS FOR REVIEW

1. What is a tort? Distinguish between a tort, a crime, and a breach of contract.
2. Explain vicarious liability and any limitation on its availability.
3. Distinguish between intentional and inadvertent torts.
4. Explain what is meant by a reasonable person and the reasonable person test.
5. Distinguish between assault and battery, and explain how this distinction might be affected by self-defence.
6. Explain what is required to establish a false imprisonment.
7. Why is trespass to land considered an intentional tort? Under what conditions does a trespass occur? What is a continuing trespass?
8. What can the occupier of land do when faced with a trespasser?

9. Explain the obligation of an owner or occupier of land for injuries suffered by a trespasser.
10. Under what circumstances might one neighbour sue another for nuisance?
11. What is meant by defamation? What is an innuendo?
12. Distinguish between libel and slander. Why is the distinction important?
13. What impact has legislation had in the area of defamation?
14. Explain the difference between privilege and qualified privileged, and when these defences will be used. What is fair comment?
15. Explain the role of fault with respect to the tort of negligence.
16. What must be established in order to successfully sue for negligence?
17. Explain the role of the *Donoghue v. Stevenson* and the *Anns* case in determining duty of care.
18. Explain the reasonable person test and where it is used.
19. What factors are taken into consideration when assessing the standard with respect to a particular case? What if experts are involved?
20. Explain what is meant by strict liability and when it might be imposed on an occupier of property.
21. How has the standard of care imposed on occupiers been modified by statute?
22. Once it has been shown that a duty of care was owed and there was a failure to live up to that standard, what else must be established to succeed in a negligence action?
23. How have the principles of contributory negligence and voluntary assumption of risk been modified in recent times?
24. Explain how the problems with remoteness in a negligence action have been substantially resolved in recent times.
25. If I were to carelessly injure the hand of a musician, on what basis would damages be determined, given the victim's occupation?
26. Why are manufacturers usually sued for negligence rather than for breach of contract? Why is an action in contract preferable for the victim?
27. Explain when a professional's liability will be based on contract and when it will be based on tort. How is the standard imposed with respect to tort determined?
28. Explain what is meant by fiduciary duty and when such a duty arises.
29. Explain the nature of the following torts: deceit, product defamation, inducing breach of contract, passing-off, trespass to chattels, and conversion.
30. Explain under what circumstances conduct amounting to tort can also constitute a crime.

QUESTIONS FOR FURTHER DISCUSSION

1. Individuals are sometimes convicted of a crime and then sued in tort for the same conduct. Is it fair or just for one person to face trial twice for the same thing?
2. Is the reasonable person test appropriate for determining what standard of behaviour should be imposed in a negligence action? Would it be more appropriate to determine negligent conduct on the basis of the average person or some other test?
3. In Canada when someone produces a defective product or performs an imperfect service he or she must be shown to have been careless—to have fallen below a community-established standard of behaviour (the reasonable person test)—before he or she can be found liable for negligence. When a person is suing for breach of contract, it is unnecessary to establish fault; the breach is enough. Consider whether the requirement to establish fault where someone's conduct causes another injury ought to be abandoned in a tort action. In other words, should it be enough to show that one person caused the injury for him or her to be liable?
4. Freedom of expression has been guaranteed in our constitution. Yet when people criticize public officials and other public figures, they can be sued for defamation, even if they believe what they say is true. Do you think we should adopt an approach similar to that in the United States and take the position that it is more important to have a frank debate with respect to such public matters, a debate free of the chill imposed by the threat of legal action? Should the protections of privileged communications be applied to all such discussions of matters of public interest, whether the statements are accurate or not? Should the media enjoy special protection in such matters?

CASES FOR DISCUSSION

1. **LEWVEST V. SCOTIA TOWERS LTD.** (1981), 126 D.L.R. (3d) 239 (Nfld. T.D.).
   Scotia Towers Ltd. was constructing a building in St. John's, Newfoundland, and in the process a crane they were operating often swung over the adjoining property owned by Lewvest. Lewvest had not given permission for such an intrusion and sued. Explain the nature of Lewvest's complaint, the arguments on both sides, and the appropriate remedy if the action is successful.

2. **JOHN V. FLYNN,** Ont. S.C.J., as reported in *Lawyers Weekly Consolidated Digest*, Vol. 19.
   An employee had a habit of drinking on the job. The employer was aware of this and did nothing about it. One day the employee drank to the point of intoxication, drove home in that condition, then immediately left again and smashed into the plaintiff's car, causing serious injury. The victim not only sued the drunken employee but also the employer. Explain the arguments on both sides and the likely outcome.

3. **HAMILTON–BURLINGTON Y.M.C.A. V. 331783 ONTARIO LTD.,** Ont. S.C.J., as reported in Lawyers Weekly Consolidated Digest, Vol. 21.

The YMCA operated a cultural and athletic activity complex, which included a sauna. This action was brought by the Y's insurer, which, after satisfying the Y's claim, assumed their rights to proceed in an action against the defendant. Because of faulty installation of the sauna, it overheated and caused a fire, resulting in considerable damage. The insurance company brought this action against the contractor that installed the sauna. The problem was that the contractor had failed to connect a backup system, including a limiter switch that would have prevented the sauna from overheating. Explain the basis for action against the contractor and the likely outcome. How would it affect your answer to know that the sauna had been installed nine years earlier and that there had been no problems during that time? That it would have been a simple matter to turn off the sauna? That the employees knew the sauna was overheating, but they either didn't bother or had never been instructed as to what to do in these circumstances?

4. **GROSS V. GREAT-WEST LIFE ASSURANCE CO.** (2000), 80 Alta. L.R. (3d) 132, [2000] 8 W.W.R. 62, 6 B.L.R. (3d) 32 (Alta. Q.B.).

Gross operated a successful rehabilitation clinic in Edmonton and was persuaded by an agent of Great-West Life Assurance Co., an insurance company with which they were working successfully in Edmonton, to open a similar clinic in Toronto. They were told that if they did open such clinic, they would have no problem filling it because of the referrals that Great-West would provide to them. Gross opened the Toronto clinic and the Great-West agent even provided a supporting letter to assist in getting the needed financing. Unfortunately, once open, no referrals were forthcoming and the clinic had to close for lack of business. Gross sued Great-West. Explain the arguments on both sides and the likely success of the action.

5. Explain the arguments of both parties and the likely outcome in the following three shopping mall cases.

SHABSOVE V. SENTRY DEPARTMENT STORES LTD., Ont. Gen. Div., as reported in *Lawyers Weekly Consolidated Digest*, Vol. 15.

One March day Mrs. Shabsove went to a shopping mall operated by Sentry to go to the bank. She parked close to a bank machine, and when she got out of the car and started to go over to to the machine she slipped and fell on the icy surface and suffered a serious injury. She sued the shopping mall for her injury. How would it affect your answer to know that she was wearing leather-soled loafers, or that the mall had a program in place to salt areas where thawing snow was known to accumulate, but this area had last been salted three weeks previously?

COOPER V. LOBLAWS SUPERMARKETS LTD., Ont. Gen. Div., as reported in *Lawyers Weekly Consolidated Digest*, Vol. 15.

Cooper was shopping in a Loblaw's store when she slipped and fell on oil that had been spilled on the floor. She suffered a broken hip. Although pylons had been placed near the obstacle and an employee was cleaning it up, Cooper slipped and fell as she tried to get past the area. How would your answer be affected by knowing that the employee had misplaced the pylons or that Cooper had been hurrying when she slipped?

LECLERC V. WESTFAIR FOODS LTD. (2000), 148 Man. R. (2d) 56, 224 W.A.C. 56, [2000] 8 W.W.R. 592 (Man. C.A.).
A shopper stepped backwards into a display of cans set up for advertising purposes that was protruding into the aisle. The cans fell down causing her to fall and suffer serious neck injuries. How would it affect your answer to know she had been distracted by another display and didn't notice the cans as she backed into them?

6. **VANEK V. GREAT ATLANTIC & PACIFIC CO. OF CANADA LTD.,** 180 D.L.R. (4th) 748 (Ont. C.A.).
A child became sick for a short time when she consumed a fruit juice drink produced by the defendant. The drink was contaminated with toxic fluid. Unfortunately, her parents, and especially her father, were particularly susceptible to nervous shock and anxiety, and he was eventually hospitalized for heart disease and unstable angina brought about by the stress caused by his daughter's injury. The daughter and her parents decided to sue for the injuries suffered. Explain the likelihood of their success and the arguments that could be presented on both sides.

7. **BRUCE V. COLISEUM MANAGEMENT LTD.** (1998), 56 B.C.L.R. (3d) 27, 165 D.L.R. (4th) 472 (B.C.C.A.).
Bruce went to a bar. After a friendly tussle with his friend, the doorman asked him to leave, as he thought the two friends were fighting. The doorman escorted Bruce out, and at the upstairs exit Bruce prevented the doorman from closing the door. Bruce was quite abusive, and eventually the doorman gave him a push that was hard enough to throw him off balance. Bruce fell down the stairs and suffered a serious injury. In this action Bruce is seeking compensation for his injuries from both the doorman and his employer. Explain the nature of his complaint, the arguments on both sides, and his likelihood of success. What factors should be taken into consideration in calculating what damages, if any, should be paid?

8. **MOISES V. CANADIAN NEWSPAPER CO.** (1996), 30 C.C.L.T. (2d) 145, [1997] 1 W.W.R. 337, 24 B.C.L.R. (3d) 211 (B.C.C.A.).
A newspaper wrote an article accusing Moises, the plaintiff, of being involved in an organization that had allegedly massacred 10 000 people in Mozambique. While the article contained accurate information, the headline was clearly false. Moises sued for libel. The publisher claimed they had a duty to report this information and had done so in good faith. Explain the defences that might be raised by the newspaper and the likelihood of success in the action.

9. **BAHNER V. MARWEST HOTEL CO.** (1970), 12 D.L.R. (3d) 646 (B.C.C.A.).
Mr. Bahner attended the defendant's restaurant with some friends and ordered some wine shortly before midnight. Unknown to Bahner, the laws then in place in British Columbia required all drinks to be removed from the table by midnight. This meant Bahner and his friends only had about 15 minutes to drink the bottle of wine which had been opened by the waiter. When Bahner learned this, he refused to drink or pay for the wine, although he did pay for the rest of his meal. When he proceeded to leave, a security guard told Bahner to remain in the restaurant and to wait until the police arrived. The situation was explained to them and they arrested Mr. Bahner who spent the night in jail. He sued both the restaurant as well as the police for false imprisonment. Explain the likely outcome.

CHAPTER 3

Formation of Contracts

The process of carrying on business involves transactions, agreements, arrangements, consultations, services, employment, and other forms of interaction—all based on contracts between the parties. An examination of contract law is fundamental to any study of business law, and most of the other topics that will be examined in this text are founded to a large extent on contract law principles.

Contract: an exchange of promises enforceable in court

A contract can be defined as a voluntary exchange of promises or commitments between parties that are legally enforceable in our courts. When people enter into such contracts, they create a world of law unto themselves. They can create new obligations and responsibilities, but they can also modify or remove obligations and responsibilities. When a ticket to an event contains a provision stating that patrons "enter at their own risk" or that the "management is not responsible for injuries or damage," an attempt is being made by contract to remove the risk of liability for negligence that would otherwise be present. Contract law was developed in the courts, and there has been little statutory interference with these common law fundamentals. As we will see in subsequent chapters, however, there are a myriad of examples of statutory modification of contract laws in specific situations, including the sale of goods and consumer protection, both of which will be discussed in the last half of Chapter 5. This chapter will examine the formation of a contract and qualifications that must be met.

FIGURE 3.1 First Element of a Contract

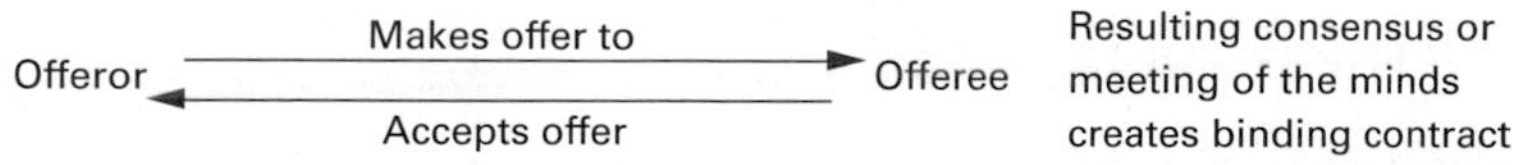

Consensus

Consensus reached through bargaining

Offer and acceptance leads to agreement

Reaching an agreement is at the heart of the formation of a contract (see Figure 3.1). Consensus is normally achieved through a process of **offer and acceptance**, which results in a shared commitment where both parties clearly understand the obligations and responsibilities they are assuming. It is a bargaining process that includes enticements, offers, questions, arguments, and counteroffers, until the parties eventually reach an agreement in which a valid offer is accepted. The courts are willing to find that a consensus has been reached by looking at the subsequent behaviour of the parties. If no specific offer or acceptance can be identified and yet the parties have obviously come to common understanding with all the other elements of contract present, it is likely that the court would still find that a contract exists. While we look at the traditional requirements of offer and acceptance here, it is important to remember that a court may find that a consensus exists even where no specific offer or acceptance can be identified. Neither is it necessary that both parties actually have a complete understanding as to what they have agreed. The only requirement of consensus is that the terms are clear and unambiguous. A basic principle of contract law is that the courts will give effect to the reasonable expectations of the parties. If one of them fails to read those terms or misunderstands them, it is not usually an excuse to get out of a contract. But agreement between the parties must be present. The court will not bargain for them. When they leave important terms to be negotiated later, there is no contract. Still, mistakes with respect to the nature, terms, or some other aspect of the contract do take place, and the courts have developed a structured approach to dealing with them. The court usually interprets and enforces those terms, rather than finding there is no agreement. The way courts deal with such mistakes will be dealt with under "Mistake" in the following chapter (see p. 76).

CASE SUMMARY 3.1

Cedar Group Inc. v. Stelco Inc.[1]

Agreement to Contract Not Binding

Stelco was negotiating with Cedar Group to sell a portion of their business and reached the point of a letter of intent being signed to that effect before negotiations broke down. Still the Cedar Group brought an action to enforce a contract based on that letter of intent. The court held that the parties had done no more than reach an agreement to negotiate a contract and such a contract to enter a contract is no contract at all. As was made clear by the correspondence, many elements, including use of trademarks, non-competition agreements, and warranties, had not yet been agreed to. Those negotiations may or may not have resulted in a contract. There is no binding contract until negotiations are completed and a consensus is reached between the parties.

1. Ont. Gen. Div., O'Leary J., December 21, 1995.

OFFER

The **offer** creates the first legal consequence. It is a tentative promise that contains the terms of the anticipated contract. It is tentative in the sense that the other party need only indicate a willingness to be bound by the stated terms (the acceptance) to create a binding contract. Before this stage is reached, however, a significant amount of communication can take place between the parties. Pre-contract communications, whether they take the form of advertising or provide product or service information, do not create contractual obligations. They are referred to as invitations to deal or **invitations to treat** and sometimes are confused with offers. It is often difficult to determine at what point we are dealing with an offer rather than an invitation. Most media advertisements, catalogues, brochures, window and floor displays, and even clearly marked and priced goods set out on shelves in self-service situations are invitations to treat rather than offers. There is some controversy over this last point, but it was the subject of a decision of the English Court of Appeal in the *Pharmaceutical Society* case.[2] Legislation required that certain types of drugs had to be sold under the supervision of a pharmacist. When the defendant, Boots, introduced self-service merchandising into the industry, by displaying such controlled drugs on the shelves, where they could be selected by the customer and brought up to the front of the store for purchase, it infringed on that legislation. Although the pharmacists were situated at the front of the store by the check-out tills, the Pharmaceutical Society argued that the contract was formed where the customer selected the goods, and thus the sale was unsupervised in violation of the Act. The judge held that the display of the drugs on the shelf was an invitation rather than an offer. The offer was made by the customer picking up the product. The acceptance took place at the front, when the cashier and pharmacist approved the sale, and thus the requirements of supervision were satisfied. Although the reasoning of the judge in this case is suspect, the decision has been followed and is thus good law in Canada, making goods displayed in such self-service situations invitations and not offers. The case is of interest because it is one of the few that makes it clear where an invitation ends and an offer begins.

Invitations do not create legal obligations

Such an invitation has no legal effect in contract law. The actual offer that leads to an acceptance and eventual contract depends on subsequent communications between the parties. It only takes place when all of the important terms are present, and it is clear that the person making the offer has reached the point where he or she is serious and expects to commit to those terms.

For the communication to be an offer, it must contain all of the important terms of the contract. This usually requires, at a minimum, the identification of the parties to the agreement, the subject matter, and the price to be paid (parties, price, and property). Other terms may also have to be understood by the parties if they have been made part of the agreement. For example, if the goods are to be purchased on credit, the payment schedule and interest payable should also be clear. An agreement to enter into an agreement is not a contract. If Joe agreed to sell his car to Sam for $10 000, "credit terms to be arranged later," there would be no contract, since no final agreement had been reached. All of the important terms of the agreement must be set out or be implied in the agreement. It must be emphasized that putting a contract in writing is always good practice. However, except for a few specific instances that will be discussed below, a written contract

An offer is a tentative commitment containing essential terms

2. *Pharmaceutical Society of Great Britain v. Boots Cash Chemists (Southern), Ltd.*, [1953] 1 All E.R. 482 (C.A.); aff'g [1952] 2 All E.R. 456 (Q.B.).

Offer/contract need not be in writing

is not a legal requirement. Because of this it is possible for parts or even the whole contract to be implied from the circumstances, including the record of dealings between the parties. Note that the object is to reach a consensus, and so the offer must be communicated before it can be accepted. The offeree cannot accept an offer that he does not know about. The problem of communication sometimes arises when the offeror wants to include an exemption clause that restricts or limits her liability in the transaction. This must be brought to the attention of the other party at the time the contract is created. For example, a sign at a parking lot may state, "Not responsible for lost, stolen, or damaged vehicles." To be a binding part of the contract, the clause must be communicated to the customer at the time she enters into the contract. Sometimes this is done by including it on the receipt issued at the time the contract is made, or by clearly posting a sign where the ticket is obtained. If it is only communicated after the fact, such as on a bill sent later, or on a sign located in a part of the business where the customer is not likely to see it, that exemption clause will not be a part of the contract.

Exemption clauses must be brought to the other party's attention

CASE SUMMARY 3.2

Boutcev v. DHL International Express Ltd.[3]

Exclusion Clause Not Properly Brought to the Attention of Customer

When two boxes that were supposed to contain computers arrived empty at their destination, the plaintiff, Boutcev, sued the shipper DHL International Express Ltd. for compensation. The shipper refused, referring to an exclusion clause contained in very small print on the back of the waybill. The judge found that the clause was illegible; he said it was "painfully small and defied reading with the naked eye." He refused to enforce it, holding in favour of the plaintiff. Parties to an agreement are only bound by the terms that are reasonably brought to their attention. To ensure that such exclusion clauses are enforceable, the party drawing up the contract should put them in bold type or otherwise highlight them in some way.

Offer will end:

- At end of a specified time

- At end of reasonable time

- Upon death or insanity of offeror

- Upon revocation

END OF AN OFFER Consistent with the bargaining model for the creation of a contract, a number of rules determine when an offer will come to an end (see Table 3.1). Where the offeror states a **specific time** for expiration, such as "at noon on May 12, 2005," the offer ends when specified. After that time it is too late to accept the offer. If no expiration time has been specified, the offer will end after a **reasonable time**. What is reasonable depends on the circumstances. If ripe fruit is being offered, a few hours might be appropriate. If property is involved, or heavy duty equipment, the offer might last a few weeks. The offer will also automatically come to an end with the death or insanity of the offeror. Because the offer is only the first step in the creation of a contract, it imposes no legal obligation on the offeror, who is free to withdraw the offer any time before acceptance, even where he or she has indicated it would remain open. This is called **revocation**, and so long as the revocation has been communicated to the offeree before acceptance has taken place, it is then too late to accept. There can be no valid acceptance after the offeree learns that the offeror has changed his or her

3. Alta. Q.B., as reported in *Lawyers Weekly Consolidated Digest*, Vol. 20.

TABLE 3.1 Bargaining

Invitation	Not an offer; not capable of being accepted to form a contract	
Offer	After expiration of specific time	Original offer ends
Offer	Where not specified, after a reasonable time	Original offer ends
Offer	After communicated revocation	Original offer ends
Offer	After counteroffer	Original offer ends
Offer	After death or insanity of offeror	Original offer ends
Offer	Where option agreement has been purchased	Original offer continues despite above
Offer	Sale to another	Original offer continues unless revocation
Offer	Qualified acceptance	This is a counteroffer; original offer ends
Offer	Effective acceptance	Results in a binding contract

mind. This power to revoke can be given up in a separate option agreement, which is explained below.

The conduct of the offeree can also cause the offer to end. If the offeree rejects the offer, it ends. The offeree can't later change her mind, accept, and hold the offeror to the deal. A **counteroffer** by the offeree has the same effect, and if that counteroffer is rejected she can't turn around and force a contract by accepting the original offer. The offeree would have to make another counteroffer, embodying the original terms, and hope that they are still agreeable to the other party. This may seem somewhat complicated, but it has the advantage of eliminating confusion as to just what offer is being accepted and forming the basis of the contract. A common mistake is to assume that selling the subject matter of an offer to someone else automatically ends that offer. This is incorrect. If anything, this is a revocation of the offer by conduct and would have no effect on the offer, unless the other party learned of the sale before accepting. This is a dangerous situation, and the offeror should make sure that the original offeree knows that he changed his mind before concluding the sale to another. Of course, if the offeree finds out the goods have been sold to someone else, that communicates the revocation indirectly, and it is too late to accept. There can be no meeting of the minds when the offeree knows that the offeror has changed his mind before the acceptance is made.[4]

- Upon rejection
- Upon counteroffer

- Selling item does not end offer

The right of the offeror to change his mind and revoke the offer anytime he wants is often an impediment to doing business. And so it is possible to create a situation where the offer cannot be revoked and must remain open until expiration at a specified time. This is called an option agreement. In effect, a separate contract is entered into where the offeree pays the offeror, usually a small sum, to

Option keeps offer open

4. *Dickinson v. Dodds* (1876), 2 Ch. D. 463 (C.A.).

hold the offer open for the designated time. The offeror is now bound in a separate contract to hold the offer open. Thus the offeror is bound, but the offeree is free to accept or reject the original offer. This gives the offeree some time without the worry that the deal will be taken up by someone else.

We don't always have the choice to bargain. In some businesses standard form agreements are in place, which create a "take it or leave it" situation. Often one-sided terms are present, including exemption clauses that favour the offeror. It must be emphasized that where such a standard contract is accepted, it is just as binding as any other contract. The only adjustment made for the lack of bargaining is that any ambiguity in a term favouring just one of the parties is interpreted in favour of the other party. Also, some statutory protection has been provided, especially where consumer contracts are involved as will be discussed under "Consumer Protection Legislation" in Chapter 5 (see p. 109).

One-sided contracts may be controlled by statute

ACCEPTANCE

Once a valid offer has been made, there is a commitment to be bound on the part of the offeror. The offeree then must make a similar commitment for a contract to be formed. Since the terms of the agreement are embodied in the offer, the offeree's commitment consists merely of an indication of a willingness to be bound by those terms. Such an acceptance must be total and unconditional. Sometimes an offer will involve several different aspects. The offeree can't pick and choose which part to accept unless that was the intention of the offeror. You have to accept all of the terms of an offer or nothing. Similarly, a conditional acceptance does not qualify. If Joe offers to sell his car to Sam for $5000, and Sam responds, "I accept, providing you fix the rust on the fender," this is a counter-offer rather than an acceptance.

Acceptance is a commitment by the offeree to terms of offer

Acceptance must be complete and unconditional

The general rule is that an acceptance must be communicated for it to be effective. A contract requires a meeting of the minds, and so there is no contract until the offeror is notified of the offeree's acceptance. This can be important since it determines when and where the contract comes into effect. When Joe in Vancouver offers to sell his car to Sam in Montreal by phone, and Sam accepts, also by phone, the acceptance is effective when and where Joe hears the acceptance—in Vancouver. Where the contract is formed can be an important consideration in determining what court has jurisdiction and which province's law should be applied to the transaction.

General rule: acceptance is effective when and where communicated

The offeror may require the offer to be accepted by some specified conduct. When this happens, the conduct required must be something unique, not part of a person's normal routine, and the offeree must respond as directed. If the specified acceptance requires the offeree to "go to work tomorrow as usual," going to work would not constitute acceptance. But if the direction is to put a red triangle on the front door, doing so would amount to acceptance of the offer. Sometimes the nature of the contract itself requires the actual performance of the contract as the method of acceptance. This is called a **unilateral** contract. The offering of a reward is a good example. When someone places an add offering a $100 reward for the return of a lost dog, the method of acceptance is the actual return of the dog.

Acceptance by conduct

Acceptance by performance

Sometimes marketers will send unsolicited goods to a prospective customer stating that if they don't send it back, they've bought it. The general rule is that silence by itself will not be construed as acceptance, and a person in receipt of such goods is not required to go to the trouble to return them. Note that care should be taken not to use such goods, as this would affirm the contract. Simply store the goods for a reasonable time, and if they're not reclaimed by the mar-

No acceptance by silence

keter, dispose of them. Only where there is a pre-existing business relationship will silence be an appropriate acceptance. If you have been receiving a regular supply of a product from a business, it is quite appropriate for that business to send a note: "If we don't hear otherwise, we will renew your order as of May 20, 2005." Because of the already established relationship, there is a duty to communicate a cancellation in these circumstances. A few years ago a company providing cable services notified their customers that they would be supplying them with extra channels at an added cost unless the customer notified the company that they didn't want the additional service. Because of the pre-existing service relationship, silence in these circumstances would have affirmed the new arrangement. The public was outraged, however, and the company was forced to back off. This is the danger of joining a CD or book-of-the-month club. Once the relationship is established, it is hard to terminate it.

Exception: Where use of mail is reasonable, acceptance is effective when and where posted

There is one important exception to the rule that an acceptance must be communicated to be effective. This is the **post box rule**. As contract law developed, the postal service was the accepted method of doing business at a distance. The inherent delay in communications created uncertainty as to what point a contract actually came into existence. The solution was the rule that if it was appropriate to respond by mail, the acceptance was effective when and where it was posted. In the example of selling a car, if the mails, instead of the phone, were used—with Joe in Vancouver sending a letter to Sam in Montreal offering to sell his car for $5000 and Sam responding with a letter of acceptance—that acceptance would be effective when it was mailed in Montreal. If Joe had required acceptance before Saturday, and the letter was mailed Friday, there would be a valid contract, even though Joe would not know of it until the letter was delivered—likely sometime in the following week. Also, since the contract was formed in Quebec, this would be an important factor in determining what court would have jurisdiction and what provincial law would apply to the contract. Note that the post box rule only applies where it is reasonable to respond by mail. There is usually no problem posting an acceptance where the offer is sent by mail. But where the offer is presented in some other way, such as in person, past dealings between the parties, as well as the nature of the subject matter of the contract, will be important factors in determining if response by mail was reasonable. If ripe fruit were being offered, a response by mail would likely be unacceptable. To avoid the problem, the appropriate means of acceptance should be specified in the offer.

CASE SUMMARY 3.3

Eastern Power Ltd. v. Azienda Communale Energia and Ambiente[5]

Post Box Rule Not Applied to Fax

Azienda, an Italian company, negotiated a cooperation agreement with Eastern Power Ltd., which was based in Ontario. When Azienda terminated the agreement and refused to pay the bill for costs submitted by Eastern Power, the Ontario company brought this action against Azienda in an Ontario court. In determining if they had jurisdiction, the Ontario court had to decide, among other things, where the

(continued)

5. (1999), 178 D.L.R. (4th) 409 (Ont. C.A.).

contract was made. Negotiations took place by facsimile. The final acceptance of the offer was also sent by fax by the Ontario company to Azienda in Italy. Claiming the post box rule exception applied, Eastern Power argued that acceptance was effective when and where the fax was sent in Ontario. The court rejected this argument, stating that the use of facsimile transmissions involved instantaneous communication, much like a telephone, and so there was no justification for applying the post box exception. Since the fax was received in Italy, the contract arose in Italy; consequently, Ontario was an inappropriate place to sue.

The post box rule will not apply where a fax is used

Exception only applies to an acceptance

In recent times there has been a profound change in the nature of business communications. The mails are still used to a significant extent, but fax and email have become commonplace. An important question faced by the courts was whether the post box rule should be extended to other forms of communications. It has been extended to the use of telegrams, but should it be extended further? The question was answered in the *Entores* case,[6] where the English Court of Appeal held that when telex (similar to a modern fax) and other forms of instantaneous communication were used, there was no need for the post box rule. Thus, where fax is used, the acceptance is only effective when and where it is received by the offeror. Although there may be some small delay when email is involved, it is not likely that any court would expand the rule in that direction. Today the post box rule is restricted to the use of the postal service, telegrams, and possibly couriers. It must be emphasized that the post box rule is an exception to the requirement that an acceptance be communicated before it is effective. There is no indication that the rule will be applied to other forms of communications between the parties as they bargain. In fact, in the English case of *Henthorne v. Fraser*,[7] which was important in establishing the rule in the first place, the court made it clear that a mailed revocation was not effective until received. See Table 3.2 for a summary of the rules of acceptance.

TABLE 3.2 Acceptance

Offer ⟶	Acceptance, general rule	Acceptance is effective when and where offeror hears of acceptance
Offer ⟶	Acceptance by performance	Unilateral contract accepted upon performance of contract term
Offer ⟶	Acceptance, post box rule	Acceptance effective when and where posted, if use of post was appropriate

6. *Entores Ltd. v. Miles Far East Corp.*, [1955] 2 All E.R. 493 (C.A.).

7. [1892] 2 Ch. 27 (Ch.D.).

Consideration

The second qualification that must be met for the formation of a contract is the exchange of consideration (see Figure 3.2). In keeping with the bargaining model, both parties must get some benefit from the deal. This may take the form of money, service, goods, or some other type of benefit. Note that it is not necessary for the consideration to actually change hands at the time of the acceptance; rather, both parties must make a commitment to give the other some form of consideration pursuant to the agreement. This is often referred to as the exchange of promises.

Exchange of promises/benefits required

People sometimes promise to give a gift or do something for someone else and expect nothing in return. Such one-sided promises (called gratuitous promises) are not legally enforceable. Of course, once a gift has been given, the giver cannot force its return; rather, it is the promise to give such a gift that cannot be enforced. If I give you a fur coat, it's yours. But if I promise to give you a fur coat and change my mind, there is nothing legally you can do about it.

In business it is sometimes difficult to tell whether there has been an exchange of consideration or not. While the court won't worry about whether the consideration is reasonable (that would be interfering in the bargaining process), the benefit must be specific. A promise to pay "something" or a "reasonable price" is generally not good enough, as there is no specific commitment and the matter will require further negotiation in the future. The exception is where services are requested. Then, on the basis of the equitable principle of *quantum meruit,* the requester is obligated to pay a reasonable amount for the services delivered. If you ask a plumber to fix a leak in your basement and he or she hands you a bill, you will have to pay it if it is reasonable, even though you didn't agree to a price beforehand.

What is promised must also be possible, legal, and of some value. A commitment to bring a pet dog back from the dead for $1000 would not be legally enforceable because, at least in the eyes of the law, it is not possible to bring a dog back to life. A promise to pay someone $500 to perform an illegal act such as buying drugs or assaulting someone also fails to qualify, because a promise to commit an illegal act is not valid consideration. Nor would a promise to return friendship or love and affection constitute valid consideration as no value can be put on such affection. As mentioned above, it is not necessary that the consideration be fair, only that there be some consideration on both sides. However, if the transaction is grossly one-sided, it may support an allegation of fraud or the claim of incapacity.

Consideration need not be reasonable but must be legal, possible, and have some value

To determine if there is consideration it is often much easier to look at the price to be paid rather than the benefit to be received. If I promise to pay $50 to John to mow my aunt's lawn, it is hard to identify what specific benefit I will get out of the deal. But if we look at it from the point of view of what is to be paid (in

FIGURE 3.2 Consideration Involves an Exchange of Commitments

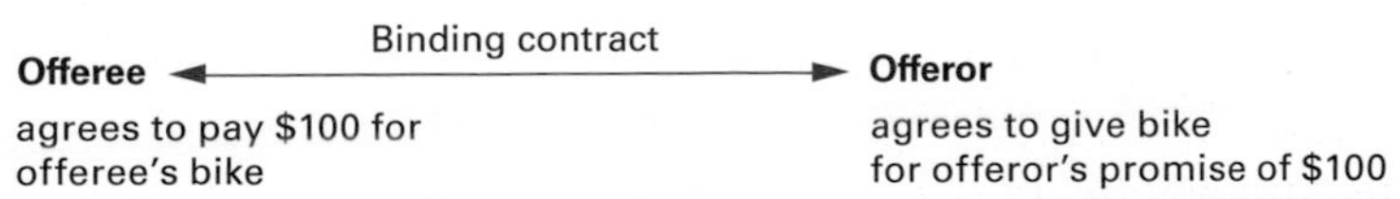

the sense of what is being given up, not just money) it is clear that both of us are paying a price. We both have by agreement changed our legal position in relation to each other. John is now obligated to mow the lawn, which he was not obligated to do before the agreement, and I am obligated to pay the $50. There has been an exchange of commitments, which constitutes consideration.

Both parties must pay a price

For example, in business one person is often required to sign a guarantee before a financial institution will loan money to a debtor. What does the guarantor get out of it? It is better to look at the commitments. The guarantor is now responsible for paying the loan if the debtor defaults. His or her legal position has changed in accordance with the agreement. The bank now commits to advance the funds to the debtor, something they otherwise would not have done. They also have changed their legal position pursuant to the deal, and so there is consideration on both sides. Both have paid a price in the sense that they have assumed obligations that they didn't have before. But if the money is advanced before the guarantee is extracted, as sometimes happens, it may well be a gratuitous promise and not binding. The guarantor has made a commitment, but the bank does not change its legal position, since it has already advanced the money. This is an example of **past consideration**. Where the benefit has been given before the deal is struck, it cannot be part of an exchange and hence the expression "past consideration is no consideration."

Past consideration is no consideration

CASE SUMMARY 3.4

Tildesley v. Weaver[8]

Debt Discharged by Bankruptcy Is Not Consideration for Promissory Note

Mr. Weir had been discharged of his previous debts through the process of bankruptcy. After Mr. Weir's death one of his old creditors approached his son, who was the executor of his estate, and demanded payment. The whole idea of bankruptcy and discharge is to remove any old obligations, so that the debtor is free to start over. With that in mind, it is clear that at the time of the demand no money was owed by the deceased or his estate to the old creditor. Still, the executor agreed to sign a promissory note, committing the estate to pay the alleged $14 900 debt. When he later refused to pay, this action was brought by that would-be creditor to enforce the promissory note. The court decided that since the debt had been discharged by bankruptcy, there was no debt outstanding at the time the promissory note was made. This made the promissory note a one-sided or gratuitous promise, since the executor of the estate had received nothing in return for signing the note. Because of this lack of consideration, there was no legally enforceable obligation on the executor or the estate to pay the funds claimed or to honour the promissory note.

GRATUITOUS PROMISES

Sometimes there is an existing legal relationship or obligation that the parties want to change. In general, any obligation created by contract can be changed

8. 1998 CanLII 6690 (B.C.S.C.) (1998-08-04).

by agreement. But there has to be consideration on both sides to support the change. If a builder had a contract to finish remodelling your house by June 10 and fell behind, you might well agree to pay an extra $2000 so that more help could be hired to get the job done on time. At first glance it looks like there is consideration on both sides, but in fact there is not. You have made a commitment to pay more, but the builder is in exactly the same legal position that he was in before you made that promise—to finish the job by June 10. He has made no new commitment and so this is a one-sided or gratuitous promise not binding on the promisor. It is true that the builder has agreed to hire extra help and this will cost him more, but he would have had to do that anyway to fulfill the original agreement. The commitment has not changed. You would not be obligated to pay the $2000 promised, unless the builder agreed to do something extra for it.

Paying less to satisfy a debt is a similar problem. If I owe you $1000 and I offer to pay you $800 if you will take it in full satisfaction of the debt, the reduction of the debt is one-sided. You get nothing out of it. Yes, you will be paid, but I was obligated to do that before you agreed to take the lesser payment. So unless I agree to do something extra such as pay early, after getting the $800 you should still be able to sue me for the other $200. But this is another one of those situations where the necessities of business overshadow the logic of the law. It is often better to settle debts this way—with certainty. As a result, legislation has been passed in most jurisdictions to the effect that if a creditor agrees to take less in full satisfaction of a debt and in fact takes the money, he or she can't turn around and sue for the remainder. The debt is settled.[9]

Taking less in satisfaction of a debt made binding by statute

EXCEPTIONS There are two exceptions to the unenforceability of gratuitous or one-sided promises (see Table 3.3). **Promissory estoppel** is a difficult concept best understood by example. Where a person contracts with another to lease property at a set rent for five years and then is persuaded to reduce the rent during the term of the lease, that would be a gratuitous or one-sided promise. If the landlord changed his or her mind, insisting on the full rent, no action could be brought to enforce the agreement to pay less. But what if the lower rental payments were made and the landlord then brought an action to enforce the original lease, demanding that the shortfall be made up? If it can be shown that the tenant relied on the promise—changed what he or she did on the basis of it—then the tenant can raise the defence of promissory estoppel. A promise has been made and the promissor is estopped or prevented from enforcing the earlier claim.

This defence is rarely available since it is the person who made the promise who has to sue, and that only happens when there is some pre-existing contract that is being modified by the gratuitous promise. Promissory estoppel, then, will only be used where there is a gratuitous promise, and then only where it can be used as a defence. The expression is that promissory estoppel can only be used "as a shield and not as a sword."

Reliance upon one-sided promise may be used as a

The second exception is the use of the **seal**. The use of the seal predates the requirement of consideration and was used to indicate a person's commitment to the deed or transaction in question. That historical recognition of seals contin-

9. Examples are British Columbia's *Law and Equity Act*, R.S.B.C. 1996, c. 253, s. 43, and Ontario's *Mercantile Law Amendment Act*, R.S.O. 1990, c. M-10, s. 16.

CASE SUMMARY 3.5

Gilbert Steel Ltd. v. University Construction Ltd.[10]

Promise to Pay Higher Price Not Supported by Consideration

Gilbert Steel agreed to supply steel at a specific price to University Construction for the construction of a number of buildings. The cost for steel went up, and upon request, University Construction agreed to pay Gilbert a higher price than previously agreed for the steel they supplied. University made regular payments as the job progressed, but not enough to cover the increase in price. When the job was completed Gilbert Steel sued University Construction for the shortfall. University Construction claimed they were not obligated to pay the agreed-upon increase based on the lack of consideration supporting the change. The court agreed. University Construction had agreed to pay a higher price, but Gilbert Steel had not agreed to do anything in return for the change. Note that promissory estoppel was raised by Gilbert Steel. This was rejected by the court since promissory estoppel can only be "used as a shield, not as a sword," and Gilbert Steel was suing to enforce the gratuitous promise. Had University Construction made the higher payments and then sued to recover the excess paid, it could well be that Gilbert Steel could have used University Construction's promise to pay the higher amount as a defence on the basis of promissory estoppel.

Where there is a seal, no consideration is required

ues, and today when a wafer or design is pressed into a document, it has a similar effect. Contract law and the need for consideration never replaced the sanctity of the seal, and today where a seal has been affixed to a document there is no need to establish consideration. Financial institutions will usually affix seals to credit transactions involving a guarantor to avoid any possible question of consideration. Note that the presence of a seal does not replace the need for consensus or any other requirement of contract law, only consideration. In some jurisdictions specialized corporate documents must be under seal to be effective, and some specialized documents prepared by lawyers and notaries are also placed under seal. But as a general rule, the seal is not a requirement in modern contract law.

TABLE 3.3 Consideration and Alternatives

A makes promise to B	Under seal w/o consideration	B can sue A to enforce promise
A makes promise to B	With mutual consideration	Result is a binding contract, so B can sue A to enforce promise
A makes promise to B	Bare promise w/o consideration	Promissory estoppel; B can defend if A sues and thus ignores promise, but B cannot sue A

10. (1976), 67 D.L.R. (3d) 606 (Ont. C.A.).

Capacity

As a rule the courts don't interfere with the parties' freedom to contract. There are, however, some people who are considered incapable of negotiating a contract.

INFANTS

The age of majority at common law used to be 21. In Canada this has been reduced to 18 or 19, depending on the province. Anyone under that age is considered to be an infant and is protected to the extent that the contracts they make with adults are binding on the adults, but voidable at the option of the infant. People understand that this protection is afforded to younger children, but they are often surprised to learn that the protection continues to age 18 or 19. The terms *void* and *voidable* will come up throughout the discussion of contract law (see Figure 3.3). **Void** means there never was a contract and both parties are free from any obligation under the agreement. A **voidable** contract is valid, but one of the parties, because of some problem, has the right to escape if he or she chooses to do so. This is the case with infants. The adult is bound by the contract, but the infant can escape if he or she so chooses. Of course, the infant can't have it both ways and must return any goods obtained under the agreement. If the infant purchases a car on credit from a merchant and then stops making payments, she has no further obligation with respect to the payments but must return the car. There are significant exceptions to the infant's right to escape from contracts. Infants are bound to pay a reasonable price when they contract for necessities. Such necessities include food, clothing, lodging, and transportation. Infants are also bound by their beneficial contracts of service. These are contracts that are determined to be in the infant's best interest such as an apprenticeship arrangement. It should be noted that once a contract has been executed—both sides have performed their obligations—it will be very difficult for the infant to escape the contract and be reimbursed unless there are gross inequities involved.

Infants not bound by contracts but adults are

Infants are bound by beneficial contracts of service and for necessities

FIGURE 3.3 Void and Voidable Contracts

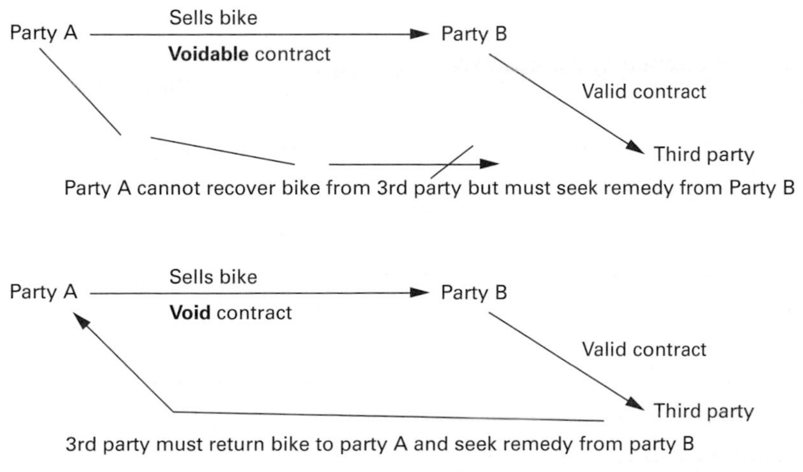

The British Columbia *Infants Act*[11] is unique in that it declares that *all* contracts with infants are **unenforceable** against the infant except those specifically made enforceable by statute such as student loans. In British Columbia even contracts for necessities and beneficial contracts of service are unenforceable against the infant. An unenforceable contract only prevents the adult from suing the infant to enforce the contract; it does not empower the infant to get out of the deal once she has performed as required in the contract. The infant has only done what he or she agreed to do, and the courts will stay out of it. Of course, this can lead to an unfair result, and the court has the power to give relief to both the adult and the infant where appropriate.

Infant can ratify when adult

In every jurisdiction, if the infant ratifies the contract after becoming an adult, he is bound by it. This may be done directly in writing or by implication, such as receiving some further benefit or making additional payments.

Infants are liable for their own torts. Parents may be made liable by statute

Note that this protection of infants in contract law does not extend to tort liability. Infants are as liable for torts committed by them as anyone else, subject of course to what reasonable standard of behaviour could be expected of that infant. The adult can't get around the protection provided to an infant in contract law by suing in tort instead. For example, if an infant damages a rented car, the rental company could not sue in contract, but may try to sue in tort claiming negligence on the part of the infant. This would not be allowed. Parents, as a general rule, are not responsible for the contracts entered into by their children unless they have authorized that contract or they have agreed to be a guarantor or co-debtor. Nor are parents responsible for the torts committed by their children. Only where the adults themselves are negligent, as would be the case if they allowed a child access to a loaded gun, will they be held personally liable. In fact, this has been changed by statute in several jurisdictions where parents have not only been made responsible for torts but in some cases responsible even for the criminal conduct of their children.

INSANITY AND INTOXICATION

A contract supposedly involves a meeting of the minds, but where one of those minds is insane or intoxicated, they may be able to escape the contract. The person or his representative trying to escape a contract for a non-necessity—something other than food or lodging—on the basis of insanity must be able to establish three things. First, it must be shown that the contracting party was so insane that he didn't understand the nature of the transaction that he entered into. Anything short of this, and the contract is binding. Second, it must be shown that the other party knew, or should have known, of the insanity. A central principle in contract law is that the courts will enforce the reasonable expectations of the parties. So if a person has no idea that she is dealing with someone whose mind is gone, and there is nothing in the situation that should have alerted her to that fact, that contract will be enforceable. In the case of *Hardman v. Falk*,[12] after terms for the sale of a property were negotiated with two daughters, the women introduced the purchasers to their elderly and sickly mother, the owner of the property. The terms were then explained to the woman and she signed the documents with an X. The daughters explained that their mother was too feeble to sign her name. Later the daughters tried to get out of the deal on

11. R.S.B.C. 1996, c. 225.

12. [1953] 3 D.L.R. 129 (B.C.C.A).

the basis of their mother's insanity at the time of the contract. The court found that her mind was gone at the time of the contract. Even though she was visibly old and sickly, there was nothing to alert the purchasers to her insanity, and so the contract for the sale of the property was valid. Third, if a person regains his sanity, that person must take steps to quickly repudiate the agreement. If the person has bought shares, for example, he can't wait to see if those shares have gone up or down in price before repudiating.

Where one party is insane or intoxicated, there is no contract if the other person should have known

This latter requirement is more important where the mental impairment is caused by intoxication, since sobriety usually follows. Whether the intoxication is caused by drugs or alcohol, the requirements for escaping liability under the contract are the same: that the person was so impaired he or she didn't understand the transaction; that the other person knew or ought to have known of the intoxication; and that the agreement is repudiated quickly upon becoming sober. Insanity will be a defence to a criminal charge where the accused didn't understand what he or she was doing or that it was wrong. Intoxication, however, in most cases will not constitute a defence to a crime. Note that where a person has been committed to a mental institution, a trustee is appointed to look after his or her affairs. The person may be given an allowance, and any contracts he or she enters into beyond that are simply not binding—not even contracts for necessities.

There are several other situations where the capacity to contract might be a problem. Where corporations and societies are involved, the extent of their capacity to contract depends on the legislation that creates them. This is not a problem where ordinary corporations are involved, but when dealing with Crown corporations, government agencies, or even universities, municipalities, and trade unions, their powers are often limited. Any doubt should be resolved by checking the appropriate statute. A different problem exists when dealing with foreign governments and their representatives. Because governments are sovereign, they may be immune from criminal prosecution or civil action in our courts. A few years ago a woman was struck and killed in Ottawa by an intoxicated foreign government official. The Canadian courts could do nothing because of diplomatic immunity. The official was recalled, however, and tried in his own country. Finally, it should be noted that the capacity of status Indians is also limited to some extent under the provisions of the *Indian Act*.[13] This was intended to protect them from exploitation and is a right that remains despite the provision of the *Charter of Rights and Freedoms*. The *Indian Act* is in the process of major revision at the time of writing.

Statutory bodies may have limited capacity

Diplomats protected

Aboriginal people are protected

Legality

Contracts that have an unlawful objective or where the consideration is illegal are void. Examples are contracts to commit a crime or tort; contracts involving an immoral act including prostitution; contracts to sell government secrets or to bribe officials; and contracts that obstruct justice, such as paying someone to go to jail and thus defeating the deterrent nature of a jail sentence. Note that where a statute prohibits a certain act, the terms of the statute itself must be examined to determine the consequences. The prohibited agreement may or may not be void, depending on the provisions of the statute. Gambling was illegal according

13. R.S.C. 1985, c. I-5.

to common law but now is permitted, providing the terms of appropriate statutes are complied with. Without such permits there are significant penalties under the *Criminal Code* for gambling in various forms, for placing bets for others, and for operating the premises involved in such activities.

Contracts to commit a crime or other illegal acts are void

Insurance arrangements also face the danger of being illegal contracts—a form of wagering—unless they are intended to cover a loss. In order to collect you must demonstrate that you have an insurable interest in what was insured, meaning that the insurance payout must compensate for a loss and not constitute a windfall. Contracts where merchants agree to sell their merchandise at a common price (price fixing) also raise questions of legality. Under the federal *Competition Act* it is only where competition is unduly restrained by such contracts that the agreements are prohibited. The *Competition Act* imposes significant criminal penalties for various forms of agreements between businesses that have the effect of unduly injuring or limiting competition, including conspiracy and bid-rigging. These provisions will be discussed in more detail in Chapter 10.

CASE SUMMARY 3.6

Agasi v. Wai[14] and 114567 Canada Ltd. v. Attwell[15]

Failure to Meet Statutory Requirements May Void Contract

Mr. Agasi did $15 000 in renovations on Mrs. Wai's property, but she refused to pay, claiming the contract was illegal because he had no business licence from the city. The court found that the purpose of the bylaw in question was not to protect consumers from unqualified workers but to produce revenue. This did not interfere with the legality of the contract, which was binding.

But compare *114567 Canada Ltd. v. Atwell*, where the opposite conclusion was drawn. Atwell bought a recreational vehicle through a financing arrangement from the plaintiff, which in turn was borrowing from the bank. In fact, unknown to Atwell, the plaintiff was not properly registered as a salesperson under the *Motor Vehicle Dealers Act* of Ontario. After signing the contract, but before taking delivery, Atwell changed his mind and refused to go through with the deal. Without Atwell's knowledge, the plaintiff made some significant modifications to the contract to satisfy the requirements of the bank providing the financing, so that the vehicle could be used as security. The bank repossessed and auctioned off the vehicle, but there was a shortfall. The plaintiff in this action was seeking to recover the $30 000 he still owed to the bank from the defendant. Mr. Atwell took the position that since the plaintiff was not a properly registered salesperson under the *Motor Vehicle Dealers Act*, the contract was therefore void, and he owed nothing. The court agreed and found that there was no enforceable contract and no obligation on Mr. Atwell to pay. This was a situation where the law requiring the registration of salespeople under the *Motor Vehicle Dealers Act* was designed to protect consumers from just this kind of situation. Because of the plaintiff's wrong doing in making changes in the con-

14. (2000), 4 C.L.R. (3d) 101 (Ont. S.C.J.).

15. Ont. S.C.J., as reported in *Lawyers Weekly Consolidated Digest*, Vol. 20.

tract, no discretion would be exercised in their favour. Both of these cases deal with non-compliance with a statute but with different results, thus illustrating how important it is to look at the purpose of the statute to determine whether contracts entered into may fail for illegality or not.

Perhaps the most important business situation where the question of the legality of an agreement may arise occurs when a business is sold and a provision is included prohibiting the seller from carrying on a similar business. Such a provision is permissible only where it is reasonable, meaning that it goes no further than is necessary to protect the goodwill of the business being sold. If Joe sells Sam a barbershop, and a term is included that prohibits Joe from carrying on the trade of a barber, this would be void. It goes too far. The idea is that if Joe were to immediately start up a new business near the old one, this would defeat the goodwill of the one sold because he would attract all of his old customers. But if Joe opens up a barbershop in another province or five years later, this poses no danger. Such a contract should include a time limitation and an area limitation that goes no further than is necessary to protect the business being sold from such unfair competition. In this example the limitations of not opening up another barber shop within two years and within 40 kilometres of the original business might be more appropriate. It must also not harm the public interest. If only one barber were left, who then could charge exorbitant prices, this might be sufficient reason to void the contract. A similar problem arises when employers impose such terms on their employees that require them not to work in a similar industry after termination. This condition may be necessary to protect trade secrets or special customer relations, but the term should also be reasonable and not go further than necessary to prevent the anticipated evil. It should be noted, however, that the courts are less inclined to enforce such restrictive covenants against employees, especially where they are prevented from carrying on their trade or profession.

Restrictive covenants must be necessary and reasonable

CASE SUMMARY 3.7

Button v. Jones[16]

Dentist Breaches Non-competition Clause

Button and Jones were dentists practising in the same city. Jones agreed to sell his practice to Button for $150 000, $84 000 of which was for the value of the goodwill associated with the practice and patient records. The two then continued on in association. Both the agreement providing for the sale of the business as well as the continuing association agreement contained clauses prohibiting the defendant from soliciting his former clients or opening up a new business in competition with the purchaser for a period of four years anywhere in that city. Before that four-year period was up, Jones terminated the agreement, opened up a new practice only 1.5 kilometres away, and told his patients of his new practice. The court held that the non-competition clause had

(continued)

16. Ont. S.C.J., as reported in *Lawyers Weekly Consolidated Digest,* Vol. 21.

been violated, that Jones had solicited his former patients in violation of the non-solicitation clause, and as such he was in breach of his agreement. This application was for an interlocutory injunction to stop Jones from the continuing breach until the trial of the action took place. But at the subsequent trial the court confirmed the breach and awarded damages of $78 000 plus costs of $38 000.

Where the sale of a business is concerned, the courts are willing to enforce reasonable non-competition clauses. Here, when dealing with a dentist practice, a four-year restriction within the city was reasonable. Note that this case also illustrates where the granting of an interlocutory injunction before the trial to prevent further damage resulting from the breach is appropriate.

Intention

Parties must intend legal consequences to result from contract

In domestic or social relationships there is presumption of no intention

In commercial transactions there is a presumption of intention

Presumptions may be rebutted

The parties must intend to be legally bound by their agreement, but a person can't get out of an agreement just by saying he or she was only kidding. As mentioned above, the court will give effect to the reasonable expectations of the parties. Therefore, the question isn't so much whether you intended to be bound, but whether the other party reasonably thought he or she was entering into a legally binding agreement. In some situations, such as family arrangements, it would not be normal for the arrangements to be legally binding. Thus, where such domestic relations are involved, there is a **presumption** that there was no intention to be legally bound. This means that unless the other party can produce evidence to rebut or overcome this presumption, there is no legally enforceable agreement. An agreement by a parent to pay a child an allowance would be such a situation. Business agreements are the opposite. There is a presumption that business and commercial contracts are legally binding, and to get out of one you would have to produce evidence that indicated an opposite intention. Sometimes people in business enter into understandings that they don't want to be legally enforceable. But to overcome that presumption, they must clearly state that the arrangement is not intended to be a binding contract or have any legally enforceable effect on the parties. Business and family affairs may intersect, or the agreement may involve exaggerated terms. For instance, during a golf game a person might say, "I'll give you a million dollars if you make that putt." Each situation must be looked at separately and the reasonable person test applied. The question is: Was it reasonable for the other contracting party to have expected legal consequences to flow from the agreement? Only if the answer is yes and the other elements necessary to form a contract are present will a legally enforceable contract exist.

Formal Requirements

Seal may be required by statute

Historically, the form of the document was important in determining whether it was binding. The use of the seal as discussed above is an example, but today these formal requirements have largely been removed.

WRITING

It must be emphasized that it is always good practice to put an agreement into written form. It is surprising how even the best-intentioned people will remember the same agreement differently. Still, people are usually surprised when they find out that a verbal contract is every bit as binding as a written one. The writing is important because it is evidence of the contract. There are a few situations, however, where a contract will not be enforceable unless it is in writing. Several statutes are in place requiring writing for specific types of transactions. The most important is the ***Statute of Frauds***, originally passed in England in the 17th century. This statute requires evidence in writing for contracts dealing with interests in land, such as the purchase and sale of land, including easements, leases, etc. as well as agreements where one person assumes responsibility for the debt of another. Other, less common provisions include contracts not to be completed within one year, a personal commitment of an executor to pay the debt of the estate, and agreements where someone promises another something if they get married. The sale of goods acts in some jurisdictions require that items sold over a given amount be accompanied by writing (a receipt). Some jurisdictions have repealed their statutes of frauds, and others have severely limited its application. In most jurisdictions it is expected that agreements dealing with land—except for a short-term lease of less than three years—and agreements to be responsible for the debt of another, such as a guarantee, will require written evidence.

Writing may be required by statute

***Statute of Frauds* requires evidence in writing in specific situations**

Sale of goods act requires writing in some jurisdictions

When written evidence is not present, such agreements are unenforceable. As discussed above this means that without such writing one party cannot sue in court to force the other to perform. But if a party has already performed her obligations under the contract she has only done what she should have and can't use the courts to get out of the deal. Also, if there has been partial payment or partial performance (providing that it is only consistent with the existence of the agreement), as a rule that will take the place of the writing requirement, and the contract will be enforceable.

Where writing is required but absent, the contract is unenforceable

Partial performance satisfies writing requirement

CASE SUMMARY 3.8

Atlantis Transportation Services Inc. v. Air Canada[17]

Various Documents Taken Together Satisfy *Statute of Frauds*

Atlantis Transportation Services Inc. provided delivery services over a number of years for Air Canada. Because the business of Air Canada grew considerably during that time, Atlantis had to expand their fleet and incur other expenses. At one point a five-year contract had been agreed to, but Air Canada terminated it after only two years. Atlantis sued. Air Canada took the position that they had never agreed to the five-year term. Secondly, they argued that even if they had agreed to the term, the *Statute of Frauds* required that any agreement to be performed beyond a one-year period had to be in writing. Since it was not, it could not be enforced. The court found first that Air Canada had agreed to a five-year term and also that the requirements of the *Statute of Frauds* had been met. Even though the actual agreement was not in writing, there

(continued)

17. Ont. Gen. Div., as reported in *Lawyers Weekly Consolidated Digest*, Vol. 15.

were sufficient other documents, including letters, invoices, and company minutes, that clearly indicated the existence of the contract; therefore, the requirement of written evidence was satisfied. This provision has since been repealed in Ontario along with other modifications made in Ontario and other provinces to their *Statute of Frauds* legislation, but it does indicate the operation of the *Statute* as well as what constitutes compliance with the writing requirement.

In summary, where there has been consensus in the form of offer and acceptance, consideration has been exchanged, both parties have capacity to contract, the agreement is legal, and there was intention to be bound, a legally enforceable contract has been created.

QUESTIONS FOR REVIEW

1. Explain consensus, its importance in contract law, and how such consensus is reached.
2. Distinguish an offer from an invitation to treat.
3. What must be contained in the offer for it to constitute an offer capable of being accepted to form a contract?
4. What role does the requirement of writing play in the formation of a contract?
5. What is meant by an exemption clause? How is one treated by the courts?
6. Explain under what circumstances an offer will end before acceptance.
7. What effect does the sale of the subject matter of the offer to someone else have on the offer?
8. Explain the requirements for an option agreement to be binding and its significance.
9. What is required for acceptance of an offer and how can such acceptance be accomplished?
10. Explain the effect of a partial or conditional acceptance.
11. When and where is an acceptance effective?
12. What is the effect of the post box rule and when does it apply? To what forms of communications does it apply?
13. When a unilateral contract is involved, how is acceptance accomplished?
14. Under what circumstances can an acceptance by silence be effective?
15. When will an acceptance sent by email or fax be effective?
16. Explain what is meant by consideration and the contract rule associated with it.

17. Explain what is meant by past consideration and why the designation is important.
18. What is the effect in most jurisdictions of a creditor taking less in full satisfaction of a debt? Why?
19. Explain what is meant by promissory estoppel and why it is important.
20. What is the relationship between a sealed contract and the requirement of consideration?
21. Explain the effect of a contract entered into between an infant and an adult on the parties to it. When will infants be bound by their contracts?
22. Contrast an infant's liability in contracts and in torts.
23. What must be proved in order to escape liability of contracts on the basis of insanity or intoxication? List other situations where capacity may be a problem.
24. What is required in order for a restrictive covenant to be enforceable?
25. Explain the presumptions in place with respect to the intention of the parties to contract.
26. Explain the provisions of the *Statute of Frauds* and when a contract must be in writing.
27. What is the effect if the requirements of the *Statute of Frauds* are not met? Will anything else other than actual writing satisfy the requirements of the statute of frauds?

QUESTIONS FOR FURTHER DISCUSSION

1. Consider the creation and use of the post box rule in terms of its original purpose, whether it met that objective, and whether its continued use can be justified today. In your answer consider whether the rule ought to be applied to communications between the parties other than acceptance and to different forms of communications such as email and the internet generally.
2. It is arguable that the requirement of consideration in a contract serves no other purpose than to indicate that the parties intend their agreement to be binding. Do you think that the continued requirement of consideration in contract law serves any valid purpose today? What about the separate requirement of intention?
3. Consider the fact that in most jurisdictions only some forms of contracts have to be evidenced in writing to be enforceable. Many jurisdictions have made important changes to these requirements. What do you think? Should only written contracts be enforceable in court? Should writing ever be required? In your answer consider the costs and use of legal resources as well as whether the purposes of justice in a broad sense are served by your recommendations.
4. People who are insane are given special treatment with respect to the contacts they enter into. If they are so insane they don't know what they are doing, the contract isn't binding unless the other party knew or ought to have known of the insanity. Should the only question be whether there was insanity? Would that be fair to merchants? Why don't we treat contracts with infants the same way and allow the infant to escape the contract only if the adult with whom they were dealing knew they were contracting with an infant?

CASES
FOR DISCUSSION

1. **MCMASTER ESTATE V. IMARK CORP.,** Ont. S.C.J., March 20, 2000, as reported in *Lawyers Weekly Consolidated Digest*, Vol. 19.

   Jannette McMaster had worked for Imark for 22 years when she was dismissed without notice. She was offered a severance package of pay equivalent to one year of work from the employer, but before she could accept it, she died. Under her will her brother was the executor of her estate and he accepted the offer on her behalf. When Imark learned she had died, they refused to go through with the contract and were sued by the executor of the estate. Indicate the arguments on both sides and the likely outcome.

2. **RE COLLINS,** B.C.S.C., October 21, 1991, as reported in *Lawyers Weekly Consolidated Digest*, Vol. 11.

   The marriage between the petitioner and her husband, Phil Collins, broke down and she moved to Vancouver with the couple's two children. She found it more expensive to live there than she had expected. Therefore, a further arrangement was made with Mr. Collins to purchase a home in Vancouver for the family. But this new home was put in trust for the minor children. Dissatisfied with the arrangement, Mrs. Collins persuaded the children to convey their interest in the house to her. Since they were minors, this needed the approval of the court. Mrs. Collins made an application to ask the court for the approval of the transfer. Do you think the court should approve such a transfer of the asset? State the arguments on both sides.

3. **HEALTH ONE INC. V. LEU,** 1998 CanLII 1846 (Ont. C.A.) (1998-10-22).

   Two doctors entered into an agreement with a health club to carry on a practice within that facility. They were to keep a percentage of their billings, with the rest going to the facility to pay overhead and profit. The contract contained a restrictive covenant prohibiting the doctors from practising their profession within a certain radius for one year. However, in violation of that provision, both doctors did open a practice within the prohibited radius before the year was up. This action was brought by Health One Inc. against them for breach of contract. Indicate the arguments that the doctors might raise in their defence. What would be the appropriate remedy if Health One is successful?

4. **GENDIS INC. V. RICHARDSON OIL & GAS LTD.** (2000), 148 Man. R. (2d) 19, 224 W.A.C. 19, [2000] 9 W.W.R. 1, 6 B.L.R. (3d) 193 (Man. C.A.).

   The chief executive officer of Gendis and the managing director of Richardson Oil and Gas met and negotiated a deal, whereby Gendis would purchase Richardson's share of a privately owned oil company for $39 million, plus certain designated incentive payments (Gendis and Richardson each owned 50 percent of that company at the beginning of the negotiations). At the end of the negotiations both men agreed that they had a deal, and they also agreed that Gendis would supply written documents to confirm the deal and add the necessary details. When the written documents were supplied, Richardson refused to sign them and refused to complete the transaction. When Gendis sued, Richardson claimed that what had been agreed at the negotiation session had not been finalized, and there was no intention to create a binding contract at this stage. What do you think? What is the likely outcome?

5. **TOOMBS V. MUELLER** (1974), 47 D.L.R. (3d) 709 (Alta. S.C.).
Mueller sold land to Toombs pursuant to an oral contract. The only tangible evidence of the contract was that Toombs paid regular mortgage payments and took possession of the land. Toombs is bringing this action and asking for specific performance to enforce the oral contract. Mueller is saying that since the contract is not in writing, he is not bound by it. What do you think? Give arguments on both sides. Consider the jurisdiction within which you reside.

What if Mueller were bringing an application to have Toombs evicted from the property? Would this make any difference to your answer? See *Re Whissell Enterprises Ltd. and Eastcal Development Ltd.* (1980), 116 D.L.R. (3d) 174 (Alta. C.A.).

CHAPTER 4

Contract Disputes

The very nature of business centres on arrangements made between participants that must take the form of legally binding contracts to be enforceable in a court. Whether these arrangements are legally binding or just understandings without legal force makes little difference to the business, so long as both parties are happy with the relationship. It's only when that relationship sours, and the parties think the agreement is not being honoured, that the legal validity of such arrangements and their enforceability in court becomes an important issue. Those disputes can revolve around the existence of the contract, complaints about the conduct of the parties at the time of agreement, or with respect to the **performance of the obligations** arising from it. The prior chapter dealt with what was needed for a legally enforceable contract to exist. This chapter looks at disputes that arise with respect to the start of the contractual relationship, including mistakes as to the nature, terms or other aspects of the agreement, misrepresentation, duress, and undue influence. The concept of privity and the assignment of contractual obligations are examined and the chapter concludes by examining problems related to the proper performance of the terms of the agreement.

Mistake

When contracts are challenged, the argument often revolves around the interpretation of particular terms. Often the parties have a different understanding of the interpretation or effect of the terms of an agreement. Such mistakes can take place in three ways (see Figure 4.1).

Parties making the same mistake may destroy consensus

When both parties have made the same serious error, the resulting **shared mistake** may destroy consensus and result in no contract between them. The contract is said to be void in such circumstances, for example, where both parties think they are dealing with one parcel of land and in fact they are dealing with another, or where both parties share a belief that an event will take place and it doesn't. This kind of shared misapprehension is serious enough to actually

FIGURE 4.1 **Mistakes in Interpreting Terms**

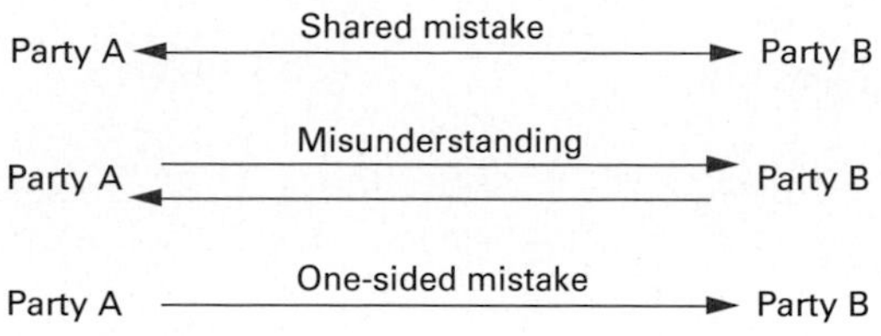

destroy the basis of the agreement and cause the contract to be void for lack of consideration. Such shared mistakes are rare. Sometimes, where a mistake is made in recording the agreement, the courts will respond to a request to **rectify** the agreement so that it corresponds to the original understanding. Thus, if the parties agreed to sell and purchase a boat for $50 000, and it was mistakenly written down as $5000, the court may be willing to supply the missing zero.

Court may correct mistake through rectification

The second type of mistake occurs when both parties have a different understanding of the terms of a contract. Such **misunderstandings** are the most common disputes in contract litigation and are usually resolved by the court imposing the most reasonable interpretation of those terms on the parties. For example, if I thought the terms of the contract required that you include the sheepskin seat covers with the sale of your car, and you refused to supply them, the court would look at the terms of the contract to determine whether they were included. The court would determine the most reasonable interpretation of the terms. If the car was shown with the seat covers on, it is likely they would be included. It is only where the court finds both interpretations equally reasonable that the mistake will destroy the contract. Thus, two British merchants who agreed on the sale and purchase of the cargo of the ship *Peerless*, on route from Bombay, India to Liverpool, England, ran into difficulty when it was discovered that there were two ships of that name making that passage. The purchaser intended one ship's cargo and the seller the other. Both positions were equally reasonable; consequently, the court found that there was no contract.[1]

When parties disagree, court will apply reasonable interpretation

The third type of mistake is where only one of the parties is in error. Such **one-sided mistakes** will normally not affect the existence of the contract. This is where the principle of *caveat emptor* (let the buyer beware) is applied. When one party has been induced to make the mistake by misleading statements made by the other, this is an actionable misrepresentation and discussed below. But when that person misleads himself or herself, normally he or she has no recourse. On rare occasions a person might sign a document by mistake, thinking it is about something different than it actually is. If that mistake goes to the nature of the agreement in its entirety, not just some aspect of it such as the price, the document may be void. The principle is *non est factum* (it is not my act), and while it used to be very important, the Supreme Court of Canada has now determined that negligence may block such a claim. The problem is that it is difficult to make an error about the essential nature of a document, for example, mistaking a mortgage for a guarantee, unless you haven't read it—and not reading it qualifies as negligence that may block the claim.

One-sided mistakes usually have no effect on contract

But *non est factum* can cause void contract

1. *Raffles v. Wichelhaus* (1894), 2 H. & C. 906, 159 E.R. 375 (E.D.).

CASE SUMMARY 4.1

Zellers, Bond v. Arkin[2]

No Contract because of Mistake in Law

Zellers Department Store caught Mrs. Bond's son shoplifting items worth about $60. She paid $225 as demanded in a letter from a collection agency employed by Zellers. The extra amount was intended to cover costs such as the salary of a loss prevention officer and various surveillance equipment. When Mrs. Bond learned that she had no legal responsibility for the crimes of her son, she brought this action to recover the money. Zellers argued that whether the original claim was valid or not, she had entered into a contract with them to pay the money in exchange for their not pursuing a lawsuit against her. The court held that since a mistake in law had taken place, there was no contractual obligation. The letter from the collection agency was misleading and led to Mrs. Bond's mistake; therefore, she was entitled to recover the amount paid to Zellers.

EXEMPTION CLAUSES

Exemption clauses limit liability

Exemption clauses strictly interpreted

One area where disputes commonly arise over the interpretation of terms in a contract involves exemption clauses, sometimes referred to as exculpatory, exclusion, or limitation clauses. These are provisions that favour one side, usually exempting that side from liability for failure to perform some aspect of the contract. A typical example would be a sign in a parking lot limiting the liability of the company for goods stolen or damage done to the vehicle, or a term in a contract with a shipper exempting it from liability for damage to the goods while in transit. Because such clauses favour one side at the expense of the other, there is some reluctance to enforce them. But the whole idea of contract law is that the parties are free to negotiate whatever they want, and it is not for the court to interfere with that bargaining process. The solution to this dilemma has been to give effect to these clauses, but to interpret them as narrowly as possible. First they must be brought to the attention of the other contracting party. Today, it is generally accepted that any unusual clause like this should be highlighted in some way and not buried in the general language of the contract. If the notification is by sign, as would likely be the case in the parking lot example, that sign must be at a location where it is clearly visible to the customer.

Secondly, any ambiguity at all will be at the expense of the party favoured by the clause. If a courier company included an exemption clause in their contract stating "not responsible for loss caused by delay or damage to goods," and the goods being transported were stolen or lost, the limitation clause would not protect the company. It may well be that we can imply that they intended the exemption from liability to cover any damage or loss of the goods, including theft, but they didn't say that, and the court will not imply such a meaning.

These exemption clauses are usually found in what are called standard form contracts. Contract law is based on a bargaining model, but, in fact, parties are

2. (1996), 138 D.L.R. (4th) 309, [1996] 8 W.W.R. 100 (Man. Q.B.).

often in unequal bargaining positions. Try bargaining with an airline over the terms included in a ticket or a car dealer over the terms included in the warranty. In those circumstances the courts are particularly vigilant in interpreting such exemption clauses as narrowly as possible.

CASE SUMMARY 4.2

Boutcev v. DHL International Express Ltd.[3]

Exclusion Clause Not Properly Brought to the Attention of Customer

When two boxes that were supposed to contain computers arrived empty at their destination, the plaintiff, Boutcev, sued the shipper, DHL International Express Ltd., for compensation. The shipper refused to pay and denied all liability, referring to an exemption clause contained in very small print on the back of the waybill. The judge found that the clause was illegible, saying it was "painfully small and defied reading with the naked eye." He refused to enforce it, holding in favour of the plaintiff. Parties to an agreement are only bound by the terms that are reasonably brought to their attention, and to ensure that such exclusion clauses are enforceable, the party drawing up the contract should put them in bold type or otherwise highlight them in some way.

Misrepresentation

Misrepresentation involves false and misleading statements that induce a person to enter into a contract. Note that false here includes half-truths, where what is *not* mentioned makes the statement misleading. Telling a prospective investor that a finance company has several million dollars in assets in the form of outstanding loans is misleading if the investor is not also told that half of those loans are unsecured and unrecoverable. The matter is simplified if the false statement becomes a term of the contract and, consequently, the injured party can sue for breach of contract. Breach of contract will be discussed as a separate topic below. Often, however, these misleading statements never become part of the contract, even though they are persuasive and the very reason the person enters into the agreement in the first place. If you purchase property because the vendor told you a new resort will open nearby, the purchase agreement would normally make no reference to the new resort. Still, if you relied on that false information to persuade you to purchase the property, you will likely have recourse under the law of misrepresentation.

Misrepresentation involves false and misleading statements

If a false statement is a term of contract, the remedy is to sue for breach

False statements that induce a contract are also actionable

For a statement to be an actionable misrepresentation, normally it must be a statement of fact, not a statement of opinion. You are entitled to have the opinion that you are selling a "great little car in good shape." It is only when an expert makes the statement that the opinion can be an actionable misrepresentation. When a mechanic says the car he is selling is a "great little car in good shape," the statement had better be true. But in most cases the false statement must be a

3. Alta. Q.B., 2001, as reported in *Lawyers Weekly Consolidated Digest,* Vol. 20.

TABLE 4.1 Remedies

Innocent misrepresentation	Rescission only
Fraudulent misrepresentation	Rescission or damages (tort)
Negligent misstatement	Rescission or damages (tort)
Misstatement—becomes a term of the contract	Rescission, damages, and other breach of contract remedies

To be actionable, a false statement must be a statement of fact, not an opinion

statement of fact to be an actionable misrepresentation. Even the non-expert will be liable if he falsely claims as a fact that the engine of the car he is selling has recently been rebuilt or replaced. When marketing products or services, legislated advertising standards must be followed. Even when those standards are adhered to, if the message is false or misleading, individual customers may be able to sue for misrepresentation. Consumer protection legislation, which is in place in all jurisdictions, broadens the responsibility of employers for misleading statements made by their salespeople. Consumer protection legislation will also be discussed under "Consumer Protection Legislation" in Chapter 5 (see p. 109).

Silence is not misrepresentation except where duty of good faith or relationship

Silence will not normally be misrepresentation. Only when there is a legislated duty or some special relationships between the parties requiring disclosure will failure to make such a disclosure constitute misrepresentation. A recent development in contract law is the recognition in a growing number of relationships that there is a **duty of good faith** between the parties. Where such a duty is present there is an obligation to disclose pertinent information. The failure to do so may well be considered misrepresentation and can be challenged in court. Even in a business transaction where someone withholds information that would lead the other party to change his or her mind, the person withholding information could be violating the duty to act in good faith. Of course, if the misleading statement did not induce the other party to contract, there is no remedy. Suppose the vendor of a property told you of a new resort opening nearby and you purchased the property to build a home or for some other purpose not affected by that claim. You will have no complaint if the statement later turns out to be false, since it did not induce you to enter into the contract in the first place. When the false statement does induce a person to enter a contract, the misrepresentation may be considered innocent, fraudulent, or negligent (see Table 4.1 for a summary of the types of misrepresentation and their remedies).

INNOCENT MISREPRESENTATION

Where misrepresentation is innocent, the only remedy is rescission

A distinction has to be drawn between someone who intentionally misleads and a situation where there is no such intention and no knowledge of the error being made. When a person misleads another without knowing, and he or she is otherwise without fault, the misrepresentation is said to be innocent. The recourse is limited to the equitable remedy of **rescission.** Rescission involves the court attempting to restore the parties to their original positions. Thus, if a seller had innocently misrepresented the year of production of a car sold to you, and this was important enough to induce you to enter into that transaction, you could seek to have the contract rescinded. You would return the car, and the seller would be required to return the purchase price as well as any incidental costs you may have incurred, such as repair and maintenance expenses. A problem arises where the goods have been destroyed, resold, or are otherwise not available to return to the other party. Rescission is then not possible. Where the misrepresentation has been innocent, no other remedy is available. The remedy of rescission will also be refused where the victim of the misrepresentation has in turn done something inappropriate, such as causing unreasonable delay or having cheated or misled the other party. To obtain an equitable remedy such as rescission, the person seeking it must "come with clean hands." Rescission will also be refused where the contract has been affirmed. This means that the victim has done something to acknowledge the validity of the contract after learning of the misrepresentation, such as trying to resell the goods to someone else.

CASE SUMMARY 4.3

Samson v. Lockwood[4]

Rescission Not Available Where Contract Affirmed

The defendants produced a brochure advertising property that stated that a building of 150 000 square feet could be built on it. Unknown to the defendants, because of a change in local bylaws, a building of only 30 000 square feet could be built. The plaintiff, after having read the brochure, agreed to purchase the property and put a substantial deposit down on the transaction. Before the actual transfer of that property, land values in the area dropped significantly. The plaintiff tried to sell the property, and when this proved impossible, he refused to go through with the transaction, claiming misrepresentation and demanding the return of the deposit. The court held that the plaintiff was not permitted to rescind the contract in this case. He knew of the error six months before the agreed upon date for the completion of the transaction, and yet he still indicated a willingness to complete. The plaintiff also attempted to sell the property to others long after learning of the error and before land values dropped. This amounted to affirmation of the contract after he already knew of the innocent misrepresentation. The result was that the purchase agreement was binding on him, despite the innocent misrepresentation in the brochure. The plaintiff was required to forfeit all of the deposit that he had paid.

It must be emphasized that where the misrepresentation has been innocent, the only remedy is rescission. Damages or the payment of monetary compensation to the victim is not available for innocent misrepresentation.

Damages are not available where misrepresentation is innocent

FRAUDULENT MISREPRESENTATION

Fraudulent misrepresentation takes place when one person intentionally and knowingly misleads another and induces him or her to enter into a contract. If it can be shown that you didn't believe that what you were saying was true, you have committed a fraud and the remedies available to the defendant are expanded. Where the misrepresentation is fraudulent, the victim can seek rescission of the contract, or he or she can seek a remedy of damages for the tort of deceit, or both.

Fraudulent misrepresentation occurs when a person knowingly misleads

4. (1998), 40 O.R. (3d) 161, 39 B.L.R. (2d) 82 (Ont. C.A.).

Remedy for fraud can be damages and/or rescission

As mentioned earlier, damages involve the wrongdoer paying money to the victim to compensate for his or her losses. The objective is to put the victim into the position he or she would have been in had the misrepresentation never taken place. In rare circumstances where the fraud is serious enough, the court will award punitive damages, which is an attempt to punish the wrongdoer rather than to compensate the victim. In such cases the victim will be awarded more money than he or she has actually lost. Victims will often sue for innocent misrepresentation, even though the presence of fraud is apparent. This can be confusing until you appreciate the strategy involved. Establishing fraud and intention is much more difficult. Where the remedy sought is only rescission, the victim will usually take the easier route of suing for innocent misrepresentation. Note also that an innocent misrepresentation can become fraud if the person who made the statement later learns it is false and fails to correct the false impression left with the victim.

Innocent misrepresentation is easier to prove than fraud

NEGLIGENT MISREPRESENTATION

Historically there was no difference between innocent and negligent misrepresentation. Since the victim was not knowingly misled, the only remedy available was rescission. In recent years, however, the courts have also awarded damages where it can be established that the wrongdoer should have been more careful. In such cases negligence is established. The legal rules associated with the tort of negligence were discussed in Chapter 2. To summarize, the remedy of rescission is available whether the misrepresentation is innocent, fraudulent, or negligent. But the remedy of damages is restricted to circumstances where it can be established that the misrepresentation was fraudulent, negligent, or where the misleading term became part of the agreement.

Damages also available where misrepresentation was negligent

CASE SUMMARY 4.4

BG Checo International v. B.C. Hydro[5]

Where Misrepresentation Is Negligent, the Victim Can Sue in Contract or in Tort

B.C. Hydro was erecting a transmission line and put out a request for tenders to erect the towers and string the required lines. BG Checo was the successful bidder, but they based their bid on erroneous information they had been given with respect to the condition of the right of way. They were informed by B.C. Hydro that it would be cleared by another party, when, in fact, they had to clear it themselves. As a result, they incurred considerable extra expense.

In this action Checo is seeking to recover those extra costs from B.C. Hydro, claiming misrepresentation and breach of contract. The main issue was whether the action should be brought in tort for negligence or for breach of contract. The matter went all the way to the Supreme Court of Canada with the defendant advocating the more traditional approach—where a contract is involved, any remedies should be restricted to breach of contract. The court rejected this position holding that Checo had the right to sue in tort for negligent misrepresentation or for breach of contract.

(continued)

5. (1993), 99 D.L.R. (4th) 577 (S.C.C.).

The importance of this decision is that the court declared that when the conduct complained of could be characterized as either a breach of contract or negligence, the victim had a right to sue in either tort or contract. "The parties may by their contract limit the duty one owes to the other or waive the right to sue in tort, but subject to this, the right to sue concurrently in tort and contract remains." The difference gives the plaintiff more options and the court more flexibility in awarding damages. The case is also interesting in that it differentiates between fraudulent and negligent misrepresentation, thus providing a remedy for both parties even when their relationship is primarily based on contract.

CRIMINAL FRAUD

Inducing someone to enter a transaction through intentionally misleading statements can also constitute a crime with potentially significant penalties. There are many specific provisions where various forms of fraudulent activity are prohibited, but for this discussion the most significant are sections 361–365 of the *Criminal Code,* which prohibit knowingly making false representations that are intended to induce someone to act on that representation. This includes obtaining credit, the extension of credit, or some other benefit for themselves or someone else under false pretenses, including misleading statements about the financial condition of the applicant or others. Knowingly paying with a cheque without sufficient funds to back it (N.S.F.) or executing some other valuable security by making false representations are also specifically prohibited. Obtaining food, beverages, or accommodation by false pretenses is also included. Section 380 contains provisions generally prohibiting fraudulent activities that cheat the public "of any property, money, or valuable consideration or service." This is followed by a number of specific offences, including using the mails to defraud and fraudulent manipulation of stock exchange transactions. A significant aspect of these provisions relates to offences involving falsifying, destruction, or manipulation of books, employee records, prospectus and other documents with intent to defraud. Impersonating others and passing-off is also prohibited. Passing-off involves leading someone to believe that he or she is dealing with one business, when they are not. For example, one soft drink manufacturer copying the distinctive bottle shape of another might well cause confusion; such an act could form the basis for a passing-off action. The penalties for such frauds vary with the value of what has been lost or the importance of the documents involved. For example, where the subject of the fraud is a testamentary document such as a will or where the amounts involved are over $5000, it will be treated as an indictable offence with a potential prison term of up to 10 years. If less than $5000, it will be treated as a summary conviction with potential imprisonment of two years.

Fraudulent misrepresentation may constitute a crime

Duress and Undue Influence

Duress and undue influence also involve disputes related to the formation of contract. Duress occurs when the free will to bargain is lost because coercion involving threat of violence, imprisonment, scandal, damage to property, or even inappropriate financial pressure is exercised by one of the parties. If someone threatens to harm your family or vandalize your business to force you to enter into a contract, the agreement would be voidable because of duress. Another example of duress would be an employer who finds an employee stealing stock or money and agrees not to report him or her to the police if the employee will agree to repay the money by working overtime at regular wage or for some other advantage. The term *voidable* means that the victim can get out of the contract unless a third party has become involved. If you sold your car to A under threat, you could sue to have it returned because you sold it under duress. But if A had already resold the car to B, you can't force B to give it up. Your only recourse is against A, the person who threatened you. A classic example of economic duress took place when a landlord put inordinate pressure on a tenant to sign a lease with unfavourable provisions. The tenant had taken over a prior lease from a tenant who had left several months' rent unpaid. She did so with the understanding that she was not obligated to pay that back rent. But the rent remained unpaid, and the landlord insisted that she was responsible for it. Under tremendous pressure, she signed a new lease where she assumed the back rent obligation. The court held that the landlord knew she had to sign to avoid "catastrophic financial losses." This economic duress made the transaction unconscionable, and released her of her obligations.[6]

Threats, a form of duress, make the contract voidable

Uttering threats of physical violence to a person, to his or her property, or even to his or her animals can amount to the criminal offence of assault. Obtaining some advantage from people by threats or intimidation can constitute extortion with serious penalties. Duress, as discussed above, may constitute criminal harassment or intimidation, which are also offences under the *Criminal Code*. These offences are also punishable by indictment up to 10 years in prison or by summary conviction up to two years in prison. The *Criminal Code* also makes it a summary conviction offence for an employer to threaten or intimidate an employee with respect to his or her trade union activities.

Note that when a person is compelled to commit an offence by threats of death or immediate bodily harm, that can constitute a valid defence except where the crime involves very serious crimes such as high treason, murder, abduction, sexual assault, or robbery.

Undue influence involves abuse of a trusting relationship making a contract voidable

Undue influence presumed in some situations

Undue influence is more common. It also involves the loss of free will to bargain. But instead of force, the unique influence of the other contracting party takes away the free will of the victim. In certain types of relationships undue influence is presumed. Examples include professionals such as lawyers, doctors, and trustees taking advantage of their clients as well as guardians contracting with wards, religious advisors with parishioners, and adults with infant children or aging parents. The presumption of undue influence means that in the absence of other evidence to the contrary, simply showing that the relationship exists is enough for the court to allow the victim to escape the contract on the basis of undue influence. Professionals doing business with their clients often find themselves in such relationships, and they are well advised to ensure that the client obtains independent legal advice before committing to the transaction. That will normally provide sufficient evidence to overcome the presumption of undue influence. There are other situations, however, where undue influence can arise based on the unique circumstances involved. For example, when Oscar learned he was dying of cancer, he transferred some of his estate to his nephew. When his brother, Arthur, found out, he got angry and demanded that Oscar transfer the rest of his estate to him and his wife. Arthur's yelling at his brother and pressuring him to go to the lawyer and

6. *Canada Life Assurance Co. v. Stewart* (1994), 118 D.L.R. (4th) 67 (N.S.C.A).

change his will the next day was clear evidence of undue influence, and the transactions and will were set aside.[7] Where there is no legal presumption based on the relationship between the parties, the person trying to escape the contract must produce evidence of actual undue influence. This is much harder to do.

The principle of **unconscionability** is related to undue influence. This is also a recently developed area of contract law that allows the court to set aside or modify the contract on the basis of vulnerability, such as poverty or mental impairment (short of incapacity) that has allowed one party to unfairly take advantage of the other. In effect, it must be shown that because of these factors the bargaining position of the parties was unequal, resulting in an unjust contract that was grossly unfair to the victim. Note that simple economic advantage will not create an unconscionable transaction. If you are charged a high rate of interest on a loan because you are a high risk, this is not an unfair or unconscionable contract. Most provinces have statutes regulating unconscionable transactions involving loans or mortgages, but unconscionability has now been expanded into contract law generally.

Unconscionable contract when vulnerable people taken advantage of

Privity and Assignment

The problems of privity and assignment are concerned with determining who has rights and claims under the contract and who can sue to enforce those claims. **Privity of contract** is a basic principle of contract law under which only the parties to a contract have rights. Strangers to the contract are not bound by it, nor can they enforce its provisions. In the example used in Chapter 2, *Donoghue v. Stevenson*,[8] Mrs. Donoghue, after finding a decomposed snail in her ginger beer, could not sue the seller because she was not privy to the contract. Her friend bought the drink for her. Her only alternative was to sue the bottler/manufacturer for negligence. The same principle of privity prevents shareholders or investors in corporations from suing accountants or others who negligently do business for that corporation, such as providing incorrect audited financial statements. The corporation is considered a separate person, and the contract is between that company and the accountant—not the shareholder or investor. The only option for the shareholder is to sue in tort for negligence.

Privity means only the parties to contract are bound by it

There have always been some specific exceptions to the privity rule. Three important exceptions are 1) interests in land that go with the land—thus a lease will bind not only the original owner and tenant but also any person to whom that land was sold during the term of the lease; 2) trust arrangements—where a person puts property in trust with a trustee for the benefit of some third party, that third party can enforce the trust through a stranger to the contract; 3) life insurance—where the beneficiary is able to enforce the policy taken out by the deceased. Note as well that in some jurisdictions the restrictions of privity have been removed by statute, allowing, for example, the consumer of a product to sue the manufacturer for breach of contract even though the original contract was with the dealer.

Privity exceptions:
- Interests in land
- Trusts
- Life insurance

Note that when agents act for principals in dealings with third parties, the principle of privity does not enter into the situation, since the resulting contract is between the principal and the third party, and the agent is merely a go-between. Similarly, where one person takes over the obligations of another in a contractual relationship with a third party (called a **novation**), there is no privity

7. *Francoeur v. Francoeur Estates*, 2001 MBQB 298 (CanLII) (Man. Q.B.).

8. [1932] A.C. 562 (H.L.).

Agency and novation do not violate the privity principle

problem since that new relationship requires a complete new contract between the newcomer and the original contracting parties. All three must agree to the change substituting a new contract for the old one.

Privity rules are changing

In addition to the statutory exceptions mentioned above, the courts have also shown a willingness to move away from the privity rule. For example, in the case of *London Drugs Ltd. v. Kuehne & Nagel International Ltd.*,[9] Kuehne & Nagel was storing valuable goods for London Drugs, and there was an exemption clause in that storage contract that limited any liability for loss to $40. Employees of Kuehne & Nagel caused considerable damage by careless handling of goods, and London Drugs sued them directly for the loss. Even though the employees were not party to the contract limiting liability to $40, the Supreme Court of Canada extended that protection to those employees, thus ignoring the rule of privity that normally would have applied.

ASSIGNMENT

Perhaps the most significant area where the rules of privity have been modified involves the assignment of contractual rights (see Figure 4.2). Assignment involves the assignor transferring a benefit to which they are entitled under a contract to a third party, called the assignee. In effect, they are selling an entitlement or claim to someone else. For example, if a debtor owes money to a creditor, that creditor can assign the claim to a third party. Merchants selling goods on credit, such as car dealerships, often do this. Their business is selling cars, not extending credit. So they assign that credit transaction to a finance company for a fee, and the payments are then made to the finance company.

Contract benefits can be transferred or assigned to a non-party

The problems arise when the person owing the obligation that has been assigned fails to perform. Because of the rule of privity, the assignee cannot sue directly; the assignor and assignee must join together to sue the debtor. This is a cumbersome process and most jurisdictions have enacted statutes that allow the assignee to sue directly if certain criteria are met. This is called a **statutory assignment** and to qualify, the assignment must be absolute. This means it must be complete and unconditional; it must be in writing; and proper notice of the assignment must be given to the person owing the obligation that has been assigned. In the example above, the car dealership would make the assignment of the original debt owed by the purchaser to the finance company in writing. The finance company would then send a copy of that assignment to the debtor, asking

Statutory assignments can be enforced directly

FIGURE 4.2 Assignment

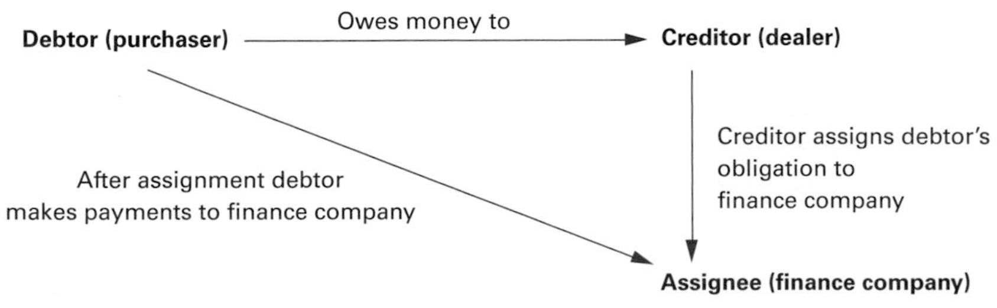

9. [1993] 1 W.W.R. 1 (S.C.C.).

that all future payments be made to them. In the event of default, the requirements for a statutory assignment have been met and the finance company can sue the debtor directly.

Only benefits can be assigned, not obligations

Finally, it should also be noted that only benefits can be assigned, not obligations. In this example, if a car were defective, the dealership would still be responsible for their breach of contract, no matter what their agreement with the finance company said. The dealership cannot assign such obligations. For that reason, in any assignment, the assignee is said to take "subject to the equities." Thus, if the car dealership doesn't honour the warranty when something goes wrong, the purchaser would have an excuse not to continue paying the finance company. The assignee can be in no better position with respect to the contract than was the assignor.

CASE SUMMARY 4.5

Trans Canada Credit Corp. v. Zaluski et al.[10]

Promissory Note Enforceable Despite Salesman's Fraud

Green was a salesman representing Niagara Compact Vacuum Cleaner Company when he persuaded and pressured the Zaluski family into signing a conditional sales agreement and promissory note for the purchase of a vacuum cleaner. Niagara, in turn, assigned their interest in the transaction to Trans Canada Credit. When Zaluski made no payments, Trans Canada Credit sued Zaluski on the strength of the assigned conditional sales agreement and on the promissory note.

The court found that Green was guilty of fraud, which tainted the sale, thus giving Zaluski a good defence against Green and his principal Niagara. This defence also extended to Trans Canada Credit, which, as the assignee of the conditional sales agreement, could be in no better position than Niagara.

But Trans Canada had sued on the promissory note, and this led to a different result. Once the negotiable instrument, such as a promissory note, gets into the hands of an innocent third party (called a *holder in due course*) they can enforce it independently of any failure on the part of the original party. Trans Canada Credit, as such a holder in due course, was in a position to enforce the promissory note, and therefore Zaluski had to pay. Negotiable instruments are extremely dangerous, and people should be careful when they enter into them. A more detailed discussion of negotiable instruments follows. Zaluski, in turn, successfully sued Niagara for the return of the money he had to pay Trans Canada Credit.

(continued)

10. (1969), 5 D.L.R. (3d) 702 (Ont. Co. Ct.).

CASE SUMMARY 4.5 Trans Canada Credit Corp. v. Zaluski et al.

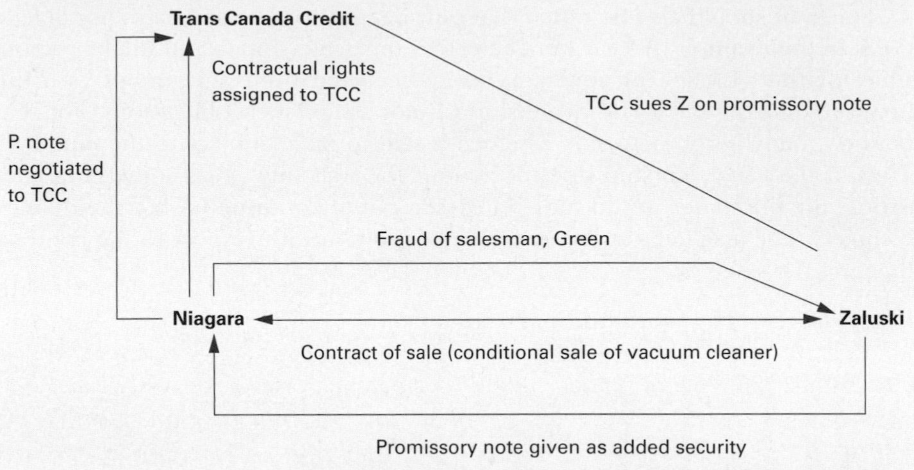

NEGOTIABLE INSTRUMENTS

Negotiable instruments include cheques, bills of exchange, and promissory notes

The position of a third party can be quite different when a negotiable instrument is involved. **Negotiable instruments** include cheques, bills of exchange (sometimes called drafts), and promissory notes. These instruments are passed between people and represent claims for funds payable. They often get into the hands of innocent third parties, and when they do, they are treated in a unique way. Such third parties, called holders in due course, can enforce these instruments against the person who made them despite any questionable transactions between the original parties. Negotiable instruments will be discussed in more detail in Chapter 5, but at this stage the position of a holder in due course of such a negotiable instrument must be contrasted with the position of an assignee of contractual rights.

The assignee is in a similar position. He is seeking to enforce a claim against a debtor that he has acquired from someone else. But as discussed above, such an assignee can be in no better position than was the original creditor. If the original creditor couldn't enforce the claim, neither can the assignee. That's why Trans Canada Credit couldn't sue on the strength of the original debt they had been assigned in the *Zaluski* case above. The transaction was tainted by the fraud of the salesman, Green. But if that assignee also has a cheque or promissory note made by the original debtor but acquired from someone else, and if the assignee is innocent of any wrongdoing, then he is a holder in due course. As such, the assignee can enforce that instrument independent of any difficulties with the original transaction. That is why Trans Canada Credit was able to successfully sue Zaluski for the amount owing—not on the strength of the assignment of the contractual rights, but on the basis of being a holder in due course of the promissory note. For this reason most credit transactions include a promissory note so that the position of any third party acquiring rights under it can be protected.

Holder in due course can enforce instrument independent of problems

Discharging Contractual Obligations

PERFORMANCE

Most disputes with respect to contracts arise because of incomplete or improper performance of contractual obligations (see Table 4.2). This is called *breach of contract*, and there is a significant problem in determining just how imperfect performance has to be before it becomes a serious enough breach to discharge the other party's obligations. A contract is **discharged by performance** once both parties have performed as required under the agreement and there are no further outstanding obligations. The terms of an agreement can be characterized as major terms, called **conditions**, and minor terms, called **warranties**. Be careful not to confuse the term warranty, as it is used here, with the assurance given by a manufacturer with respect to the quality of a product produced by them and sold to consumers (a **manufacturer's warranty**). That is a specialized use of the term. The more correct use of warranty refers to any term of lesser importance (a minor term) in all contractual relationships. You can tell if a term is a condition or a warranty by asking the contracting party if, had he or she known ahead of time that the term was going to be breached, he or she would still have entered into the contract. If he or she would have walked away, the term is a condition, but if it is likely that the contracting party still would have entered into the contract, the term is of lesser importance or a warranty.

Contractual obligations can be ended by performance

If a condition is breached after the contract is in place, the other party can elect to treat the contract as discharged. He or she doesn't have to perform the obligation under the agreement since the contract has been discharged by breach. But if a warranty is breached, the failure is not considered serious enough to discharge the contract or end the obligations of the non-breaching party. Thus, the contract is still in effect, and the non-breaching party must still perform his or her side of the agreement. There has been a breach, however, and the non-breaching party does have the right to seek compensation in the form of damages from the breaching party.

Breach of warranty still considered performance

A similar result takes place when a condition is breached in some minor way. Even though a major term has been breached, the failure is so minor that the contract is considered **substantially performed** and the non-breaching party is

TABLE 4.2 How to End Contractual Obligations

Performance	Discharge by performance takes place where there is complete performance or where failure to perform is minor.
Breach	Breach of a condition (important term) discharges the victim of his or her obligations under the contract.
Frustration	Discharge by frustration takes place where performance is made "impossible" by some outside event
Agreement	Obligations can be modified or ended by a new agreement.

still required to perform his or her obligations under the agreement. Of course, here there is also a right to seek compensation for the loss from the breaching party. If you were to order a new car from a dealership and it was delivered with regular wheels rather than the racing rims you specified, this would be a breach of warranty. You could not refuse to take delivery of the car and would have to pay the agreed-upon price, reduced by what it would cost to replace the wheels. If the car was delivered without an engine or a different model altogether was sent, this would be a breach of condition, and you could refuse delivery and would not have to pay for the car. If you operated a fleet of cars and ordered 1000 cars from the dealership and only 999 were delivered, this would be substantial performance of a condition of the contract (the delivery of 1000 cars). You would still have to pay, but only for the 999 delivered cars.

Substantial performance still considered performance

When money is involved, there are some special rules. A cheque, even a certified cheque, is not the same as cash. If the contract calls for the payment of a specified amount of money, that means Canadian legal tender unless otherwise specified. Cheques can be used if that has been agreed to or has been the accepted method of doing business in the past. But when in doubt, make sure that actual Bank of Canada bank notes are delivered. Even Canadian coins do not qualify as legal tender over a specified amount. For example, under the *Currency Act*[11] anything over 25 pennies is not considered legal tender. All coins have restrictions in this way; the amount that can be used varies with the denomination of the coin. However, there is no similar limitation on bills.

Note limited definition of legal tender

It should also be noted that one party can't prevent the other from performing and then claim to be relieved of her obligations because the other party has failed to properly perform her contractual obligations. As long as the performing party is ready, willing, and able to perform and has attempted to do so, that **tender of performance** is considered equivalent to proper performance of the contract. Suppose I agree to paint your house and arrive at the time specified with the appropriate paint and brushes, and you refuse to let me in. I have lived up to my contractual obligation. If you fail to pay me, you are the one in breach, not me. Again, money is treated differently. If I owe you money and come ready to pay it at an appropriate time and place, and you refuse to take it, I still owe you the money. But there is one significant change in my obligation. Normally, it is the debtor's obligation to seek out the creditor to make payment. But I have done that, and now the obligation will be upon you to seek to collect the money from me. You must bear any expenses (including court costs) arising in that process.

Except with money, proper tender is considered performance

BREACH

As noted, a serious breach of contract can discharge the other party of his or her obligations under the contract. This breach of contract could take place by incomplete or improper performance of the contractual obligations. The breach can also occur through **repudiation**. This involves one of the parties informing the other that he is refusing to perform his contractual obligations, or doing something that makes proper performance impossible (implied repudiation). Where the repudiation takes place before performance is due, it is called **anticipatory breach**, and the victim of that breach has two options. He can either ignore the repudiation and continue to demand performance or treat the contract as

Repudiation involves refusal to perform

11. R.S.C. 1985, c. C-52.

discharged and make other arrangements. Treating the contract as ended allows the victim to make other arrangements and to sue right away rather than waiting for the actual failure before suing. If the victim must hire someone else to do the job, for example, any higher costs can be recovered in that action. On the other hand, if the victim continues to demand performance, the damages recovered may be higher, but there is also the danger that some unexpected event such as a fire, natural disaster, or even sickness may make it impossible to perform. Such an event would discharge both parties of their obligations. Worse, the victim of the repudiation may find that he is no longer in a position to perform, making him the one in breach.

Anticipatory breach: can treat contract as ended by breach or demand performance

- But is bound by choice

If the refusal to perform comes after performance is due, this is just another form of breach through failure to properly perform contractual obligations. The remedies available for such a breach will be discussed below.

CASE SUMMARY 4.6

Long House Trading Co. v. Nagaard Sawmills Ltd.[12]

Making Performance of a Contract Impossible Amounts to Repudiation

Long House had a five-year contract with Nagaard to sell cedar siding manufactured by them as their commissioned agent. After two years of successfully selling the product, Nagaard increased the price of the cedar siding by 25 percent. The increase made it impossible to compete in the market and brought sales for the product to a halt. Receiving no commissions, Nagaard treated the contract as repudiated and sued for compensation. The court agreed, finding that the decision of Nagaard to increase the price by 25 percent was entirely within the control of Nagaard and made it impossible to sell the product. This was inconsistent with the terms of the contract and constituted repudiation by conduct on the part of Nagaard. The court awarded damages of $62 000 to Long House for breach of contract. Note that this is quite different from the kind of frustration discussed below, where the events that make performance impossible must be unexpected and not within the control of either party. The Nagaard decision was reversed on appeal, but for reasons that don't affect its value as an illustration of repudiation by conduct.

As noted above exemption clauses are often included in contracts in order to lessen the liability of one party at the expense of another. This is an attempt to make something that would normally constitute a breach of contract imposing liability on the breaching party only a minor breach of warranty—if indeed a breach at all. The idea is that even in the face of some failure on the part of the party benefited by the term, the other party is still obligated to perform his or her side of the bargain with no claim or a reduced claim to compensation. The courts have responded by interpreting such clauses very narrowly; only in the clearest of cases have the courts given effect to them. In some instances, where the conduct has been particularly damaging, the courts have gone further and have applied the principle of fundamental breach. For example, where a purchased vehicle is so defective as to make it essentially worthless to the purchaser, the court would

12. B.C.S.C., as reported May 16, 1997 in *Lawyers Weekly*, Vol. 17.

TABLE 4.3 Performance and Breach

Performance and Breach		Options of the Other Party
Repudiation		
Before performance due	Election	Can treat obligations as ended and sue or wait for performance
After performance due	Breach	Can treat obligations as ended and sue
Failure to perform	Breach	Can treat obligations as ended and sue
Partial performance		
Serious failure	Breach	Can treat obligations as ended and sue
Minor failure	Performance	Must perform obligations, but can sue for compensation
Complete performance	Performance	Must fulfill contractual obligations
Performance tendered but refused		
Goods and services	Performance	Must fulfill contractual obligations
Money		Money still owed, but no obligation to seek out creditor

find that the contract of purchase has been fundamentally breached. Further, the warranty provision exempting the seller and manufacturer from liability does not apply in this situation on the basis that the parties never would have intended such a complete exclusion of responsibility when they originally entered into the contract. The warranty exclusion, then, is interpreted to apply only to lesser shortfalls in performance. This is referred to as the *interpretation approach* to fundamental breach.

Finally, it should be noted that under rare circumstances a breach of contract can amount to a criminal offence with serious penalties. For such a breach to constitute a crime under section 422 of the *Criminal Code,* the breaching party must know, or have reasonable cause to believe, that the breach will result in danger to human life, serious bodily injury, or serious property damage, or that the breach will delay a train, or even deprive a city (or a significant part of it) of light, power, gas, or water. See Table 4.3 for a summary of the types of performance and breach.

FRUSTRATION

Frustration ends contractual obligations

Frustration involves impossibility of performance or fundamental change

A contract **discharged through frustration** is a recognition that the parties should not be penalized when events happen that are out of their control. Frustration usually takes place when performance becomes impossible, such as when the subject matter of the contract is destroyed through no fault of the parties. A contract can also be frustrated when performance is still technically possible, but would lead to a completely different result because of the changing circumstances. This is illustrated in the case of *Cassidy v. Canada Publishing Corp.*[13] discussed below.

13. B.C.S.C., as reported February 3, 1989 in *Lawyers Weekly Consolidated Digest,* Vol. 8.

The kinds of situations that can lead to a contract being frustrated are personal illness or destruction of the subject matter, an event the contract was based on being cancelled or changed, and interference by government (such as changing the law, refusing permits and licences, or expropriating property). For a contract to be frustrated the changing events leading to frustration must be outside the control of either party. Suppose that Jones contracted to build a house for Smith, but was denied a permit due to a change in government regulation. That would likely be frustration. But if he was denied that permit because of his failure to supply necessary plans or other documentation, that would be breach of contract, since the matter was within his control. This is referred to as *self-induced frustration*, which is simply a breach of contract.

Self-induced frustration is breach of contract

Sometimes a provision will be put into the contract stating what will happen and who will bear the loss in the event of such frustrating events. If that is the case, the provisions of the contract will prevail. For a contract to be discharged by frustration, there must be an outside, unforeseen event that is out of the control of either party and that renders the contract impossible to perform. Such events destroy the foundation of the contract and make performance something completely different from what was contemplated.

CASE SUMMARY 4.7

Cassidy v. Canada Publishing Corp.[14]

Change of Curriculum Frustrates Contract

Ms. Cassidy had a contract to work as part of an authoring team to produce a social studies text to be used in the public schools. Her contribution, among other things, was to provide a chapter on criminal law. But the Ministry of Education changed the curriculum requirements so that a criminal law chapter was no longer required. In response, the defendant dropped the plaintiff from the writing team and provided no compensation for the considerable amount of work that she had already done. The court found that there was a contract here, but that it had been frustrated by the change in curriculum. Although it was still technically possible for the arrangement to continue, "the substantial revision of the curriculum amounted to a frustrating event," excusing the parties of further performance. It is interesting to note that although the court found frustration, they ordered a considerable amount of compensation for the work she had already done and which benefited the publisher to be paid to the plaintiff as required under the *Frustrated Contracts Act* discussed immediately below.

Historically, the effect of a frustrated contract was simply "let the loss lie where it falls." Both parties were discharged of any further obligations, keeping any benefits and bearing any losses that had been incurred to that point. But that was seen to be unfair, and today all jurisdictions have enacted frustrated contracts acts that overcome much of this unfairness. Essentially, if either party has benefited by a partially performed contract, he or she will have to pay for that benefit as was

Frustrated contracts acts require payment for benefits received and the return or apportionment of any deposit

14. *Ibid.*

the case in *Cassidy v. Canada Publishing* above. If a deposit has been paid and no benefit has been received, the deposit must be returned. Note that a portion of that deposit can be retained to compensate for costs incurred in preparing to perform the contract. The British Columbia *Frustrated Contracts Act* goes further by requiring the parties to share equally any costs incurred, even where no deposit has been paid.

AGREEMENT

Changing legal relationships through agreement is the basis of contract law. Just as contractual obligations are created by agreement, they can be modified or ended by agreement as well. But for a **discharge by agreement** to take place, all of the elements necessary to form a contract must be present. The problems usually arise with respect to the requirements of consensus and consideration. One party cannot impose such changes on the other without his or her consent. If one party decides to pay less or not go through with the contract without the agreement of the other party, that is simply a breach of contract.

Contract can be modified by new contract

The lack of consideration is a more difficult problem. Where both parties are relieved of some obligation—or get something more by the change—there is no problem. But sometimes the parties agree to changes to end or modify a contract that benefit only one side. In these circumstances the party benefited must agree to do something extra for the changes to be binding; otherwise, the person benefiting from the gratuitous promise cannot enforce it. Still, where the person making the gratuitous change to the agreement changes his or her mind and then brings an action to enforce that original provision, the other party, who has relied on the change, may be able to raise promissory estoppel as a defence. It should be noted that in almost all instances where promissory estoppel has been applied by the court, the gratuitous modification of a prior contractual obligation was involved. Consideration and promissory estoppel are discussed in detail in Chapter 3.

But all ingredients including consideration must be present

Finally, it should be noted that the original contract might include conditions that will end or modify the obligations. In some circumstances the contract may include an option for one of the parties to terminate under certain specified conditions, but more commonly there will be a condition precedent or a condition subsequent included. When someone buys a house subject to selling his or her old one or subject to arranging financing at a particular rate, that is a **condition precedent**. Until it is met, there is no obligation under that contract. Contracts involving continuing obligations will often include terms specifying when that obligation will end, such as a contract to supply food services until a particular construction project is finished. This is a **condition subsequent**.

Note condition precedents and conditions subsequent in contract

REMEDIES FOR BREACH

When a dispute arises over the formation of a contract, judicial remedies are designed to put the parties in the position they were in before the contract was entered into. Thus, where there has been misrepresentation or the contract is void or voidable, the court will usually grant rescission and attempt to put the parties back to their pre-agreement positions. But when the dispute relates to improper or incomplete performance, the remedies attempt to put the injured party in the position they would have been in had the contract been properly performed. In the first case the courts look back, and in the second they look forward. Note that rescission is also used as a remedy for breach of contract in combination with damages. This nullifies the original contract and excuses the victim from any further contractual obligation.

CASE SUMMARY 4.8

968703 Ontario Ltd. v. Vernon[15]

Early Failure Justifies Termination of Contract

Vernon agreed to have the assets of his business sold at auction. The terms of the contract required all proceeds to be deposited in a bank account and then Vernon was to get the first $450 000, the auctioneer was to get the next $150 000, and the rest was to be split between them on a 70/40 basis. But after the first two days of the auction, the auctioneer kept the entire $100 000 brought in, and Vernon refused to allow the auctioneer back on his property. The auction company continued to hold onto the money and sued for lost profits resulting from the breach of contract. Vernon countersued, also for breach of contract. The court held that the auctioneer's continued failure to deposit the money as agreed was a substantial breach of contract. The auctioneer had also breached a fiduciary duty that he or she had to Vernon by selling some of Vernon's assets at a lower price than was appropriate to a company with which the auctioneer was associated. These failures entitled Vernon to rescind the contract and treat it as if there never was a contract, thus undoing any obligations Vernon had in association with it.

DAMAGES The primary remedy for a breach of contract is the awarding of damages. This is an order for the breaching party to pay monetary compensation to the victim of the breach in an attempt to put her in the position she would have been in had the contract been properly performed. Where someone agrees in contract to sell his yacht to one person for $100 000 and then sells it to another, then he might well be sued for breach of contract. If the victim of the breach had to pay $110 000 to obtain a similar yacht, the damages awarded would be the difference ($10 000) plus any costs incurred. These amounts are usually given to compensate for monetary loss, but in some cases, where appropriate, the courts today are also willing to provide monetary compensation for emotional stress or pain. For example, in medical malpractice actions and in wrongful dismissal cases, the courts will often take into consideration any pain and mental upset in their damage award. A classic example where damages for mental distress were awarded involved a hospital that in breach of contract improperly disclosed confidential information that implied the plaintiff may have been infected with AIDS.[16] Normally, punitive damages designed to punish the breaching party rather than compensate the victim for the loss are not available for breach of contract. They are sometimes awarded where a tort such as fraud is also involved, or in other special circumstances.

Remedy of damages involves money payment

The parties can agree in the contract to limit the amount of damages to be paid in the event of a breach. These are called **liquidated damages**. A pre-paid

Liquidated damages are pre-agreed payments for breach in contract

15. 2002 CanLII 35158 (Ont. C.A.).

16. *Peters–Brown v. Regina District Health Board*, [1996] 1 W.W.R. 337 (Sask. Q.B.).

deposit is a form of liquidated damages. When someone purchases a new car, he or she will usually be required to pay a certain amount as a deposit before delivery. If the purchaser fails to go through with the deal, that amount will be forfeited as a pre-estimation by the parties as to what damages will be paid in the event of breach. Another form of prepayment that must be distinguished is a **down payment**. This is simply the first payment of the purchase price and is not forfeited in the event of breach. The terms used are not conclusive, but where the contract does not provide that the prepaid amount is to be forfeited upon breach, it is a down payment and is not directly available as damages.

Mitigation requires victim to keep damages low

There are significant limitations on the availability of damages in contract law. First, the victim must mitigate her loss. That means the victim must take all reasonable steps to minimize that loss. Failure to do so will reduce the damages awarded to what should have been lost had there been proper **mitigation**. For example, when someone is wrongfully dismissed from his employment, he has an obligation to mitigate by trying to find another job. Any damage award for wrongful dismissal will be reduced by what the person earns (or should have earned) from that alternate employment. Second, the victim of the breach can only receive compensation in an amount that was reasonably foreseeable by the breaching party at the time they entered into the agreement. This means that unreasonable or unexpected losses are too **remote** and cannot be claimed. In one case a victim of fraudulent misrepresentation was induced to enter a franchise agreement to purchase and service soft drink and food dispensers. The court awarded compensatory damages, including the recovery of the initial investment, and also awarded punitive damages for the fraud. But the plaintiff had also put a deposit down on a van to be used to service the dispensers, which had to be forfeited when the franchise arrangement failed. He also sought compensation for the loss of his deposit on the van, but the court held that the purchase of the van was not part of the franchise agreement and was therefore too remote and could not be recovered.[17]

Damages only payable where reasonably foreseeable

Equitable remedies require good behaviour of victim

Sometimes monetary compensation will not sufficiently compensate the victim of a breach. The Courts of Chancery developed several remedies that are still available when a contract is breached. Note, however, these **equitable remedies** are not available when money damages would provide adequate compensation, where there has been wrongdoing on the part of the person seeking the remedy (including unreasonable delay), and when some innocent third party would be adversely affected.

Specific performance requires carrying out original contractual obligation

Specific performance is an equitable remedy that requires the breaching party to perform his or her part of the contract. Where the goods involved are unique, such as a painting by a famous artist, no amount of money will compensate if the seller changes his or her mind. A specific performance remedy involves the court ordering the breaching party to actually transfer the painting to the buyer. Land transactions are often remedied by an order for specific performance because each plot of land is unique.

Injunction requires the end of conduct that is breaching a contract

An **injunction** is used in contract and in tort to stop a person from doing something that is wrong. If the party breaching a contract is involved in some activity inconsistent with the proper performance of the contract, the court may order him or her to stop doing it. If I rented a hall from you to put on a concert and you changed your mind, I could seek an injunction to prevent you from rent-

17. *Lapensee v. First Choice Industries Ltd.* (1992), 46 C.P.R. (3d) 115 (Ont. Gen. Div.).

TABLE 4.4 Remedies

Remedies	Type	Nature
Damages	Common law	Money compensation limited by mitigation and remoteness
Liquidated Damages	Contract	Deposit forfeited or contract terms limit damages to be paid
Specific Performance	Equitable	Order to perform contract terms
Injunction	Equitable	Order not to act inconsistent with contract terms
Accounting	Equitable	Order to disclose and pay over profits to victim
Quantum Meruit	Equitable	Order to pay reasonable amount for services supplied

ing that hall to anyone else. I could also seek an order of specific performance forcing you to let me use it as per the original contract.

There are other types of specialized equitable remedies. An accounting is available when profits have been diverted and it is difficult to determine just what injury has taken place. The court can order the breaching party to disclose financial records and dealings, and to pay any profits obtained through their wrongdoing to the aggrieved party.

Accounting requires disclosure of profits and their surrender to victim

Quantum meruit is applied where the contract is breached before all work has been done or when no specific consideration has been agreed upon for services rendered. Here, the court orders a reasonable amount to be paid for what has been done. If you seek help from a plumber or mechanic, often you don't agree on a price ahead of time. You are then required to pay a reasonable price on the basis of *quantum meruit,* which is what you are billed, unless you immediately protest and dispute the amount claimed. See Table 4.4 for a summary of the remedies for a contract breach.

***Quantum meruit* requires reasonable payment for services given.**

QUESTIONS FOR REVIEW

1. Distinguish between a shared mistake, a misunderstanding, and a one-sided mistake and explain how each one of these problems is dealt with by the courts.
2. Explain what factors must be present for a contract to be challenged on the basis of misrepresentation.
3. Distinguish between innocent, fraudulent, and negligent misrepresentation, and indicate the remedies available for each.
4. When will an opinion or silence qualify as a misrepresentation?

5. Explain why it is easier to succeed with an action for innocent misrepresentation than for fraudulent or negligent misrepresentation.
6. Distinguish between duress and undue influence.
7. Distinguish between a void and voidable contract. Why is this important to the discussion of duress and undue influence?
8. Explain what is meant by a presumption with respect to undue influence, the effect of such a presumption, and under what circumstances those presumptions will occur.
9. When will the courts find a contract to be unconscionable? What effect will that have on the position of the parties?
10. Explain what is meant by privity of contract and the role it plays today.
11. Explain the exceptions to privity. Explain why agency and novation are not considered true exceptions to the privity rule.
12. Explain what is meant by assignment in contract law, and indicate any limitations on what can be assigned.
13. What is necessary for an assignment to qualify as a statutory assignment? What is the importance of such a designation?
14. What does it mean to say the assignee is "subject to the equities"?
15. Define a negotiable instrument and distinguish between a cheque, a bill of exchange, and a promissory note.
16. Explain the position of an endorser of a negotiable instrument.
17. What is necessary for a person to qualify as a holder in due course? Why is that designation significant?
18. Distinguish between conditions and warranties, and explain how this can affect the discharge of contractual obligations.
19. Explain what is meant by substantial performance and how that can affect the discharge of contractual obligations.
20. Explain what is meant by repudiation and, in particular, the effect of anticipatory breach on the position of the parties to a contract.
21. Define frustration and explain what is necessary for a contract to be considered discharged though frustration.
22. What is the effect of finding the frustration to be self-induced?
23. How has the effect of a frustrated contract been modified by statute?
24. What is necessary for a contract to be discharged or modified by agreement?
25. Explain the role promissory estoppel sometimes plays in discharge by agreement.
26. Distinguish between a condition precedent and a condition subsequent.
27. Explain the remedy of damages as it applies to breach of contract.

28. Explain how damages for breach of contract are calculated and any limitations on their availability.
29. How are equitable remedies treated differently from an award of damages for breach of contract?
30. Distinguish between specific performance and an injunction.
31. Explain what is meant by an accounting and *quantum meruit.*

QUESTIONS FOR FURTHER DISCUSSION

1. The law of contract is to a large extent based on the barter model. The guiding principle of this model is that the parties are in an equal bargaining position negotiating balanced terms with which the courts shouldn't interfere. But in recent years the courts are showing an increasing willingness to overturn terms such as exculpatory clauses, or they are stepping in to protect individuals on the basis of good faith or unconscionability. Consider whether in the process of attempting to ensure fairness in contract law the courts and legislatures have interfered to such an extent as to defeat the underlying principle of the parties' freedom to contract as they wish. Should the guiding principle or the assumption that the parties are in an equal bargaining position be abandoned and the courts take on more of a protective role?
2. Discuss the principle of privity of contract and whether it has any place in modern law. In your answer consider the problems it presents when the person injured by products or services supplied under contract is not the party who originally contracted for that product or service. Also look at the growing number of exceptions, including assignment of contractual rights and negotiable instruments, and consider whether the retention of privity causes more harm than it overcomes.
3. Consider the discharge of a contract through frustration. There are several restrictions on the application of frustration such as the fact that the interfering event must be unexpected and out of the control of either party. Also legislation has been passed modifying the common law position of "let the loss lie where it falls." Consider whether anyone should be allowed to escape his or her contractual obligations on the basis of frustration. Should the application of the principle be broader so that there are not so many limitations involved? Does the statutory interference reduce the problem or make it worse? Is there any place for the doctrine of frustration in modern contract law?
4. It makes little difference to the nature of the injuries suffered by the victim of false statements if they were misled intentionally or inadvertently. However, it makes a significant difference to the remedies available to the victims if they were misled intentionally or innocently. The victims of intentional misrepresentations can sue for damages, whereas the victim of an innocent misrepresentation can only ask for rescission. Should a distinction be drawn between fraudulent and innocent misrepresentation in determining the availability of damages as a remedy? In your response consider the appropriateness of all remedies available for misrepresentation in any form and where negligence should fit into the mix. There are different remedies available depending on the nature

of a misrepresentation. Damages are only available in some situations. From the point of view of the victim it doesn't matter whether the misleading statement was intentional or not; the damage is the same. Discuss the various remedies available for misrepresentation however it happens, and consider the appropriateness of the variation of remedies given from the point of view of both parties.

CASES
FOR DISCUSSION

1. **BUCHANAN ET AL. V. CANADIAN IMPERIAL BANK OF COMMERCE** (1979), 125 D.L.R. (3d) 394 (B.C.C.A.).

The Buchanans had very limited business experience and were persuaded to grant a mortgage on their home in order to secure a pre-existing loan to their son-in-law. The bank then called that pre-existing loan now secured by the mortgage immediately after the mortgage was arranged. The Buchanans had no idea that the bank was planning to do this. They had assumed that the mortgage would keep the bank happy, and they would continue to support a new real estate venture that the son-in-law was trying to get going. When the Buchanans originally arranged the mortgage the bank manager gave no indication that the bank intended to call the loan. In this action Mr. and Mrs. Buchanan are applying to have the mortgage set aside (declared invalid). Explain what arguments they can raise to defeat the bank's claim against them.

2. **KETTUNEN V. SICAMOUS FIREMEN'S CLUB,** B.C.S.C., as reported in *Lawyers Weekly Consolidated Digest*, Vol. 19.

Kettunen attended a campground where a "mud bog race" was being held. Even though she was some distance from the race course, one of the drivers lost control and the vehicle struck Mrs. Kettunen, causing her injury. She sued Sicamous Firemen's club, the operators of the campground, and the race. When Kettunen signed in as a camper, one of the documents contained a waiver of liability and indemnity. This is a particular kind of limitation clause exempting one party from liability for failure to perform what would otherwise be an obligation under the contract. Should the victim be precluded from seeking compensation on the basis of this waiver of liability? How would your answer be affected by knowing that the clause was long, in small print, was difficult to read, and was not drawn to her attention?

3. **KOROL V. SASK. FEDERATION OF POLICE OFFICERS,** 2000 Sask. Q.B. 367, 198 Sask. R. 181, [2000] 11 W.W.R. 364. (Sask. Q.B.).

The Saskatchewan Federation of Police Officers was a non-profit organization set up to serve the interests of seven different community police forces. In 1995, this body decided to become involved in collective bargaining and hired Korol, a retired police officer, as their labour relations manager. This contract was for three years at an annual salary of over $44 000. One of the police forces withdrew their support and Korol's employment was terminated. When he sued for wrongful dismissal, the defendant claimed that they couldn't perform without the financial support of the member organizations. Was their contractual obligation to pay Korol discharged because of this turn of events? Give arguments on both sides. What is the likely outcome of the action?

4. **MCDERMID ET AL. V. FOOD-VALE STORES (1972) LTD. ET AL.** (1980), 117 D.L.R. (3d) 483 (Alta. Q.B.).

When Food-Vale Stores (1972) Ltd. bought a food store from McDermid, a provision of the purchase agreement required Food-Vale to supply heat to a neighbouring store for 10 years. Unfortunately, five months later a fire destroyed the Food-Vale store, along with the equipment needed to generate and supply the heat to the neighbouring store. As a result, Food-Vale ceased to supply the promised heat and was sued by McDermid. Explain what Food-Vale might raise in its defence. Explain the arguments on both sides and discuss the likely outcome.

5. **CANLIN LTD. V. THIOKOL FIBRES CANADA, LTD.** (1983), 142 D.L.R. (3d) 450 (Ont. C.A.).

Canlin manufactured swimming pool covers and purchased their material from Thiokol Fibres. Unfortunately, one batch of material was defective, but this was not discovered until dissatisfied customers complained and demanded compensation. Canlin not only had to meet these expenses, but also lost a considerable amount of future business because of the harm to their reputation. In this action they are asking for compensation from Thiokol for these losses. Explain the arguments that Thiokol might raise in its defence. Explain the likely outcome.

6. **BYLE V. BYLE** (1990), 65 D.L.R. (4th) 641 (B.C.C.A.).

Various members of the Byle family were involved in a real estate business that went sour when one son physically threatened one of his siblings. Fearing for their other children, the parents conveyed certain land to the verbally abusive son and gave him other advantages. This action is being brought by the parents and other family members to overturn those transactions. What arguments can be raised by the various parties to this action? Explain the likely outcome.

CHAPTER 5

Legislation in the Marketplace

Statutes modify business law

Our economic system is, to a large extent, based on a free market system, which in turn depends on the capacity of contracting parties to bargain freely. The courts, as a rule, will not interfere with people's freedom to make whatever bargain they want. Still, there are a number of situations where statutes have been passed to modify or interfere with that process. This chapter will examine some of the special situations where legislation controls or imposes special rules on sales transactions. The *Sale of Goods Act* applies to all contracts where goods are sold, whether they involve consumers or business transactions. **Consumer protection** legislation in its various forms is aimed at policing the marketplace, adjusting the balance between consumer and merchant, and establishing recourse for the worst abuses. A significant portion of business and consumer transactions involve some form of security to ensure payment, and a significant portion of this chapter sets out the general principles involved in such **secured transactions**. Because cheques, promissory notes, and bills of exchange are often used to advance credit and play such a prominent role in most transactions, a portion of the chapter will be devoted to examining such negotiable instruments. Unfortunately, businesses fail and individuals often find themselves overwhelmed by debt. A brief discussion of the *Bankruptcy and Insolvency Act*, which provides relief for the debtor and protection for the creditor, is the final topic of this chapter.

The *Sale of Goods Act*

People entering contracts often don't think to include important terms that may later turn out to be necessary. This is especially true with respect to the sale of goods; consequently, the courts have developed a large body of rules to imply those missing terms into contracts. In the 19th century, as part of a general movement to encode the common law, a *Sale of Goods Act* was passed in England that summarized and simplified that body of case law in one legislative enactment.

Similar acts were subsequently adopted in each of the common law provinces of Canada. The primary purpose of the sale of goods acts is to supply missing terms that the parties would have included, had they thought about them. It is important to remember, however, that the parties to a contract can override the provisions of the *Sale of Goods Act* simply by including a different provision in their agreement. Remember, the *Sale of Goods Act* applies to all transactions where goods are sold, not just retail sales; therefore, it has important implications for all levels of business.

***Sale of Goods Act* supplies missing terms**

GOODS OR SERVICES

It must be emphasized that for the *Sale of Goods Act* to apply, there must be an actual sale where the goods are transferred from a seller to a purchaser. Simply using goods as security for a loan is not a sale, even though a bill of sale may be involved. **Chattel mortgages** involve the debtor transferring title of goods to the creditor as security for a loan, and title will be returned upon proper payment of the debt. Since no actual transfer of goods is involved, no sale has taken place. **Conditional sales** look similar to chattel mortgages, but there is an actual sale, with the goods actually transferring to the purchaser. The seller sells the goods on time to the purchaser, holding title as security until the last payment is made. Title is then transferred and the two-staged sale is completed.

The transaction must also involve **goods**. Goods or chattels are tangible, movable property such as pens, cars, boats, and even locomotives. Generally, it is simple to differentiate between transactions involving goods, land, or services. The problem arises where mixed goods and services are involved. For example, when a person orders a meal in a restaurant or an artist paints a portrait for a client, is that a service or the sale of a good? Where the main component is a service, as is the case with an artist painting a portrait, the *Sale of Goods Act* will not apply. But where the service is incidental to the supply of the goods, as with the meal in a restaurant, the *Sale of Goods Act* does apply. If the person who buys a custom painting from an artist subsequently resells it, then it is a good and the Act would then apply. Sometimes the good and service components of a contract can be separated. When a mechanic repairs a car, the *Sale of Goods Act* applies to the parts supplied but not to the labour. When an electrician wires a house, the receptacles and wiring are covered by the Act, but the actual work of the electrician is not. It should also be noted that as a holdover from the *Statute of Frauds* some provinces require evidence in writing, such as a receipt, for sales over a specified amount.

For the Act to apply, goods must be transferred/sold

CASE SUMMARY 5.1

Gee v. White Spot Ltd.; Pan et al. v. White Spot Ltd.[1]

Contaminated Food Covered by *Sale of Goods Act*

Two customers suffered botulism poisoning from consuming food they obtained at the White Spot restaurant in Vancouver; they sued. They relied on section 18 of the B.C. *Sale of Goods Act* that requires goods to be of merchantable quality and fit for

(continued)

1. (1986), 32 D.L.R. (4th) 238 (B.C.C.A.).

normal use. The restaurant claimed they provided a service—not a good—and that the Act did not apply. The judge however agreed with the plaintiff:

> I agree with counsel's submission that an item on the menu offered for a fixed price is an offering of a finished product and is primarily an offering of the sale of a good or goods and not primarily an offering of a sale or services.

The contaminated food was not fit for the purpose for which it was sold and was not of merchantable quality. The contract of sale, therefore, had been breached and the White Spot was liable for the injuries. This case shows how important the implied terms of the *Sale of Goods Act* can be, especially since the damages awarded were substantial.

TITLE AND RISK

Under the Act risk follows title, except . . .

People often neglect to specify at what point title will transfer in their transaction. This is important since "risk follows title," meaning the person with title bears the loss if the goods are destroyed or damaged. This is one area that is often overridden by the parties in the agreement. For example, with **CIF** (cost, insurance, and freight) contracts, one party is designated to be responsible for arranging and paying for the insurance and transportation of the goods, thus assuming the risk of damage or loss. In **FOB** (free on board) contracts, the parties specify that title and risk will transfer at a specific place, for example, FOB the seller's loading dock or a particular ship in Vancouver harbour. **COD** contracts (cash on delivery) require the purchase price to be paid when the goods are delivered to the purchaser. The risk also transfers at that time. **Bills of lading** can also be used to control risk and title. These documents are used when a third party or carrier transports goods. If the seller names himself or herself to receive the goods when they reach their destination then the seller retains control of those goods but also bears the risk during their transport. But if the purchaser is named as the receiver, the purchaser bears the risk.

- in the case of CIF, FOB, COD, and bill of lading

In situations where such provisions are not made, risk will follow title and the transfer of title (the property in the goods) will be determined by the operation of five rules set out in the *Sale of Goods Act* (see Table 5.1).

Five rules determine when title transfers

Rule #1 Where the goods sold are specific, identified, and nothing further has to be done to them, title transfers immediately upon the contract of sale being made. The purchaser bears the risk even though payment or delivery may take place at some later date and the goods continue in the hands of the seller.

Rule #2 If something has to be done to those goods to put them in a deliverable state, such as fixing a scratch or adjusting a part, title transfers when the repair is made and the customer is given notice that the goods are ready.

Rule #3 If the goods have to be weighed or measured to determine price, title will transfer once that has been done and notice given.

If I came into your store and purchased a particular bolt of cloth at a specified price, arranging to pick it up and pay for it the next day, it would remain in your store, but at my risk. If you agreed to wash the cloth before I picked it up, or if the price was to be determined by measuring the amount of cloth on the bolt, title and risk would transfer only when that had been done and I was notified.

TABLE 5.1 Title and Risk

Situation	Rule	Result
The sale of specific goods in a deliverable state	#1	Title transfers immediately upon creation of the contract of sale.
The sale of specific goods needing repairs, etc.	#2	Title transfers when work is done and the purchaser is notified.
The sale of specific goods needing to be weighed or measured	#3	Title transfers when this is done and the purchaser is notified.
The sale of goods on approval	#4	Title transfers to the purchaser with - Notification to seller of approval - Passage of a reasonable time -Treatment of goods as the purchaser's own
The sale of goods that are not yet selected (from many) or not yet made at the time of contract	#5	Title transfers when goods are unconditionally committed to contract with assent (expressed or implied)

Rule #4 When goods are taken on approval or sale with the right to return them if not satisfied, title and risk transfers when the purchaser notifies the seller of his or her acceptance, or when the purchaser acts towards those goods in a way consistent with having accepted them. For example, if cloth is involved and you make a dress out of it, the cloth is yours. You can no longer return it.

Rule #5 When goods have not yet been made, or where they have been selected from a sample or a floor model, etc., title only transfers after the particular goods to be purchased have been made (or selected and committed to the transaction) with the assent of the other party (usually the purchaser). In rules #2 and #3, actual notice is required, but the wording in #5 is broader; therefore, assent or approval can be implied. Suppose I were to leave my car at a tire store specifying four new tires were to be installed while I was shopping in the mall. Title would not transfer immediately. While I was shopping, the seller would select four tires of that specification from stock, and when they were installed on my wheel rims, they would be committed (unconditionally). My assent would be implied and title would transfer. Remember that the parties can include overriding provisions in their purchase agreement with respect to these rules if they wish. Note also that when goods are sold in a retail situation, the seller will normally have insurance coverage. If the goods are damaged or something else happens to them while in their care, the seller will assume responsibility no matter what these rules say about title or risk.

OBLIGATIONS OF THE SELLER

Some of the most important provisions in the *Sale of Goods Act* relate to the seller's responsibility for the goods sold. Although the Act varies to some extent from province to province, there are usually four sections imposing conditions and warranties on the seller with respect to the nature of the goods supplied. *Conditions* are major terms which, when breached, allow the victim to treat his or

Breach of condition ends contractual obligations

Breach of warranty does not end contractual obligations

Obligations of seller under the Act:

- To deliver good title

- To deliver quiet possession

- To deliver goods free of liens

her obligations as over. *Warranties* are minor terms which, when breached, do not end the contract, but permit the victim to seek compensation for the breach. This may make the difference between the right to return the goods to the seller for a refund or only to have the goods repaired or replaced. Note that the parties are free to designate a provision as a condition, thus making it important, when otherwise it would only be a warranty. For convenience the Ontario *Sale of Goods Act* will be referred to in the following discussion. Section 13 implies terms with respect to title. Section 13(a) makes it a condition of the contract that sellers deliver **good title** to the goods to the purchaser. If it turns out later that the goods were stolen, whether the seller knew it or not, the purchaser can get his or her money back. Section 13(b) implies a warranty requiring the purchaser to provide **quiet possession** with respect to the goods supplied. This means that the goods have to be usable as intended without interference. For example, if you purchased an automobile that you couldn't drive because the model had not met road safety standards, that would interfere with your right to quiet possession of the vehicle. Section 13(c) also implies a warranty requiring the goods sold to be free of any **charge or encumbrance**. We usually refer to these as liens, and they are imposed when a creditor lends money and takes the goods as security for the loan, thus giving the creditor a prior claim against the goods. Such a lien, if properly registered, gives the creditor the right to repossess the goods in the event of a default, even when those goods have been resold to a subsequent purchaser. Since these last two provisions are only implied warranties, their breach only gives the victim the right to seek compensation, not rescind the contract.

CASE SUMMARY 5.2

Gencab of Canada Ltd. v. Murray–Jensen Manufacturing Ltd.[2]

Breach of Quiet Possession Provides Remedy

Dominion Electric sold dies and equipment and the right to produce a particular product to Gencab, which in turn sold those dies and equipment to Murray–Jensen Manufacturing. When Dominion Electric relied on their patent rights and prevented Murray–Jensen from using the dies and equipment to produce the product in question, Murray–Jensen sued Gencab for breach of contract, claiming that their right of quiet possession of the goods sold had been breached under section 13 of Ontario's *Sale of Goods Act*. The court held that Dominion's patent rights, which prevent the use of the goods sold, did interfere with their quiet possession and found Gencab liable for the breach. This case illustrates the nature of the right of quiet possession.

CASE SUMMARY 5.2 Gencab of Canada Ltd. v. Murray–Jensen Manufacturing Ltd.

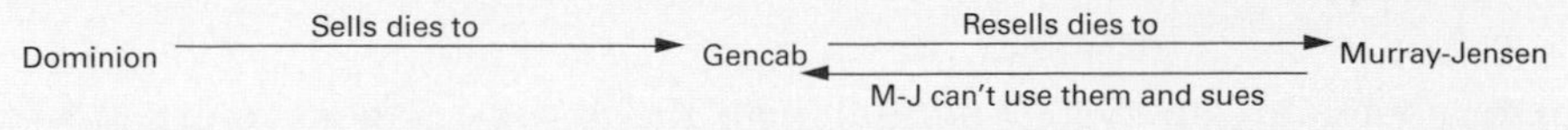

2. (1980), 114 D.L.R. (3d) 92 (Ont. H.C.J.).

If the goods are bought by **description** or by **sample** and what is delivered does not match the description or sample, the *Sale of Goods Act* implies conditions into the contract that permit the purchaser to refuse delivery (sections 14 and 16). A purchaser buying a truckload of apples based on a sample Spartan would be able to refuse delivery if Macintosh apples were delivered. Sale by description not only covers situations where goods are bought through a catalogue or ordered from an advertisement, but also includes any purchase of goods that have been mass-produced. Since you don't choose one particular item over another, as they are all the same, you are relying on specifications (description) to make the purchase, and the goods must match that specification, picture, box, pamphlet, etc.

Goods must match description or sample

Perhaps the most important implied obligation of the seller relates to the **fitness and quality** of the goods sold. Section 15 of the Ontario *Sale of Goods Act* requires that when goods are sold by description (which now is taken to mean all mass-produced goods), those goods must be of merchantable quality. This means essentially that the goods must be free of any defects that would render them unusable or interfere with their effectiveness. If they are defective in some way or fail earlier than expected, a condition of the contract has been breached, and a refund can be demanded. British Columbia has taken this even further, requiring the goods to be "durable." Section 15 also provides that when goods for a particular purpose are requested and the purchaser relies on the recommendation of the seller who deals in those goods, the goods have to be suitable for that job. If you go to a paint store asking for a product to cover a concrete floor and the product supplied then peels off the floor, a condition has been breached and you can recover not only the purchase price but also any costs you incur in stripping and repainting the floor. Note that the particular provisions relating to fitness and quality only apply to goods sold in the normal course of business and not to private or "as is" sales.

Goods must be of merchantable quality

Goods must be fit for the purpose purchased

Sellers often attempt to override these implied conditions of fitness and quality (see Table 5.2). A new product warranty is an attempt by the seller and manufacturer to limit the liability that would otherwise be implied by the provisions of the *Sale of Goods Act*. These warranties usually limit the time of the obligation to 90 days for electronic products, for example, or to a few years for automobiles. They

TABLE 5.2 Implied Conditions and Warranties

Seller's obligations with respect to title	Seller must deliver property/good title	Condition
	Seller must deliver quiet possession	Warranty
	Goods must be free of charge or encumbrance	Warranty
When goods bought by description	Goods must correspond to description	Condition
Purchaser relies on advice of seller	Goods must be reasonably fit for purpose required	Condition
When goods bought by description	Goods must be of merchantable quality	Condition
When goods bought by sample	Goods must correspond to sample and be free of hidden defects	Condition

also typically restrict the remedy available to repair or replace the product, and specifically exclude all other warranties express or implied.

Limited warranties try to override these obligations

As discussed in Chapter 4, in contract law these limited warranties are referred to as exculpatory, exemption, or limitation clauses, and their sole purpose is to limit the liability or responsibility of one of the parties under the contract. The courts have always been careful of such clauses and when there is any ambiguity, they resolve it in favour of the party disadvantaged by the provision. As a result such provisions must be very carefully worded. Thus, if a restaurant displayed a sign stating "not responsible for lost or stolen goods," it would not protect it if the goods were damaged in a fire. The courts would not be willing to imply a broader meaning. Also, the other party will not be affected by any exculpatory clause that is not reasonably brought to their attention at the time of the agreement. If the limitation clause is on a sign, it must be in a place where it is readily visible to all parties. If it is on a ticket, it should be on the front in clear type or there should be a direction on the front to refer the purchaser to other important provisions on the back of the ticket. The practice of burying such clauses in a contract's fine print and complicated legal language has been challenged, and now such clauses are often highlighted in some way to ensure they are brought to the attention of the other party to the contract.

Exemption clauses must be clear and brought to purchaser's attention

The importance of such clauses as well as the extensive application of the *Sale of Goods Act* is illustrated by *Hunter Engineering Co. v. Syncrude Canada Ltd.*[3] In this case massive gears were sold as vital components of the huge conveyor belts used to convey the oil sands as they were extracted in the tar sands project of northern Alberta. The gears were defective, and the court held that the fitness and quality provision of the *Sale of Goods Act* applied, making Hunter Engineering liable to Syncrude for the defective parts. They had failed to contract out of that provision by including a carefully worded, limited warranty. It is interesting to note that another supplier of identical defective gears, Allis Chalmers, was not responsible because they had effectively limited their liability. It should also be noted that sometimes where a failure to perform goes right to the very root of the contract, the courts will avoid applying an exemption clause, even though technically it is worded broadly enough to exempt a party from liability for the failure. In these situations, the court interprets the term more narrowly, concluding that the parties never would have intended the exculpatory clause to exempt liability for such a fundamental breach.

Some provinces have prohibited sellers from overriding these implied conditions in consumer transactions, making such limited warranties void. Others have imposed obligations of fitness and quality in a separate statute. This will be discussed below under "Consumer Protection Legislation."

If the purchaser defaults, the seller can stop goods in transit

The Acts imply many other important terms into sale of goods transactions. We can only mention a few here. Where no purchase price is stated, a reasonable price is implied. Where no date is specified, payment is due at a reasonable time, which is normally taken as the time of delivery. If the purchaser defaults and fails to take delivery of the goods or fails to pay for them, the seller is entitled to the normal contractual remedies discussed in Chapter 4. In addition, the seller has the right to ***stoppage in transitu***. This means that if the goods are in the hands of a transporter and being delivered to the purchaser, the seller can intercept those goods and recover them from the transporter. Even if they do get into the hands of the purchaser, the seller has a limited right to recover them in the event of the

3. [1989] 1 S.C.R. 426 (S.C.C.).

purchaser's bankruptcy under the federal *Bankruptcy and Insolvency Act.* Where title has transferred and the full price is due and payable, the seller can sue for the whole price in the event of a default—not just for lost profits and costs—a much more attractive remedy. Finally, it should be mentioned that each province has passed an international *Sale of Goods Act* covering international sales transactions.

If bankruptcy, seller has limited right to recover goods

Consumer Protection Legislation

As we use the term here, **consumer** refers to someone purchasing a product for his or her own use, not for resale and normally not for use in a business activity. Historically, the common law approach to consumer transactions has been *caveat emptor*, sometimes translated as, "let the buyer beware." However, this is one area where the many abuses have prompted governments at both the federal and provincial levels to enact legislation designed to protect the consumer. While the legislation varies substantially from province to province, in the next few pages we will highlight some of the basic principles that the different provinces' legislation has in common.

Both federal and provincial consumer protection legislation

The first type of protection provided relates to the quality of products and services supplied. As mentioned above, the *Sale of Goods Act* implies certain conditions and warranties related to title, fitness, quality, and nature (description) of goods supplied. Normally, the parties can override these provisions, but where consumer transactions are involved, several provinces, including British Columbia, have prohibited any attempt to do so. Saskatchewan and New Brunswick have enacted specific statutes imposing similar obligations of quality and fitness. Thus, products must be fit for their purpose and of an acceptable quality, and are liable for any failure, no matter what other provisions may be included in a limited warranty or other limitation clause in the contract. People suffering injury or loss because of defective products have the right to sue the supplier or manufacturer of the goods in tort for negligence. The advantage of this legislation is that it provides a contract remedy where it is not necessary to show fault, only that the contract was breached. As mentioned in Chapter 4, where the product is dangerous and the seller breaches while knowing there is a risk to health or injury to property, criminal prosecution may result.

Consumer goods must be of minimum quality

CASE SUMMARY 5.3

Frey v. Sarvajc[4]

Purchaser Duped

In this case the plaintiff purchased a used truck from the defendant in a private sale. The defendant had not informed him that the truck had previously been written off as a total loss, even though the plaintiff had asked several questions with respect to the truck's condition and whether it had ever been "smashed up." After

(continued)

4. [2000] 8 W.W.R. 74 (Sask. Q.B.).

acquiring the truck, the plaintiff paid for several major repairs. When he discovered that the truck had been totalled prior to his purchase, he brought this action to recover the purchase price and the cost of the repairs. It should also be noted that an odometer with a significantly lower mileage figure had been installed. When the truck was transferred, the registration did state "previous total loss vehicle," but the plaintiff did not notice this at that time.

This case took place in Saskatchewan where, in addition to the implied terms with respect to fitness and quality found in the *Sale of Goods Act,* the *Consumer Protection Act* also implied similar terms that could not be contracted out of. However, these provisions did not apply since this was a private sale. The judge also observed that since the truck was still roadworthy, it could not be said that a fundamental breach had taken place. Even the fact that the serial numbers of the engine and body did not match was not a factor, since they were readily visible on easy inspection. The principle of *caveat emptor* applied. But that was not the case with the odometer reading. It contained important information for a purchaser, and it had been tampered with. Section 15 of the Saskatchewan *Sale of Goods Act* requires that any goods bought by description must match that description. Because of the misleading information on the odometer in this case, the description did not match the actual truck. Consequently, the plaintiff was awarded damages. This case not only illustrates the limitations of consumer protection legislation, but also the long reach of the *Sale of Goods Act*—even to private sales.

Abusive and deceptive trade practices are controlled

Unconscionable transactions are controlled

Salespersons' statements form part of the contract

Abusive merchants subject to fine, injunction, and loss of licence

Cooling-off period for door-to-door sales

Statutes, variously called a *Trade Practices Act* or *Business Practices Act,* are designed to protect consumers from unacceptable practices. They prohibit misleading and deceptive practices generally, and then list a number of unacceptable practices specifically. All involve different ways that merchants may deceive the consumer, whether intentionally or by mistake. These statutes also control unconscionable transactions where the consumer is taken advantage of because of factors such as undue pressure, a particular vulnerability results in the victim paying an unfair price, or some other harsh or adverse terms that are imposed in the contract. Such unconscionable transactions are unenforceable against the consumer. Some jurisdictions limit this unconscionability protection to mortgage contracts. Only the courts have the power to modify, limit the obligations, or otherwise change the terms of the agreement to make them more equitable. In most provinces, legislation also makes any false or misleading statement made in the course of the sale, whether in advertising or by the salesperson, a term of the contract, thus making it actionable as a breach with all of the normal remedies available. Other remedies against the merchant engaging in unacceptable business practices include injunctions and damages, fines, and other penalties. These provincial statutes aimed at consumer protection are typical examples of statutes creating provincial offences.

Consumer protection acts in place in most provinces are designed to control specific types of businesses that are prone to abuse. Where door-to-door sales (direct sales) are involved, cooling-off periods, as well as other protections, are provided. Where **executory contracts** are involved (contracts to be performed in

CASE SUMMARY 5.4

Director of Trade Practices v. Gerald Mason Ltd. et al.[5]

The Danger of Door-to-Door Sales

A number of businesses participated in a coupon book promotion where people paid $12 for a book of coupons providing various bargains. One of these coupons provided a $30 credit on carpet cleaning services provided by Gerald Mason Ltd. But this was just a ruse to get salesmen into the homes of potential customers so they could demonstrate vacuum cleaners. Selling these appliances was the true nature of Gerald Mason's business. The only cleaning that was done was as part of that demonstration.

Kathy Kelly used the coupon and arranged for a carpet cleaning. But the salesman who came to her home didn't clean anything—he only demonstrated the use of the vacuum cleaner, which she then purchased. She later changed her mind; consequently, the director of trade practices in British Columbia asked the court to declare the coupon produced by Gerald Mason a deceptive trade practice and to stop the practice with an injunction. The court agreed that the coupon was designed to "deceive and mislead" and ordered a permanent injunction as requested. This is an older case, but it illustrates the misleading marketing schemes that the *Trade Practices Act* is designed to remedy.

the future), a written contract is required and the consumer's obligations, before performance, are limited. Referral selling, pyramid schemes, and the delivery of unsolicited goods are also controlled. Referral selling involves giving a discount when the purchaser provides a list of names for the seller to contact. Pyramid sales involve multi-level organizations where people buy into the organization and the money is distributed up the chain, much like a chain letter. Pyramid schemes must be distinguished from multi-level marketing organizations where the funds distributed are obtained from the sale of a product, not an entrance fee. Pyramid schemes have been made crimes under federal legislation. Responsibility for unsolicited credit cards, and for lost and stolen credit cards, is also severely restricted. Legislation that requires the true cost of borrowing be disclosed in all loan transactions is also in place. Sometimes the practice of including bonuses or using different methods of calculating the effect of compounding interest will lead people to pay much more for their loans than they expected. Now the actual rate and costs associated with the transaction, including the total amount to be paid, must be made clear at the outset. Most jurisdictions also control organizations that supply their customers' credit information to others, as well as debt-collecting practices. These are just some of the provisions that are typically included in such consumer protection statutes.

Pyramid schemes and referral selling are prohibited

True cost of borrowing must be disclosed

5. (1978), 90 D.L.R. (3d) 695 (B.C.S.C.).

These provincial statutes aimed at consumer protection are typical examples of statutes that create provincial offences. Government agencies are set up to investigate abusive practices and to resolve disputes. Typically, such organizations have the power to investigate, to search and seize records, to assist the consumer to obtain remedies, and to impose fines and other penalties in their own right. Large fines can be effective, but these bodies also often have the right to take away a licence and put the offender out of business. In many cases these consumer protection statutes provide for dual enforcement. The consumer, or even the designated government official, is given the option of proceeding in a civil action seeking damages and/or seeking an injunction to stop the offending conduct. But that government official will usually also have the power of treating the offending conduct as an offence punishable by fine and imprisonment. Although these offences are not criminal in a technical sense (only the federal government can pass criminal law) they can have the same impact and are referred to as **quasi-criminal offences**. The procedure involved for prosecution is set out in provincial legislation such as Ontario's *Provincial Offences Act*.[6] Because there is the potential of a significant fine and imprisonment, the *Charter of Rights* protections relating to legal process (sections 7–14) and other criminal prosecution requirements, including the "presumption of innocence" and "proof beyond a reasonable doubt" discussed in Chapter 1, generally apply.

Powerful government agencies enforce rules

CASE SUMMARY 5.5

Director of Trade Practices v. Ideal Credit Referral Services Ltd. et al.[7]

The Power to Enforce Is Considerable

Ideal Credit resided in British Columbia and advertised to U.S. customers that they would provide guaranteed credit, even for bad risks. They used phrases such as "bankruptcies O.K.," and "guaranteed results." This was a scam. The customers were required to pay $300 as a processing fee. Ideal would then do a $15 credit check and invariably turn down the credit application and pocket the difference. The director of trade practices applied to the court under the *Trade Practices Act* for an injunction to stop this "deceptive or unconscionable act." But Ideal countered that since the customers were in the United States, the B.C. Act did not apply. The trial court agreed with Ideal, but on appeal the court held that the *Trade Practices Act* prohibited any deceptive or misleading practices that took place in the province, even where the victims were elsewhere.

This case shows the extensive reach of the *Trade Practices Act* but raises the question of just how far this should go. What about providing gambling services for other locations, or offering pornographic or other materials considered immoral in this province to those in other provinces or countries?

6. R.S.O. 1990, c. P. 33.
7. (1997), 145 D.L.R. (4th) 20 (B.C.C.A.).

Ontario has recently enacted a comprehensive consumer protection statute,[8] which likely points the way that consumer statutes will go in other jurisdictions as well. It not only ensures that warranties for fitness and quality set out in the *Sale of Goods Act* cannot be overridden in a consumer purchase agreement by a limited warranty, but also extends that protection to leases and services as well.

The new Act includes the provisions previously found in the former *Consumer Protection Act* and *Business Practices Act* of that province. Thus, there is a list of specified unfair practices that are prohibited, including unconscionable representations as well as the remedies and procedures to follow when these provisions and others are violated. Extensive powers are given under the Act to search, seize, make orders, create offences, etc. The new *Consumer Protection Act* also sets out regulations and prohibitions with respect to specific businesses and business activities, including agreements requiring future performance (such as the payment of price) time-share agreements; personal development agreements such as provided by fitness clubs; agreements made over the internet; the repair of motor vehicles and other goods; and credit transactions in general. The new *Consumer Protection Act* and regulations also have extensive provisions to govern internet consumer transactions. At the time of writing, the *Consumer Protection Act* is not yet in force and is waiting on the completion of extensive regulations that must be in place for it to be operative.

Non-government agencies also help consumers

There are other non-government, consumer-oriented organizations, both profit and non-profit, that can be helpful to the disadvantaged consumer. The Better Business Bureau is a unique organization consisting of and supported by member businesses. The idea is that reputable businesses are served by weeding out unscrupulous businesses that damage other members of the business community. The bureau issues reports, but also provides a service directly to the public where they can inquire about specific businesses to learn of any complaints that have been made.

The federal government also has significant consumer protection legislation enforced by government departments. These control hazardous products, govern the bankruptcy process, and control anti-competition business practices. They also investigate and resolve consumer complaints. They have considerable power and funds to support research, investigation, hearings, and education. The *Competition Act* controls anti-competitive merchandising and advertising practices such as predatory pricing (low prices are used to drive competitors out of business); anti-competitive mergers; agreement between competitors to control prices; bid rigging; and misleading advertising. An important recent example where the competition tribunal found that misleading advertising had taken place in violation of the *Competition Act* was committed by Sears when they advertised a particular brand of tires as being on sale. The ad said, "Save 45%," when in fact they regularly sold only about 2 percent of those tires at the posted cost. The ad inflated the regular cost of the tires making the sales price appear more attractive. This constituted misleading advertising, which could bring "harm to consumers, business competitors, and competition in general." The penalty included a payment of $500 000 and a commitment not to do it again.[9] The *Competition Act* will be discussed in some detail in Chapter 10.

The federal *Competition Act* controls anti-competitive merchandising and advertising practices

8. *Consumer Protection Act, 2002,* S.O. 2002, c. 30, Sch. A.

9. *Commissioner of Competition v. Sears Canada Inc.,* Comp. Trib., No. CT-2002-004.

Other federal statutes include the *Food and Drugs Act*, which regulates dangerous food and pharmaceuticals, and the *Hazardous Products Act*, which regulates dangerous products, prohibits some products, and requires appropriate warnings on others. These federal statutes also create specific criminal offences for certain kinds of prohibited conduct.

Secured Transactions

Security arrangements assure creditor of repayment

Real property and personal property used as security

As a general rule, the simple promise embodied in a contract to repay debt is not good enough for a creditor to loan money. Whether in the consumer world or arranging business financing, some extra assurance is required to ensure that the creditor will be repaid. This is usually accomplished by the debtor providing security, and giving the creditor first claim on some asset at least equal to the value of the debt. In the event of default the creditor has first claim on that asset (see Figure 5.1). Any form of property can be used to create such security. Real property (land and permanent structures built on that land) is normally the preferred form of security, but other forms of property can also be used. The use of real property as security will be discussed in a subsequent chapter.

_P.P.S.A._ accommodates all forms of personal property as security

In a conditional sale the seller is a creditor

Chattel mortgage involves title going to creditor as security

Personal property, both tangible in the form of goods or chattels, and intangible in the form of a right or claim one party has against another, can also be used as security. Share certificates, bonds, and negotiable instruments such as cheques and promissory notes are examples of intangible personable property. The documents involved merely represent the actual claim or right. The personal property security acts (*P.P.S.A.*) in place in all English-speaking provinces control secured transactions involving personal property. Where tangible personal property or goods are involved, the normal method of creating the security relationship is through a conditional sale or a chattel mortgage. Ordinarily, both of these situations involve the creditor taking title to the goods as security while the debtor had possession. A conditional sale takes place in a two-stage process; the debtor gets possession right away, but the creditor keeps the title (or property in the goods) until the final payment whereupon the title is also conveyed. A chattel mortgage involves the debtor surrendering title to goods that he or she already owns to the creditor to hold as security for debt. Upon repayment, the title is returned to the debtor. In both cases in the event of default the creditor realizes his or her secu-

FIGURE 5.1 Secured Transactions

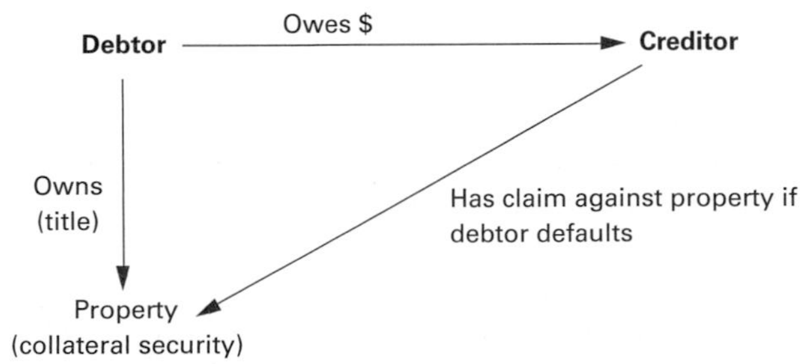

rity by taking possession of the goods and reselling them if payment is not forthcoming. In the past, conditional sales and chattel mortgages as well as other forms of personal property used as security were all controlled by separate statutes. This was cumbersome, and one of the advantages of the *Personal Property Security Act* is to bring all transactions involving personal property as security under one statutory umbrella, with one consistent approach—no matter what form the security takes. A second advantage is that the Act allows any form of personal property—tangible or intangible—to be used. This flexibility creates a much more comprehensive system. An important change under the Act is that title now stays with the borrower, but the rights given to the creditor remain the same as with traditional conditional sales and chattel mortgages.

Now all forms of personal property used as security are covered by *P.P.S.A.*

Now title remains with the borrower

A security is created by giving the creditor first claim against the assets used as security. This is accomplished in a unique way under the Act. The transaction should be viewed in three stages—first the agreement; second, attachment; and third, perfection (see Figure 5.2). In fact, these steps often take place simultaneously, but conceptually distinguishing among the stages makes it easier to understand. The contract sets out the rights and obligations between the parties and designates the asset (such as a vehicle) to be used as security. The creditor still has no claim against the car, having provided no actual benefit to the debtor at this stage. **Attachment** takes place when value is given under the contract to the debtor. At that point the creditor obtains a claim against the asset. If money is involved, attachment takes place when the money is provided to the debtor. But what happens where the debtor resells those assets to some third party or uses them as security in another transaction? The whole idea of security is to give the creditor a first claim in these circumstances. It would be unjust to allow the creditor to retake those goods from the third party, who has no way of knowing of the creditor's claim in the asset. To solve this problem a registry has been created so third parties dealing with the assets can check to see if someone else has a claim against them. There is, therefore, an obligation on the creditor with the secured interest in the asset to register that claim in the appropriate registry. This second stage is called **perfection**, which is primarily accomplished through **registration**. Anyone dealing with such goods is well advised to search the registry before purchase. Perfection gives the creditor a prior claim to the property that is good against any subsequent holder or claimant. If Jones, through a chattel mortgage agreement that uses his car as security, borrows money from Ace Credit Union, the credit union has no claim against the car until they advance the funds. At that point their security attaches. This gives them a claim against the car while in Jones' possession, but not if it is resold. The credit union then perfects their secured interest by registering the claim. This is accomplished by filing a simple, standard form at the appropriate registry. Now anyone interested in buying or taking the vehicle as security in another transaction can search the registry to determine if there are any prior claims (called liens or charges). Finding such a claim should dissuade the buyer from the transaction because the credit union's registered claim now has priority.

Attachment gives the creditor rights against the debtor

Perfection by registration

Perfection gives the creditor rights to security good against all subsequent claimants

Perfection can also take place by the creditor taking possession of the property used as security. This is usually done where intangible claims, such as stock certificates, bonds, or negotiable instruments, are used to secure the loan. However, the original document, not a photocopy, is required to accomplish perfection by possession. The key to understanding the *Personal Property Security Act* is to understand the process of attachment and perfection: Attachment gives the creditor a claim to the property or goods against the debtor, and perfection gives the creditor a claim to the property or goods against all others.

Perfection by possession

CASE SUMMARY 5.6

Mitsui & Co. (Canada) Ltd. v. Royal Bank of Canada et al.[10]

Even Big Deals Can Go Sour

Mitsui provided two leased helicopters to Pegasus, which subsequently became bankrupt. The trustee in bankruptcy claimed the helicopters as assets for the benefit of the creditors, primarily the Royal Bank. If this was a true lease, Mitsui would retain ownership of the helicopters. The problem was that the lease contained a provision where Pegusus, at the end of the lease period, could purchase all of the helicopters at the reasonable fair market value of the helicopter as established by the lessor. Under the Nova Scotia *Conditional Sales Act*, if the lease contained an option to purchase, it was a conditional sale and had to be registered as such—something Mitsui had failed to do.

This case went to the Supreme Court of Canada, which held that even though there was no firm price, the transaction was a true option to purchase. As a result, Mitsui's claim had to be registered under the *Conditional Sales Act* of Nova Scotia. Mitsui's failure to do this caused the claims to the trustee in bankruptcy and the Royal Bank to come first. They were given priority with respect to the helicopters. Similar results would take place under the current *Personal Property Security Act.*

In actual practice the operation of the *Personal Property Security Act* can be quite complicated, especially where a variety of claims are involved. But once the principles of attachment and perfection described above are understood, the basic principle is relatively straightforward.

Creditor has the right to repossess and resell upon default

In the event of default, the essential right of the creditor is to obtain and resell the property used as security. Where the tangible personal property involves goods that are not in the possession of the creditor, this process entails repossessing those goods from the debtor. It must be emphasized that where the contract gives the creditor this right upon default, there is no need to get a court order or otherwise involve official government services. Repossession is usually accomplished through employees or the services of a private agent called a bailiff. It is important to note that no force or violence can be used. Where a car is locked in a garage or furniture is in a house, a court order must be obtained to get them.

Court order not needed to repossess

But force cannot be used

FIGURE 5.2 The Process

Creation of contract	Attachment	Perfection
Contents of agreement determine rights of parties	Value given for security taken	1. By registration or 2. By taking possession of property (security) (not repossession)

10. (1995), 123 D.L.R. (4th) 449 (S.C.C.).

Once possession has been acquired, the goods can be sold to recover the debt. But anyone who has an interest, including the original debtor, must be notified of the sale and given a chance to redeem the goods by making appropriate payment. The seller must make an effort to obtain a fair price upon sale. This is usually done at public auction, although it can be done by private sale, providing the process is "commercially reasonable." Any excess obtained from the sale over the amount owing, less the costs of the process, must be paid to the debtor. If there is a deficit or shortfall, that amount is still owed by the debtor. If the sale was done properly, further steps can be taken to collect the debt. Note that in some provinces, where consumer sales are involved, such a shortfall will not be recoverable.

Creditor must give the debtor notice and the opportunity to redeem the goods before resale

If resale is properly handled, creditor has the right to sue for deficit

CASE SUMMARY 5.7

General Motors Acceptance Corp. of Canada Ltd. v. Snowden et al.[11]

A Creditor's Right to Deficit Can Be Easily Lost

Snowden purchased a car and arranged financing though General Motors Acceptance. When he defaulted on the payments, they repossessed and resold the vehicle under the *Conditional Sales Act* of New Brunswick. They sold the vehicle at an auction restricted to licensed automobile dealers; the amount recovered fell short of what was owed by about $6000. Snowden refused to pay the difference, claiming that the sale had not taken place in good faith. The court found that the creditor failed to satisfy the court that they had obtained the best price for the car. This auction involved wholesale prices, with the dealers purchasing at a lower price so they could resell at a profit. A retail sale would have brought a better price for the car. The creditor's action to sue for the remainder of the outstanding debt was refused. Although this is an older case and the result may not apply in other jurisdictions, it illustrates just how careful creditors have to be to comply with the requirements of notice and process of sale when reselling goods used as security after a default and repossession.

OTHER FORMS OF SECURITY

A problem has always existed in the construction industry where suppliers of labour and materials deal with contractors. Because the contractor normally doesn't own the property, the suppliers of goods or subcontractors have nothing to claim against if they are not paid. This has been remedied in all provinces with builders' lien/construction lien/mechanics' lien acts, which give suppliers and subcontractors a claim against the property if they are not paid (see Figure 5.3). A subcontractor can now register a lien against the property, which can eventually force a sale of the property if the subcontractor is not paid. The property owner is protected from this possibility by retaining a **holdback** (7–20 percent of the amount owing to the contractor, depending on the province) and making this available to satisfy the claims of the subcontractors or suppliers. Upon payment of the funds held back, an application can be made to the court to have the liens

Builders' liens protect contractors, subtrades, workers, and suppliers

11. (1990), 76 D.L.R. (4th) 519 (N.B.C.A.).

FIGURE 5.3 Builders' Liens

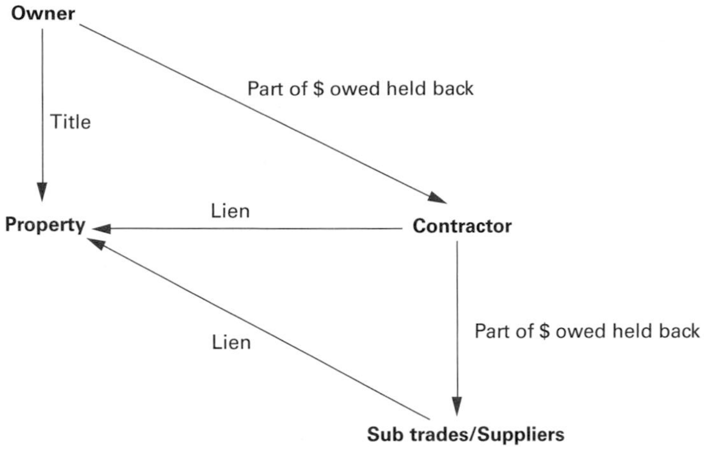

removed, and thus the property owner will have no further obligation even where the amounts claimed exceed the amount of the holdback.

Guarantee: One person agrees to pay if debtor does not

The **guarantee** is another way to create security. It involves three parties—the creditor, the debtor, and the guarantor who agrees to pay the debt if the debtor defaults (see Figure 5.4). This is a contingent obligation, with the guarantor having no liability until default. It also must be evidenced in writing to be enforceable. Often these agreements are put under seal to avoid any problem with consideration.

CASE SUMMARY 5.8

Bank of Montreal v. Wilder et al.[12]

A Bank's Breach Discharges the Guarantees

The Wilder family had been involved in several businesses over the years that required more and more credit. Eventually, they attended a meeting at the Bank of Montreal. The bank agreed to provide further funding and honour their line of credit until a particular road building project was completed—if they would inject a further $250 000 into the company. This was done by a debenture issue, and the Wilders were also required to sign personal guarantees for the line of credit, which was in the form of a demand loan against their company. One month later, and well before the completion of the project, the bank suddenly refused to honour any more of the Wilders' cheques and demanded payment of the loan ($860 920.30)—on 20 minutes' notice. When payment was not forthcoming, a receiver/manager was appointed to take over the business. He refused to finish the road building project, thus caus-

(continued)

12. (1986), 32 D.L.R. (4th) 9 (S.C.C.).

ing the company to fail. This action was brought by the bank to enforce the guarantees signed by the Wilders.

This case went to the Supreme Court of Canada which found in favour of the Wilders. The bank's action of failing to honour the cheques and demanding payment on the loan amounted to a breach of the understanding between the parties: that the line of credit would be honoured at least until the road building project was finished. Because upon payment the guarantor takes over the position of the creditor, the bank had an obligation to the Wilders to protect the value of a security such as the debentures. The bank's actions seriously undermined the value of that security, in turn harming the position of the guarantors. Consequently, the Wilders were released from their personal guarantees. This case shows how careful creditors have to be to consider the position of guarantors.

It should be noted that because this is a contingent liability, any defence that the debtor has against the creditor is also available to the guarantor, with the exception of bankruptcy and infancy. Thus, if the debtor purchases a car on time and there is a default, the creditor can turn to the guarantor for payment. But if the car is defective, the creditor/seller cannot demand payment from the guarantor instead of the debtor. Both can claim the defective product as a defence. If the guarantor is called upon to pay the creditor, he or she steps into the shoes of the creditor and assumes the rights of the creditor. If, for example, there is some additional form of security involved such as a chattel mortgage, the guarantor assumes the creditor's right to repossess those goods from the debtor. It is also important to note that if the creditor and debtor get together and change the terms of the agreement to advance more credit, change the interest rates, or otherwise modify the agreement without the permission of the guarantor, the guarantor will not be bound by the new terms and will also be released from the original obligations.

Guarantor has the same defences as debtor

Guarantor steps into the shoes of the creditor upon payment

FIGURE 5.4 Guarantee

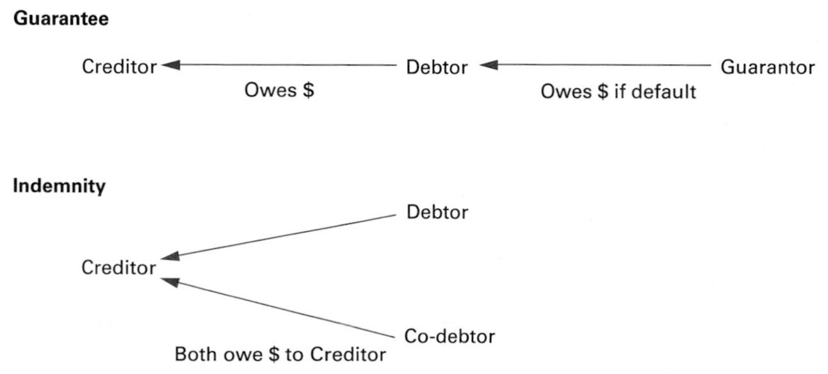

Negotiable Instruments

Negotiable instruments take the form of:
- Promissory notes
- Cheques
- Bills of exchange or drafts

Negotiable instruments are often used in conjunction with other forms of security as well as to advance credit and transfer funds. They have an ancient origin but are now controlled by the federal *Bills of Exchange Act*.[13] The three types provided for in the Act are promissory notes, cheques, and bills of exchange (often referred to as drafts).

A **promissory note** is an instrument whereby one person promises another to pay a certain sum of money at some future date or on demand (see Figure 5.5).

A **cheque** involves three parties. The drawer orders a bank where he or she has an account to pay a certain sum of money to a third party, who is called the payee. The drawer delivers the cheque to the payee, who normally then takes it to the bank and presents it for payment (see Figure 5.6).

A **bill of exchange** or a *draft*, which also involves three parties (drawer, drawee, and payee), is similar but broader. A cheque must be drawn on a bank, but the bill of exchange can be drawn on any person or business. Also, the bill of exchange can be made payable at some future time, whereas the cheque must be payable on demand (see Figure 5.7).

FIGURE 5.5 Promissory Note

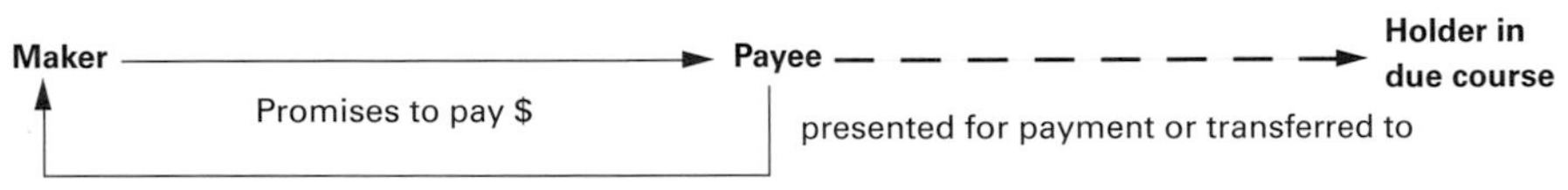

FIGURE 5.6 Cheque

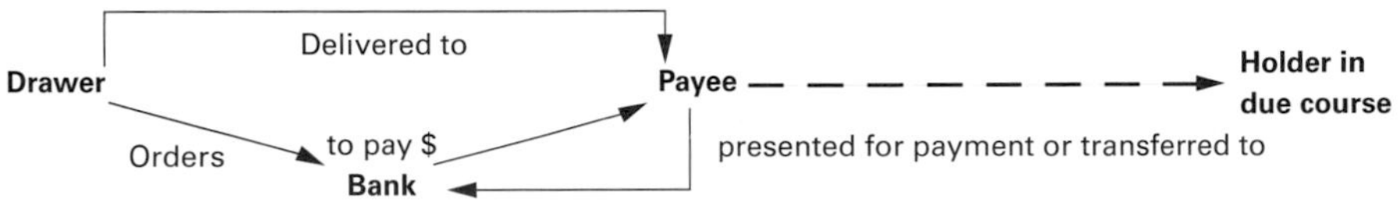

FIGURE 5.7 Bill of Exchange

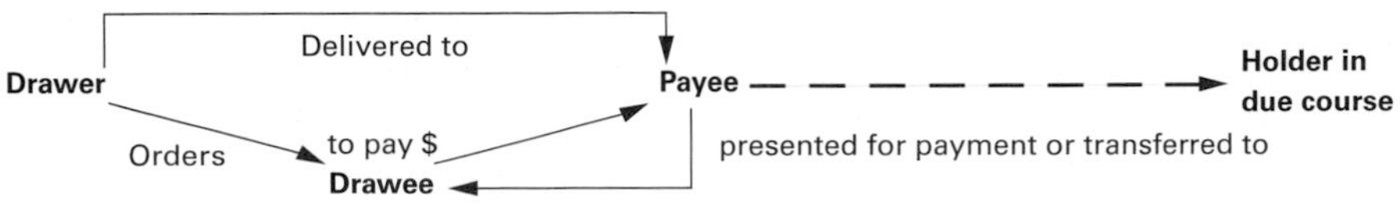

13. R.S.C. 1985, c. B-4.

The key to understanding the unique nature of negotiable instruments is in their free transferability from person to person. As discussed in Chapter 4, this is accomplished by giving an innocent party, who acquires possession of the instrument and is called a **holder in due course**, a right to collect on it whether the original contractual obligations have been met or not—short of outright fraud or forgery. They can also collect even though no notice of the various transfers that may have taken place has been given to the original debtor. These two factors make such instruments easily negotiable from person to person—hence, the name negotiable instruments. Thus, where a purchaser gives a cheque in payment for a car and there has been misrepresentation, he or she can stop payment on the cheque as long as it is in the hands of the person to whom it is made out. But if that cheque is transferred to an innocent third party, including the payee's bank, the purchaser/drawer will have to pay, even though there has been misrepresentation.

Holder in due course must be innocent

Holder in due course gets better rights than parties

It must also be emphasized that when one of the persons in possession of the cheque or other negotiable instrument endorses the back before transferring it, he or she can also be held liable for the amount of the cheque if the original drawer fails to pay. There are several different types of endorsement, but where the holder merely signs his or her name (a blank endorsement), it becomes a bearer instrument negotiated simply by passing it from one person to another. Where the holder adds the words "pay to the order of" it is an order instrument and the next person must also endorse it before transferring. In both cases the endorser has added his or her credit to the instrument and must be prepared to pay if the drawer fails to do so.

Normally, the endorser adds credit to a negotiable instrument

Bankruptcy

No discussion of creditor/debtor relationships would be complete without an examination of the law of bankruptcy. People often confuse the terms bankruptcy and insolvency. When a person is **insolvent**, it simply means that he or she is unable to pay his or her bills as they become due. **Bankruptcy**, on the other hand, involves a process whereby the debtor's assets are actually transferred to an official, who then distributes them to the unpaid creditors. Bankruptcy is becoming much more common today with personal bankruptcies far outstripping corporate bankruptcies as personal credit becomes so much easier to obtain. The federal *Bankruptcy and Insolvency Act*[14] provides a uniform process of bankruptcy across Canada. The object of the legislation is to preserve as much of the assets of the bankrupt debtor as possible for the benefit of the creditors. At the same time, the intention is to promote rehabilitation of the debtor so that he or she will have an insurmountable burden of debt removed and will again become a productive member of society.

Bankruptcy involves transfer of debtor's assets to a trustee

There are two ways that bankruptcy can be accomplished. When a debtor voluntarily transfers his or her assets to a **trustee in bankruptcy** (a private professional authorized to act in the area), it is called an **assignment in bankruptcy**. When the debtor is forced into bankruptcy by his or her creditors, they must obtain a **receiving order** from the court to forcibly transfer those assets to the trustee. To obtain a receiving order the debtor must owe at least $1000 and have

Assignment is voluntary, but bankruptcy may also be forced by a receiving order.

14. R.S.C. 1985, c. B-3.

committed an act of bankruptcy such as a fraudulent preference (paying one creditor in preference to another), a fraudulent conveyance (transferring property to a spouse or friend to keep it out of the hands of a creditor), or fleeing the jurisdiction to avoid debts. These also constitute bankruptcy offences and are discussed below. However, the most common act of bankruptcy is insolvency, where the debtor has simply been unable to pay debts as they come due.

The function of the trustee, in addition to counselling individual debtors, is to look after the assets and preserve them, doing whatever is necessary to protect their value. This may involve making repairs, doing maintenance, or, where an operating business is involved, actually managing that business. But usually a trustee will determine the priorities among the creditors, sell assets where necessary, and distribute the proceeds to those creditors on the basis of their entitlement.

Assets are distributed:

- First to secured creditors

Secured creditors, as discussed above, retain their privileged position with respect to the assets taken as security. The trustee must surrender the asset to them or pay out the amount owed. Where there is a shortfall and the amount obtained in selling the security does not cover the debt, the secured creditors will become unsecured creditors for the remaining amount owed. In such cases, they usually only obtain a percentage of that amount along with the other unsecured creditors.

- Then to preferred creditors

Preferred creditors are paid next. Some examples include funeral expenses, costs of the bankruptcy process itself, some taxes, and other fees such as employment insurance and workers' compensation. Also included are a limited amount of unpaid wages of employees and up to three months' back rent owed to a landlord.

- Finally to unsecured creditors

Finally, any amount left over is distributed to the **unsecured creditors**. Each receives a percentage of what was originally owed. Often the amount the unsecured creditors receive is a very small portion of the actual debt; this underlines the wisdom of taking security when a debt is created, as discussed above. Note that the trustee will often allow the bankrupt to keep certain assets that are difficult to sell and some assets such as tools and furniture, and that in some provinces RRSPs and even the equity held in a home are exempt from seizure.

Some possessions are exempt

Bankruptcy offences prohibited and penalized

If the bankrupt commits a **bankruptcy offence**, such as failing to disclose information, lying, or transferring property to a spouse or friend, this is a punishable offence and may ultimately interfere with him or her being discharged from the bankruptcy. The listed offences under the *Bankruptcy and Insolvency Act* are criminal offences with fines up to $10 000 or three years in jail, if treated as indictable offences. False claims made by creditors face similar penalties. The fraudulent transfer of property with the intent to defraud creditors is also an indictable offence under section 393(1) of the *Criminal Code* with a maximum term of imprisonment of two years.

Discharge ends obligations

Note exceptions

Where the bankrupt is an individual, after nine months an application is automatically made to the court for the discharge of the bankrupt. If it is the first bankruptcy, the individual will automatically be discharged, unless the discharge is opposed by one of the creditors or there has been a bankruptcy offence committed. If less than 50 cents on the dollar is paid, the court will sometimes impose a **conditional discharge**, requiring the bankrupt to make further payments. But usually once a person has been discharged, he or she is then free of any former indebtedness. This means that even if that person were to win a lottery worth millions, those former creditors would have no claim, since the debts would have been discharged through bankruptcy. Note that some debts survive the bankruptcy process and will not be eliminated by a discharge. These include student loans less than 10 years old, family maintenance obligations, and court-imposed fines.

A corporation can also go through the bankruptcy process but will not be ultimately discharged. After the bankruptcy process all assets are distributed and the corporation is left as an empty shell or dissolved, although this is normally not worth the expense. Creditors, shareholders, and others may have other recourse against the directors, principals, and officers of the corporation. This will be discussed in Chapter 7.

Corporations do not survive bankruptcy

CASE SUMMARY 5.9

Re Southwick, Trask and Trask[15]

Bankrupt Must Make Payments after a Conditional Discharge

This case illustrates bankruptcy and the principles taken into consideration in discharging the bankrupt. The bankrupt operated a call centre that employed a number of people. There were considerable debts, both secured and unsecured, that totalled about $2 million. When a significant client failed to pay a large account, the business became insolvent. As a result, personal bankruptcy was forced upon Mr. Trask and his wife, who had signed personal guarantees. Because the assets were less than 50 cents on the dollar, the court agreed that there would be a conditional discharge; this meant the bankrupt should be required to make further payment after discharge.

The trustee and other creditors recommended that Mr. Trask and his wife should pay a further $54 000. This amount was claimed on the basis that the couple had $354 000 in RRSPs that were exempt, and they had managed to borrow $160 000 from their family to pay off claims on their home and cottage, which had been used as security for the business loans. The judge, however, rejected this recommendation.

He made it clear, first, that the bankruptcies resulted from business misfortune, not from any wrong doing. He found that the legislature had specifically exempted RRSPs from the bankruptcy process, and so they should not be taken into consideration nor forced into liquidation when deciding what should be paid in a conditional discharge. He looked at the superintendent of bankruptcy guidelines, which stated the bankrupt should be left with 25 to 30 percent of his or her income per month to live on. The Trasks' income was calculated to be about $1000 per month, and so the payment would be only $750 for a period of 24 months or a lump sum payment of $18 000 (the present value of that amount). The judge acknowledged that one of the purposes of a conditional discharge was to accomplish a fair distribution to creditors, but this had to be balanced against the goal of rehabilitating the bankrupt. Clearly, in this case the judge looked at the lack of blameworthiness of the bankrupt and what the Trasks could afford to pay, more than at the losses of the creditors.

15. 2003 N.S.S.C. 160, 44 C.B.R. (4th) 134, 216 N.S.R. (2d) 190 (N.S.S.C.).

There are alternatives to the bankruptcy process, the most obvious consisting of simply negotiating alternative arrangements with creditors, including consolidating one's obligations. Where that fails, the *Bankruptcy and Insolvency Act* provides a formal alternative to the bankruptcy process. If individual debtors owe less than $75 000, they can make a proposal to their creditors to pay less than the full amount owed, and/or over a longer time. If the offer is accepted and properly fulfilled, a certificate is issued and the debtor is then released from those obligations without having gone through bankruptcy. Debt counselling is involved and the arrangements are usually made through the trustee/administrator. This is a **Division Two proposal**.

Division Two proposal is an alternative for individuals

The arrangements for companies and larger debtors owing over $75 000 is more formal and complex; they involve more oversight and fall under a **Division One proposal**. A singular advantage for both is that any action being taken to seize property is stopped until the time allotted for the proposal process has been completed. Even then, an application can be brought to the court to extend this time. This has led to some abuses. Large corporations with very large debt obligations often proceed using a different federal statute, the *Companies' Creditors Arrangement Act* (*C.C.A.A.*),[16] which has a similar effect and allows some additional flexibility.

Division One proposal is an alternative to bankruptcy for a company

C.C.A.A. **also provides alternative to bankruptcy for company**

Usually secured creditors of large corporations will include terms in the original contract that give them the right to take over the management of that corporation in the event of default. This is called **receivership** and is often confused with bankruptcy. Receivership eliminates the need to go through the bankruptcy process, but the effect can be just as devastating on the business. A professional **receiver** is appointed by the creditor and literally takes over the business, displacing the directors and other managers in the process. Table 5.3 provides a summary of the consequences of bankruptcy.

Receivership is not bankruptcy

TABLE 5.3 Consequences of Bankruptcy

Debtor	Options	Result
Debtor owing under $75 000	- Voluntary assignment	Loss of assets and ultimate discharge
	- Receiving order (forced)	Loss of assets and ultimate discharge
	- Division Two proposal	Pay as agreed; no bankruptcy
Debtor owing over $75 000	- Voluntary assignment	Loss of assets and ultimate discharge
	- Receiving order (forced)	Loss of assets and ultimate discharge
	- Division One proposal	Pay as agreed; no bankruptcy
Corporations	- Receiving order (forced)	Loss of assets but no discharge; corporation dies
	- Division One proposal	Pay as agreed; no bankruptcy; corporation survives
	- Receivership (Forced)	No bankruptcy but creditors take over company

16. R.S.C. 1985, c. C-36.

QUESTIONS FOR REVIEW

1. Explain the role played by the *Sale of Goods Act* and the qualifications that must be met for the Act to apply to a particular transaction.
2. How is the person who bears the risk determined under the *Sale of Goods Act?* Explain how this can be modified by the parties.
3. Explain the five rules that determine when title will pass under the *Sale of Goods Act.*
4. Explain the obligations imposed on a seller with respect to title, sale by sample and description, and fitness and quality.
5. Explain what is meant by merchantable quality.
6. Discuss the nature of exculpatory or exemption clauses and their effect on the provisions of the *Sale of Goods Act.*
7. When a default takes place, what are the rights of the seller with respect to goods that are in transit? With respect to goods that are in the hands of a bankrupt?
8. Explain how consumer protection legislation can affect the operation of exemption or exculpatory clauses, e.g., limited warranties.
9. Describe the abusive business practices that are controlled by trade practices or business practices statutes. Describe how the statutes' provisions are enforced.
10. Explain what is meant by a cooling-off period and explain how pyramid and referral selling schemes are controlled under consumer protection legislation.
11. Explain the nature and objective of the federal *Competition Act,* and provide a list of prohibited or controlled practices under that Act.
12. Indicate other federal statutes that have a consumer protection aspect to them.
13. Explain what is meant by a secured transaction, indicating the special position of the creditor.
14. Distinguish between a conditional sale and a chattel mortgage, and indicate the effect of the *Personal Property Security Act* on such transactions.
15. Why was the passage of the *Personal Property Security Act* so important to secured transactions?
16. Distinguish between attachment and perfection, and describe how perfection can be accomplished.
17. Describe the rights of the creditor when there is a default under the *Personal Property Security Act.* What must the creditor do to protect his or her right to sue for a deficit?

18. Explain the significance of a holdback under the builders' liens or construction lien statutes.
19. Explain who is protected—and how—under the builders' liens or construction liens statutes.
20. Distinguish between an indemnity and a guarantee.
21. Explain the position of a guarantor with respect to the debtor's obligations and how those obligations are affected by subsequent dealings between the parties.
22. Explain the rights of the guarantor once he or she has paid the debtor's obligations.
23. Distinguish between insolvency and bankruptcy, and between an assignment and a receiving order.
24. Explain the role of a trustee in bankruptcy.
25. Distinguish between an act of bankruptcy and a bankruptcy offence.
26. Explain the positions of secured, preferred, and unsecured creditors in the event of a bankruptcy.
27. Explain the differences between the position of an individual and a corporation at the end of the bankruptcy process.
28. Explain the effect of a discharge on the bankrupt.
29. Explain the difference between the provisions of the Division One and Division Two proposals.
30. Explain the difference between a bankruptcy and a receivership.

QUESTIONS FOR FURTHER DISCUSSION

1. The purpose of the *Sale of Goods Act* is to imply terms into any contract of sale where the parties haven't specifically agreed otherwise. In some provinces a few of these terms are imposed and any attempt to override them is void. Some other provinces accomplish the same thing through separate consumer protection legislation. Consider whether the parties should be able to contract out of any of the terms of the *Sale of Goods Act*. Should such restrictions apply to both consumer and business transactions? Should there be any provision of the *Sale of Goods Act* that the parties can't override in their own agreement? In your answer consider both consumer and business transactions. Consider also consumer legislation generally. Should such legislation ever interfere with the parties' rights to have whatever terms they deem appropriate in a contract, whether it relates to a consumer transaction or not? Do such restrictions unduly interfere with the commercial process?

2. Does the process of taking collateral security unfairly assist secured creditors over unsecured creditors? Does the requirement of registration sufficiently answer any criticism? In your answer consider the process of bankruptcy and how secured creditors are given preferred treatment, often leaving an unsecured creditor with nothing.

3. Consider the bankruptcy process. It seems to be inconsistent with every principle of fundamental contract law and commercial relations. Is it fair to the creditors and debtor? What about discharge? Should debtors be allowed to escape their obligations in this way? Can you come up with a better alternative? Why prohibit student loans from being discharged through bankruptcy? Should there be other exceptions?

CASES
FOR DISCUSSION

1. **STUBBE ET AL. V. P.F. COLLIER & SON LTD.** (1977), 74 D.L.R. (3d) 605 (B.C.S.C.).
Stubbe was an electrician living in the Kelowna area when he was approached at his home by Wilhelmina Scott and Gary Neufeld, representatives of the defendant, who tried to sell him a set of encyclopedias. At first they didn't disclose to Stubbe that they were selling a product. Rather they claimed to be conducting an educational survey, which gained them access into Stubbe's home. As part of their sales pitch they claimed that Mr. Stubbe was qualified to receive a special benefit, which allowed him to get the encyclopedia at minimal cost. In fact, he would have to pay the same price as all customers. They also claimed that the product was a new edition, when it was simply a revision of an older version of the encyclopedia. Mr. Stubbe didn't purchase the books, but he did make a complaint to the police. Explain what statute would be applicable here and the arguments available to both parties. Would it make any difference to your answer to know that Mr. Stubbe was the president of the local branch of the Consumer Association of Canada and already had a set of the *Colliers Encyclopedia*? He made it a practice to let all door-to-door salespeople go through their presentation to see if he could catch them doing anything wrong. What would be an appropriate remedy in these circumstances?

2. **LASBY V. ROYAL CITY CHRYSLER PLYMOUTH** (1987), 37 D.L.R. (4th) 243 (Ont. H.C.J.).
Mrs. Lasby bought a used car from a dealer when the salesman, Mr. McDonald, told her that it had been driven by one of the dealership's executives and had a powerful six-cylinder engine. She had refused other cars because she wanted a six-cylinder car. The next day when she noticed the car was only a four-cylinder engine, she called the salesman. He told her that Chrysler no longer made a six-cylinder and that a four-cylinder was the biggest engine they made. In fact, that was false, as Mrs. Lasby found out later from her mechanic. It turned out that the car had not been executive-driven; it had been leased and had only a 2.2-litre, four-cylinder engine (instead of the larger

2.6-litre engine). She demanded her money back, but the sales manager refused, saying she "had bought the car and that was that." The salesman denied ever having made false statements to her, and the company refused any remedy. Mrs. Lasby brought this action and continued to drive the car. By the time it got to court 22 months after the purchase, the car had 40 000 kilometres on it. Explain the likely outcome of the action and the appropriate remedy if Mrs. Lasby wins.

3. **REGINA V. TAMBLYN LTD.** (1972), 26 D.L.R. (3d) 436, [1972] 2 O.R. 704 (Ont. C.A.).
A sign was placed in the window of a Tamblyn Drug store containing the following statements:

    FREE KODAK FILM A FRESH ROLL OF KODAK FILM WITH EVERY ROLL
    OF BLACK AND WHITE OR KODACOLOR PROCESSED

The cost of processing, including the free film, was $7.50 but an investigator asked the store manager for the film processing without the free film and was charged $6. Charges were laid. What is the problem with the actions of Tamblyn Drugs in this situation? Can you think of any defence they might raise?

4. **GOODFELLOW INC. V. HEATHER BUILDING SUPPLIES LTD.** (1996), 141 D.L.R. (4th) 282 (N.S.C.A.).
Heather Building Supplies Ltd. sold and delivered lumber to Goodfellow Inc., but made it clear that the lumber was not theirs until it was paid for. Goodfellow failed to pay. Heather seized the lumber, but before they could move it back to their premises, a notice was served on them that Goodfellow was making a proposal under the *Bankruptcy and Insolvency Act*. Explain the position of the parties under the Act. What is the likely outcome of the case? Would it affect your answer to know that no attempt was made by Heather to register their interest in the lumber?

5. **RE M. C. UNITED MASONRY LTD.** (1993), 142 D.L.R. (3d) 470 (Ont. C.A.).
Goldfarb, Shulman, Winter and Co. were a firm of chartered accountants providing various accounting and consulting services to M.C. United Masonry Ltd. and other related companies. The amount owed to the accountants was over $100 000. M.C. United guaranteed this amount and conveyed certain share certificates they held in another company (Palm Hill Investments Ltd.) to the accounting firm to be held by them as security for the guarantee. The security arrangement was not registered under the *Personal Property Security Act*. M.C. United Masonry Ltd. was forced into bankruptcy and the trustee demanded the return of the share certificates, effectively denying Goldfarb their position as a secured creditor as claimed on the basis of the share certificates. Discuss the arguments available to both parties. Have the requirements for priority under the *Personal Property Security Act* been satisfied in this case?

6. **VAN NORMAN V. VAN NORMAN** (1993), 100 D.L.R. (4th) 341 (B.C.C.A.).
Mr. and Mrs. Van Norman had separated. After the sale of their house, they signed a separation agreement, which required Mr. Van Norman to make a lump-sum payment of $245 000 to his wife. There were to be no on-going payments for support or maintenance. After the agreement, but before the payment was due, Mr. Van Norman made an assignment in bankruptcy and was eventually discharged. In this action Mrs. Van Norman is seeking to hold Mr. Van Norman to his commitment to make the lump-sum payment. What are the arguments on both sides?

7. **PEARCE V. PITTOCK** (1994), 113 D.L.R. (4th) 749 (Ont. Gen. Div.).
Would your answer be different if the debt due the wife was based on an obligation the couple had acquired jointly to a bank before the separation? She assumed the obligation, and he committed to make regular payments ($250 per month) to her to pay it off. He was making regular payments to that effect when he made an assignment in bankruptcy and was eventually discharged. Should the obligations to make these payments survive the bankruptcy?

CHAPTER 6

Agency and Employment

An essential aspect of any business activity is the various relationships through which business transactions are accomplished. These relationships may involve owners, managers, employees, and independent contractors. They may also include consultants, lawyers, and accountants, as well as those who carry out the various functions associated with corporations such as directors, officers, and shareholders. Employees perform designated tasks like cleaning a floor or word processing a letter. Those who represent the business/employer in dealings with others, including customers, suppliers, and the government, are referred to as agents. Each of these relationships involves unique responsibilities, rights, obligations, and benefits. All of these should be taken into consideration when a person makes decisions with respect to his or her business, including whether that business should be carried on through a proprietorship, a partnership, a corporation, or a combination of these methods. The functions and relationships associated with the different methods of carrying on business (proprietorship, partnerships, and corporations) will be the subject of the following chapter. In this chapter we will look at agency and employment.

It is important to distinguish between independent contractors, employees, and agents. An **independent contractor** performs a specific service described in a contract. Normally, this is not an ongoing obligation. The contractor does the job and moves on. Essentially, a contractor works for himself or herself, as when a builder agrees to build a house for someone or a lawyer incorporates a company for a client. Consultants and auditors are other examples of independent contractors who provide a contracted service to a business. The nature of these relationships is governed by the general rules of contract law discussed in prior chapters.

An independent contractor works for him- or herself

An **employee**, on the other hand, is more committed to an employer in an on-going relationship and is subject to specialized rules governing employment. There is much more control exercised by employers over the activities of their employees, hence the

An employee works for the employer in an ongoing relationship

term *master/servant,* which more accurately captures the true nature of the relationship. Most people earn their income through a wage or salary paid by an employer. Employment will be discussed below, but the first topic to be examined in this chapter is the law of agency.

Agency

Agency refers to the nature of the service being provided rather than to the degree of control or the on-going nature of the relationship. An agent is someone who represents another person (the principal) in dealings with a third party (see Figure 6.1). The relationship is normally created by contract, although this is not always the case.

An agent represents a principal in dealings with a third party

A significant portion of this chapter is devoted to the examination of the agency relationship, because agency principles are integral to business law and most business activity is carried on through agents. Agency also forms a significant component of the law of partnership and corporations to be discussed in Chapter 7.

It is important to emphasize at the outset that an agent can be either an employee or an independent contractor, but not all employees and independent contractors are agents. For example, a plumber may be acting as an agent for the general contractor or the owner of the building when he is ordering materials to do the job, but not when he is installing the fixtures. Some examples of independent contractors who act primarily as agents are travel, insurance, and real estate agents. Similarly, an employee may or may not be an agent, depending on the assigned task. A clerk selling groceries to a customer is acting as an agent, but an employee sweeping the floor is not.

An agent may be an employee or an independent contractor

Usually agents enter into contracts with third parties on behalf of their principals, but sometimes the agent's services may not involve the creation of a contract at all. For example, lawyers file documents for a client or accountants file tax returns. Real estate agents find buyers and facilitate negotiation, but contracts are usually made directly between the purchasers and sellers.

Agents usually enter into contracts on behalf of their principals

An agency relationship is created when a principal, usually in a contract, grants authority to an agent to act on his or her behalf (see Figure 6.2). In rare circumstances the agency function is performed gratuitously, for example, by a volunteer. The key is to find some indication that the principal has granted authority to the agent to act on his or her behalf. In special situations an agency relationship is created by a formal contract put under seal (called a **power of attorney**). Normally, however, there are no formal requirements, and an agency relationship can even be inferred from the conduct of the parties.

Agency depends on granting of authority

Agency is usually created by contract

FIGURE 6.1 Agency Relationship

(The principal contracts through an agent with the third party)

FIGURE 6.2 Agent Relationships

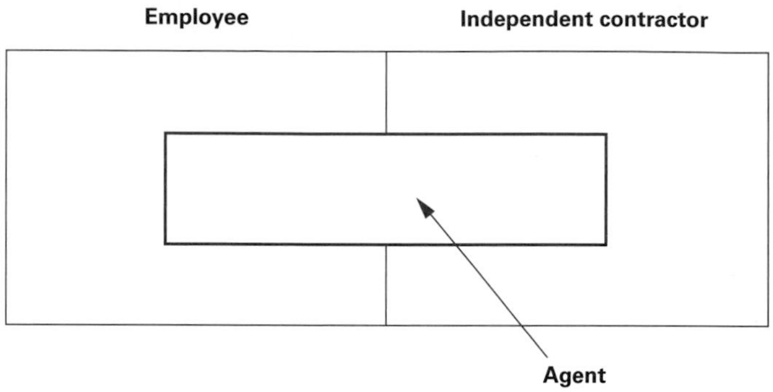

(An agent may be an independent contractor or an employee)

PRINCIPAL/THIRD-PARTY RELATIONSHIP

The unique aspect of agency law relates to the relationship between a principal and a third party, created when an agent functions as an intermediary. The primary consideration is to determine under what circumstances the third party will be able to hold the principal responsible for the conduct of the agent in contract law and/or in tort law.

AUTHORITY What is the responsibility of a principal for contracts entered into by an agent? A principal is liable for contracts entered into on his or her behalf by an agent who has been granted the authority to do so (see Figure 6.3). That authority may consist of the specific authority granted by the principal called **actual authority**, but may also be based on what the principal has led others to believe (called *apparent authority*). The actual authority granted may have been specifically stated but may also be implied from some position given to the agent. For example, a gasoline attendant would have the implied authority to sell gasoline, whether it has been specifically stated by the principal or not. Of course, there would be no implied authority for the gasoline attendant to sell the actual gas station. Understanding an agent's apparent authority is a little more difficult.

Principal also bound where agent acts within apparent authority

Apparent authority involves a principal being held responsible for the representations they make to third parties with respect to the authority of their agents. For example, the manager of an auto supply store might give a sales clerk specific instructions not to sell anything over $200 without first getting approval from the manager. If, despite those instructions, the clerk sold an engine block to a customer for $400 without getting approval, that contract would still be binding on the store. There would be no actual authority for the clerk to make such a sale, since authority cannot be implied in the face of clear instructions to the contrary. Rather, the principle of estoppel prevents the employer from denying that the clerk had authority in the circumstances. Where a principal does something to lead a third party to believe that the agent has authority to act for him or her, the principal cannot later deny that such authority exists. If the principal has held out the agent to have such authority, the agent does have that authority. Putting the clerk into a position where a customer would expect him to have the authority to sell the engine block would constitute such a holding out.

FIGURE 6.3 Agent's Authority

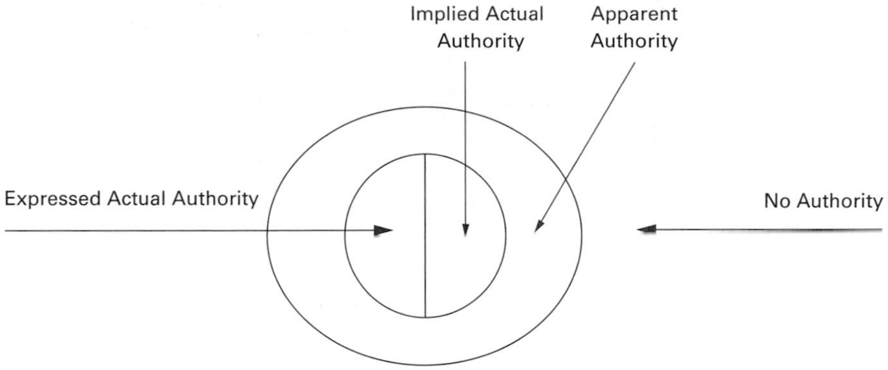

(An agent may have actual authority [expressed or implied] or apparent authority)

Note that *estoppel*, as it is used here, must be distinguished from *promissory estoppel* discussed in Chapter 3. Promissory estoppel or equitable estoppel involved the making of a promise, whereas this involves an assertion of some fact indicating the agent has authority. Once the principal leads another to believe that fact and it is relied on, he or she cannot simply deny its validity later when convenient. In this situation, the manager has put the sales clerk into a position where others dealing with that clerk would think he had the authority to make sales with respect to the items in the shop. The manager is then held responsible for creating that impression.

Agent has apparent authority when principal leads another to that belief

CASE SUMMARY 6.1

Doiron v. Devon Capital Corp.[1]

The Consequences of Allowing Others to Believe Someone Is Your Agent

The plaintiffs wanted some short-term investments and turned to Mr. Demmers, who had looked after their pension fund and insurance matters as a representative of Manulife. He persuaded them to invest in Devon, calling the corporation "a no-risk investment." This proved to be bad advice and the plaintiffs lost all of their funds. They sought compensation from Demmers, who had become bankrupt. In this action the plaintiffs sought compensation from Manulife. It was clear that the plaintiffs thought Demmers was an employee of Manulife and that the Devon investment was one of their products. In fact, Manulife had taken pains to set out in their contract that Demmers was not an employee, but was an independent contractor.

(continued)

1. [2002] 10 W.W.R. 439, 2002 ABQB 664 (Alta. Q.B).

Even though the Devon investment was not one of Manulife's products and their contract with Demmers made it clear that he was an independent contractor, the court held Manulife liable for Demmers' negligence in recommending this investment. Demmers had offices in the Manulife building and was encouraged to refer to himself as their representative. When someone phoned him, the call went through the Manulife operator. Demmers was required to work for Manulife exclusively. These factors encouraged those dealing with him to believe he was working for Manulife. This gave Demmers apparent authority to act for Manulife and created the impression that Manulife was responsible for his actions. This case illustrates the difference between an independent contractor and an employee, but it also shows the importance of finding apparent authority, which can make the principal responsible for the agent's actions even when there is no actual authority.

There is an obvious overlap between apparent authority and implied authority. The distinction is only important where the authority of the agent cannot be implied because of specific instruction to the agent otherwise. The principal could still be bound by the apparent authority of the agent. On the other hand, if the sales clerk were to attempt to sell the whole store, or the gasoline attendant the gas station, that transaction would not be binding on the principal. A purchaser would not expect the agent to have that kind of authority, and so there is neither implied authority nor any apparent authority to support the purchase.

A principal, then, will be bound by transactions entered into by an agent where that agent has acted within the actual authority given expressly or by implication by the principal or within apparent authority based on the principal's representations to the third party.

Agent can be given authority by ratification either intentionally or by implication

In circumstances where the agent has exceeded both his or her apparent and actual authority, the principal can still enforce the transaction and be bound by it through ratification. **Ratification** involves some act by the principal lending validity to the transaction after the agent has acted. This can be done intentionally by the principal expressly ratifying the transaction, or it can be done inadvertently by the principal taking some benefit under the agreement. For example, if after the clerk sold the store the principal liked the deal, he could ratify the sale and the purchaser would be bound by it.

Ratification works retroactively

Note that the effect of such ratification is retroactive. The contract comes into effect, not at the time of ratification, but at the time of the original transaction when the agent purported to act for the principal. Thus, ratification involves the agent's authority being confirmed after the fact, but the result is as if the agent always had that authority.

Restrictions on ratification

Because the power to ratify puts the third party at some disadvantage, there are some restrictions on ratification. First, the third party can specify a reasonable period of time within which that ratification must take place. Also, the principal cannot ratify a transaction if at the time of the ratification it would be impossible to enter into the agreement. Thus, after the principal's house has burned down, it is too late to ratify a contract of insurance put through by an unauthorized agent. Similarly, the principal cannot ratify a contract that he or she could not have entered into at the time the agent purported to act on his or her behalf. Thus, a contract entered into on behalf of a company before incorporation could not be ratified by that company after incorporation. It should be noted that by statute some jurisdictions allow these pre-incorporation contracts.

CASE SUMMARY 6.2

John Ziner Lumber Ltd. v. Kotov[2]

Ratification Is a Two-Edged Sword

A contractor agreed to build a house for Kotov and made arrangements with Ziner Lumber to supply the materials. At first Ziner wasn't aware of Kotov's involvement, since all of their dealing was with the contractor. However, Ziner became suspicious of the contractor's credit and started sending their bills directly to Kotov's company, the registered owner of the property. Eventually, Kotov fired the contractor but did nothing to stop Ziner from delivering more lumber, which was incorporated into the house. Kotov then refused to pay for the lumber, claiming the contractor had exceeded his authority. This action was brought by Ziner, who was seeking payment for the lumber. Kotov took the position that he was an undisclosed principal and was not responsible for the debt.

The court found that while that may have been the case in the beginning, Kotov's identity did eventually become known to Ziner. At the time the lumber was delivered and incorporated into the building, Kotov was no longer an undisclosed principal. Although the contractor may not have had the authority to order the lumber, because it had been incorporated into the building, Kotov had in effect ratified the agreement and was therefore obligated to pay. In this case the ratification was implied from the conduct of the principal and worked retroactively to bind Kotov to the contract.

CASE SUMMARY 6.2 John Ziner Lumber Ltd. v. Kotov

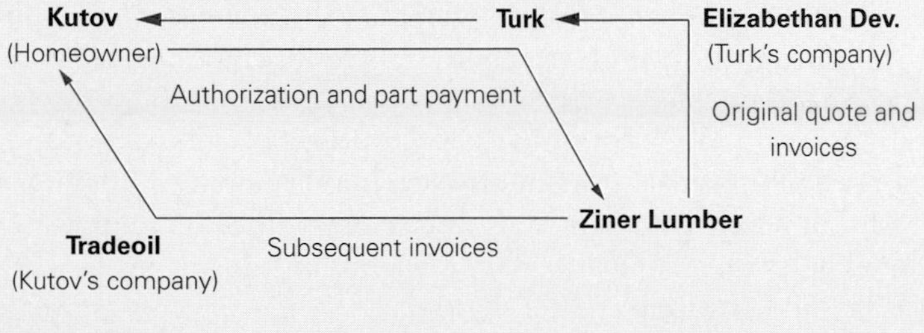

It is clear that great care should be taken to inform an agent of just what authority he or she has been given; any limitation on that authority should be made absolutely clear. Also, when an employee is dismissed or the services of an

Agent's authority should be carefully specified

2. 2000 CanLII 16894 (Ont. C.A.) (2000-10-17).

agent are terminated, all customers, clients, and suppliers with whom that individual has dealt should be notified of the termination.

Vicarious liability will be imposed where an agent is also a employee and . . .

Where employee/agent commits tort in course of employment

VICARIOUS LIABILITY What is the responsibility of the principal for torts committed by the agent? When one person is held responsible for the torts committed by another, it is referred to as **vicarious liability**. This is found primarily where an employment relationship exists (see Figure 6.4). An employer is vicariously liable for torts committed by an employee that take place during the course of that employment. When the agent is also an employee, vicarious liability will apply whenever that agent commits a tort while on the job. For example, if a purchasing agent were to carelessly run over someone while driving her own car to a meeting with suppliers, the employer would be vicariously liable since the tort was committed while the employee was doing what she was employed to do.

But if that employee were to divert and go home to check on her family, and in the process carelessly ran over someone, the employer would not be vicariously liable. The purchasing agent was not doing what she was employed to do, but was on a "frolic of her own." The fact that the accident took place during or after working hours is not the determining factor. Rather, what determines vicarious liability is whether the employee/agent was doing what she was employed to do at the time of the accident. A store clerk who took it upon himself to eject an unruly customer and caused injury would likely not impose vicarious liability on his employer since he was acting beyond the scope of his employment. But if the same ejection was performed by a bouncer, that conduct would be well within his duties, even if he was doing the job improperly.

It is not always clear just when employees are improperly performing what they were employed to do or when they are acting outside the scope of their employment altogether. Nothing will substitute for careful training and clear instruction as to the nature of the job assigned. It should be noted that in two recent Supreme Court of Canada cases dealing with sexual abuse committed by an employee, the court took a broader approach and imposed vicarious liability on the two institutions involved, based on policy consideration even where the sexual abuse of the employees did not take place within the "scope of their employment." Justice Beverley McLachlin said that in cases where there are no clear precedents, rather than hiding behind semantics such as "scope of employment," an employer's vicarious liability should be determined on policy considerations. "The fundamental question is whether the wrongful act is sufficiently related to conduct authorized by the employer to justify the imposition of vicarious liability." She then listed several policy considerations to be taken into consideration in determining the answer to that question.[3]

Liability of principal for agent's torts are limited where the agent is an independent contractor

The more difficult question relates to when a principal will be liable for torts committed by an agent who is not his or her employee. Liability for the acts of independent contractors such as lawyers, accountants, insurance agents, and real estate agents is much more restricted. They are working for themselves and so are responsible for their own wrongful conduct. The principal will only be liable if the tort causing injury took place during the actual exercise of the authority that the principal has given the agent. The agent has to be in the process of actually transacting the business he or she was authorized to do. Usually this is restricted

3. "Supreme Court lays down rules for finding vicarious liability," *Lawyers Weekly*, Vol. 19 No. 8 (June 25, 1999).

FIGURE 6.4 Vicarious Liability

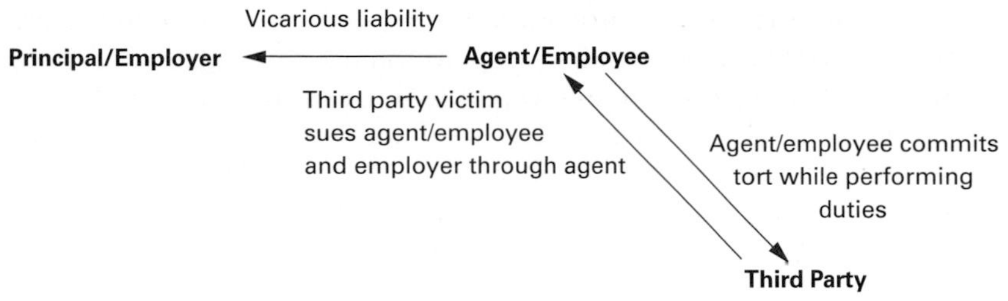

to the tort of fraud and negligent misstatement associated with the negotiation or enactment of the contract itself. This was discussed in Chapter 4 under "Fraudulent Misrepresentation" and "Negligent Misrepresentation." Where my real estate agent negligently runs over someone on the way to show my house, I would not be held vicariously liable for her tort, as she was working for herself at the time. But if she fraudulently or negligently misrepresented that the house was zoned for multiple family residences when it was not, that would be the commission of a tort while actually acting for me and exercising that authority as agent. Consequently, I could well be held vicariously liable for the fraud or negligent statement. Remember, with vicarious liability both the agent and the principal would be liable for the tort.

Principals will be responsible for their own torts committed through the agent

Of course, if the principal gave the false information to the agent, who then innocently passed it on, the agent would be completely innocent and it would be the principal alone who would be directly liable for the fraud or negligent statement.

In many jurisdictions vicarious liability is imposed on the owner of a motor vehicle when they lend it to someone, even where the permission to use it is implied. The British Columbia *Motor Vehicle Act*, for example, states:

> **86.** (1) In an action to recover loss or damage sustained by a person by reason of a motor vehicle on a highway, every person driving or operating the motor vehicle who is living with and as a member of the family of the owner of the motor vehicle, and every person driving or operating the motor vehicle who acquired possession of it with the consent, express or implied, of the owner of the motor vehicle, is deemed to be the agent or servant of that owner and employed as such, and is deemed to be driving and operating the motor vehicle in the course of his or her employment.
>
> (2) Nothing in this section relieves a person deemed to be the agent or servant of the owner and to be driving or operating the motor vehicle in the course of his or her employment from the liability for such loss or damage.

Vicarious liability imposed on car owners by statute

Essentially, if you loan your car to a friend and he gets into an accident that is his fault, you are responsible. If the purchasing agent, in the example above, were using a company car, the company would be vicariously liable even if she were checking on her family instead of going to the meeting with suppliers. Although she was on a frolic of her own, she has acquired the car with permission, and so the company would be vicariously liable.

THE AGENT/THIRD-PARTY RELATIONSHIP

Normally, the agent can neither sue nor be sued under the contract

As a general rule, the third party has no claim against the agent since the agent simply acts as an intermediary. The resulting contract is between the principal and a third party, and if not satisfied, the third party must look to the principal for a remedy. For the same reason, the agent has no claim against the third party and must look to the principal for any payment for services rendered.

Exception: Agent may be sued for breach of warranty of authority

It is only when the agent has exceeded all authority to act that the third party can sue the agent for claiming authority not possessed. This is a tort action for "breach of warranty of authority," and gives the third party the right to obtain compensation from the agent for what was lost because of the unauthorized transaction.

CASE SUMMARY 6.3

Biondich v. Kingscroft Investments Ltd.[4]

The Nightmare of Dealing with a Fraudulent Agent

Carmichael made investments on behalf of the plaintiffs in Kingcroft Investment Ltd., claiming he was a partner in that firm and that the money was "safe as money in the bank." In fact, the company had been dissolved several years earlier and there was little likelihood the money would ever be recovered. Carmichael claimed to be acting for a company that didn't exist. The court found that Carmichael had not only committed fraud and was liable for it, but he had also breached a warranty of authority by claiming to be a representative of Kingcroft and signing investments on its behalf, knowing all the while that the company no longer existed. The court not only awarded compensation but punitive damages as well. An agent can be personally liable when he claims to have authority he does not have.

Exception: Agent may be sued where acting for undisclosed principal

Third party can sue agent or undisclosed principal, but bound by choice

Sometimes it is not always clear that someone is acting as an agent. For example, if a church group decided to sell one of their buildings, it may be reluctant to sell it to a well-known nightclub operator in the town. The purchaser then could employ an agent to make the purchase without disclosing that the agent is acting for someone else. Large land acquisitions are often done this way in order not to disclose what is to be built on the property, which might affect the asking price for the individual plots of land. These are called undisclosed principals. Where the facts are ambiguous as to whether the agent is acting as agent or principal, either party can be sued if the deal goes sour. The third party can commence action against the agent, but once the identity of the undisclosed principal is learned, a choice must be made to continue the action against the agent or to sue the principal instead. Once the choice is made, the third party is bound by it and cannot change his mind, even if it turns out that the party being sued has no funds. It must be emphasized that in this scenario the agent's conduct must be unclear as to whether he is acting as agent or principal. If the agent signs as a pur-

4. 2002 CanLII 24606 (Ont. S.C.J.) (2002-12-04).

chaser, for example, only he can be sued, since his conduct was not consistent with acting as an agent. On the other hand, if the agent clearly signs as an agent, even if he does not disclose the identity of the principal, he is not a party to the agreement and cannot be sued on it.

It should also be noted that there are some situations where a contract entered into by an agent for an undisclosed principal will not be binding—in contracts where identity is important, for instance. Thus, a famous tenor cannot agree to perform a concert and then send an understudy claiming he was acting as an agent for an undisclosed principal. The same principle would apply to a contract of employment. But in the example above where the church group sold its building to a nightclub owner, it is likely that the church would be bound, since what the property was used for after it was sold was not their concern.

Third party not bound where identity of undisclosed principal is important

THE AGENT/PRINCIPAL RELATIONSHIP

The relationship between the third party and the principal is governed by the contract creating the relationship. The rights of the agent to payment for services and expenses for the specific things that the agent is authorized to do should be set out in that agreement.

FIDUCIARY DUTY Although the principal has some obligations to the agent, such as the payment of expenses, salaries, and any fees already agreed to in the contract itself, the more interesting obligations in this relationship rest on the agent who has a fiduciary duty to the principal. A f2act in the best interests of the principal (see Table 6.1). This is referred to as an "utmost good faith relationship" and arises where trust has been placed in another by someone particularly vulnerable if that trust is broken. As a fiduciary, the agent cannot take advantage of a business opportunity that comes to her because of her position. That business opportunity belongs to the principal. Where there is a conflict between the agent's personal interests and that of the principal, the agent must disclose it and put her own interest aside. If the agent has an interest in the property being offered to the principal, she must fully disclose that fact and not make a profit on the deal without the consent of the principal. Similarly, any information the agent acquires with respect to transactions she is involved in belongs to the principal and must be communicated to the principal. This is forcefully illustrated in the *Ocean City Realty* case discussed below.

Agent has fiduciary duty to principal

Agent must exercise utmost good faith to principal

Agent must make full disclosure to principal

An agent must act for only one principal and cannot take a benefit from both sides. These are called kickbacks and for an agent to take even a small gratuity such as liquor, a trip, or some other benefit from a supplier would be a violation of this fiduciary duty.

The agent cannot make a personal profit from the deal, other than the commission or other payment coming from the principal. For example, if a real estate agent finds an unsophisticated principal willing to sell a house at a low price, he cannot purchase the property himself, even if done through a partner or a company. The agent's duty is to get the principal the best price possible and that duty would conflict with his own interests in this situation. Also, the agent cannot compete with the principal. If the agent is selling one particular product for the principal, he cannot promote his own product or someone else's product instead. To continue with the real estate example, if the real estate agent is selling a house for a principal and finds an interested buyer, the agent will be in violation of his fiduciary duty if he tries to sell the prospective purchaser his own property instead.

Agent must put principal's interest ahead of his or her own

TABLE 6.1 Agent's Fiduciary Duty

- Must not take advantage of principal's business opportunities
- Must submerge his or her own interests in favour of principal's
- Must disclose conflict of interest
- Must not take benefit from both parties
- Must disclose information to principal
- Must not compete with principal
- Must not make profit at expense of principal

Where such a fiduciary duty is breached the principal can demand an accounting. He can require the agent to disclose any profits personally made from the transaction and then to pay those profits to the principal. The agent would also be deprived of any commission in these circumstances.

Section 426 of the *Criminal Code* makes it a criminal offence for agents or employees to accept a secret commission or other benefit (or indeed for anyone to pay or offer such a secret commission), to act against the interests of their principal or employer, or to show favour or disfavour to a particular party in the business dealings of their principal. This is an indictable offence, and the penalty imposed can be up to five years in prison with both the agent/employee and the person making the offer subject to be charged. In addition, there are specific offences related to agents involved in unique activities such as fraudulently dealing with minerals; title documents to land; or participating in, acquiring, or operating premises used for gambling or other prohibited activities. Thus, these agents not only face civil action, including the loss of their commissions for such breaches of fiduciary duty, but also may face criminal prosecution in certain circumstances.

Agent must also exercise reasonable competence and appropriate skill

In addition to a fiduciary duty, the agent also has an obligation to act competently in carrying out those duties. An employee or agent who carelessly performs

CASE SUMMARY 6.4

Ocean City Realty Ltd. v. A & M Holdings Ltd. et al.[5]

An Agent Has a Duty to Disclose

Mrs. Forbes was a salesperson working for Ocean City Realty when she arranged for Halbower to purchase commercial property in Victoria from A & M Holdings. But in order for the deal to proceed, the purchaser, Halbower, insisted that Mrs. Forbes surrender half of her commission to them. She agreed to do this but did not inform the seller. When A & M Holdings found out about this secret deal between her and the purchaser, they refused to pay her any commission, claiming she had breached her fiduciary duty. Even though A & M Holdings didn't lose any money because of

(continued)

5. (1987), 36 D.L.R. (4th) 94 (B.C.C.A.).

this arrangement, the court agreed that she had breached her duty to her principal. Mrs. Forbes had a fiduciary duty to disclose all pertinent information, and it was up to the principal to decide what information was important. Because of this failure, she was not entitled to any commission on the deal. This case illustrates just how far a fiduciary is required to go in looking after the best interests of the principal.

CASE SUMMARY 6.4 Ocean City Realty Ltd. v. A & M Holdings Ltd. et al.

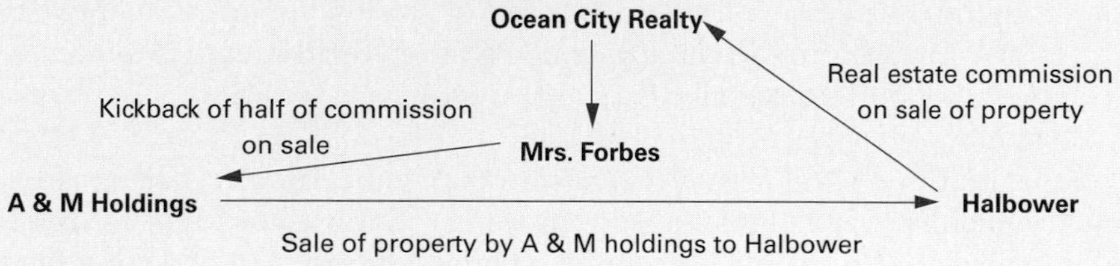

his or her responsibilities, causing the employer or principal losses, may be required to pay compensation in a negligence or breach of contract action brought by the principal or employer.

It should also be noted that it is the agent's job to carry out the responsibilities assigned to him or her. As a general rule the agent cannot delegate those responsibilities to others. There are many exceptions to this rule, usually based on industry practice. Thus, it is common for real estate agents to use sub-agents to fulfill their responsibility. Accountants and lawyers will also normally involve others in fulfilling their responsibilities to their clients.

In general, an agent cannot delegate

ENDING THE AGENCY RELATIONSHIP

An agent's actual authority to act for the principal will normally be terminated when the job is finished, when the agent receives different instructions from the principal, or when the employment or agency relationship is changed or terminated. The authority to act will also end where the project involved becomes illegal or the principal dies, goes bankrupt, or becomes insane.

Agency ends with termination of authority

Death, bankruptcy, or insanity terminates authority . . .

Many jurisdictions now permit a power of attorney to be created that will continue after the principal becomes mentally incapacitated, thus allowing a trusted friend or relative to manage the incapacitated principal's affairs. This usually must be done under the supervision of a public trustee or some other government official.

Although an agent's actual authority may be terminated in this way, that is not to say that the principal will avoid being responsible for the agent's actions under the principle of apparent authority. This is one reason the principal should avoid the creation of such apparent authority in the first place. Where that is not possible, the employer must take steps to notify all customers and suppliers who would normally deal with the agent that the relationship has been terminated. Letters, faxes, or emails indicating that the agent or employee in question no longer represents

But apparent authority may continue

the business should be sent to all those potentially dealing with the business. Direct notification is best, but where that is not possible an advertisement to that effect may help to avoid future difficulties. Often this is done in trade publications associated with the particular industry or by placing a notice in a local newspaper.

Employment

Contract law applies to employment

To review, employment is based on a special relationship that is historically recognized as one of master and servant. That term catches the essence of this special relationship, which involves unique obligations of commitment, duty, and loyalty. Today, the employment relationship is based on contract, and normal contract law applies—especially to the employment's creation, the duties to be performed, and the consideration. As well, the special rules associated with master/servant law still apply.

There are three main areas with which we are concerned regarding employment. The common law of master/servant applies in those areas that are not covered by collective bargaining and where no unions are involved. It deals primarily with the law of termination and wrongful dismissal. There has also been a considerable amount of legislation passed that deals with employee rights and benefits, and this will be the second topic of discussion in this section. Finally, we will look at those special relationships where collective bargaining determines the workplace environment, and where unions and management must comply with the law set out in specialized statutes.

Specialized statutes have own definitions of employment

The first question to be determined is whether or not an employment relationship exists. Today there are many statutes in place that provide a definition of employment, such as the *Employment Standards Act,* the *Workers' Compensation Act,* and the *Employment Insurance Act.* These are important, but the definition given is restricted to the operation of the particular statute within which it is found. No general statutory definition of employment is provided. The reason it is important to determine whether an employment relationship exists outside of these statutes is usually to determine the extent of the employer's liability for wrongful acts committed by their employees. As discussed above, such vicarious liability is usually restricted to the employment relationship, with the employer being responsible for wrongful acts of employees that are committed in the course of carrying out that employment. The injured victim can seek redress from both the employee who caused the injury and the employer who profited from the work being performed. Since the employer is usually in a much better position to pay such compensation, it is vital, from the point of view of the victim, that an employment relationship be established.

Vicarious liability based primarily on employment

Historically, the test used to determine employment was based on the degree of **control** exercised. Independent contractors work for themselves, doing the job agreed to in the contract. They control their own hours and how they do the work. Employees, on the other hand, work for and under the direction of the employer and can be told not only what to do, but how to do it. If a painter was hired as an employee to paint an apartment building, he would be expected to come to work at a specified time, take limited breaks during the day, and leave for the night when instructed. He could also be told which rooms to do first and even the length of brush stokes to use in the process, whereas a painter hired as an independent contractor would have agreed to do the job and to meet certain specifica-

Employment exists when employee can be told what to do and how to do it

FIGURE 6.5 Employee v. Contractor

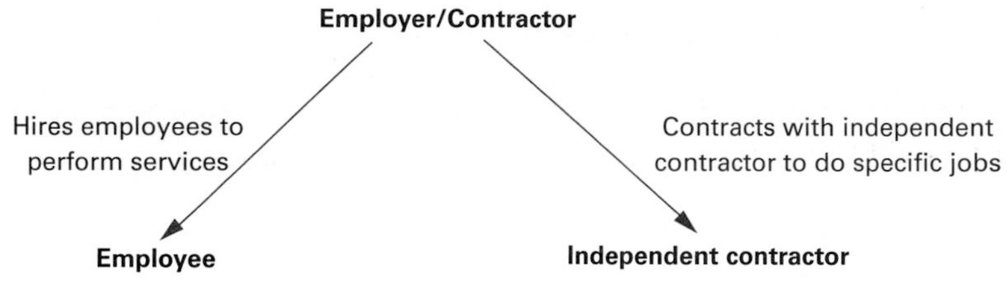

tions such as colour, number of coats, and quality of paint. But since the painter would be working for himself, he would determine the hours of work and process used. So long as the painter finishes by the time specified and does an adequate job, the owner of the property would have no complaint. Thus, the employee is subject to rules and control whereas the contractor is independent of those controls (see Figure 6.5).

Sometimes this control test is not adequate for determining employment, and so a supplemental test has been developed based on an employee's relationship to the business. This is called the **organization test**. If the individual is found to be an integral and essential part of the business organization, he or she is an employee for purposes of vicarious liability, even though the actual control exercised over him or her is limited. A salesperson may look like an independent contractor selling by commission only, supplying her own car, and determining her own hours. But if she can only sell for that one business, must report to it for sales meetings, has an office or desk located at the business, and is part of the main sales force, then she can be said to be an integral part of that organization and an employee of the business. The employer will be held vicariously liable for wrongful acts committed in the process of this employment. But remember that the employer will only be responsible for conduct that takes place while on the job and not when the employee is "on a frolic of her own."

Employment exists when employee is an essential element of employer's organization

Employer liable for torts of employee within scope of employment

As far as the liability for contracts entered into by an employee, that is entirely based on the principles of agency discussed above. If the employee were acting within the authority given, either actual or apparent, the employer is responsible for contracts entered into by that employee.

Employer liable for contracts of employee/agent acting within authority

Few disputes arise with respect to the on-going employment relationship outside of organized trade union activity, which will be discussed below. That is not surprising, since it is doubtful that the employment relationship would survive such a dispute. Consequently, most disputes resolve with the ending of the employment relationship. In general, one can say that an employer has an obligation to provide a safe workplace, appropriate direction, tools where appropriate, wages, and reimbursement for expenses as well as any other specific obligations set out in the employment contract. The employee must be reasonably competent, have the skills claimed, and must also be honest, punctual, loyal, and perform the work agreed to. Where the employee is a manager or key employee, there may be a fiduciary duty owed to the employer, but generally there is no fiduciary duty owed by an ordinary employee.

Only managers or key employees have fiduciary duty

CASE SUMMARY 6.5

Barton Insurance Brokers Ltd. v. Irwin et al.[6]

When Does an Employee Owe a Fiduciary Duty?

Mrs. Irwin left Barton Insurance Brokers Ltd., where she had worked several years as an office administrator, and went to work for a rival company. Barton claimed she was misusing confidential information—Barton's customer lists—in her new job. It turned out that she was simply using her memory to solicit Barton's customers, but they still sought an injunction to stop her. The court had to determine whether there was a general obligation on an employee not to use information obtained in prior employment. The court held that there was no general fiduciary duty in these circumstances. Free competition was encouraged and required that no such general restrictions be imposed. Note that had there been a restrictive covenant in Mrs. Irwin's employment contract or if she had been a key employee or manager, the results could have been different. Also, if she had actually taken a copy of the customer list when she left her former employment, the action brought against her would likely have been successful.

EMPLOYMENT STANDARDS

It should be noted at this stage that there has been a considerable body of specialized legislation passed in all jurisdictions to govern the workplace. Human rights legislation prohibits discrimination and harassment in the workplace; workers' compensation provides health and safety regulations and compensation where accidents take place. Employment insurance provides benefits to workers between jobs, but most importantly employment standards legislation sets minimum standards that employers must adhere to with respect to hours worked, overtime, minimum wages, termination allowance, pregnancy and other leaves, and other similar on-the-job restrictions and requirements. This will be expanded on under "Other Legislation" on page 156.

Termination

For our purposes the most important aspect of the law of master/servant relates to the termination of that employment and the notice that must be given, usually by the employer (see Figure 6.6). Normally, in the absence of "just cause" the employer is required to give an employee reasonable notice of termination, unless there has been agreement otherwise. The employment contract itself sometimes contains terms with respect to the ending of the employment relationship. Often a person will be hired for a set time or for the duration of some project such as the building of a bridge. When that time expires or the project is completed, the employment will end according to the terms in the agreement. No further notice is necessary, unless required by statute. Of course, the parties can always mutually

Employment contract may be for specific period

But statutory requirements must be met

6. (1999), 170 D.L.R. (4th) 69 (B.C.C.A.).

FIGURE 6.6 Notice of Termination of Employment

Common law notice period may be up to 2 years if long employment

Statutory period is less but common law prevails

Contract provision is void if less than statutory period, otherwise it prevails over common law

agree to end the employment relationship, and providing both agree, there will be no further obligation unless imposed by statute. Sometimes the contract will provide for a set amount of notice that must be given in the event of termination by either the employee or the employer, and that agreed-upon period will prevail over the "reasonable notice" normally required under the common law. For example, where an employer gives an employee only three months' notice of termination as specified in the employment contract, that provision will prevail even where long-term employees working for 20 or 30 years are being terminated. Normally, they would be entitled to considerably more notice but they will be bound by the terms of the employment contract, providing no statutory minimum notice requirement is breached. The employment standards acts in place in most Canadian jurisdictions set out a minimum amount of notice that must be given by an employer when terminating the employment of an employee. This ranges usually from one week up to a maximum of eight weeks in British Columbia and Ontario, for example, depending on the length of employment. Note that in British Columbia this eight-week period is referred to as a maximum, but in section 9 of that Act it makes it clear that all standards set out in the Act are only a minimum. If there are higher standards, either in other statutes or at common law, those higher standards will prevail. This is the essence of the decision of the Supreme Court of Canada in the *Machtinger* case set out below. These statutes also make it clear that any attempt to contract out of their provisions will be void.

Notice requirement may be set out in contract

CASE SUMMARY 6.6

Lefebvre v. HOJ Industries Ltd.; Machtinger v. HOJ Industries Ltd.[7]

Contractual Attempts to Limit Notice Period Must Be Very Carefully Drafted

After working for HOJ Industries for seven years, Lefebvre's employment was terminated with only four weeks' notice. In fact, an employment contract he had signed entitled him to only two weeks' notice, but the employer extended this to four weeks,

(continued)

7. (1992), 91 D.L.R. (4th) 491 (S.C.C.).

which was the stated minimum amount required at that time under the Ontario *Employment Standards Act*. Lefebvre sued, claiming he should have been given reasonable notice under the common law which would have been seven and one-half months. The Supreme Court of Canada determined that the contractual notice period was void, as it was in conflict with the statute and had no effect on this case. Since the common law notice (reasonable notice) was higher then the statutory minimum and under the statute the higher standard was to prevail, Lefebvre was awarded damages amounting to seven and one-half months' notice or pay in lieu. Note that had the stated contractual notice requirement been greater than that required in the *Employment Standards Act*, that contractual period would have prevailed.

Employer must provide reasonable notice of termination

Or provide pay in lieu of notice

Reasonable notice requirement can be extensive

In most situations an employment relationship will be on-going with no provision made for the termination of that employment. In these circumstances, under the common law an employer must give the employee **reasonable notice** of the termination, unless there is just cause. Most of the litigation with respect to wrongful dismissal involves disputes over the adequacy of the notice to terminate given to the employee. It should be noted at the outset that it is notice or pay in lieu of notice that must be given. Where six months' notice is required, the employer is free to pay the employee what would have been earned in that six-month period and terminate immediately. Many employers, especially those subjected to American influences where notice periods are shorter, are surprised to discover that notice periods of four or five months for long-term employees are inadequate. In Canada the required notice will be based on such factors as length of service, the importance of the job, the age of the employee, and the likelihood of finding other employment. The longer the service and the more important the job, the longer the notice period must be. Where long-term employment is involved, the required notice can approach two years. A very rough rule of thumb might be one month for every year of employment, but remember that other factors may affect the amount of notice required. Don't confuse the statutory notice periods discussed above with this higher level of reasonable notice required under the common law. People often think when they are given the shorter statutory notice that is the extent of their entitlement. But that statutory notice period is only a minimum and will be overridden by the longer reasonable notice requirement under the common law. Only where there is a contractual provision that is equal to or greater than the specified statutory notice requirement will the common law reasonable notice requirement be overridden. These relationships are illustrated in Figure 6.6 above. Note as well that the amount that must be paid is more than just the actual wages that would have been earned; it also includes benefits and even bonuses when they are normally paid to all employees and not based on merit.

It would be a mistake for an employer to assume that these extreme amounts must be offered to all terminated employees. Often the employee will be willing to settle for considerably less, since he or she will get the money right away, avoid the costs of litigation and lawyers' fees, and will avoid having his or her payout reduced by income from other employment (the obligation to mitigate). Still, if the matter does go to court, it is important to consider that judgments involving these considerable amounts are a potential outcome. It is also important to make the parting of an employee as painless as possible, not just to avoid confrontation and potential lawsuits, but because it is the right thing to do. Great care should be taken not to add to the trauma of the terminated employee, but to provide assistance in counselling, upgrading, and in finding alternate employment. Just as there are consulting services that provide assistance in finding and hiring key personnel, there are also those that assist in the process of easing redundant employees out the door with as little pain as possible. Human resources departments today should have specialists in place to assist in this process.

An employer is not required to give any notice of termination where there has been **just cause** on the part of the employee. If the employee has stolen from or otherwise been dishonest with the employer, has acted immorally, or has been convicted of some crime that will interfere with his or her ability to perform the job, has disobeyed a lawful instruction from the employer, or has committed some actionable wrong while on the job, these can amount to just cause supporting immediate dismissal without notice or other compensation. Where an employee lies on a resumé and the employer finds out, that destroys trust and amounts to just cause.

No notice required where just cause]

Employee incompetence will also be just cause, but employers often lose the right to dismiss an employee on this ground because of their own past conduct. Where they have given annual raises or bonuses to the employee, they have led that employee to believe that the level of performance was adequate. In the process employers lose the ability to claim incompetence. When faced with such a problem, the employer should clearly inform the employee of his or her shortcomings with respect to the job and give the employee a chance to improve before proceeding to termination. Hopefully, there will be in place some form of regular employee evaluation, which will identify problems before they become too serious. The employee will then be invited to participate in making a plan to overcome that problem or shortcoming, including making concrete attainable goals such as taking courses, sensitivity training, and the like. Where the employee follows through and overcomes the problem, the business has regained a valuable employee. But where that employee fails to meet the goals after being given the opportunity and help to improve, the employer is on much more solid ground when the employment is terminated.

Incompetence often difficult to establish

Historically, illness that prevented an employee from working provided just cause for dismissal. Although this is not the fault of the employee, if he or she can no longer do the job, the employment contract has been frustrated. Today, human rights legislation requires that the employer make all reasonable efforts to accommodate a disabled employee. If that employee can do some work, the employer should find the individual a job that he or she can do—even if it is part time—providing it doesn't place an unreasonable burden on the business. Today, long-term disability plans and pensions go a long way to overcome the dilemma posed by sick employees who can no longer work.

Reasonable accommodation required for disabled workers

Lack of work because of a downturn in the economy does not amount to just cause for dismissal. That is not to say that an employer cannot terminate employees when the need arises, but the employer must provide reasonable notice and satisfy other statutory requirements. Often such conditions prompt a layoff where the employment is suspended until there is more work to do. Note that the employee is entitled to treat such long-term lay-offs as termination, which triggers the above-mentioned employer obligations of notice and severance pay.

Lack of work is not just cause

WRONGFUL DISMISSAL

A wrongful dismissal action in Canada almost always involves a dispute over whether an adequate amount of notice or pay in lieu has been given by the employer to the employee. Either the employer is claiming just cause and has given no notice at all, or the employee is claiming that although she received some notice or severance, it was not enough. When just cause is claimed, the court must determine whether that was enough to constitute just cause for termination of the employment. What constitutes just cause was outlined above. If any of these elements are present, even if discovered after the termination has taken place, the employee will fail in her wrongful dismissal action. However, if the employer has done something—such as the payment of a bonus—to encourage the employee to think that her level of performance was adequate, the employer will be prevented from relying on incompetence to justify the termination.

Wrongful dismissal damages based on what notice should have been given

When an employee does sue for wrongful dismissal, the compensation claimed is usually based on what should have been earned, given the difference between the amounts of notice the employee was given and what she should have been given. Thus, if the employee received two months' notice and should have been given 10, the employee will claim an amount of damages equivalent to what she would have earned in that extra eight months. The compensation may also be increased on the basis of how that termination took place. Employers sometimes try to justify the termination on the basis of just cause such as theft or lying, when there is none. The employer may also degrade the employee or otherwise harm her reputation, publicly causing further mental anguish. Today, the courts will take these aggravating factors into consideration and award a longer period of compensation. The Supreme Court of Canada in *Wallace v. United Grain Growers Ltd.*[8] decided that it was appropriate for the court to take into consideration the way that the employee was terminated—including any mental distress caused—and extend the notice period required accordingly. The amount of compensation awarded will also take into account regular bonuses that would have been given as well as the benefits that have been lost such as pension contribution and medical coverage. Sometimes individuals, such as managers, will defame the employee making untruthful allegations to justify the termination. When that happens, the employee may be able to bring a separate defamation action against that individual.

Bad faith of employer may justify extended notice period

Terminated employee must mitigate loss

On the other hand, the employee must make a reasonable effort to mitigate her losses. The employee must try to get another job; damages will be reduced by whatever she earns from this other employment during the notice period. The employee who should have received ten months' notice and only received two would have a right to claim for the difference. But if the employee made the required attempt and found other employment after three months at the same rate of pay or higher, she would be entitled to only one month's additional compensation, making the wrongful dismissal action a waste of time and resources.

Note that reinstatement is generally not an option in a wrongful dismissal action because in most cases the employer could have dismissed the employee by giving proper notice. Hence, the remedy given is the award of the amount of payment needed to compensate for the lack of notice. Reinstatement is a possibility where a statutory requirement has been breached, such as dismissing an employee because of pregnancy or some other human rights violation. Also, where collective bargaining is involved and an employee is terminated, often the grievance procedure gives the arbitrator the power to reinstate. Even in these situations, there is usually a reluctance to order reinstatement because of the serious deterioration that has taken place with respect to the relationship between the parties.

---

8. [1997] 3 S.C.R. 701, 152 D.L.R. (4th) 1 (S.C.C.).

CASE SUMMARY 6.7

Simpson v. Consumers' Association of Canada[9]

Inappropriate Sexual Comments and Conduct Can Constitute Just Cause for Termination

Mr. Simpson was the executive director of the Consumers' Association of Canada and over the years had been involved in many sexually inappropriate situations with several different female employees. After several complaints, he was dismissed from his employment for cause. He sued for wrongful dismissal, claiming he should have been given reasonable notice. At trial it was held that since these activities took place outside the workplace, they were not just cause for dismissal and he was awarded damages equivalent to 18 months' notice. On appeal, the court rejected this position finding that the various incidents did take place at job-related activities and constituted just cause. His conduct could not be justified as part of a sexually charged atmosphere at work since he was the cause of that situation. Nor could he rely on the fact that there was no sexual harassment policy in place, since it was his obligation as manager to prevent this sort of thing from happening. Even long-term senior employees can be terminated without notice if they sexually harass other employees.

CONSTRUCTIVE DISMISSAL

Sometimes by demoting, transferring, or otherwise changing the employment conditions, an employer will try to make an employee so uncomfortable that he or she will quit, thus avoiding the requirements of notice and termination. This is a dangerous course of action, since the courts recognize such subterfuge as *constructive dismissal*. Whether done intentionally or simply as part of the restructuring of the business, it is the employer who has created a situation that makes it difficult or impossible for the employee to continue. Consequently, it is the employer who has breached the employment contract, not the employee, by refusing the change or by quitting. The employee can successfully sue for wrongful dismissal in such circumstances. Of course, if the employee agrees to the change, there is no problem. Also, the employee's obligation to mitigate may require him or her to take the alternate position unless the atmosphere has been so poisoned or the potential harm to his or her reputation makes such an option impractical.

Wrongful dismissal may take form of constructive dismissal

Examples of constructive dismissal include: dismissal of an employee for refusing to relocate when that was not included as a term of the contract when hired; termination upon refusal of a foreman in a paper mill to be on call every sixth weekend without pay; and the refusal of an employee to take a lower paying position because of company downsizing. But a refusal by the employer to allow an employee to change her work hours to attend bible college was not constructive dismissal. The following case is also a good example of constructive dismissal as well as other things.

9. (2001), 209 D.L.R. (4th) 214 (Ont. C.A.).

CASE SUMMARY 6.8

Lane v. Carson Group Inc.[10]

Change in Territory Amounts to Constructive Dismissal

Patrick Lane had worked as a salesman for the defendant for 25 years; he had a territory covering all of the Atlantic Provinces. Some adjustments had been made over the years, but all with consultation and his consent. In 2000, a new sales manager first refused to pay for Mr. Lane's travel expenses that had been paid in the past and then reduced his assigned territory substantially by assigning Newfoundland and Cape Breton to another salesperson. That represented 25 to 30 percent of his income. In response to these actions by the new sales manager, Mr. Lane resigned. He then brought this action for wrongful dismissal.

The court held that the change in the payment of travel expenses and the reduction of Mr. Lane's territory without consent amounted to a breach of his employment contract and constituted constructive dismissal. Since Mr. Lane had been employed for 25 years, he was entitled to 24 months' notice. On that basis the plaintiff was awarded $333 000. Note that the original employment contract provided that Mr. Lane was entitled to only two weeks' notice, but the judge determined that this provision was harsh and ludicrous considering the plaintiff's 25 years of employment. Also, because of subsequent changes in that contract without any reference to this two-week notice provision, the judge said that that provision "had been overtaken by events" and no longer applied. Failure to mitigate was also argued, but the judge found that Mr. Lane had made every reasonable effort to find alternate employment but was unable to do so.

This case not only illustrates constructive dismissal, but also the amount of notice considered reasonable, and how damages are calculated where long-term employment is involved.

TERMINATION BY THE EMPLOYEE

Finally, it is necessary to look at termination of employment by the employee. The employee has a right to quit for cause when he or she is given dangerous or illegal instructions, is not properly paid, is put into dangerous situations, can no longer perform his or her duties because of disability or illness, or where important terms of the employment contract are otherwise breached. Where the employment contract or other subsequent agreement provides for notice or has other terms relating to termination, those provisions will prevail.

Employee can quit where just cause

Or pursuant to contract provision

Usually, however, there is no such provision and the employee, like the employer, is required to give reasonable notice of termination. What constitutes reasonable notice on the part of the employee, however, is considerably less, unless that employee plays some special role so that his or her leaving on short notice would be particularly damaging to the employer. This might be the case

10. 208 N.S.R. (2d) 60, 2002 NSSC 218, [2002] N.S.J. No. 428 (N.S.S.C.).

where the employee is a manager or salesperson having exclusive dealings with the company's customers or where the employee had some particular skill or expertise that would be difficult to replace. Even then, it is unlikely that lengthy periods of notice would be required. It is normally easier for a company to replace a long-term employee than it is for that employee to find another job.

Otherwise employee must also provide reasonable notice

Often, however, employees are liable to their employers for wrongful or inappropriate conduct when leaving. When they leave to work for a competitor they sometimes take with them confidential customer lists, secret formulas or practices, or other information the disclosure of which causes harm to the former employer's competitive position. Sometimes employees, while still employed, will approach the customers and try to persuade them to go with them to their new business. Such activities may amount to a breach of trust, a breach of fiduciary duty, or a violation of the duty of confidentiality and could be the cause of legal action by the employer.

Employees liable for misuse of confidential information or other wrong

Often an employment contract will contain a restrictive covenant preventing an employee, upon termination, from working in a similar industry for a period of time. Such provisions are designed to prevent unfair competition by those employees or the disclosure or misuse of confidential information to competitors. As discussed in Chapter 3, such restrictive covenants must be reasonable in that they must be necessary to protect a valid interest of the employer and go no further than necessary to accomplish that goal. In determining the reasonableness of the provision in the employment contract, the court will also look at the effect it has on the employee. If it prevents the employee from working in his or her profession, it is less likely to be enforced. The case set out below illustrates the reluctance of the court to enforce such provisions on employees.

CASE SUMMARY 6.9

947535 Ontario Ltd. v. Jex[11]

Unreasonable Restrictive Covenants Void

The defendants were employed as tax consultants in an H & R Block franchise owned by the plaintiff in Owen Sound, Ontario. They were long-time employees but were terminated every year at the end of tax season and later rehired for the next. In 1993, the franchise was sold and when the employees were hired back they were required to sign a non-competition agreement as part of their renewed employment. This provision required them not to prepare any tax returns or solicit any of the company's clients for two years after termination within the city or for a distance of 40 kilometres from the city limits. In January 2000, instead of going back to work for the owners of the franchise, they opened up a new business in direct competition next door to where they used to work. That year they served 562 former clients of their previous employer. This action was brought by the current owner of the franchise seeking an injunction. Among other things the court had to deal with the reasonable-

(continued)

11. (2003), 37 B.L.R. (3d) 152 (Ont. S.C.J.).

ness of the restrictive covenant. The court held that not only was the distance limitation unreasonable, but also the two-year restriction. The actual franchise from H & R Block only gave the plaintiff a right to operate within the city limits of Owen Sound. And although the distance included a department store where the plaintiffs operated another similar business, the defendants never worked at that location and so could not unreasonably compete. The court determined that the 40 kilometre distance from the city limits was too broad and unreasonable. The court also found that since the defendants were only temporary employees hired and terminated each year, the two-year restriction was also too broad and unreasonable. There were additional reasons for the decision, but the case clearly illustrates how such non-competition provisions must go no further than necessary to protect the goodwill of the business. Where such provisions are found to be unreasonable they are void, leaving no restrictions at all. Note that the fact that these were only temporary employees was taken into consideration in determining the reasonableness of the provisions.

Collective Bargaining

Workers band together to combat poor working conditions

Violence associated with trade union movement

Canada follows American approach

Certification process reduces confrontation

Low wages and poor working conditions prompted workers to band together in the 19th century in an effort to improve their lot. The resulting trade unions were initially resisted, sometimes violently, but throughout the 20th century they managed to achieve respectability and acceptance The passage of the U.S. *National Labor Relations Act* (the *Wagner Act*) of 1935 (after which Canadian labour legislation was patterned) was designed to put an end to labour strife. The Act recognized the employees' right to organize collectively, but required the union to show they had the support of a majority of the workers. Once majority support was established, the union was certified as the exclusive bargaining agent for the employees, and the employer could then deal only with the union. In all jurisdictions in Canada labour relations boards have been established to handle disputes arising with respect to collective bargaining and related labour matters. See Table 6.2 for a summary of the types of disputes and their consequences.

ORGANIZATION

Employees have right to bargain collectively

All Canadian jurisdictions recognize that there is a general right for employees to be members of a trade union and to bargain collectively through a bargaining agent. Management, however, is normally excluded from the bargaining unit and some categories of employees such as police, firefighters, and health workers who provide essential services will usually have only limited rights to take job action.

A trade union seeking recognition as the bargaining agent for a group of employees must make application to the labour relations board for **certification**. They must show that they have a certain portion of the designated workforce signed up as members of the union, for example, 45 percent in British Columbia and 40 percent in Ontario and similar percentages in other provinces. The process usually begins with disgruntled employees approaching a union such as the Teamsters, or union organizers will approach the employees to sign them up as members. In most cases, this won't take place on the employer's premises or during

TABLE 6.2 Types of Disputes and the Consequences

Recognition dispute	To get the employer to bargain with the union instead of individual employees	Certification process
Jurisdictional dispute	Rival unions contend over who should do what job or who should represent workers	Certification process or application to board
Rights dispute	Disagreement over the meaning of terms in the collective agreement	Grievance procedure and ultimately arbitration
Interest dispute	Disagreement over what should be included in the next collective agreement	Mediation and ultimately strike, lockout, and picketing

working hours, although an employer will sometimes allow it to keep on good terms with the union and to be aware of what is happening. Historically, most of the violence took place at this stage in the process (called a **recognition dispute**), but today this is all dealt with through the certification process. Often a company will have several different categories of employees, and they will be represented by different unions. Disputes can arise between these different trade unions as to which body should represent a particular group of workers or which union's members ought to be doing a particular job. For example, should the member of the carpenters' union install the new metal studs in a building or should this be done by a steelworker? This is called a **jurisdictional dispute** and is also resolved by application to the labour relations board. Once the particular bargaining unit has been identified and the requisite number of employees signed up, an application is made to the board for certification of the union as the bargaining agent for that group of employees. In some jurisdictions if the union can show they have signed up a large number of employees (over 50 percent federally[12]), the union can be certified without a vote. But in most jurisdictions the next step requires that a government supervised certification vote take place. There are some jurisdictional differences, but normally if a majority of those voting support union representation, the union is then certified as the official bargaining agent for those employees. The result is that the employer from that point on must deal with the union exclusively, and can no longer make separate deals with individual workers.

Recognition disputes reduced through certification process

Jurisdictional disputes also resolved through certification or by application to board

Certification requires signing up members and making an application

Followed by government supervised vote

Certification granted with majority vote

Even though it is a right for employees to be represented by a union and to bargain collectively, some employers will attempt to interfere with the process. Trying to intimidate or threaten employees, creating employer-dominated bargaining units, or even changing pay or conditions of work to undermine the certification drive are usually considered **unfair labour practices** and prohibited. Firing employees for their union activities is not only a violation of labour legislation, but under section 425 of the *Criminal Code* it is a criminal offence for an employer to fire or refuse to hire someone because of his or her trade union activity or to threaten or otherwise intimidate employees from joining a trade union. It is also a criminal offence for employers to conspire together to do those things. This refers to the past practice of creating a blacklist of employees in a particular industry. These acts are punishable as summary conviction offences with the

Intimidation and coercion prohibited

12. *Canada Labour Code,* R.S.C. 1985, c. L-2, ss. 28-29.

potential of up to a two-year prison term. In the face of such unfair labour practices, in some jurisdictions the board can certify the union without a vote if it is convinced that it is no longer possible to determine the true feelings of the workforce through a representative vote. Still, freedom of speech is guaranteed in the *Charter of Rights and Freedoms* and the employer retains the right to make comments and express opinions with respect to the organization process and its effect on the business, providing those comments don't amount to threats or intimidation.

But employer free to express honest opinions

In some jurisdictions it is possible for a group of employers to band together and be certified as an association for bargaining purposes. An example in British Columbia is the Forest Industrial Relations or FIR, an association of forest companies that bargain with the forestry unions through a common bargaining agent.

BARGAINING

Once certified, the process of collective bargaining begins. Either party can serve notice on the other to commence bargaining. Then representatives from both parties meet and negotiate with the object of reaching a collective agreement. When they do reach an agreement, it must be presented to the members of the union—the employees—for a ratification vote. If there is an employer association involved, they too must ratify the contract, and once ratified there is a binding collective agreement in place. Often, however, there is a deadlock. One of the important developments in Canadian law has been the imposition of mediation, sometimes referred to as conciliation, into the process. Either party or the government can request the intervention of a mediator who will assist the parties in their efforts to reach an agreement. The mediator acts as a go-between, trying to find common ground between the parties. During this mediation process neither party can take any further job action. If mediation is successful, a collective agreement will result, but if the mediator feels that his or her efforts are no longer helpful, the mediator will "book out" of the dispute. The parties are then free to take further job action.

Parties must bargain in good faith

Mediation available to assist bargaining

If they do reach an agreement, there are some mandatory provisions that must be included. For example, any dispute that arises after the agreement is in place (called a **rights dispute**) must be handled through a grievance process set out in the contract itself and culminating in arbitration of the dispute. Strikes and lockouts are not permitted to resolve disputes with respect to current collective agreements. When such a strike does take place it is referred to as an illegal strike or a wildcat strike, and the court will have little hesitation in issuing an injunction to bring it to an end. A collective agreement must be for a period of at least one year. Normally, a prior agreement will expire before serious bargaining takes place. As a result, when a new agreement is finally reached, it will be applied retroactive to the expiration of the prior agreement. Thus, even with the minimum one-year requirement, the parties can find themselves back into bargaining almost immediately.

Contract must provide for arbitration of rights dispute

Agreement must be at least for one year

Once an agreement is in place and the parties have become used to bargaining with each other, subsequent collective bargaining will often be accomplished in a more orderly fashion. But often reaching the first agreement poses difficult if not insurmountable obstacles; because of this, in most jurisdictions the labour relations board retains the right to impose a first contract. Often just the threat of this will encourage the parties to be reasonable and conclude an agreement without the need for such intervention.

First contract can be imposed

Unions will often insist that a **union shop** clause, which requires any future employees to join the union, be included in their agreements. Sometimes the contract will require that only members of a union be hired. This is called a **closed shop** agreement. Dockworkers, who are sent out to a job from a union hiring hall, are an example of this arrangement. A compromise where employees don't have to join the union is referred to as a **Rand Formula** agreement. In this form of collective agreement employees need not be members of the union, but they must pay dues and are subject to the terms of the collective agreement negotiated. Most collective agreements will also have a clause requiring the employer to deduct union dues directly off the employees' pay (a **check-off** provision). This has the advantage of saving the union from the trouble of collecting dues directly from their members, some of whom may not be enthusiastic about contributing.

Employees can be required to join a union, with the employer collecting dues

JOB ACTION

If the parties cannot reach an agreement, normally a strike or lockout will follow. Such actions are only permitted where there is an **interest dispute**, which is a dispute over the terms to be included into the new collective agreement. After the parties have bargained in good faith, and all mediators involved have booked out without an agreement reached, each party is free to serve **notice** (72 hours in British Columbia) on the other of a strike or lockout. A **strike** involves the employees withdrawing their services by stopping work, although this may not involve closing down the whole operation. Often only some workers will be pulled off the job in different locations for study sessions, rotating, or escalating strike action, to put further pressure on the employer. A **lockout** involves the employer closing down the operation and denying work to the employees. This is often done to control the timing of the work stoppage, so that it will have the least possible impact on the business, for instance, when stockpiles of products have been accumulated. Note that once such notice has been given, the job action need not necessarily commence at the expiration of the notice period. Often the continuing threat of immediate job action will be used as a pressure tactic at the bargaining table during negotiations. Employee benefits such as health, dental, and insurance coverage will normally continue while the strike or lockout continues, but the union will have to pay the entire amount.

Interest dispute may lead to strike or lockout

Employees must give notice of strike

Employers must give notice of lockout

CASE SUMMARY 6.10

United Food and Commercial Workers, Local 1518 v. KMart Canada Ltd. et al.[13]

Right of Expression Protected by *Charter*

Employees lawfully on strike at one KMart department store decided to pass out leaflets at another KMart location. This was determined to be secondary picketing, and an injunction was imposed to stop the practice. The matter went to the Supreme Court of Canada. The court first determined that handing out leaflets in this way did constitute picketing as defined in the B.C. *Labour Relations Code* and that picketing at a location other than the one struck constituted secondary picketing, which was prohib-

(continued)

13. (1999), 176 D.L.R. (4th) 607 (S.C.C.).

ited under the statute. The court then looked at the definition of picketing in the statute and determined that it was too broad and interfered with the *Charter of Rights* guarantee of freedom of expression. There was no intimidation or physical confrontation here, which was often present with normal picketing, but just the communication of accurate information persuading people not to deal with the store. It was argued that this was a reasonable limit under section 1 of the *Charter* but the Supreme Court found that while restricting secondary picketing might well be upheld as a reasonable limit under section 1, the prohibition against distributing leaflets extended this restriction further than was necessary. The B.C. government was given six months to change the definition of picketing in the statute so as to not include this type of activity.

Employers will usually try to keep the business running with management personnel doing all of the essential jobs, or in those jurisdictions where it is permitted, with replacement workers. Aside from the strike, one of the strongest weapons in the union arsenal is **picketing**. This involves the employees and often other sympathetic union members posting themselves at strategic entrances to a job site (or marching around the job site) carrying signs displaying their grievances and trying to persuade customers, suppliers, and other employees not to deal with the employer. The idea is to shut the business down completely during the duration of the strike or lockout.

Union members can picket during lawful strike

Note that people have the right to cross a picket line if they want to. But sometimes frustration will prevail, and violence or intimidation will take place. Courts and labour boards usually will not tolerate this, and upon application by the employer, they will order the number of picketers limited to a reasonable amount. But there is a strong ethic among union members never to cross a picket line; truck drivers, rail workers, and other union members who would be picking up or delivering will normally not cross a picket line, effectively cutting the business off with the possibility of preventing its continued operation. That is the strength of the strike and picketing process. It is usually very difficult in most jurisdictions for a company to continue its operations once a picket line has been established. In some jurisdictions only the location where the particular group of employees on strike works can be picketed. In others the union can picket anywhere the employer carries on business.

Strong tradition of honouring picket line

Trade unions must be democratic, not discriminate, and properly represent members

Note that trade unions must be democratic and free of discrimination and other human rights violations. They are also required to properly represent their employees in dealings with the employers. If they fail to do so, the legislation permits the dissatisfied employee/union member to bring an action against the union itself for compensation.

Other Legislation

Only a fraction of workers are represented by trade unions, and so a considerable body of employee welfare legislation has been passed in all jurisdictions to protect employee rights and curb abuses by employers. There are many examples of statutes that have been passed to better the plight of workers, both socially and on the job. The original factory conditions that employees found themselves working in during the industrial revolution were often dangerous and unhealthy in the extreme. Employees who became sick or were injured because of conditions on the job were simply terminated and left without recourse or compensation. **Workers' compensation** statutes were designed to overcome those problems. Employers are required to contribute to a fund that works like insurance, providing compensation to workers who become ill or are injured on the job. Sick or injured employees make a claim against the fund for compensation. Workers injured on the job cannot normally sue the employer or a fellow employee who causes them injury. Rather, their recourse is to seek compensation under the workers' compensation legislation.

Workers' compensation statutes compensate injured workers

A second aspect of workers' compensation legislation, often contained in a separate statute, authorizes a government-appointed body to set and enforce health and safety standards in the workplace. This includes rules with respect to matters such as ventilation. The use of safety equipment (including hard hats, safety shoes, railings, harnesses, and the like) is enforced by inspectors who have the authority to levy penalties and even close the job down where necessary.

Occupational health and safety statutes ensure worker safety

Employment insurance legislation is designed to provide a soft landing for those who are laid off. Both the employer and employees contribute to a fund. When laid off, the employee makes a claim and receives a set payment for a designated number of weeks to help bridge the gap until he or she finds other work. Also the **human rights legislation** discussed in Chapter 1 has its greatest application in the field of employment. Discrimination on the basis of race, religion, ethnic origin, gender, disability, and sexual orientation with regard to hiring, promotion, or any other aspect of employment is prohibited, as is sexual harassment. All complaints go to human rights boards, which have broad powers of investigation and enforcement.

Employment insurance statutes helps workers between jobs

Human rights statutes protect workers discriminated against in employment

CASE SUMMARY 6.11

Central Okanagan School District No. 23 v. Renaud[14]

Both Employer and Union Must Respect Human Rights

As part of his employment with the Okanagan School District, Mr. Renaud was required to work on Friday nights, contrary to his beliefs as a member of the Seventh Day Adventist Church which prohibit working at this time. When other arrangements that Mr. Renaud made with the employer to accommodate his beliefs were presented to the union, it refused to agree because they conflicted with the terms of the collective agreement. Mr. Renaud complained to the Human Rights Commission and the dispute eventually went to the Supreme Court of Canada, which found that the school board had a duty to accommodate Mr. Renaud's religious beliefs and that they had failed to do so. The fact that the union did not agree to the change in shift was not sufficient reason for the refusal, since the union's only recourse would have been to file a grievance, which they knew that they would lose. The court pointed out that the employer had a duty to accommodate such religious requirements unless it placed an unreasonable burden on them, and the fact that the union would file a grievance did not constitute such an unreasonable burden. Note that the Supreme Court also found that the union had a duty to accommodate Mr. Renaud's religious beliefs, and their refusal to cooperate with the change of shift was a violation of that duty.

14. (1992), 95 D.L.R. (4th) 577 (S.C.C.).

There were once many statutes that imposed standards on the workplace. In each Canadian jurisdiction they have been brought together into one statute (called the ***Employment Standards Act*** in British Columbia and Ontario). The Acts set up standards that apply to all employees and cannot be waived by contract. The only exception is where a collective agreement sets higher general standards. In most jurisdictions these are minimum standards, and if the common law sets a higher standard, for example, with respect to the amount of pay in lieu of notice that must be paid upon termination, that common law standard will prevail. These statutes cover such areas as the amount of notice or pay that must be given in the event of termination; the number of hours to be worked in a day, a week, or a month; what amount of overtime must be paid if these figures are exceeded; pay for statutory holidays and annual vacation; and specified leaves for pregnancy, bereavement, parenting, and the like. These statutes also set up government boards that have the power to hear complaints, investigate, enter the workplace, gather evidence, inspect records, impose penalties, and otherwise enforce the legislation. This discussion is intended to give just a summary of the kinds of provisions that have been enacted. For specifics you should look up the particular statutes that apply in your jurisdiction. Note that contravention by employers of the provisions and standards established under these statutes can constitute a provincial offence and expose the offending party to significant fines, and, in some cases, imprisonment. For example, in the Ontario *Workplace Safety and Insurance Act* fines of up to $25 000 can be imposed on an individual and $100 000 on a corporation. In that province's *Employment Standards Act* the maximum penalty for repeated serious offences can be as high as $500 000 and up to a year in prison.

Employment standards statutes provide for holiday pay, leaves, overtime, termination, etc.

Agency and employment are two of the most important relationships found in business. For most of us employment is the legal relationship that defines our lives and careers. It is hoped that this brief discussion has helped the reader to understand that relationship and encouraged further study.

EMPLOYEE THEFT AND SHOPLIFTING

One of the greatest challenges to many businesses is to deal with shoplifting and employee theft. Shoplifting is generally restricted to retail businesses, but employee theft can apply to almost any endeavour including retail, transportation, and production businesses. In addition to the general offence of theft (section 322 of the *Ciminal Code*), there are a number of specific offences that deal with unique situations and relationships such as theft of telecommunication services, theft by someone holding a power of attorney, and misappropriation of money held as part of the job. There are also a number of offences listed that resemble theft that might be committed by an employee or by someone dealing with the business. Examples include taking a vessel or a motor vehicle without consent; committing a criminal breach of trust involving a trustee by redirecting the subject to the trust for an unauthorized purpose; taking and re-branding cattle; taking possession of drift logs; fraudulently obtaining computer services; and committing various credit card offences. Employees also sometimes sabotage the business by causing some form of physical damage to tools and equipment; interfering with software, data, or computer equipment; or contaminating information or goods. This constitutes mischief (section 430) or one of the various property-related offences discussed in Chapter 8. Most of these theft-like offences, including mischief under section 430, expose the perpetrator to a maxi-

Examples of theft and theft-like activity

mum term of imprisonment of 10 years where the amounts involved exceed $5000 and the Crown proceeds by way of indictment. Shoplifting is also theft, but it usually involves lesser amounts and is punishable by indictment or summary conviction with a term of imprisonment of up to two years.

The challenges for the business relate to detection and prevention. All businesses have to balance the costs of security, surveillance, and enforcement against the losses incurred. Of course, too tight security can also have the negative effect of destroying employee morale and loyalty, and damaging customer goodwill. No one likes going into a store and having his or her bags searched, and the presence of security cameras and other forms of surveillance are sometimes taken by employees as an invitation to try to beat them. It is likely that the best counter to employee theft is the promotion of employee loyalty, but this will depend on the nature of the business. Where small valuable items are involved such as precious jewels, watches, or valuable tools, most employees and customers would expect and tolerate a reasonable amount of surveillance and security, providing it is not too intrusive.

Extensive surveillance often resented

In all cases where surveillance is involved, it is important that employees are made aware of it from the outset; otherwise, there is not only the danger of losing employee loyalty but also of being accused of violating that employee's right to privacy. When countering shoplifting, well-trained security people and other employees are vital. A business will often lose much more as a result of a judgment of assault, defamation, or false imprisonment brought on by an overzealous or misguided employee than from the shoplifting itself.

Employee training vital to avoid litigation

Employee theft and fraud has to be treated somewhat differently. Often the existence of the theft is discovered before anyone in particular is suspected. At this stage the police can be brought in to investigate, but sometimes it is better for internal security people to investigate first. Again, the rights of employees have to be respected. There is no general right to search employees, their lockers, or computers unless there is reasonable grounds to suppose that a particular employee committed the theft being investigated. Police can obtain a search warrant, but that option is not available to managers or even their security services without involving the police. If it is made clear when employees are first employed that there is surveillance in place and that telephones and computers will be monitored, there is little likelihood of infringing on an employee's rights, providing the business owns the phones and computers. But it is doubtful that such notice will entitle an employer to search an employee or his or her locker without police involvement.

Often better to involve police

Of course, where shoplifting or employee theft is involved, prosecution is often not effective due to the high standard of proof that must be established by the prosecution. Another serious disadvantage is the disruption to the business caused by the investigation, evidence gathering, and prosecution process; the long delays; and the damage that the publicity can bring to the business. Often it is better where employees are involved to simply terminate the employee, assuming enough evidence has been gathered to establish just cause. Unless the amounts for a particular individual are significant, it is generally not worth the trouble, time, and expense to pursue theft or frauds by customers in a civil action. For this reason businesses often simply include such shoplifting, customer fraud, and employee theft as a cost of doing business, and add it to the cost of the merchandise or service provided. This, of course, is entirely unsatisfactory but does drive home the importance of putting the emphasis on prevention rather than enforcement.

Termination often only effective remedy for employee theft

If a decision is made not to involve the police, there is the danger of the business itself, the managers, or the owner who made that decision being charged with the criminal offence of obstructing justice. This comes with the potential of 10 years' imprisonment when treated as an indictable offence. For example, suppose an employee has been stealing for some time. When he or she is found out, the employer promises not to tell the police if that employee agrees to repay the money by working longer hours. Or suppose a youthful shoplifter is caught and the parents promise to repay the amount and a fee for overhead if the police are not brought in.[15] This case is likely an obstruction of justice, as it amounts to withholding evidence of a crime from the police. Similarly, where an ad is placed in a newspaper offering a reward for the return of stolen goods "no questions asked," both the person who placed the ad and the business that published it have committed a summary conviction offence under section 143 of the *Criminal Code.*

Legal pitfalls when legal advice or police involvement is lacking

15. *B. (D.C.) v. Arkin* (1996), 138 D.L.R. (4th) 309, [1996] 8 W.W.R. 100 (Man. Q.B.).

QUESTIONS FOR REVIEW

1. Explain why the topics of agency and employment are important with respect to the study of business law.
2. Distinguish between independent contractors, employees, and agents. Explain why that distinction is important.
3. Distinguish between an agent's actual and apparent authority, and explain how that apparent authority may arise.
4. Distinguish between apparent authority and implied authority.
5. Explain what is meant by ratification, how ratification may arise, and its effect on the contracting parties.
6. Explain under what circumstances a principal will be responsible for the wrongful acts committed by an agent who is an employee and by an agent who is an independent contractor.
7. Explain what is meant by breach of warranty of authority and the effect on the position of the third party.
8. Explain what is meant by an undisclosed principal. What options are available to a third party when an agent acts for such an undisclosed principal?
9. Explain the nature of an agent's obligations to the principal, and what is meant by fiduciary duty. Give examples.
10. Define employment and distinguish between the control test and the organization test.
11. Explain under what circumstances an employer will be responsible for the torts committed by an employee and for contracts entered into by an employee.

12. Explain how the employment relationship may be terminated. In the absence of contractual provisions, how much notice is required? Include a discussion of constructive dismissal and what effect that will have on the requirement of notice.
13. Define just cause, give examples, and explain what effect it has on the requirement of notice.
14. What are an employer's obligations with respect to disabled workers?
15. What are an employer's options with respect to termination when there is no more work to do?
16. How are damages assessed in a wrongful dismissal action, and how is that award affected by bad faith on the part of the employer or an employee's failure to mitigate?
17. When an employee decides to leave, how much notice must be given?
18. Explain the employee's obligations with respect to fiduciary duty and confidential information.
19. Describe the certification process in your jurisdiction.
20. Distinguish between recognition, jurisdiction, interest and rights disputes. Indicate how each of these types of deputes must be resolved.
21. Explain what is meant by unfair labour practices and how they are dealt with in Canadian law.
22. Explain what is meant by the obligation for the parties to bargain in good faith and the role mediation plays in the collective bargaining process.
23. How must disputes arising under a collective agreement be resolved?
24. Distinguish between a strike and a lockout, and indicate how much notice must be given and any other restrictions or requirements on strike or lockout in your jurisdiction.
25. What is meant by picketing? Why is it so effective and what limitations on the right to picket are there in your jurisdiction?
26. Explain what is meant by a union shop, a closed shop, and the right of "check off."
27. Explain the purpose and effect of workers' compensation legislation, occupational health and safety statutes, employment insurance statutes, and human rights statutes with respect to employment.
28. Describe the nature of the standards imposed by employment standards statutes in your jurisdiction.
29. Explain effective strategies to avoid employee theft and shoplifting.
30. What dangers does a business face with respect to the investigation and enforcement aspects of employee theft and shoplifting?

QUESTIONS FOR FURTHER DISCUSSION

1. Employers are held vicariously liable for torts committed by their employees in the course of their employment. Some have questioned the fairness of this process since it is the employee who is committing the wrongful act, not the employer. This is an example of holding the employer strictly liable for the employee's wrongdoing even though they are completely innocent. We don't even impose that kind of liability on parents for the wrongful acts committed by their children. Discuss the appropriateness of holding one person such as an employer responsible for the acts of another. Look at the question from the point of view of all parties involved and also consider the public interest.

2. In Canada we have developed the practice of requiring employers to give employees extensive notice or pay in lieu of notice when terminating without cause. Most provinces have enacted employment standards acts where the required statutory notice is much less than the common law requirement. But these statutes also provide that the longer term (in either the statute or the common law) should prevail. Is it appropriate or fair to employers to impose such lengthy notice periods? Should the declared statutory period simply override any prior common law approach, as would normally be the case with statutes? On the other hand, do you think that when a term is included in the employment contract which reduces this notice period, it should be allowed to stand? Think about the relative bargaining positions of the employer and employee at the time of hiring when these special terms are normally agreed to.

3. Do you feel that unions have too much power today? Look at the legislation in place in your jurisdiction and discuss whether it accomplishes a balanced approach between the needs of employees and their right to bargain collectively, and the freedom of action required by an employer to carry on its business.

4. A principal who enters into a contract that specifically limits the agent's authority to act still faces the possibility of being bound by acts the agent performs outside that actual authority. This is because of the agent's apparent authority. Why should the principal bear responsibility to the third party when it was the agent who violated the authority limitation? Would it not be more appropriate for the third party to turn to the agent for compensation for any losses suffered when the agent violates his or her authority? In your discussion consider the matter from the point of view of the principal, the agent, and the third party.

CASES
FOR DISCUSSION

1. **CALGARY HARDWOOD & VENEER LTD. ET AL. V.CANADIAN NATIONAL RAILWAY CO.** (1979), 100 D.L.R. (3d) 302 (Alta. S.C.).

Thomas Young worked as an Industrial Development Officer for the Canadian National Railway Company. For two years he had been dealing with Calgary Hardwood & Veneer Ltd. to sell them certain lands owned by the C.N.R in Calgary. Finally, he made an offer to the purchaser to the effect that if they could get municipal approval for the use they were intending to make of the land, then the C.N.R. would "agree to sell" it under the terms negotiated. Calgary Hardwood did obtain the necessary approval and accepted the C.N.R. offer presented to them by Mr. Young. But the C.N.R. then took the position that Mr. Young didn't have the necessary authority to make such an offer, and they refused to go through with the sale. For the entire two years, the C.N.R. officials were aware of the negotiations Mr. Young was carrying on with the purchaser, but they said nothing. Indicate the arguments on both sides as to the validity of the contract of sale of the land. Would it affect your answer to know that on some of the negotiation sessions with the purchaser Mr. Young was accompanied by other C.N.R. officials?

2. **CANSON ENTERPRISES LTD. ET AL. V. BOUGHTON & CO. ET AL.** (1991), 85 D.L.R. (4th) 129 (S.C.C.).

The facts of this case have been somewhat simplified for clarity. Mr. Treit, along with another person, agreed to purchase land through a company for $410 000, resell it, and split the profit. Mr. Treit then made arrangements with certain purchasers to buy the land for $525 000. The purchasers agreed to pay Treit a 15 percent commission on whatever profit they made when they in turn developed and resold the land in question. Mr. Treit falsely represented to these purchasers that he would be making no other profit on the deal. Mr. Wollen, who was the solicitor acting for Treit and the purchasers in this transaction, was aware of this secret profit to be made by Treit but failed to inform the purchasers. The deal went ahead and the land was developed, but because of negligence on the part of an architect and a pile driving firm, the resulting building was severely damaged, which caused considerable loss to the purchasers. The damage suffered could not be completely recovered from those defendants. It was at that point that they learned of the secret profit by Treit and the knowledge of it by the lawyer, Mr. Wollen. Do you think that the purchasers should be able to recover their loss from Treit or Wollen? Explain the reasons that would be advanced by both sides. The damages claimed were for the secret profit, for the 15 percent commission on the resale, and for the unrecovered losses for the damaged building. Just how far do you think that the lawyer and Treit's responsibility for the loss should go?

3. **MITCHELL-CLAPHAM V. FULLARTON** (1974), 46 D.L.R. (3d) 766 (N.B.S.C.).

Mr. Fullarton agreed to purchase an only partially finished house from Mr. Jewet. The agreement provided that Jewet would finish the house and that Fullarton would be able to select certain materials to be used in the process. Following Jewet's instructions, Fullarton went to Gunter's Flooring Ltd., made the appropriate selections, and returned with the quotation to Jewet for his approval. This was acceptable and, with Jewet's authority, Fullarton returned to the flooring store. He dealt with Mr. Mitchell-Clapham and his secretary when he made the purchase. Fullarton signed the quotation, which Jewet had approved, using his own name. There was nothing on the written document indicating that Fullarton was acting as an agent; however, he did instruct Mitchell-Clapham to send the bill to Jewet. In subsequent dealings it was clear to Mitchell-Clapham that Fullarton was acting on behalf of Jewet. In fact, Jewet failed to pay and in this action Mitchell-Clapham is suing Fullarton for the cost of the flooring materials ordered and supplied. Is Fullarton liable in these circumstances? What are the arguments that each party might raise? What is the likely outcome?

4. **BEGUSIC V. CLARK, WILLSON & CO. ET AL.** (1992), 92 D.L.R. (4th) 273 (B.C.S.C.).
Mrs. Begusic purchased a residential unit in Cedarbrooke Village from the defendant, the vendors of the unit. The project was unique in that each unit was purchased as part of a cooperative, which held the property under a long-term lease. This meant that the rent to be paid under that lease had to be renegotiated on a regular basis. This imposed considerable uncertainty, although Mrs. Begusic was unaware of it when she bought the unit. In fact, the arrangement was all spelled out in a prospectus, but the real estate agent, as well as the solicitors involved, failed to give her a copy of the prospectus or to tell her that one was available. When she discovered that the rent was to be revised upward on a regular basis, she sued the vendors, claiming that they were responsible for the negligence of the lawyers and the real estate agent in failing to disclose this important information. Further, she claimed that if she had known of the rent revision provisions, she never would have purchased the unit. What is the nature of her complaint? Explain the likelihood of her success and the arguments to be raised by the various parties. Assuming the value of her unit would not increase as would other real estate investments because of the rising rent, what would be an appropriate remedy?

5. **MCKINLEY V. BC TEL ET AL.** (2001), 200 D.L.R. (4th) 385 (S.C.C.).
Martin McKinley was a chartered accountant who worked as a controller for several BC Tel companies. He developed high blood pressure, a condition which at first was controlled by medication. Eventually, under his doctor's advice he had to take a leave of absence from his employment. He discussed with his superior his desire to return to work in a less responsible position, but no such position was offered even though such positions opened up in the organization. The company made him a severance offer that was rejected. His employment was terminated and this action for wrongful dismissal was brought against BC Tel. At the time of his termination McKinley had been employed by B.C. Tel for 17 years. When his employment was terminated, he lost his short-term and long-term disability benefits. He complained to the Human Rights Commission and brought this wrongful dismissal action. He also claimed that the company had dismissed him in a "high handed and flagrant manner," amounting to "intentional infliction of mental suffering." This was denied by the company. They claimed that the employment relationship had been frustrated and that they had offered a reasonable severance package. What would McKinley's complaint to the Human Rights Commission consist of? Did the company have just cause for termination? If not, what would be an appropriate remedy in these circumstances? If the com-

pany had been guilty of bad faith in the termination process, how would this affect the remedies to be awarded? How would it affect your answer to know that well into the trial the company was allowed to change their defence to just cause for dismissal? The new defence was based on a letter they discovered, which indicated that the doctor had recommended a type of medication that would allow him to return to work and that McKinley's withholding of this letter amounted to dishonesty justifying the termination.

6. **VANDERLEEST V. CITY OF REGINA** (1992), 91 D.L.R. (4th) 538 (Sask. Q.B.).
Mrs. Vanderleest had worked for the City of Regina for 17 years in various positions. She was working as manager of the city's Social Development Division, a very responsible position involving the supervision of 10 professional, technical, and clerical employees when she resigned. There is no question that she was a dedicated and competent employee, but her supervisor made clear to her that the Social Development Division was to be incorporated into another department and that she would no longer continue as manager. Her supervisor told her that she would continue as an employee of the city but in a non-management capacity. This prompted her resignation. She also claimed that her supervisor made the working environment so unpleasant that she had to resign. He had interviewed her staff behind her back and made disparaging remarks about her to them. When he told her that she would work in a non-management position, he also informed her that he had no confidence in her management ability and he did this in a "haughty and derisive" manner. In this action she is suing for wrongful dismissal. Indicate on what she would base that claim and the arguments that could be raised by the city in its defence.

7. **PEPSI-COLA CANADA BEVERAGES (WEST) LTD. V. R.W.D.S.U., LOCAL 558** (2002), 208 D.L.R. (4th) 385 (S.C.C.).
The union in question obtained certification as the bargaining agent for the employees working at the Pepsi-Cola bottling plant in Saskatchewan. The employer and union bargained collectively but were unable to reach an agreement, and a legal strike took place, followed by a lockout. A bitter confrontation ensued, including employees taking over the company's warehouse facilities. An injunction was issued and the company resumed business with replacement workers. The union members then extended their picketing to secondary locations, including retail outlets where Pepsi products were sold, as well as a hotel where several replacement workers were staying, and in front of the homes of several Pepsi managers. They carried placards, chanted slogans, screamed insults, and uttered threats of harm at these locations. This action was brought by the employer; they applied for an injunction to stop picketing at these secondary locations. Explain the grounds for their complaint and the likelihood of their success. Indicate any arguments that might be raised by the union in their defence. Would it affect your answer to know that there was no statute prohibiting secondary picketing in place in Saskatchewan as there is in some provinces?

8. **INTERNATIONAL LONGSHOREMEN'S ASSOCIATION, LOCAL 273 ET AL. V. MARITIME EMPLOYERS' ASSOCIATION ET AL.** (1978), 89 D.L.R. (3d) 289 (S.C.C.).
Three trade unions had entered into a collective agreement with the employers' association (Marine Employers' Association), which included a provision not to strike dur-

ing the term of the collective agreement. During that time frame, a legal strike commenced by the National Harbour Board Police against that employers' association. A picket line was established and the members of the three unions (International Longshoremen's Association, et al.) refused to cross that picket line. This application is brought for an injunction ordering those employees to cross the legal picket line and return to work. Discuss the arguments to be raised by both sides. How would it affect your answer if there was also a provision in the collective agreement stating that it would not be considered a strike if employees chose not to cross a legal picket line?

CHAPTER 7

Methods of Carrying On Business

Choosing a method for doing business is one of the most important topics in this text. The methods have been developed to facilitate the commercial needs of society by spreading the control and risk of doing business amongst those involved. People should exercise great care when starting a business to ensure that the structure chosen is the best one for their particular needs.

Take care in choosing method to carry on business

Although there are other business models, we will look primarily at sole proprietorship, partnership, and incorporation. The sole proprietor involves one person operating a business alone without going through the process of incorporation. A partnership involves two or more people carrying on business together without going through the process of incorporation. And the corporation involves any number of people going through the process of incorporation where documents are filed with a government agency and a certificate is issued, thus creating a new entity—the corporation—which is the vehicle for carrying on the business. It shouldn't be assumed that a corporation is the best way to carry on a business. Each structure has its advantages and disadvantages, but it is important to point out that often what is a disadvantage to one person is an advantage to another. As a result, we discuss business structures, except in a few instances, more in terms of their characteristics rather than advantages or disadvantages. In this chapter we will first examine the general characteristics that apply to all business approaches. Then unique methods will be identified along with the rights and obligations of those involved in the business and those who do business with them.

Common Elements

Each one of these structures is designed for the purpose of carrying on business and making profits for those involved. Government regulations present a series

Government regulations impact all businesses

of hurdles that all businesses must face. For example, both federal and provincial income taxes must be paid and business people must keep sufficient records of their dealings to account for those tax obligations. There may also be property taxes owed to a city or municipality. Where services or products are offered to the public, federal GST must be collected from customers, and, depending on the jurisdiction, there is an obligation to collect provincial sales tax. Those funds must then be remitted to the appropriate level of government. A certain portion of employees' pay must be retained for income tax purposes, and employers must pay employment insurance, workers' compensation and Canada Pension Plan premiums. In some cases, depending on the nature of the business, it is necessary to obtain a provincial or municipal licence and adhere to the regulations associated with that licence. For example, most businesses dealing with the public will need a municipal business licence, and some businesses such as real estate, insurance, and travel agencies will need a provincial licence to operate. Professionals such as lawyers, doctors, dentists, accountants, and real estate agents must also meet stringent qualifications and maintain membership in good standing in their respective professional organizations.

In addition, there are privacy and confidentiality obligations, human rights regulations, pollution controls, and health and safety standards that must be complied with. Carrying on business today is highly regulated and government regulation will be discussed as a separate topic in Chapter 10.

The Sole Proprietor

Sole proprietor works for himself or herself

A sole proprietor works for himself or herself (see Figure 7.1). There are no special processes or formalities that must take place to create a sole proprietorship other than the registration of a business name. Even that is only required when the business name is different than the sole proprietor's. A person is a sole proprietor as soon as she embarks on some business activity alone. When a child opens a lemonade stand she is a sole proprietor. Sole proprietor then is the term used to describe someone who starts up a business on her own without going through any formal process such as incorporation.

No formal process required

As a general rule the sole proprietor has complete control of the business. There is no one else to tell her what to do and she is answerable only to herself. The record and reporting burden is lighter and there are fewer government regulations. Any profits made from the business belong to the sole proprietor, and any obligations of the business are those of the sole proprietor. Thus, the sole proprietor and the business are one.

FIGURE 7.1 Sole Proprietor Relationship

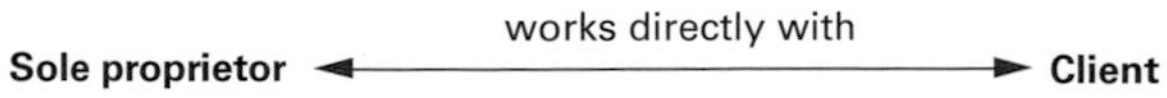

The main problem with a sole proprietor is that there is unlimited liability. This means that any debts associated with the business are those of the sole proprietor, and her personal assets will be vulnerable to creditors. There is no separation made between the sole proprietor and her business activities. The sole proprietor will be vicariously liable for an employee's wrongful conduct that takes place within the scope of the employment. It is usually this unlimited liability that discourages people from carrying on business as a sole proprietor. However, many of these disadvantages can be offset by obtaining adequate insurance coverage.

Sole proprietor has unlimited liability

Personal assets are at risk for business debt

Perhaps the primary disadvantage of operating a business alone is also its greatest advantage. While others can invest in the business, they become creditors of the sole proprietor, not participants in the business. The sole proprietor remains in control. To become participants, a partnership or corporation must be created. In many jurisdictions professionals cannot incorporate. A dentist may incorporate a company to hire the staff, assistants, and supply the office space and equipment, but not the performance of the dental service itself. If such a professional is by himself, he must act as a sole proprietor. If the professional decides to band together with other professionals who then carry on business together, they must do so as a partnership. Some jurisdictions now allow such professionals to form professional corporations, but in most cases they retain personal responsibility for their professional activities.

Some professionals can't incorporate

One of the greatest disadvantages to a sole proprietor involves income tax. Since the income of the business and that of the person owning it are one, it is considered personal income and taxed at that rate. Most business people will pay a much higher rate of personal taxes than they would if they operated through a corporation. Through the corporation the business person has the advantage of paying at a lower rate and then reinvesting the funds, thus delaying personal taxes so that there is more money available for investment. Funds to be distributed can be taken out at a more convenient time when personal income is low. Also, there are mechanisms available so that the corporation can be used to redirect income to a spouse or other family member. Such income splitting allows the parties to take advantage of the lowest personal tax rates.

CASE SUMMARY 7.1

Atlantic Glass and Storefronts Ltd. v. Price[1]

Unlimited Liability Continued after Incorporation

Mr. Price originally operated "Fins, Furs and Feathers" as a sole proprietor but neglected to register the change under the *Partnerships and Business Names Registration Act* when he incorporated the business as P.R. Enterprises Ltd. When the company failed to pay their supplier—Atlantic Glass and Storefronts Ltd.—the supplier sued Mr. Price directly instead of the company. Price clamed he was protected as a shareholder of the company, but the court found against him since he was still registered as

(continued)

1. (1974), 48 D.L.R. (3d) 471 (N.S. Co. Ct.).

a sole proprietor. As far as Atlantic Glass and the court were concerned that was still the case, and Price was personally liable for the debt. This case shows how important it is to follow the correct procedures when incorporating a business. It also illustrates the different responsibilities of a shareholder and a sole proprietor.

Partnership

Partners work together to earn a profit

No formal process needed to form partnership

Common law case law is codified by partnership acts

A partnership is defined as "the relation between persons carrying on a business in common with a view to profit."[2] Essentially, they are a group of sole proprietors who have agreed to carry on their business together without going through the incorporation process (see Figure 7.2). No formal process is needed other than, in some cases, registration with the appropriate government agency. Historically, this was the common method of carrying on business and a considerable body of judge-made law was developed to deal with partnerships. In 1890, as part of the movement towards codifying commercial law in England, this body of law was summarized in partnership acts. Each common law province in Canada has adopted a version of the *Partnership Act*. Today, in many jurisdictions doctors, lawyers, dentists, and accountants can only carry on business as sole proprietors or in partnerships.

CREATION

Partnership should be created by contract

Some provisions of partnership can be modified by contract

Partnership acts govern relations between partners where there is no contract

Partnerships should be created by express contract where the parties clearly indicate in writing the nature of the rights and obligations between them. Many of the provisions of partnership acts that deal with the relationship between the partners can be modified by agreement. Considerable deliberation and negotiation should be devoted to determining just what changes should be made. For example, under the *Partnership Act* all partners have an equal share of the decision-making power, and are entitled to an equal share of the profits. This can be modified to create different classes of partners with the senior partners having more control and receiving a greater share of the profits. The provisions of the Acts will apply, unless the partners have agreed otherwise.

FIGURE 7.2 Partnership Relationship

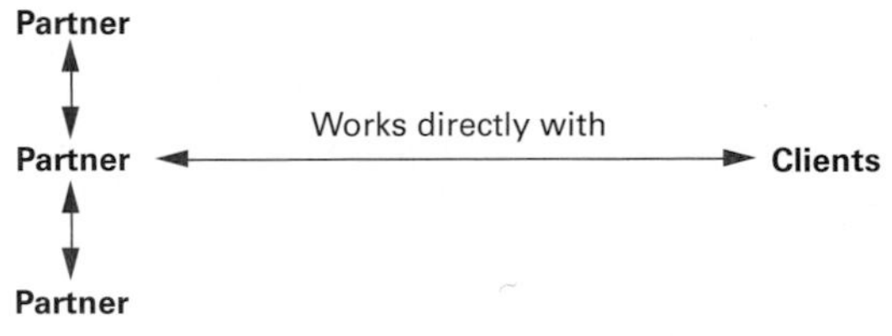

2. *Partnership Act*, R.S.O. 1990, c. P.5, s.2.

CASE SUMMARY 7.2

A.E. LePage Ltd. v. Kamex Developments Ltd. et al.[3]

Not All Common Activities Create a Partnership

Several individuals invested different amounts in an apartment building and, after costs, received a share of the profits based on that investment. At a regular monthly meeting they discussed selling the property, and one of the group, unknown to the others, entered an exclusive listing agreement with A.E. LePage. The investors did sell the property under an open listing through another agent. A.E. LePage demanded their commission and sued all the co-owners, claiming they were partners and bound by the exclusive listing contract entered into by their partner. The court held that they were not partners, and although they owned the property together and shared the profits, they fell under the exception set out in the Ontario *Partnership Act,* which states that owning property together "does not in itself create a partnership." This is only one of several exceptions listed under the *Partnership Act* whereby sharing profits will not, by itself, create a partnership.

Partnership can be created inadvertently

Carrying on business together can create a partnership

Sharing profits indicates partnership

But note exceptions listed in *Partnership Act*

A contract, whether it is expressed or implied, is not necessary for the creation of a partnership. The definition in the Act simply requires that the parties work together in some business where they are trying to make a profit. Such a relationship can be created inadvertently. What has to be determined is what constitutes carrying on business and when is that done in common. Clearly one event, such as a group of students getting together to put on a dance or party, will not constitute carrying on a business. But if a series of dances are promoted by that group of students and they do it for profit, then they are engaged in the business of promoting dances, and a partnership has been created. This has important consequences in terms of liability for those students. A court will usually find that they are carrying on the business in common where it can be shown that the parties have contributed to the capital necessary to carry on the business, and where they each participate and have a say in the management of the business, or where they will share in the profits from the enterprise. Profit, as used here, means the net proceeds of the business after expenses have been deducted. The sharing of fees (gross receipts) is not enough. For example, if a lawyer were to kick back a given percentage of what she was paid for transferring property to the real estate agent who referred a client to her, this might be unethical, but it would not by itself establish a partnership. But if the lawyer paid over a given percentage of her profits (after expenses have been deducted), that would be evidence of a partnership. The *Partnership Act* specifically lists a number of activities that by themselves will not establish a partnership. For example, sharing rental profit from a jointly owned property, or an employee commission or bonus based on the performance of a business will not cause the person being paid to be considered a partner in the business.

It should also be noted that the liability of a partnership will be imposed on a person who represents himself or allows himself to be held out as a partner. If an

3. (1977), 78 D.L.R. (3d) 223 (Ont. C.A.).

accountant introduces his friend to a client, referring to him as his partner in circumstances where it is reasonable for the client to believe that there is a business relationship between them, and the friend does not correct the statement, that friend will not be able to deny it later if the client sues him as a partner. This is an example of the principle of estoppel, which was explained in the previous chapter in the discussion relating to the apparent authority of an agent (see p. 133).

Representation of partnership can create liability

LIABILITY OF PARTNERS

All partners are liable for all debts and obligations of partnership

Each partner is responsible for the debts and obligations of the partnership. This includes obligations based on tort, breach of trust, or contract. Each partner is vicariously liable for the torts of employees and other partners that are committed in association with the partnership business. If one partner carelessly injures a pedestrian while delivering documents, the other partners will be responsible for those injuries. When one partner commits a breach of trust, such as diverting money she is holding in trust for a client for her own use, the other partners are responsible. And with respect to contracts, each partner is considered an agent of the other partners, so that any contract entered into by one partner with respect to the partnership business is binding on them all. If one partner in a flower store purchases flowers from a distributor, the other partners are parties to that contract and liable under it, even though they may not have authorized the purchase and have no knowledge of the transaction. This liability is unlimited. Just as with the sole proprietor, the debts of the partnership are the debts of the individual partners.

Liability of partners unlimited

CASE SUMMARY 7.3

McDonic et al. v. Hetherington et al. [4]

Other Partners Are Liable for Their Partner's Negligence

Watt was a partner in a law firm and lost money on several imprudent investments he made for two elderly sisters. When they died, their estate sued all of the partners for the money lost. Watt had used the firm's trust accounts to transfer the money; the partners were aware of the investments; the other partners sometimes signed the cheques; and some of the money was loaned to employees and their relatives. As a result, the court found that the investments were made as part of the partnership business, and all partners were liable for the loss.

If the resources of the partnership business are not enough to meet its obligations, each partner will be required to pay them out of his or her personal assets. If the business fails, the partners will not only lose their business but may lose their homes, cars, and other personal assets to satisfy the claims of the creditors. In the example where a partner injures a pedestrian while carrying out company business, if the injuries are significant and there is inadequate insurance, it is quite likely that all the partners would have to pay from their personal assets. If there are several partners and only one of them has assets, that partner will be required to pay the entire claim and will be left with the hollow hope of collecting

Personal assets are at risk for partnership debts and liabilities

4. (1997), 142 D.L.R. (4th) 648 (Ont. C.A.).

from the others as their circumstances improve. Thus, it is vitally important that business people exercise great care in choosing partners who are trustworthy and financially sound. The great danger about unlimited liability in partnership is that one partner will not only be liable for his or her own mistakes but also completely responsible for the mistakes of the other partners and employees as well.

Unlimited liability unaffected by partnership agreement

While many of the provisions of the *Partnership Act* can be modified by the partners, they cannot change provisions that relate to their liability to outsiders. Thus, the partners could set out a term in their partnership agreement that a particular partner would only be responsible for 15 percent of any losses. But if a customer, creditor, or outsider had a claim of, for example, $50 000 against the partnership, and the other partners had no funds, that partner could be required to pay the entire $50 000, despite the provision of the agreement to the contrary.

A new partner coming into the partnership will not be responsible for prior debts and obligations unless he agrees to take on that responsibility. But a retiring partner is not in as favourable a position. As a general rule he will not be responsible for debts that are incurred after he ceases to be a partner. However, as long as people dealing with the partnership still think that person is a partner, he will be liable to them on the basis of apparent authority. Every partner is an agent of every other partner. For this reason it is vitally important that the retiring partner provide notification to others that he has left. This usually requires specific notification to current customers, suppliers, and clients as well as a public notice of the retirement published in a newspaper or trade publication. It is also a good idea to get the remaining partners to agree to indemnify the retiring partner for any obligations that arise after he leaves.

Retiring partners should notify customers and public

It is usually this threat of unlimited liability that persuades business people to avoid the partnership model of doing business and to incorporate. But much of the liability risk associated with partnership can be overcome by acquiring sufficient insurance coverage. As will be seen below, often the advantage of limited liability found in corporations is more of a myth than reality. Also, there is a growing trend to use limited partnerships and the newly developed limited liability partnerships to overcome this liability problem. These modified partnerships will be discussed below.

Insurance can alleviate unlimited liability problem

THE RELATIONSHIP BETWEEN PARTNERS Even though some terms of the *Partnership Act* can be modified in a partnership agreement, it is the relationship between the partners and their rights and obligations to each other as set out in the *Partnership Act* that makes partnership unique. With respect to the day-to-day operation of the business, a majority vote prevails, but one of the most significant features of a partnership is that no major decisions can be made without unanimous agreement of the partners. Where a decision must be made to admit a new partner, to borrow or invest money, to dissolve the partnership, or to embark on some new business venture—even if only one partner out of 10 opposes the decision—that one veto will prevail. All partners are equal. They share the profits equally; they have equal access to the partnership books and records; and they all share in the management of the partnership with an equal say in its operation. Because partners carry on business together, they cannot earn a salary from the business. Each partner is entitled to an equal share of the profits, and arrangements are usually made so that they will take a monthly draw against those profits. An end-of-the-year adjustment is then made so that the draws equal each partner's profit entitlement. Any expenses incurred should also be repaid before the profits are determined.

Majority vote governs day-to-day activities

Major decisions require unanimous consent

Partners share equally in profits

Partners don't get a salary but can take a draw against the profits

Partners owe fiduciary duty

One of the most important features with respect to partners' obligations is the special duty owed by each partner to the others. Partners are agents of each other and as such owe a fiduciary duty to their principal (the other partners) as was discussed in Chapter 6. They must act in the best interest of the partnership, even to the extent of putting the interests of the partnership business ahead of their own. Thus they can't take advantage of business opportunities that come to them because of their position, but must make them available to the partnership. If a partner in a real estate agency learns of a particularly good deal on commercial property, she must bring it to the partnership rather than make the investment alone. If she fails to do this and makes a profit on the deal, she may be required to pay over that profit to the partnership. If she loses money, the losses are hers alone. Similarly, the partner must disclose any conflict of interest; avoid competition with the partnership; not use any partnership property for her own purposes; and properly account for all expenses, income, and benefits received. Of course, where one partner sets out to cheat others, she will be subject to damages and other civil remedies. In serious cases of intentional fraud, she may also be subject to criminal prosecution and the imposition of significant fines or imprisonment. This applies whether she is committing that fraud against a fellow partner or a client.

CASE SUMMARY 7.4

Rochwerg et al. v. Truster et al.[5]

Partner Must Account for Secret Profits

Mr. Rochwerg was a partner in an accounting firm, and while he paid over some of the remuneration he received from serving as a director on two associated companies, he failed to disclose the fact that he was also entitled to stock options. When the other partners discovered the existence of the stock options, they demanded an accounting. The court held that these amounted to secret profits that Mr. Rochwerg made while carrying out partnership business and required him to pay any profits for distribution to all the partners. Rochwerg retained only that portion he was entitled to as a partner. The case illustrates the obligations of partners to each other and how any gains from activities related to the profession must be paid to the business.

Relations between partners can be modified by agreement

This is the default position as set out in the *Partnership Act,* but it is often modified by agreement. The importance of a carefully negotiated partnership agreement cannot be overemphasized. Partnership agreements are often used to create different classes of partners so that they are no longer equal. Senior partners will have a greater say in the operation of the business. Also, a partner's right to an equal share of profits may be modified by agreement. In a partnership of 10, for example, the two senior partners may be entitled to 20 percent of the profits each, while the six junior partners would only be entitled to 10 percent. Partnership agreements often contain terms restricting a partner's authority to act on behalf of the partnership and limiting their responsibility for losses. It is

5. [2002] O.J. No. 1230 (C.A.).

important to remember that these provisions only give rights to compensation from each other after claims by outsiders have been satisfied. The partnership agreement will not affect the rights of the people with whom the partners are dealing. Other provisions often included in partnership agreements establish the contribution expected from each partner in terms of capital and service, the maintenance and access to books and accounts, how disputes between the partners are to be resolved, provisions relating to the retirement of partners, and the dissolution of the partnership.

It should also be noted that the same tax considerations apply to the partnership as with the sole proprietor. Because the income of the partnership business is also the income of the partners, they must pay taxes on it at their personal rate. For this reason many professionals create professional corporations to provide services to the practice. While they may not be able to incorporate the actual practice of their profession, they create a corporation to handle the rental or ownership of property, to employ secretaries, managers and other staff, and to rent or purchase the equipment needed. The partnership pays a fee to the corporation for these services. The shareholders of the service corporation can be the partners' spouse or other family members, thus effectively splitting income for tax purposes.

DISSOLUTION

Partnership dissolves upon death or bankruptcy

Under the partnership acts a partnership is dissolved automatically upon the death or bankruptcy/insolvency of a partner. Where there are more than two partners this can have disastrous consequences for the business. This is one of the areas where the provisions of the partnership acts vary from province to province. For example, in British Columbia when there are more than two partners and one of them dies or becomes bankrupt, the partnership only dissolves with respect to that one partner, but the firm continues.[6] In Ontario, where there are more than two partners and one dies the whole partnership dissolves in the event of the "death or insolvency of a partner."[7] In fact, just what will cause a partnership to be dissolved is one of the most important provisions of the *Partnership Act* that is normally modified in a partnership agreement. Usually, the partners will agree that the partnership will not dissolve except with respect to that one partner, and they will arrange sufficient insurance to pay out the claims of that partner or his or her estate.

Partnership dissolves upon notice

Partnership dissolves upon court order

The normal way for a partnership to dissolve is simply by one partner serving notice to that effect on the others. Of course, if the partnership was created for a specific period of time or for a particular project, the completion of the specified time or project will also cause the partnership to dissolve. It will also dissolve if the activity becomes illegal or a court orders it to be dissolved. This normally happens where there has been misconduct, breach of the partnership agreement, or where one partner becomes incapable of fulfilling his or her partnership obligations.

Assets first go to pay off liabilities and expenses

When the partnership is dissolved, all of the firm's resources must be devoted to paying the debts and liabilities of the partnership. If there are not enough funds, the individual partners will be required to use their own personal resources to meet those obligations. Where there are excess funds, they are first

6. *Partnership Act*, R.S.B.C. 1996, c. 348, s. 36.1.

7. *Partnership Act*, R.S.O. 1990, c. P.5, s. 33.1.

Assets then return capital and then divided equally

used to pay back expenses incurred by the partners. Then the partners will divide the capital, assets, and excess profits equally among them. This distribution, after meeting the debts and liabilities of the partnership, can also be modified by the terms of the partnership agreement.

CASE SUMMARY 7.5

Kucher v. Moore [8]

When Partners Lose Trust in Each Other

Moore was a dentist who was suspended from practice when he became seriously depressed, overbilled his patients, and failed to keep proper records. He and his partner had acquired disability insurance with the understanding that any payments would go to the partnership. But Moore misled his partner, claiming the benefits received were only $19 000 per year, when in fact he was receiving $90 000 per year. Upon application to the court by his partner, the partnership was dissolved, and Moore was ordered to pay over half of the proceeds from the disability insurance. Any property included on the partnership books was also to be divided between them. Although the partnership agreement did not allow for it to be dissolved upon notice, the court always has the power to dissolve a partnership when it is "just and equitable to do so." Here the fraud and deceit destroyed the trust required for a partnership to continue.

An important similarity between a partnership and a corporation is that the partnership can sue or be sued in the name of the business, but unlike a corporation, each partner is individually responsible for the debt. It is this characteristic of unlimited liability that separates partnerships and sole proprietorships from corporations. Still, there are two ways that limited liability can come about in a partnership arrangement.

LIMITED PARTNERS

Limited liability refers to an investor's risk of losing only the amount invested. Thus a shareholder in a corporation can lose what he or she has paid for shares, but is not responsible otherwise for the debts and liabilities of the corporation. This same protection is available to a limited partner. Limited partners are essentially investors in the partnership who don't actually take part in the partnership business. If they do participate in the management, they will lose their status as limited partners and risk the same unlimited liability as the other general partners.

Limited liability given to limited partners if:

- They don't take part in management

The following requirements must be met for such a limited partnership to be created.

- There is one general partner

- The limited partnership must be registered

- there must be at least one general partner in the firm,
- the limited partnership must be registered as such with the appropriate government agency, and

8. (1991), 3 B.L.R. 50 (Ont. Gen. Div).

- the name of the limited partner must not be listed as part of the name of the partnership business.

This allows individuals to invest in the partnership business without assuming any responsibility. But limited partners are in a precarious position and can easily lose their limited liability status by participating in the partnership or failing to meet one of the other qualifications. Often, through carelessness, the limited partnership will not be properly registered. Also, when the business gets into trouble there is a great temptation for the limited partner to get involved. And there are considerable dangers associated with the actual agreement creating the limited partnership. For tax reasons these agreements often contain a provision subjecting the limited partner to the payment of further funds if required by the business. This defeats the limited liability objective of a limited partnership. The investor should exercise great care to read the contract carefully before investing, and then be careful to avoid the pitfalls that could change the status of a limited partner to a general partner.

Limited partner can become general partner with unlimited liability

CASE SUMMARY 7.6

Haughton Graphic Ltd. v. Zivot et al.[9]

When Limited Partners Lose Their Protection

Zivot and another individual were limited partners in *Printcraft* (a new magazine) with Lifestyle Magazine Inc. which had been incorporated so that it could be the only general partner. Zivot was also the president of Lifestyle Magazine Inc. and as such played an active role in controlling the business of *Printcraft*. Houghton was an unpaid supplier and sought payment directly from Zivot. The court held that under the Alberta *Partnership Act*, Zivot lost his limited partnership status when he participated in the *Printcraft* business. It didn't matter that he was acting as an employee of Lifestyle or even if he had informed the suppliers that he was a limited partner. Because he was taking part in the control of the *Printcraft* business, he lost his status as a limited partner and was liable as a general partner. This case shows the nature of a limited partner and how easily that status can be lost.

LIMITED LIABILITY PARTNERSHIP Because professionals face much broader and more extensive liability for their mistakes, they have brought pressure on government to pass legislation reducing the unlimited liability feature of partnerships. Since professionals are not allowed to obtain limited liability through incorporation, Ontario and several other provinces have passed legislation permitting the formation of limited liability partnerships. To create such a firm, the partners need only enter into an agreement designating the relationship as a limited liability partnership and stating that the Act relating to limited liability partnerships governs the agreement. Also, the name of the partnership must be registered and must end with the words "Limited Liability Partnership" (LLP). Only members of professional organizations governed by a separate statute such as Ontario's *Law Society Act* are eligible, and then only where the organization permits its members

Some provinces allow limited liability partnership

Must be registered and use LLP designation

9. Ont. S.C.J., as reported in *Lawyers Weekly Consolidated Digest*, Vol. 6 (May 1986).

Must be permitted by professional organization and have insurance

to carry on business as limited liability partnerships. Those organizations must also require their members to maintain a minimum amount of liability insurance. At the time of writing, in Ontario only accountants and lawyers are permitted to form LLPs; however, other professional bodies including those for doctors and dentists are considering allowing their members to do so.

Negligent partner retains unlimited liability

But other partners are not liable

Carrying on business as a limited liability partnership protects a partner from liability for the negligent acts or omissions of the other partners. Where one partner, or a person supervised by him, acts negligently, that partner will still be personally liable to compensate the victim. Essentially, the partner acting negligently is in the same position as any partner in a normal partnership faced with unlimited liability to compensate. All of his personal assets are exposed to risk, but the other partners will not be responsible for that partner's negligence. In this sense their liability is limited to their own negligence, not that of their partners. Thus, if one accountant makes a mistake with respect to an audit and causes significant losses to investors, only that one partner, along with his insurers, will be required to compensate the victims. In this way the risk faced by professionals doing business in professional partnerships is considerably lessened. But some would argue that it defeats the whole principle of professional responsibility. Finally, it should be noted that in some provinces professionals have been given the right to incorporate, but these professional corporations do not grant the professional the limited liability that would be present in a standard corporation.

Where professional incorporations allowed, they don't give limited liability

Corporations

A corporation is a legal fiction

But recognized by the courts as a separate legal person

The essential thing to remember about corporations is that they are artificial creations of government, which have no existence in reality. It is merely a convenient legal fiction that is properly referred to as the corporate myth. A sole proprietor consists of one legal personality—the sole proprietor. Likewise, a partnership is not a legal person separate from the partners. But if there are 10 shareholders in a corporation there are 11 legal personalities—the 10 shareholders and the corporation itself. The corporation is considered a legal person, separate and apart from the shareholders that make it up. It is in that last legal personality—the corporation—that we find the corporate myth or the legal fiction. It is an artificial legal personality recognized by the courts and all other official bodies as well as the various elements of our business communities, but in reality it has no existence separate from its parts (see Figure 7.3).

Corporations have been created by royal charter

The first business corporations were created by royal charter to deal with large trading expeditions that required many investors. Incorporation proved a popu-

FIGURE 7.3 Corporate Relationships

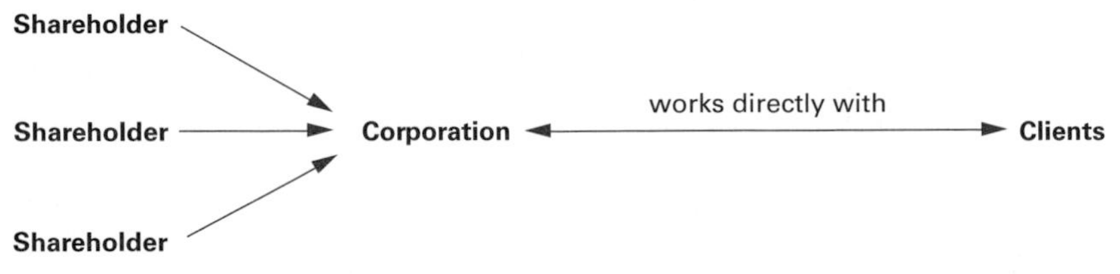

lar and efficient way to do business, and eventually smaller corporations were formed and used in regular business activities. In fact, there are many such legal entities in our society, including cities, universities, and societies as well as banks, trust companies, and special act companies such as the Canadian Broadcasting Corporation (CBC) and the Canadian National Railroad (CNR). We will concentrate our discussion on closely-held and broadly-held corporations that ordinary business people can use to carry on their business. Still, much of what is said is applicable to all of these various legal entities.

Corporations have been created by special act

CREATION

Federal or provincial companies

In Canada these corporations can be created either under the federal or various provincial and territorial statutes. There are three different methods used to incorporate. Nova Scotia still uses the registration method of incorporation where a **memorandum of association** and **articles of association** are submitted to the appropriate government agency, which in turn issues a certificate of registration recognizing the corporation. Quebec and Prince Edward Island are the only provinces still using the **letters patent** method of incorporation. Upon application by subscribers, letters patent are issued, thus granting a charter creating a corporation. Most provinces and the federal government have adopted the American approach where incorporation is accomplished by the filing of **articles of incorporation** and the issuance of a certificate of incorporation by the appropriate government agency.

Creation by registration

Creation through letters patent

Creation through articles of incorporation

These incorporating documents, in most provinces called articles of incorporation, are essentially the constitution of the company setting out such things as the name, the registered office, and the share structure, which includes different classes of shares, the number and power of directors, and any restriction on the types of business that can be engaged in. In addition, each corporation creates bylaws setting out the normal operating rules of the company such as the notice required and procedures for an annual shareholders' meeting, the responsibilities of directors and officers, and the management organization of the company. British Columbia recently changed from the registration method to the articles of incorporation method, but added to the confusion by their use of the term *articles*. Table 7.1 below is intended to clear up some of the confusion with respect to the use of this term and to show what has to be filed when incorporating in the various jurisdictions. Note that it is at this initial stage of incorporation that shareholders will often enter into a shareholders' agreement. Such agreements can be extremely important and are described below.

TABLE 7.1 Jurisdictional Differences

Jurisdiction	Method of Incorporation	Charter Documents	Bylaws
P.E.I. and Quebec	Letters Patent	Letters Patent	Bylaws (not filed)
Nova Scotia	Registration	Memorandum	Articles (filed)
British Columbia	Certificate of incorporation	Notice of articles	Articles (not filed)
Federal and other provinces	Certificate of incorporation	Articles of incorporation	Bylaws (not filed)

No matter what method of incorporation is used, the outcome is essentially the same: the creation of a corporation that is a separate legal entity from the members that make it up. This has developed into an extremely efficient method of doing business, both on a large and on a small scale. In all jurisdictions the basic structures, including rights and responsibilities of directors, officers, and shareholders and the methods of financing, are the same. Although incorporation in one jurisdiction allows the corporation to carry on business in others, a registration fee must be paid to do so. For this reason incorporation should take place in the jurisdiction where the business will be carried out, or federally, which allows the corporation to carry on business in any province.

Result is creation of separate legal person

A company incorporated in one province may register to do business in another

STRUCTURE

Business corporations can be either **broadly-held** or **closely-held**. Broadly-held corporations are also referred to as reporting, public, or offering corporations. A private or closely-held corporation is more like an incorporated partnership with only a few shareholders. Such a business is likely to be small. The directors, officers, shareholders, and managers are likely to be the same people, and the reporting and accounting requirements are much simpler and less stringent. It is in these smaller corporations where a shareholders' agreement becomes so important (much like a partnership agreement as discussed above). Closely-held corporations also have restrictions placed on the free transferability of shares. Usually the shareholder will have to sell the shares to current shareholders or get permission from the directors to sell them to someone else. A broadly-held corporation has many more regulations and controls that must be met. The rules relating to the protection of shareholders' rights, the responsibilities of directors, the requirements for annual meetings, and the reporting requirements are much more stringent. These larger corporations are likely to be traded on the stock market, which imposes even more regulations.

Closely-held corporations are smaller with fewer regulatory controls

Closely-held corporations have restrictions on transfer of shares

Broadly-held corporations are larger and more regulated

SHAREHOLDERS

The membership of the corporation is made up of shareholders. While they are separate from the corporation itself, they have very significant rights with respect to control of the corporation. Shareholders have the right to vote in shareholder meetings, and their vote controls what happens in the corporation. The supervision of the management and operation of the corporation is controlled by the **directors**, who are chosen by a vote of the shareholders usually at an annual general meeting. The shareholders have a vote based on the number of shares that they have. For example, one shareholder holding 200 shares would outvote 10 other shareholders holding 10 shares each. The majority shareholder in a corporation has ultimate control, and the minority shareholder has very little say in the operation of the corporation. This is sometimes referred to as the tyranny of the majority. In fact, the shareholders will likely not actually attend the shareholders' meeting but will give representatives their right to vote, which is called a **proxy**. The exercise of those proxies allows a few individuals who have gained the confidence of the shareholders the power to control the meeting and choose the directors and vote on the various proposals presented.

Shareholders are separate from corporation

Shareholders control corporations through their votes

Majority rules

In a corporation different classes of shareholders can be created, giving different rights and restrictions with respect to the shares. These usually take the form of preferred and common shares. **Common shares** normally give the right

Common shareholders have the right to vote and to dividends, once declared

to exercise control of the corporation through voting and to share in dividends when they are declared. **Dividends** are the method used to dispense the profits of the corporation to the shareholders. If the directors choose to pay out these profits rather than use them for other company purposes, they make a declaration to that effect, and the shareholders receive a payment based on the number of shares they hold. The shareholders also have the right to see certain documents, including financial statements and the company's annual report. Holders of **preferred shares** usually are denied voting rights, but have a commitment from the company to receive a specific dividend payment each year. It should be noted that whether preferred or common shares are involved, there is no legal right to a dividend; the shareholder cannot sue if a dividend is not declared and paid. The best that the preferred shareholder can do is to demand to be paid the promised dividend before a dividend is paid to the common shareholders. They can't force the corporation to pay the dividend promised. However, if the promised dividend is not forthcoming, this often triggers other rights for the preferred shareholder, such as obtaining the right to vote and to have a say in the operation of the company. A company will often have a mixture of common and preferred shares.

Preferred shareholders have no right to vote but are promised a regular dividend

Shareholders have no legal right to a dividend

But where no dividend is paid, other rights can be acquired by the preferred shareholder

Preferred and common shares are just one way that the share structure can be designed. Sometimes different classes of shares are created for estate purposes, with one class of shares (voting, non-participating shares) giving voting control but no dividends to the person setting up the estate. The other class of shares (participating, non-voting) gives dividends to the heirs but no say in how the company is run. These various specialized shares can take many different forms fulfilling the unique needs of the enterprise; careful consideration should be given to their design when first incorporating a company.

Shares with special rights and restrictions may take other forms

SEPARATE LEGAL PERSON

The key to appreciating the nature of a corporation is to understand the consequences of it having a separate legal personality. A corporation has the same powers of a natural person to carry on business. It can employ others, it can be an agent, and it can even be a partner. Since it is an artificial creation without a body, everything it does is done though agents. Although the incorporating documents can place restrictions on the types of business activities these corporations can be involved in, they are for internal purposes only. An outsider dealing with such a corporation doesn't have to worry about these restrictions unless they have actual notification of them. The exception is where the dealings are with a company that has been created by a special act of Parliament or by a provincial legislature (special act companies such as the CBC and the CNR). It may well be that in the incorporating statute the capacity of a special act company is restricted in the type of business activity they can do. If someone acting on the corporation's behalf enters into such a prohibited contract, it will not be binding on that corporation, whether or not the outsider knows of the limited capacity. People having dealings with such bodies that seem unusual or out of place should check the legislation under which they were incorporated first to determine any restriction on their capacity to do business. They should exercise the same caution with banks, trust companies, trade unions, insurance companies, as well as government agencies and departments. Of course, since all dealings with a corporation are through agents, people should always ensure the agent has been given the appropriate authority to act.

A corporation is a separate legal person

A corporation has the same powers and capacity of a natural person

Capacity may be limited with special act companies

Agents acting for corporations may have limited power

LIMITED LIABILITY

Shareholders are not liable for the debts and liabilities of the corporation

Perhaps the most important consequence of the separate legal entity status of the corporation is limited liability. Since the corporation is a separate legal personality, any debts, liabilities, or other obligations of the corporation are those of the corporation itself, not the shareholders. This was established by a famous case, *Salomon v. Salomon & Co.*,[10] where Mr. Salomon operated a shoe business, which he subsequently incorporated with himself holding all but a few shares. He then sold the assets of the business to the corporation and became a secured creditor for the debt. Through no fault of his, the business ran into financial difficulties and the creditors turned to Salomon for payment. The court held that the debts were those of the corporation, not Mr. Salomon, and that only the corporation was responsible for payment. Thus, Mr. Salomon had limited liability. To make matters worse for those creditors, Salomon as a separate person could also be a creditor, and as a secured creditor, he had first claim on the remaining assets of the corporation ahead of those other creditors.

Shareholders have limited liability

Limited liability then means that the debts, liabilities, and other obligations of the corporation remain with the corporation. In normal circumstances they will not be imposed on the shareholders, directors, or other participants in the corporate business. But it is always important to remember that the separate legal person aspect of the corporation is a myth or fiction created for the convenience of doing business. As a result, in rare circumstances, the courts are willing to look behind the corporate structure (lift the corporate veil) and impose liability on the shareholders directly. This approach is usually restricted to situations where the corporation is being used by the shareholder to commit a crime, fraud, or some other wrong.

Court may lift corporate veil where there is crime or fraud

One important advantage of a corporation is that its separate legal personality makes it responsible to pay taxes on its earnings, while the shareholders only have to pay taxes on dividends when declared by the corporation. Because of the lower rates of taxation for smaller corporations, there is sometimes a temptation to create a number of smaller corporations that are taxed at a lower rate than one big one.

Several corporations may be treated as one for tax purposes

But this is not permitted, and these corporations will all be treated as one for taxation purposes. This is another example of the consequences of ignoring the separate legal entity status of different corporations. It should be noted that the position of the director is not always as protected as that of a shareholder. Because directors have a more direct involvement in decision-making, they have a significant duty of care to the corporation, and many statutes also hold them directly responsible for the decisions made. Directors' liability will be discussed below.

Directors do not have the same protection

CASE SUMMARY 7.7

Nedco Ltd. v. Clark et al.[11]

But the Corporate Veil Can Be Lifted

Employees of Nedco were involved in a lawful strike when they extended their picket lines to Northern Electric, Nedco's parent company. The Alberta legislation permit-

(continued)

10. [1897] A.C. 22 (H.L.).

11. (1973), 43 D.L.R. (3d) 714 (Sask. C.A.).

ted secondary picketing, but Northern Electric asked for an injunction to stop the picketing, arguing that although Nedco was a wholly owned subsidiary of Northern Electric they were separate companies, and as such, were legally independent of each other. The court held that this was one of those rare cases where the court could ignore the separate entity status of corporations and found that Nedco was an integral component of Northern Electric's business operation. The corporate veil was lifted, and the employees of Nedco were allowed to extend their pickets to the Northern Electric operations. The case shows that, while generally reluctant, courts are willing to ignore the separate legal entity of corporations where it is appropriate to do so.

CASE SUMMARY 7.7 Nedco Ltd. v. Clark et al.

But the corporate veil can be lifted

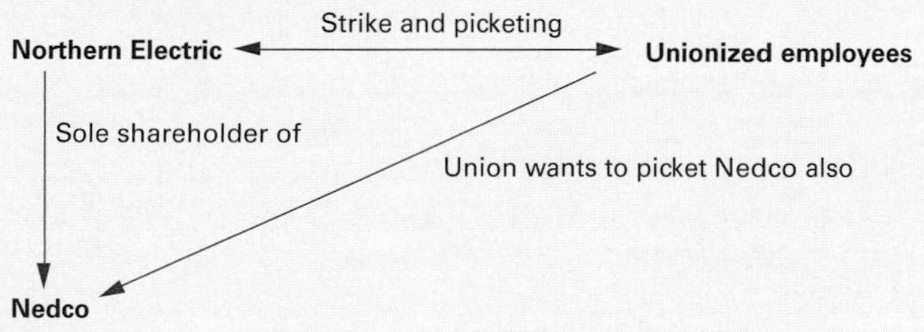

Another consequence of the corporation being a separate legal person is that it doesn't die. Because the company is a fiction, it doesn't die of natural causes like a normal person, although it can be dissolved voluntarily or by court order. As a result, there are many corporations that have been in existence for hundreds of years and are still going strong. The Hudson's Bay Company (the Bay), established over 300 years ago, is an example. Also the corporation doesn't end when the shareholders die. The shares are merely assets held by the shareholders that are passed down to their heirs. The company carries on. Once issued, shares are assets that can be bought and sold without directly affecting the corporation. This has led to the creation of that venerable institution—the stock market. It is this characteristic of independence from the corporation that makes shares such an attractive tool for investment.

Corporation does not die

The corporation does not end with deaths of shareholders

Another effect of the nature of a corporation as a separate legal person is the ability to have management that is separate from the owners or shareholders. In a partnership the partners are the management, but in a corporation a separate management group can be hired to manage the corporation. The management can even be from the shareholders themselves. They can be hired as employees, since unlike a sole proprietor or a partnership, the shareholders are separate and independent from the corporation. This management team is answerable to the directors who are, in turn, answerable by election to the shareholders, who maintain ultimate control of the corporation but do not manage it. Note that "ownership" as it is used here is a little misleading. The shareholders don't technically

Management and shareholders are separate

Managers are answerable to directors

own the corporation or its assets. The shares only give the shareholder control of the corporation through voting. It is only upon dissolution of the corporation that the shareholder may have a claim to the assets of the company. Note, however, that there is a Supreme Court of Canada decision holding that the shareholder has a sufficient interest in the assets of a corporation to take out insurance and collect in the event of damage.[12]

Such separate management can have a downside as well. Often in large corporations the management side is separate and apart and develops different interests from the shareholders. As a result, it will sometimes act against the best interests of the shareholders to protect its own position. For example, frequently one corporation will attempt to take over another by offering a generous amount for outstanding shares. But the managers of the corporation to be taken over may see this as a threat to their jobs and do what they can to resist, even though the shareholders would be better off with the takeover.

Managers sometimes act against interests of shareholders

Another important result of the shareholders being separate from the company is that it allows the shareholders to carry on their own business activities without reference to the company. A partner has to be careful not to compete with the partnership and to always put the interests of the partnership ahead of his own, but a shareholder has no similar duty to the corporation. A shareholder is free to sell his or her shares, to compete, to hold shares in other similar or competing businesses, to withhold information, and to pursue other business or personal interests that may even be detrimental to the corporation. Only where the shareholder becomes a director, officer, or other employee of the corporation may fiduciary or other duties be imposed. Note also that where a shareholder holds enough shares to be classed as an insider in a publicly traded company, there are also important limitations placed on his or her ability to purchase and sell those shares because of the privileged information the shareholder is presumed to possess.

Shareholders are not required to act in best interests of corporation

Insiders must not act on privileged information

SHAREHOLDERS' RIGHTS

Shareholders have:
- **Right to vote**
- **Right to dividend**
- **Right to assets upon dissolution**
- **Right to inspect records**

Although there are very few duties imposed on the shareholder, there are several mechanisms built into the corporate structure designed to protect the interest of the shareholders and their investment. As discussed, shareholders have a right to vote at the annual shareholder meeting and a right to a dividend if one is declared. They also have a right to a share of the assets of the corporation if it is wound up (dissolved). Also they have the right to inspect certain financial and other records of the corporation that are kept at the company's registered office for that purpose. In addition to these rights, there are several mechanisms designed to protect them from abuse. Sometimes the elected directors will make decisions that negatively affect the shareholders (usually a minority shareholder in particular). If the decision involves a major change for the good of the corporation that will have a negative impact on minority shareholders, the minority shareholders may have a right to **dissent** and have their shares purchased by the corporation at a "fair value." Sometimes the directors representing the majority shareholders will make decisions that have a negative impact on both the corporation and the minority shareholders. Usually there has been a falling out and the majority shareholders are simply using their power to hurt the minority shareholders. Sometimes the majority shareholder may strip assets from the company for his own benefit or transfer, sell, or otherwise bestow a benefit onto a company he owns, all at the expense of the

- **Right to dissent**

12. *Kosmopoulos v. Constitution Insurance Co. of Canada*, [1987] 1 S.C.R. 2 (S.C.C.).

corporation and the oppression of shareholders. When this happens, the minority shareholder can apply to the court seeking protection from such **oppression**. If the court agrees, there is considerable latitude in what they can do. This includes stopping the offending conduct, compensating the victim, setting aside the offending contract or transaction, or altering its terms. It may also declare that new directors or a receiver be appointed, that terms in the articles or shareholders' agreement be changed, or that the corporation be wound up.[13] Note, as well, that the remedy of oppression is not limited to shareholders but can be brought by any "security holder, creditor, director or officer of the corporation."[14]

- Right to be free of oppression

CASE SUMMARY 7.8

400280 Alberta Ltd. v. Franko's Heating & Air Conditioning (1992) Ltd.[15]

When a Director's Breach of Fiduciary Duty Constitutes Oppression

Watts and Franco started up Franco's Heating and Air Conditioning Ltd. (a metal fabrication business) to support Watts' successful plumbing and mechanical contracting business. Because Franco generated some business directly, Watts held only 30 percent of the shares. Unknown to Watts, Franco incorporated another company (Franco 92 Inc.) where he owned all of the shares and diverted as much business as he could to it. When Watts discovered this, he brought an action for oppression against Franco. The court found that as a director Franco owed a fiduciary duty to the original company, and he breached that duty when he opened up the new company in competition and diverted business to it. Watts was a victim of oppression, and Franco had to pay 30 percent of the profits of the new company to Watts. This case illustrates the nature of a director's duties to the company and what happens when a majority shareholder manipulates the affairs of a corporation in order to oppress a minority shareholder.

CASE SUMMARY 7.8 **400280 Alberta Ltd. v. Franko's Heating & Air Conditioning (1992) Ltd.**

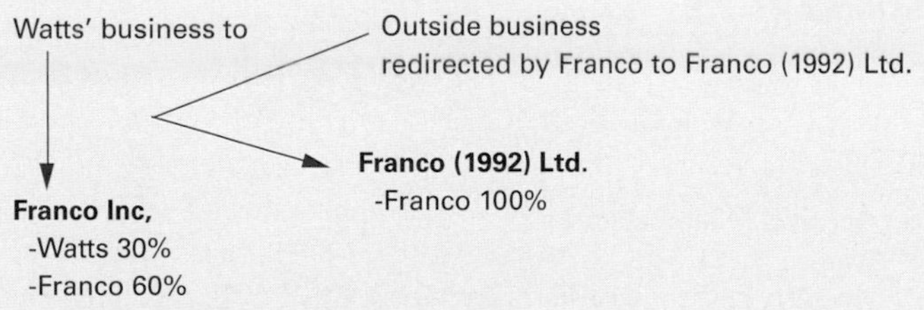

13. *Business Corporations Act* R.S.O. 1990, c. B.16, s. 248.
14. *Ibid.*, s. 207.
15. [1995] 4 W.W.R. 558 (Alta. Q.B.).

Another way that the interests of a minority shareholder could be adversely affected is through the issuing of more shares. When incorporated, a company will be given authority to issue a large number of shares (authorized share capital) but, in fact, will actually issue only a portion of those shares. The company is free then to issue more shares in the future. Issuing more shares can have an adverse effect on the position of the present shareholders, if they're not offered to them first. For example, suppose 10 000 shares have been issued and a minority shareholder holds 4000 of them. If 5000 more shares were issued but not offered to that minority shareholder, his or her share of the company would drop from a 40 percent interest to a 27 percent interest. If there were a number of shareholders, none with a clear majority, the issuing of such shares could completely alter the control structure of the company, depending on to whom they were issued. To prevent this abuse, corporations are allowed to state in their incorporating documents whether or not a portion of any newly issued shares must be offered first to the present shareholders sufficient to maintain their percentage control of the corporation. These are called **preemptive rights**. In this example it would mean that the minority shareholder having 40 percent of the outstanding shares would have to be offered 2000 of the newly issued shares to maintain his or her position. In those jurisdictions where such preemptive rights are not included in the statute, they are usually built into the incorporating documents or into a shareholders' agreement.

Shareholder may have preemptive rights

Perhaps the most important right of the minority shareholder is the right to bring a **representative action** (sometimes called a derivative action). The corporation may have the right to sue someone and the directors may choose not to do so. This may be the result of the majority shareholder obtaining some benefit from the decision as would be the case where the majority shareholder has an interest in the offending company or is seeking some other advantage from them. Or it may be the directors themselves who have failed in their duty to the corporation and, not surprisingly, refuse to sue themselves. Sometimes the victim company is a subsidiary, and it is the parent company that is the major shareholder and the wrongdoer. In these circumstances any shareholder has a right to bring an action on behalf of the corporation (a representative action) and pursue the claim. Note that it is still the company that is doing the suing, but the shareholder is the one acting on that company's behalf, much like a parent would bring an action on behalf of an injured child.

Shareholder has right to bring representative action

CASE SUMMARY 7.9

Re Richardson Greenshields of Canada Ltd. and Kalmacoff et al.[16]

Derivative Action Used to Thwart Directors

Security Home Mortgage Investment Corporation had both common shares held privately and preferred shares sold to the public. A management company involving some directors and the CEO of Security Home ran the company. Dissatisfaction

(continued)

16. (1995), 123 D.L.R. (4th) 628 (Ont. C.A.).

arose with the arrangement. A vote was held amongst the shareholders, including the preferred shareholders; it was decided to terminate the services of the management company. The board complied, but then simply rehired all of the same people to manage Security Homes directly.

Richardson Greenshields, which had been involved in the public offering of the preferred shares and the successful vote, protested. They stated that rehiring the managers went against the stated wishes of the shareholders. When their protest was ignored, they bought several preferred shares of Security Home and brought this derivative (representative) action against the directors.

Was Richardson Greenshields an appropriate complainant with the right to bring such an action? The trial judge said they were not, since they had purchased the shares after the rehiring had taken place. But the Court of Appeal disagreed. They found that even though they had purchased shares after the action complained of had taken place, and with the express purpose of launching this derivative action, they were still entitled to do so and qualified as a proper complainant under the Act.

This case dramatically shows that any shareholder can bring such a derivative (representative) action on behalf of the company with the court's permission as long as he or she was bringing the application in good faith, and there was a legitimate issue to be tried. Here the court held that it was in the best interests of the company to determine whether the rights given to the shareholders had been "improperly extinguished or rendered meaningless by the directors."

DIRECTORS

While shareholders owe no duty to the corporation, the same is not true of the directors. Directors approve all the important decisions with respect to the operation of the corporation. They are the ultimate decision-makers and essentially the alter ego of the corporation, and they are only answerable to the shareholders in the sense that they must face re-election. Directors must function at a high standard when performing their responsibilities. They are required to "exercise the care, diligence and skill that a reasonably prudent person would exercise in comparable circumstances."[17] In the past the standard of care expected was much lower, and when it was increased, it caused many to resign—especially token directors who were given the positions because of their name and reputation, but didn't really function as directors. It is important to note that this duty is owed to the corporation, not to the shareholders. Only the corporation can sue the directors when they cause a loss through their carelessness or wrongdoing. It is for this reason that the representative action discussed above is so important. Although the shareholder can't sue the director, they can bring an action on behalf of the corporation and bring the director to account by that means.

Directors must exercise skill of reasonably prudent person

Director's duty owed to corporation

17. *Business Corporations Act*, R.S.O. 1990, c. B.16, s. 134 (1)(b).

Directors owe duty of honesty and good faith

Director must act in best interest of corporation

Information must be passed on to corporation

Business opportunities must be passed on to corporation

Hidden payments violate fiduciary duty

Conflict of interest must be disclosed

Where violation director must pay over any profit

Directors liable to creditors for improper dividends

Directors must also "act honestly and in good faith with a view to the best interests of the corporation."[18] Thus, the director has a fiduciary duty, which is owed to the corporation, rather than the shareholders. As was the case in the discussion of partnership above and agency in Chapter 6, a fiduciary duty imposes an obligation on the directors to act in the best interests of the corporation, even to the point of putting the corporation's interests ahead of their own. Any information or business opportunities that come to a director because of his or her position in the corporation belong to the corporation, not the director. All such information must be disclosed to the corporation (the other directors), and any such business opportunity must be passed on to the corporation. Only where the board of directors rejects the opportunity and gives permission to the director to pursue it should he or she take advantage of the deal. Secret profits, commissions, kickbacks from suppliers, or other under-the-table dealings are all violations of this fiduciary duty and may also constitute a criminal offence. If the director finds himself in a position where the corporation's interests conflict with his own, he must disclose that conflict and not participate in the discussion of the matter in question or influence the decision. For example, if the corporation of which he is a director is considering the purchase of land and he has an interest, is part owner, or would otherwise be benefited by the purchase of one of the properties being considered, he would have to disclose this conflict of interest and excuse himself, leaving the room as the other directors discussed and voted on which property to purchase. Where this fiduciary duty is breached the director is liable to the corporation for any losses suffered and must account for any profits received.

In addition to these obligations owed to the company, there are other important duties and liabilities imposed on the directors by statute for the wrongdoings of the business. First, directors will be liable to creditors if they declare dividends when the company is insolvent. The capital of the corporation must be preserved

CASE SUMMARY 7.10

UPM-Kymmene Corp. v. UPM-Kymmene Miramichi Inc. et al.[19]

A Director Breaches His Fiduciary Duty

Mr. Berg arranged through a company that he controlled to acquire majority control of Repap Enterprises Inc. This included the change of a number of old directors and the appointment of new ones under his control. As part of the process he had himself appointed as a director and senior executive officer of Repap. He then arranged for Repap to pay him an exorbitant compensation package, including a huge salary, stock options, bonuses, pension provisions, and a generous termination allowance. Eventually the old shareholders regained control of the company, appointed new

(continued)

18. *Ibid.*, s. 134 (1)(a).

19. (2002), 214 D.L.R. (4th) 496 (Ont. S.C.J.).

directors, terminated Mr. Berg's contract, and refused to pay the $27 million he claimed he was owed for those services. This action is brought by the new directors for a declaration that Mr. Berg had breached his fiduciary duty to the corporation. In fact, he had not disclosed all the pertinent information to the new board members who had approved the compensation contract. There should have been an independent evaluation, which was not done. The company couldn't afford such an exorbitant amount for his salary and benefits, and Mr. Berg should have known it. This was a breach of his fiduciary duty and also amounted to oppression. The court set the contract aside, and Berg was deprived of any claim against the company under it.

Directors must forward taxes and deductions

Directors are responsible for unpaid wages

Director responsible for pollution and other statutory offences

and dividends can only be declared out of profits. Also, the corporation has an obligation to collect and forward PST and GST taken from customers and the deductions from the wages of employees for income tax, employment insurance, and workers' compensation assessments. The directors have the responsibility to see that this is done. They are even responsible directly to the employees for several months' unpaid wages, the actual number varying with the jurisdiction. Directors can also be held liable for environmental damage caused by the corporation, for offences under the *Competition Act,* and other federal and provincial legislation as well as direct liability for fraud or criminal activity. It is because of this potential liability that we often see directors resign in mass from large corporations that have run into financial difficulty. Even the director's claims that he or she didn't participate in the questionable decision or that he or she missed the meeting will not provide a sufficient excuse. Only where the directors can show that they exercised due diligence might they avoid such responsibility. Due diligence has become a very important concept in law, especially when dealing with government regulation. This topic is covered in Chapter 10. For the purposes of this chapter, due diligence can be expressed as the requirement that an individual, usually a corporate officer, must exercise all reasonable care to ensure that some prohibited event or conduct does not take place, or that the legislation in question is complied with. Note that this is a defence, and so the company or the individual director or manager is usually facing a charge, such as an environmental offence resulting from the escape of pollutants. The individual who was in control at the time might be charged personally, or the corporation itself might be charged for the director or other employees' actions, where that individual can be said to be the directing mind of the corporation or acting within his or her assigned duties or authority, or with the knowledge of superiors when the offending conduct took place. The due diligence defence requires the corporation or officers charged to show that they have taken reasonable steps to ensure the violation didn't take place or to comply with the regulations. This may require putting systems in place to ensure that the complained of event will not happen, for example, proper selection and training programs for employees and the establishing of policies and procedures that will avoid the problem.

A classic example involves a shoe manufacturing company that failed to properly store liquid waste. It was stored in barrels, which began to leak. Three executives were charged with environmental offences, but only one was able to raise due diligence as a defence and avoid responsibility. The plant manager made inadequate inspection of the site, and the director charged knew of the problem and failed to correct it. Only the president of the company was able to successfully claim due diligence on the basis of establishing appropriate procedures to avoid the problem, and reasonably relying on the competence of those given the responsibility to implement those procedures.[20] Note that in addition to environmental legislation, due diligence defences have been raised in many situations. These include failing to forward taxes (GST) and other funds collected on behalf of government; violations of the *Competition Act*, privacy legislation, and safety legislation for workers; food and drug act violations; building code violations; and even parking ticket violations. Note, also, that under many of these statutes both the corporation and the directors themselves can be held responsible. Due diligence on the part of the directors, who are the guiding minds of the corporation, or the manager or employee responsible for the area will protect the corporation as well.

Directors appoint and control managers

An important responsibility of the directors is to appoint the various officers of the corporation that make up the management team. These are typically the chair of the board of directors, the president, vice-president, secretary, treasurer,

CASE SUMMARY 7.11

Machula v. Her Majesty the Queen [21]

Director Responsible for GST Payment

This case is a good example of a director's obligation of due diligence. Machula was a director in three separate corporations, all of which failed to properly remit the goods and services tax (GST) owed. He claimed that he had exercised due diligence in all three cases and so should not be held personally liable. But the court held that he had only exercised due diligence with respect to one of the three corporations. For the first company he signed all cheques and received all benefits and so should have known of the GST owing and that it was not being paid. For the second company he was involved in on-going litigation, and since he was thoroughly informed about its financial dealings, he should have known that the GST had not been paid. In the case of the third corporation there were 800 employees, an up-to-date accounting system with current computers, software, and supervision in place, and he received financial reports every month with no indication that the GST was not being paid. In the case of the first two corporations, he should have known that the GST was not being paid. He had failed to exercise due diligence to ensure that it was properly paid and, therefore, was personally liable for that failure. But for corporation number three he had ensured that there was a proper system in place, which he should have been able to rely on. He was not in a position to know of the failure to pay and so, because he had exercised due diligence, was not personally responsible for that corporation's failure to pay the GST.

20. *R. v. Bata Industries Ltd.* (1992), 9 O.R. (3d) 329 (Ont. Prov. Ct).

21. [2003] T.C.J. No. 481 (T.C.C.).

general manager, and any others so designated. Their responsibilities are determined by the bylaws, but they bear a similar duty to the corporation as do directors—to perform their duties with the care, diligence, and skill of a reasonably prudent person, and to act honestly and in good faith in the best interests of the corporation. In a closely-held corporation it is common for these offices to be reduced to a minimum and held by the directors and shareholders.

Managers have similar duties to directors

It should also be noted that when a corporation is first formed, those promoting it have the same responsibilities to it as subsequent directors and officers, but they also have an obligation not to misrepresent or conceal information from future shareholders and not to sell property they hold to the corporation at an inflated price.

Promoters have duty not to mislead

Financing

RAISING FUNDS

Perhaps the major advantage to incorporation after limited liability is the flexibility that structure allows with respect to raising funds. The company can obtain such funds through equity financing where investors purchase shares, and through debt financing where money is loaned to the corporation by creditors (see Figure 7.4). As already mentioned, a company is incorporated with an authorized share capital and then a portion of those authorized shares are issued to investors. In most jurisdictions no value is put on these shares when issued; the selling price and future trading price are simply determined by the market. These are called **no par value shares**. It is quite unusual, even in those jurisdictions that still allow it, for a share to be given a nominal value (**par value**) when issued, although there may be some tax advantage to doing so.

Corporations allow flexible financing

Equity financing involves the issuing of shares

Issued shares usually much less than authorized share capital

The corporation may issue different classes of shares with special rights and restrictions that usually take the form of preferred shares and common shares. Common shares are the normal shares with all of the rights normally given to the shareholder, including the right to vote, to choose directors, and to set important policies, as well as the right to a dividend once declared. Such common shares will also have no unusual restrictions placed upon them. Preferred shares appeal to investors expecting a specified return on their investment. There is usually a commitment to pay a specified dividend each year, but it is important to remember that, like all shares, there is no right to such a dividend. The preferred share-

Common shares have no special rights or restrictions

FIGURE 7.4 Corporate Funding

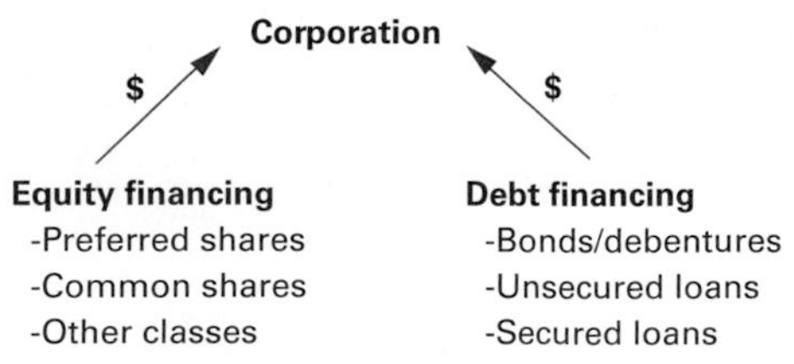

Preferred shareholders are usually promised dividend but can't vote

Unpaid dividends accumulate

holder cannot sue the corporation if he or she doesn't declare a dividend in any given year. When that happens, however, these preferred shares are usually designed so that the failure triggers other rights, such as the right to vote, which is normally denied a preferred shareholder so long as dividends are being properly paid. Where dividends have not been paid, the preferred shareholder usually has **cumulative rights**, requiring that all missed dividends must be made up to the preferred shareholder before any dividends can be paid to the common shareholders. But a preferred share is not a debt obligation of the corporation, and the preferred shareholder is an investor rather than a creditor.

Debt financing involves corporation borrowing money

Shareholders often loan funds to a corporation

Creditor usually takes security for loan

Personal guarantee defeats limited liability

A corporation is a separate person in the eyes of the law, and, like anyone else, the corporation can borrow money. Thus, debt is another important method of financing the business. Often the shareholders will loan the corporation money to get it started. This is normally a preferable way to invest, since issuing more shares to all of the shareholders will not change their proportional control of the company. For example, if three shareholders wish to start a business that needs $60 000 for equipment to get started, they may incorporate a company and issue only a few shares (say 10 shares each) for which they pay $1 per share. They would then loan the corporation $20 000 each for a total of $60 000 debt and take out a security against the equipment purchased with the money. They then each have one-third control of the company and are secured creditors for the other funds supplied. Or the company can borrow from some other creditor such as a bank. Creditors will usually require some security that will ensure the repayment of the money advanced if the business fails. This is often difficult for a new business, even where there are significant assets, and so the creditor will usually insist that the shareholders, directors, or some other financially stable person sign a personal guarantee, usually in addition to other forms of security, to repay the loan. If the corporation fails and cannot repay the debt, the individual guarantor is personally responsible for that debt (see Table 7.2). By this single stroke the major advantage of incorporation, limited liability, is defeated. And, in fact, most new businesses are in this position, much to the dismay of the entrepreneurs starting them.

TABLE 7.2 Liability Summary

	Nature of Business	Individual Liability
When victim sues	Sole proprietorship	Sole proprietor faces unlimited liability
	Partnership	Partner faces unlimited liability for obligations of firm or other partners
	Limited partnership	Limited partner faces only loss of investment (limited liability only)
	Limited liability partnership	Only partner directly responsible faces unlimited liability
	Corporation	Shareholders face only the loss of investment (limited liability only)
	Corporation with personal guarantee	Guarantor liable for debt to victim

Another more unusual form of debt financing involves the creation of a large debt obligation, either secured or unsecured, which a trustee is then named to manage. Small portions of this debt (called **bonds** or **debentures**) are issued to the public and then traded on the market much like shares. Whether a standard loan is negotiated with a bank or other institution or bonds or debentures are involved, these instruments usually include a unique right to the creditor in the event of default. Of course, the creditor can sue the corporation, but that is usually an empty remedy. They can also realize on their security or seek repayment from a guarantor, but they also usually have a right to appoint a **receiver** in the event of default to take over the management of the business to protect their investment. This is known as going into receivership. It has the effect of displacing the directors, shareholders, and managers of the corporation and removing them from control, while putting all decision-making power into the hands of the receiver. This form of receivership must be distinguished from bankruptcy. The appointment of a receiver is a right generated by the loan contract, and default on the debt is enough to trigger the appointment of the receiver. No court order is required, although this may be sought. Bankruptcy, on the other hand, is the procedure set out in the *Bankruptcy and Insolvency Act* whereby the bankrupt's assets are transferred, either voluntarily or by force, to a trustee in bankruptcy. The trustee then takes over the business and usually distributes the assets to the creditors. Note that, as discussed in Chapter 6, one of the options under the *Bankruptcy and Insolvency Act* is to make a proposal to the creditors. When this is done, the rights of the creditors are frozen, giving the debtor a chance to reorganize his or her affairs and solve the financial difficulties. Such a proposal would also prevent a receiver from taking over the management of the business until the expiration of the protection period. An application by large companies to the court under the *Companies' Creditors Arrangement Act* would have a similar delaying effect. Creditors can also sue for oppression, as illustrated in the following case.

Bonds are debt obligations traded like shares

Creditor usually has right to appoint receiver if loan defaulted

A receiver takes over the control of the corporation

Receivership distinguished from bankruptcy

Proposals delay actions by creditors

CASE SUMMARY 7.12

Re S.C.I. Systems, Inc. and Gornitzki Thompson & Little Co. et al. [22]

Oppression Can Also Be Claimed by a Creditor

S.C.I. Systems was a creditor and held a promissory note against Gornitzki, Thompson & Little Co. Ltd. (G.T.L.). Instead of paying the note, the director and sole shareholder of G.T.L. had the company declare and pay dividends, pay down loans to themselves, and transfer funds to other related corporations so that there was no money left to pay S.C.I. As a result, S.C.I. sued the sole shareholder of G.T.L. for oppression against them as creditor. The court found that paying out dividends while insolvent was a violation of law, and that, combined with their other manipulations, was unfair and oppressive. The shareholder of G.T.L. was required to pay compensation to S.C.I. Both shareholders and creditors can sue for oppression when company affairs are manipulated in such an unfair way to their detriment.

22. (1997), 147 D.L.R. (4th) 300 (Ont. Gen. Div.).

THE SHAREHOLDERS' AGREEMENT

Position of shareholders can be further refined through shareholders' agreement

Shareholders' agreement can protect minority shareholder

Shareholders' agreements can ensure employment and restrict control

Throughout this discussion several references have been made to shareholders' agreements. These usually are included where there are only a few shareholders and they want to set out rights and responsibilities with respect to each other that are not included in the incorporating documents. For example, three shareholders may get together to set up a restaurant: one the investor supplying cash; one an accountant supplying business expertise; and one a chef supplying experience in operating this type of business. Let us say that the one supplying cash takes 60 percent of the shares and the other two 20 percent each. This may reflect the individuals' relative commitments and how they want to share the profits, but not how they want the control of the business to be exercised. In such an organization the two minority shareholders would be completely at the mercy of the majority shareholder, who would exercise complete control with respect to the affairs of the corporation. In our example, however, the understanding is that each will have an equal say in the business and that the chef and accountant will also be full-time employees of the business. If the number of directors were set at three, the shareholders' agreement could provide that each one of the three shareholders would fill these positions and be a director. Thus the actual control would be shared equally. Also the shareholders' agreement would provide that the chef and the accountant would be full-time employees of the business. It is likely that the agreement would also provide for the resolving of disputes, such as a method to buy out a disgruntled shareholder and a method to establish a fair value for the shares. The agreement might also provide an arbitration process for the resolution of such disputes. In fact, these shareholders' agreements serve much the same purpose as a partnership agreement (discussed above), in that they allow the shareholders to set up special rights and obligations that better suit their unique relationship. Such a shareholders' agreement might also set out restrictions on when and to whom shares could be sold. In such small corporations the relationship between the shareholders is important, and so having some control over who can become a shareholder is equally important. It should also be noted that the terms of the shareholders' agreements must be unanimously agreed upon among all shareholders. They must be consistent with the legislation governing corporations in the jurisdiction in question. The agreement should be viewed as supplementary to the incorporating documents.

CASE SUMMARY 7.13

Philo Investments Ltd. v. Toronto Paramedical Management Inc.[23]

Shareholders' Agreements Can Cut Both Ways

Philo held 70 percent of Med-Chem Laboratories Ltd. shares, while Toronto Paramedical Management Company (T.P.M.C.) held the other 30 percent. There was a shareholders' agreement between them containing a "shotgun" clause. This pro-

(continued)

23. Ont. Gen. Div., as reported in *Lawyers Weekly*, Vol. 15 No. 45 (April 5, 1996).

vided that where one party offered to purchase the shares of the other at a specified price, the other shareholder could either sell at that price or turn the tables and purchase the offering shareholder's shares at that same stated price. Philo triggered this clause when they offered to purchase the shares held by T.P.M.C. for $3 million. To their surprise Toronto Paramedical opted to purchase the Philo shares instead of selling theirs. To accomplish this, T.P.M.C. attempted to arrange financing with its bank and another institution, but Philo did all they could to undermine that process. They informed the lenders that T.P.M.C. couldn't afford it. Several anonymous phone calls were made to both institutions telling them that T.P.M.C. was under police investigation; that an exposé on CBC was about to take place; and that their workforce was going on strike. Not surprisingly, T.P.M.C. was unable to arrange financing by the deadline, and this action was brought by Philo to force T.P.M.C. to sell them their shares, since they were not able to purchase those held by Philo. The court, however, agreed with T.P.M.C. that Philo had an obligation at least not to interfere with T.P.M.C. exercising their rights under the contract. "In any event, the applicants did everything they could to stop them and made their task almost impossible." Their request was refused and the court ordered that T.P.M.C. be given more time to arrange for financing the purchase and that Philo do nothing to interfere with the process. This case shows just how important a shareholders' agreement can be.

FLEXIBILITY

Finally, it is important to point out that partnerships and corporations as set out above are the basic building blocks of modern business. There are many different combinations of these basic building blocks that can be constructed to satisfy the needs of various enterprises. For example, it is common for companies to engage in **joint ventures** with each other. These are contractual relationships where two or more businesses get together for some project, usually of limited duration. In fact, joint ventures can take many different forms. They can be no more than a contractual arrangement, but they can also involve partnership arrangements, corporations, corporations in partnership, holding companies, etc. For example, two different oil companies might cooperate to develop a pipeline or combine their resources to open a particular gas field. They might incorporate a separate company to take on the project, each making a financial contribution as a shareholder in that new corporation and each appointing directors to run it. There would likely be a shareholders' agreement and the money might well be put forward as a shareholders' loan. Or the two companies might enter into a partnership to carry on the project, again with particulars set out in a partnership agreement. Remember that although the partnership conveys unlimited liability, the partners themselves are corporations each with the advantage of limited liability for the shareholder.

Corporations and partnership can be used in combination

Companies can come together in a joint venture

Another common way these organizations are combined is with a holding company. One individual might have 51 percent of the shares in a company that, in turn, has 51 percent of the shares in another company that, in turn, has 51 percent of the shares in a third company. That individual, with only a fraction of the actual equity ownership of the third company, still retains complete control of all

Holding companies ensure control

of them. Preferred shares, shareholders' loans, and shareholders' agreements can also be used, giving the business person a very flexible canvas on which to create a structure to do business that is completely unique to his or her needs. As a result there is no specific form that a joint venture can take, and the liability of the participants will be based on agency, partnership, and corporation principles, depending on the vehicle chosen.

Franchise

Another common method of doing business today is through a **franchise**. A franchise is not a specific legal structure of carrying on business, but has become an important vehicle, especially for retail business in Canada. In a franchise arrangement one business enters into contract with another to sell its product exclusively with appropriate names, logos, and advertising exclusive to the chain. From the point of view of the franchisor it is a very effective way to expand their business with little risk, and from the point of view of the franchisee they become part of a successful business enterprise. It must be emphasized that the franchisee and the franchisor are two different corporations, and they are normally not considered to be in partnership with each other.

Typically the franchisor will sell the right to do business in a given area to a smaller corporation (the franchisee). The franchisor provides the product and other supplies and equipment; advertising; a licence to use the name, trademark, and logos; any secret formulas as well as training and careful supervision, including management help. They sometimes even provide financing to the franchisee. Usually a standardized accounting system is supplied, likely more to protect the franchisor than to assist the franchisee. The franchisee must comply with rules, standards, and specifications with respect to the preparation of products, prices, advertising, and accounting so that there is a commonality among the various franchisees and different locations.

In addition to an initial investment of capital, the franchisee is normally required to pay a substantial franchise fee as well as regular payments to the franchisor for supplies and services, and often a percentage of the profits. Common examples of franchises in Canada range from fast food outlets like Tim Hortons, A & W, KFC, and Starbucks to other forms of businesses, including Budget and other car rental agencies, computer stores, and the like. The franchisee, of course, gets the advantage of the advertising, the right to use the trademarks, company logos, and other promotional materials, and to participate in promotions and other activities generated by the parent company.

One important drawback to these arrangements is the unequal bargaining position of the parties. Typically, the franchisor is a very large organization and the franchisee is a small entrepreneur who is not in a position to insist on favourable terms in any agreement. Standard form contracts are thus imposed on the franchisee, usually greatly favouring the parent franchisor with the inclusion of restrictive covenants and limited liability exemption clauses. Still, it is in the franchisor's interest to do all they can to ensure the success of the franchisee outlet, and so many of these arrangements have proved a very successful method of carrying on business.

There are many different variations of this kind of arrangement, and likely many more will be developed by creative business people. The point is that these various methods of doing business as described in this chapter are only the basic organizations. They can be combined and varied to such an extent that most business needs can be accommodated.

Many variations accommodate business

Corporate and Commercial Crime

Although shoplifting and employee theft can have a significant impact on businesses, they are essentially minor crimes. In this chapter we will look at major criminal activity in corporations, which are essentially variations of theft and fraud that are prohibited under the *Criminal Code*. Section 397 of the *Criminal Code* states that anyone who "destroys mutilates alters, falsifies, makes a false entry in or omits forms in a valuable security, book or document with an intent to defraud is guilty of an offence and liable to imprisonment for up to five years." There are also many other specialized sections dealing with serious internal and external embezzlement and fraud.

Internal offences against the business can include forgery, falsifying of documents, fraud associated with insurance, credit card abuse, cheques, and computers. Falsifying and abusing expense accounts, insider trading, and breach of trust are also specifically prohibited in the Code. External threats to the business include overcharging or duplication of invoices by suppliers, theft by joint-venture partners, non-payment for goods or services, counterfeit cheques, and abuses associated with the bidding process. These are a few examples of the most common offences, but there are many other ways that a business may be cheated. These efforts to defraud may be made by employees against their employer, by external perpetrators against the business, or by managers on behalf of the corporation against others, such as making false financial disclosures.

There are many examples of corporate crime

In fact, the instances of such fraud are increasing, partly due to corporate downsizing, which weakens internal controls and creates employee uncertainty. These, in turn, affect loyalty. And mergers often lead to problems with integrating people from different organizations into a new one. Additional risks have been created by the communications revolution and the global economy. The combination of these things contributes to fewer mechanisms of detection and control, and more opportunity to defraud a business from within and without. It shouldn't be surprising that much internal fraud is committed by long-term employees in positions of trust, since they have the opportunity to divert company funds. Fraud increases when the ethical structure of a business weakens. Technology and globalization contributes to the risk due to increased opportunity, dealing with strangers, and dealing with people with a wide range of values and business ethics. Business practices that are illegal here are sometimes common in other cultures. Another significant factor contributing to the increase in corporate crime is the increased role played by organized criminal organizations both in Canada and in other countries where Canadian corporations deal. These organizations are often involved in laundering funds from other criminal activities, counterfeiting, forgery, and various forms of computer and internet fraud.

Mergers and downsizing contribute to increase in corporate crime

Technology and globalization contribute to the increase in corporate crime

Recent high-profile cases have drawn even more attention to corporate fraud and brought changes to legislation, creating a greater risk of criminal prosecution for corporations and their managers. Multi-million dollar frauds at Enron and WorldCom, and trading scandals at the New York branch of the Daiwa Bank and the Barings Bank are only a few examples. Corporate fraud at its extreme can bring down the whole corporation.

A major objective of a business should be the prevention and detection of corporate fraud. Management must take responsibility and institute appropriate measures. Often the appointment of a specific loss-prevention team will focus efforts in this area, enabling managers to buy into the loss-prevention process, even though it is unpleasant. Management that includes risk assessment and developing pro-active strategies for risk avoidance is vital. Having good ethical standards and a published and distributed statement of the company's policies and code of conduct, combined with appropriate training for employees and staff, may go some way to avoid internal fraud. It may also serve to establish a due diligence defence by showing that reasonable efforts were made on the part of a corporation to avoid illegal activity.

Risk management strategies can combat corporate crime

Careful credit and reference checks, including a background and criminal record check as well as verification of all claimed credentials and degrees, should be made with all new hires. For senior positions such checks should go further, with interviews of former colleagues and employers, database checks—including public records and legal proceedings—as well as searches of published articles in newspapers and magazines. When dealing with other firms, especially foreign corporations, an effort should be made to get to know the parties with appropriate research of the people, cultures, and companies. Firms should never be taken at face value. When dealing with fraud, simple surveillance will not be as effective as appropriate internal controls such as dual signatures on cheques and close supervision of people with power to order and deal with corporate funds. Careful internal audits, designed to detect fraud and followed by external audits, are necessary. Most such frauds are detected internally by supervisors and fellow employees—usually by accident—rather than by external means.

Research and reference checks can avoid problems with employees, partners, and other businesses

While prevention is important, detection of fraud is vital. Often such crimes, committed by trusted employees, go on for years because there is no structure in place for detection. Proper processes of supervision and control, including appropriate security and surveillance, serve the double purpose of discouraging crime and detecting it when it takes place. Here again, care must be taken not to infringe on the privacy rights of employees. Whether there is simple abuse by an employee who makes personal use of a company's tools, equipment, or other facilities, or whether these resources are being used to commit a criminal act or to defraud the company, the practice will likely be reduced with proper surveillance. A business is more likely to have the right to monitor an employee's use of company equipment such as computers, phones, and other telecommunications equipment if they inform the employees that they are subject to such monitoring at the outset. They also have the right to use closed circuit TV to monitor various plant and office locations, again with appropriate pre-notification. In fact, such notification should be made a term of the contract of employment. This might be more difficult where a union is involved, and their agreement and cooperation are required. It is likely that anything beyond normal supervision of unionized employees will be considered a breach of an employee's privacy rights, unless there are reasonable grounds for launching an investigation. Note that such privacy legislation varies from province to province. While such close monitoring of an employee's activities and use of equipment may be taken as distrust and reduce loyalty, if the expectation is made part of the corporate culture from the outset, it will likely be more readily tolerated by all levels of employees.

Careful supervision, security, and surveillance can avoid problems

Employers must take care not to infringe the rights of employees

Even when no crime has been detected, there are often telltale clues that should alert management to a potential problem. When an employee shows a marked change in personality or there is evidence of a serious drinking problem or drug abuse, this should at least trigger concern for the employee's welfare, but it may also indicate a serious problem with reference to his or her job performance or some criminal activity. High debt load or other financial difficulties, gambling problems, and even an employee avoiding taking a vacation may also be symptoms of a serious job-related problem, especially if the opportunity is present for the misappropriation of funds.

When an individual employee is suspected of criminal activity or other wrongdoing, great care must be taken in the investigation and punishment process. The first stage is usually a forensic audit to determine the extent of the fraud and find evidence of the wrongdoing. Lawyers should be brought in at this stage to ensure that evidence is preserved and the investigation does not interfere with the rights of the employee. Overenthusiastic investigators have been known to breach privacy rights, defame individuals, and trespass, putting at risk any further action and subjecting the corporation to a wrongful dismissal action. Sometimes a gentler, less threatening approach will be more productive.

Expert help should be obtained when a crime is suspected

A decision has to be made at this stage whether the goal is simply the dismissal of the employee, the recovery of what has been lost, or an actual criminal prosecution. If the goal is simply to get rid of the employee, there is the danger of a wrongful dismissal action or even an action for defamation if the grounds for the dismissal are theft or fraud and that is made public. Such an unfounded accusation can significantly increase the damages awarded. The employee should be given an opportunity to respond to any charges against him or her, and any other employees involved must be made to understand that everything associated with the investigation is completely confidential. The dismissal process itself should be done privately, preserving the dignity of the terminated employee so as to avoid defamation by innuendo.

Improper process can have serious repercussion to business

If the goal is to recover the money, great care must be exercised not to intimidate or coerce the employee by threats of prosecution. Any agreement not to inform the police in return for the employee's cooperation and the return of the money is an indictable offence under sections 141 and 142 of the *Criminal Code* and is punishable with imprisonment up to five years. Also, if there is any chance of recovering the funds, action must be taken immediately to preserve those funds and any evidence of the wrongdoing. This may include police involvement, obtaining *ex parte* injunctions and court orders to freeze assets.

Employer should move quickly when fraud discovered

Where internal fraud or theft is involved, the corporation often will not be interested in pursuing a criminal prosecution because of damaging publicity, the disruption of the business and time-commitment of key personnel, the disclosure of confidential corporate information, the lengthy legal process, and the difficulties of getting a conviction. Still, it may well be that for the preservation of the company's reputation or as a deterrent to others, criminal prosecution will be appropriate. In this case it is advisable to involve the police at the earliest stage. Police have greater powers of investigation and greater investigatory expertise. They can obtain search warrants and are more likely to ensure that the process followed is correct and does not interfere with the rights of the suspected wrongdoer. While the primary focus of criminal prosecution is conviction and punishment, the prosecution process also has the potential of a restitution order in the event of a conviction. If the matter can be settled with the cooperation of the prosecutor before that stage, the restoration of the funds taken can be a condition of the settlement. The threat of jail might be a stronger inducement to return the funds, since doing so can significantly reduce any sentence imposed by the court.

Police involvement and prosecution can have beneficial results

One considerable problem with involving the police is that the corporate crime specialists are often overextended and overworked and may not have the resources to properly investigate the complaint in a timely manner. Private professional legal and forensic experts can be hired by the corporation to investigate. They then provide information to the police, thus overcoming this problem to some extent. But in some cases the police simply do not have the resources and will refuse to get involved, especially where there is a civil remedy available. Still, insurance policies usually require that at least a police report be filed.

A considerable amount of corporate crime takes place with the corporation as the perpetrator rather than the victim. Employees commit the crime while acting on behalf of the corporation to further business interests. In such circumstances the corporation will not only face civil liability but may also face criminal prosecution along with the offending employee.

Internal fraud and theft as well as other unique criminal acts by employees can be committed against other businesses or the public. People are cheated; government regulation is flaunted; trademarks, patents, and copyrights are infringed; software is pirated; businesses conspire to limit competition; misleading ads are published; pollution and other toxic wastes are discharged; stock markets are manipulated; insider information is misused; and illegal proceeds of crime are laundered, to name a few.

Corporate liability for criminal acts broadened

In the past a company could only be liable for regulatory offences committed by employees, but generally not for crimes. The company that benefited was usually not pursued, unless it could be determined that the individual who committed the crime was also the directing mind of the corporation. This was seldom the case. But amendments have been made to the *Criminal Code* making it much easier to prosecute the corporation or other organization for crimes committed by directors, employees, members, agents, partners, and contractors. Note that organizations include trade unions, societies, partnerships, and associations as well as corporations.

It is important for the business to implement prevention strategies to avoid prosecution

Where the crime was committed by one of these parties, the corporation can be found criminally negligent if it can be demonstrated that a senior officer departed "markedly" from the standard of care required to prevent the offence, and the offending individual was acting within the authority given. For offences requiring intent the corporation can be prosecuted where a senior officer was acting within his or her authority on behalf of the corporation when committing the offence; where that senior officer directed another to commit the crime; or, knowing that a representative of the corporation was about to be a party to such an offence, failed to take reasonable steps to prevent it. Such senior officers include the president, directors, and chief financial officer of a corporation. These amendments were made in reaction to the Westray mine disaster and a special section was added to the *Criminal Code* [section 217(1)] providing for prosecution for criminal negligence of anyone who has a duty to direct workers and fails to take reasonable steps to protect that person or others from bodily harm arising out of that work. Penalties extend to life imprisonment with a minimum of four years where a death results. Because a requirement for conviction of the corporation is that the senior officer be shown to have failed to take reasonable steps or to have departed markedly from the reasonable standard, there is considerable incentive for a corporation to have policies, training, and follow-up procedures in place to ensure that such departures don't occur.

These and other amendments to the *Criminal Code* and other regulatory statutes have imposed a greater responsibility on the corporation to police itself rather than be monitored and controlled by outside agencies.

QUESTIONS FOR REVIEW

1. Why is it so important to take care in choosing the method used to carry on a business?
2. Explain the nature of a sole proprietorship and the liability of a sole proprietor. Why do professionals often do business in this way?
3. Describe the nature of a partnership, the purpose and effect of the *Partnership Act*, and the effect a partnership agreement can have on the relationship between the parties as set out in that statute.
4. What factors will indicate the existence of a partnership?
5. Explain the nature of the liability of partners and the effect of a partnership agreement on a partner's liability to outsiders. How will the retirement of a partner affect those obligations?
6. Explain how major decisions are made in a partnership and how partners get paid.
7. What is the nature of a partner's duty and to whom is that duty owed?
8. Explain what will bring a partnership to an end and how the assets of the partnership are to be distributed upon dissolution.
9. What is meant by a limited partner? What is the extent of that limited liability? What qualifications must be met for such a limited partnership to exist and how it can be lost? Distinguish such a limited partnership from a limited liability partnership.
10. What is the effect of incorporation and what is meant by the term corporate myth?
11. Distinguish between the registration system, the letters patent system, and the articles of incorporation systems of incorporation. Distinguish between broadly-held and closely-held corporations.
12. What is contained in the articles of incorporation? What are the bylaws and how are they enacted?
13. Explain the right of a shareholder with respect to control of the corporation, how that right is exercised, and what is meant by shareholders' limited liability.
14. Explain under what circumstances the courts may "lift the corporate veil," and the consequences of that happening.
15. Under what circumstances can a corporation be brought to an end, and what happens to a corporation when all of the shareholders die?
16. Describe the advantages and disadvantages of having the ownership and management of a corporation separate.

17. What is meant by a shareholder's right to dissent, to be free from oppression, and pre-emptive rights with respect to the corporation?
18. Explain what is meant by a representative action, when it arises, and who can bring such an action.
19. What are the duties of a director and to whom are those duties owed? What standard of care is required of that director? What constitutes a director's duty of good faith?
20. What are the various ways a director can breach his or her fiduciary duty? Explain the consequences of such a breach.
21. Explain a director's liability for improperly declared dividends, failure to collect deductions from employees, and the consequences of such a failure. How does due diligence affect those obligations?
22. Distinguish between authorized and issued share capital, and common and preferred shares. Explain what is meant by cumulative rights with respect to preferred shares.
23. Distinguish between equity and debt financing. Explain the nature of bonds and how they differ from shares.
24. Explain what is meant by a company going into receivership. How does receivership differ from bankruptcy? Explain how a proposal under the *Bankruptcy and Insolvency Act* may affect the position of a creditor.
25. Describe the kind of corporations where a shareholders' agreement would likely be found and the effect it will likely have on the position of a minority shareholder.
26. Explain what is meant by a joint venture, a holding company, and a franchise. Why are they attractive ways of doing business?
27. Describe effective strategies for a corporation to avoid being the victim of fraud and theft.
28. What are the advantages of involving the police when internal corporate crime is discovered?
29. Explain what problems can arise from overdone security and surveillance.
30. Explain how Canada's law with respect to corporate responsibility for crimes committed on the company's behalf has been expanded.

QUESTIONS FOR FURTHER DISCUSSION

1. One of the great advantages of a corporation over a partnership is the limited liability of the shareholder investors. If the business runs into trouble, the debts are the corporation's rather than the shareholders', who can only lose what they have invested. This is one of the most important characteristics of a corporation and one of the significant limitations of a partnership. Discuss whether such limited liability is appropriate from a business point of view. Is it fair to all parties? What about creditors or others who have claims against the business because of poor decisions that have been made? Who

should be responsible? In your response consider the movement toward creating limited liability partnerships (LLPs) and whether this is a forward or a backward step. Also consider the creation of the corporate myth, which is the basis for the limited liability of shareholders.

2. While shareholders are isolated from liability for the careless actions of corporations, this protection is not always carried through to directors who may be held criminally and civilly liable for the actions of the corporation, especially when they cause physical injury to others. Directors, like partners, also owe a fiduciary duty to the corporation and can be personally sued when they violate that duty. Discuss the relative obligations of directors and partners to each other, to the business, and to outsiders. Consider whether the imposition of such liability goes too far or not far enough from a business and ethical point of view. In your discussion consider the nature of fiduciary duty and whether such an overwhelming obligation has any place in the business world.

3. A corporation is considered a legal entity, separate and apart from the shareholders who make it up. This is a myth or fiction and has no basis in reality. Most of the unique characteristics of corporations result from this separate legal entity status. Discuss whether this bit of make-believe in our legal system is justified, considering the result. In your answer consider the recent well-known events involving corporate crime, swindles, and other abuses such as Enron or WorldCom. Do you think doing away with the corporate myth would make any difference?

4. It is possible to be in partnership with someone else without knowing it, simply by getting into some sort of cooperative business venture. The burdens associated with partnership, especially unlimited liability for a partner's actions, can be very onerous. Discuss whether people should ever have partnership imposed on them in this way or whether this relationship should be limited to those situations where there is a clear understanding between the parties to create such a partnership relationship.

CASES
FOR DISCUSSION

1. **OLSON V. GULLO ET AL.** (1994), 113 D.L.R. (4th) 42 (Ont. C.A.).
Olson worked as a manager for Gullo. Together they entered into a scheme to purchase and develop a particular 1000-acre tract of land near the town of Keswick, Ontario. They both were to contribute their business skills and contribute equally with respect to the capital investment. After this discussion and an oral agreement to create a partnership, Gullo convinced Olson that the project was not viable and they agreed to abandon it. Afterward, Gullo secretly bought 90 acres of the property and sold it for a very large profit. When Olson found out, he quit his position in Gullo's organization and brought this action for a share of the profits. He claimed he was a partner in the enterprise and entitled to at least half of the proceeds. Consider whether a partnership has been created. If so, what are the obligations of the parties?

2. **LAMPERT PLUMBING (DANFORTH) LTD. V. AGATHOS ET AL.** (1972), 27 D.L.R. (3d) 284 (Ont. Co. Ct.).
Mr. Agathos was the owner of a Toronto radio station that catered to the Greek community. Mr. Margoulas contracted for certain advertising with that radio station on behalf of his business, Alpha and Omega Construction Company. Mr. Agathos did much to help out Margoulas and often would represent the business in dealings with customers. He even signed contracts and cheques on behalf of the company. He did this gratuitously with no extra remuneration other than the hope of keeping the business going so that he would be paid for the advertising purchased by the company. One of the suppliers to the construction company (Lambert Plumbing) was not paid. They then sued Agathos as a partner in the business. In fact, the principal of the supplier had been dealing with Agathos and thought that he was the principal of Alpha and Omega Construction. What are the arguments that can be advanced by both sides with respect to the existence of a partnership and Mr. Agathos' liability for these debts? Note that Agathos claimed he had never carried on business with Magoulas and that there was no partnership contract or agreement between them.

3. **PUBLIC TRUSTEE V. MORTIMER ET AL.** (1985), 16 D.L.R. (4th) 404 (Ont. H.C.J.).
Mortimer was a partner in a law firm and acted as the executor for the estate of Mrs. Amy Cooper. When she died, he distributed the proceeds of the estate to a series of beneficiaries. He also stole over $200 000 of the estate, keeping it for himself. The problem here was whether the other partners were also liable for Mr. Mortimer's wrongful conduct. Discuss the arguments on both sides. What kind of information is needed in order to answer the question?

4. **MACDONALD V. SCHMIDT,** B.C.S.C., as reported in *Lawyers Weekly*, Vol. 11 No. 41 (1992).
A group of four partners were carrying on business together when one of them (Schmidt) was found liable for certain careless conduct while acting on partnership business. The victim of that wrongdoing sued all four partners for compensation and was successful in his action. In this case Schmidt's three partners are demanding that he reimburse them for what they had to pay out in that judgment. Do you think Mr. Schmidt should be obligated to pay back his partners in these circumstances? Discuss the arguments available to both sides.

5. **RICH V. ENNS,** [1995] 6 W.W.R. 257 (Man. C.A.).
Rich was the sole shareholder in a company (Sargent Properties Ltd.) and used that company to arrange a purchase of certain property that was being sold after a foreclosure. His company purchased the property, and then Rich arranged to resell it from Sargent Properties Ltd. to Enns. Before the deal could go through, Enns changed his mind, repudiated the contract, and refused to go through with the purchase. Note that at all times the purchaser and reseller of the property was clearly stated in the contracts as Sargent Properties Ltd., not Rich. Subsequent to the purchase of the property Rich discovered that the company had actually been dissolved by the Alberta Registrar of Companies for failure to file annual reports and technically did not exist at the time of the transaction. Rich brought this action in his personal capacity (not in the name of the company). He sued Enns for damages for breach of the contract of purchase and sale for the property. Explain the arguments that Enns might raise in his defence. Discuss the likely outcome of the case.

6. **MILLS-HUGHES ET AL. V. RAYNOR ET AL.** (1988), 47 D.L.R. (4th) 381 (Ont. C.A.).
Canadian Admiral Corporation was a successful and viable business entity when it was taken over by York Lambton Inc. Under this new ownership a large loan was taken out against Admiral's assets and that, combined with escalating interest costs, drove Admiral into insolvency. When Admiral could not pay its debts, it was petitioned into bankruptcy by its creditors. That left 19 middle and senior managers of Admiral with claims for unpaid wages, bonus entitlements, vacation, and severance pay. The *Canada Business Corporations Act,* under which this application is brought, provides that directors are personally " . . . liable to employees of the corporation for all debts . . . for services performed for the corporation." Which of the above claims do you think the directors of Admiral at the time of the bankruptcy would be personally liable to pay? In this case the bonus was a guaranteed part of the compensation package of the employees. How would your answer be different if the bonus was dependant on the profitability of the corporation or on the performance of the employee?

7. **SWALE INVESTMENTS LTD. V. NATIONAL BANK OF GREECE (CANADA),** Ont. Gen. Div., 1997, as reported in *Lawyers Weekly Consolidated Digest*, Vol. 17.
Swale Investments Ltd. brought an action against the National Bank of Greece (Canada) Ltd. Because of their breach of a loan agreement, they had to provide funds to Swale. But at the time the action was to be tried, the defendant checked and discovered that Swale had been dissolved as a corporation. Consequently, the defendant brought this application to have the action dismissed. Discuss the arguments of the parties and the likely decision of the court. How would your answer be affected with the knowledge that there was a section of the Ontario *Business Corporations Act* that allowed the plaintiff company to be revived by filing the appropriate documentation, and that the effect was to give that company "all of the rights privileges and liabilities it would have had if it had not been dissolved"?
Compare this case to the following one.

8. **MEDITRUST HEALTHCARE INC. V. SHOPPERS DRUG MART** (2001), 15 B.L.R. 221 (Ont. S.C.J.).
Here Meditrust operated a mail order business selling pharmaceuticals through several subsidiary corporations. Meditrust owned all of the shares of those corporations and exercised control over them through their boards of directors. Meditrust brought this action in their own name against Shoppers Drug Mart, claiming that Shoppers had conspired to interfere with the drug distribution business of the subsidiaries. One of the accused conspirators brought this application to have the action dismissed. What do you think would be the most effective arguments given these facts?

CHAPTER 8

Property

Real property consists of land and buildings

Personal property may be tangible or intangible

One of the most important decisions that business people face relates to their investment in, acquisition, and use of property (see Table 8.1). The monetary amounts are significant, so that mistakes can have a very serious negative impact on a business. **Real property** consists of land and the things permanently affixed to it such as buildings, bridges, dams, and other structures. The other major category of property is called **personal property**, which consists of tangible and movable things called **chattels** or **goods.** Various forms of intangibles are referred to as **choses in action**. Today we often hear reference to another type of property called **intellectual property**. In fact, intellectual property is another form of intangible personal property. In this information age, however, intellectual property has become extremely important for businesses, and will be dealt with as a separate topic in Chapter 9. In this chapter we will briefly look at personal property and then do a more thorough examination of real property including landlord–tenant relationships and mortgages. No matter what form of property is involved, it is always important to reduce risk by anticipating damage to or loss of that property. A brief discussion of insurance has been included in this chapter with reference to that risk management objective.

TABLE 8.1 Property

Real property	• Land • Things affixed to the land
Personal property	• Chattels (tangible goods or movables) • Choses in action (intangible claims) • Intellectual property (ideas and information)

Personal Property

The term *property* does not refer to the thing itself; rather, it refers to a person's rights in relation to that thing. For example, a person's property is not the house or car, but the property rights that person has in the land or in the car. This allows us to separate the thing from the title or right to it, so that you can loan your car or rent your house and still be the owner. This is a difficult but vital concept to keep in mind as we discuss all forms of property in this and the next chapter.

Property relates to your rights to something rather than the thing itself

As mentioned, personal property includes both tangible and intangible personal items. Tangible personal property comprises movables called chattels or goods as opposed to real property or land, which by its nature is always fixed in one location. We have already dealt with tangible personal property when we discussed its transfer under the *Sale of Goods Act* in Chapter 5. In that chapter we also discussed the various forms of personal property being used as collateral security for a loan under the *Personal Property Security Act,* and in Chapter 4 we talked about negotiable instruments as an example of intangible personal property. Cheques, drafts, and promissory notes have no intrinsic value but represent claims or rights. Below we will examine some other aspects of personal property.

Tangible personal property is called chattels or goods

WHO HAS THE RIGHT TO THE GOODS?

Because chattels are movable, they often find their way into the hands of others, and the question arises as to who has the ultimate right to them. Basically, the person in possession of the goods has the right to them over anyone else, except someone with a prior title that has not been extinguished (see Table 8.2). A person's right to the chattel will largely depend on how it was acquired. If it was purchased or received as a gift, title has been conveyed from the prior owner to the new owner. But if the chattel was found, the basic principle is "finders keepers." This means that the finder of the goods will have a better claim to them than anyone, except the rightful owner who lost them. If you find a watch or camera in the public part of a shopping mall and take it to the lost and found, if the rightful owner doesn't claim it, you, as the finder, would have a better claim to it than the owners of the mall. If the person who lost it requested its return, however, that claim would override any claim you have to it. Note that if an employee of the mall found the watch, or you found the watch in an area where the public did not go (a private part of the mall), then the owner of the mall would have a prior claim over anyone else except the rightful owner. An off-duty police officer recently found a paper bag in a park containing $1 million and turned it in. After some dispute and once it became clear that no actual owner was going to come forward to claim the funds, the police officer was able to claim and keep the money. Of course, if it could have been established that the money had come from an illegal drug transaction, or some other prohibited activity, those funds would have gone to the government. Who the rightful owner is will depend on the history of the item in question. The rules with respect to transfer of title as set out in the *Sale of Goods Act* are discussed in Chapter 5. Any other contractual provisions that may affect who has claim to those goods, any other legislation that may affect those rights, such as the *Personal Property Security Act,* and whether the goods were stolen or wrongfully converted to another in the past, would all have an effect on who is ultimately entitled to the item. The person who finds the item also has an obligation to take care of those goods as a bailee.

Possession gives right to goods over all but someone with prior claim

Rightful owner has title

TABLE 8.2 Rightful Owner Depends on Where Goods Are Found

Order of Priority	First Claim	Then
Goods found on public property	Rightful owner	Finder
Goods found on public part of employer's property by non-employee	Rightful owner	Finder
Goods found by employee doing job on employer's property	Rightful owner	Employer
Goods found on private part of employer's property by non-employee	Rightful owner	Employer

CASE SUMMARY 8.1

White v. Alton-Lewis Ltd. et al.[1]

Finders Aren't Always Keepers

Mrs. White found a valuable ring on the floor of the store where she worked and handed it over to her manager. It was turned over to the police, but the true owner never came forward. Both the employer and Mrs. White claimed the ring. The judge found that if the rightful owner could not be found, then the finder of the ring had the right to it. Since Mrs. White was on the job and acting on behalf of her employer when she found the property, the employer had the better claim to the ring.

BAILMENT

Bailment involves one person holding goods of another

A **bailment** takes place when one person takes possession of and cares for the goods of another. The person delivering the goods is the **bailor** and the person taking care of them is the **bailee**. With such bailment the important question is the extent of the duty of the bailee to look after and care for those goods while they are in his or her possession. Historically, the nature of a bailee's obligation to care of the goods varied with the nature of the bailment. When the bailment was voluntary, the duty varied with whoever was benefited (see Table 8.3). If someone were to borrow your tools to work on her house, this is a **voluntary bailment for the benefit of the bailee** and the duty imposed to look after those tools is quite high. On the other hand, if you agreed to store a friend's tools at your home because there was no room in his new apartment, this would be a **voluntary bailment for the benefit of the bailor**, and the duty to look after the tools would be lower. Of course, the nature of the thing being stored also affects the obligation. The duty would be higher with respect to a valuable violin than with a rake or a shovel. When a person forgets a coat at a friend's home or even at a restaurant, this is an **involuntary bailment**, and the duty of care required of the bailee is only what would be expected of him with respect to caring

Duty higher where voluntary for bailee's benefit

1. (1974), 49 D.L.R. (3d) 189 (Ont. Co. Ct.).

TABLE 8.3 **Bailment**

Duty of Bailee	Low	High		Per Contract		Per Statute
Gratuitous bailment for bailor	X					
Gratuitous bailment for bailee		X				
Bailment for value		X	or	X		
Innkeepers/common carriers				X	or	X

Note that these standards vary with the nature of goods and application of the reasonable person test.

for his own goods and then only if the bailee takes control of the item in some way such as putting it away. In practice, the judge will impose the reasonable person test and take into consideration which party benefits from the bailment.

If the bailment is of mutual benefit or pursuant to a contract, it is referred to as a **bailment for value**, and the duty of care imposed on the bailee is that of the reasonable person in the circumstances, which is usually determined by the normal standards expected in the particular industry involved. Leaving a fur coat with a storage company for the winter or a ring with a jeweller for repair are examples of such a bailment for value. In such commercial relationships the bailee will usually limit his or her obligations of care in the bailment contract, which often specifies a maximum responsibility for the loss, for example $50. As has been discussed, these exculpatory clauses limiting the liability of one party at the expense of the other are very strictly applied by the court in favour of the person disadvantaged by the provision. Also, if the failure is substantial enough, a court may be persuaded that such an exculpatory clause, even though worded broadly enough, was never intended to cover such a fundamental breach. (Fundamental breach was discussed in Chapters 4 and 5.)

Where bailment for value, duty is determined by contract or industry standards

Common carriers and innkeepers have a particularly high standard imposed on them to care for the goods of their customers. A common carrier is a bus line, railroad, or trucking company in the business of taking goods from the general public and shipping them to other locations for a fee. Innkeepers provide transient accommodation (food and lodging) to travellers. Under the common law they were responsible for any damage to their customers, even where there was no negligence involved. This liability would be imposed unless the problem was caused by some defect in the goods themselves or the fault of the bailor. Today, legislation now places limits on such liability, either by reducing the standard imposed, or by allowing the bailee to limit the maximum amount that can be claimed. In Ontario, for instance, the innkeeper's liability is limited to $40 unless the loss is caused by the negligence of the innkeeper or an employee or if the lost or damaged goods were actually left with the innkeeper for safekeeping.[2] When a bailee for value is not paid for the services rendered, the common law provides the right of a lien against the goods, even allowing their sale to recover the bailee's costs. Today specific statutes extend or enhance these common law liens in specific businesses such as storage warehouses or repair services. This allows

Duty of common carriers and innkeepers now determined by statute

Bailee for value can hold goods when not paid

2. *Innkeepers' Act*, R.S.O. 1990, c. I.7, s. 4.

them to hold onto the goods if they're not paid for their service. Note that it is a criminal offence for a bailee not to surrender property to a sheriff or other official who is properly seizing it under a valid agreement (*Personal Property Security Act*) or court order. The *Criminal Code* also makes it a crime to possess stolen property and has created several offences relating to how personal property is used. Thus, a considerable part of the Code is directed to firearms offences. The Code also makes it a crime to possess the paraphernalia used for illicit drug production (Part XII.1), equipment to forge credit cards (section 342.01), various break-in instruments (sections 351 and 352), and equipment used for other prohibited uses. The penalties for these indictable offences can range from two years to 10 years, depending on the offence.

CASE SUMMARY 8.2

Manitoba Public Insurance Corp. v. Midway Chrysler Plymouth Ltd.[3]

Cars Left on Lot Only Sometimes Create a Bailment

An employee parked a car left for repairs in a locked compound but left the keys in the ignition instead of following the normal practice of putting them in the locked office. The car was stolen and found later with significant damage. The insurer compensated the customer and then sued the employer, Midway Chrysler, to recover that amount. The court found that as a bailee for reward, unless the contract said otherwise, they had a duty to care for the goods to the same standard as would be expected of a person who borrows property for his or her own use. Leaving keys in the ignition of a car, even in a locked compound, fell below that standard, and Midway was liable for the loss.

In a similar case, *Hertz Canada Ltd. v. Suburban Motors Ltd.,*[4] a car was stolen from a locked compound, and the bailee for reward was not liable. Unlike the case above, the keys were not left in the ignition, and the thief had to not only break into the compound but also break open and enter through two locked doors to get the keys. In this case the bailee for reward had lived up to the relevant standard.

Real Property

Personal property can become part of real property when affixed to it

The acquisition and use of real property can be one of the most important problems facing businesses. Real property consists of the land and things permanently attached to it. This usually involves buildings, but may also include other types of structures such as dams, aqueducts, bridges, and the like. It can also include heavy-duty machinery that has to be affixed to the land for it to operate. Prior claims on such items can cause problems since they are personal property (movable) until attached. Special rules have been developed with respect to such fixtures.

3. (1978), 82 D.L.R. (3d) 206 (Man. C.A.).

4. (2000), 1 M.V.R. (4th) 214 (B.C.S.C.).

Another problem relates to just what the land includes. The old theory that it extends vertically out into space has been modified; now the land itself only extends as high as the owner can make use of it. Thus, you can't sue the owner of an airplane that flies over your property for trespass. Still, there is a right not to have some other structure permanently intrude onto the property. If your house is located next to a tall building and your neighbour puts up a sign that hangs over your property, it would constitute a trespass, and you could force your neighbour to remove it. The same applies to under-the-surface rights. A property owner only has a right to that part of the land beneath the property that can be used. Mines, caves, and other underground activities that don't interfere with the surface will not give rise to a complaint. When the right to land is acquired, normally the under-surface mineral rights, as well as oil and gas rights, are not conveyed with the title. The owner of the land will not have the right to minerals and other valuables found under the land. As a result, the owner may have to tolerate prospectors looking for minerals and even have to submit to some interruption on the surface to accommodate a mine or oil well. As well, the owner will get little compensation when such valuables are discovered.

Real property above and below ground is limited to what the holder can reasonably use

Mineral rights usually withheld by Crown

FEE SIMPLE ESTATES

The law of real property is based on rules developed in feudal times and still incorporates some aspects of that ancient law. For example, in those days all land belonged to the king. Others had a right to hold it and use it—called an estate in the land—which was based on various types of services given to the king. An estate, then, is different from the land itself. It is a right to the land or a right to use the land. In fact, there were many different types of estates in land, based on different forms of service to the king, but today the only type of estate remaining that is equivalent to ownership is the fee simple estate. We still don't "own" our homes or property; rather we have an estate or interest in the land called a fee simple, which gives us the same kinds of rights as ownership, including the right to develop, use, sell, and will it to others. The difference is more theoretical than practical (see Table 8.4). But we should always be aware of the overriding power of government to control and restrict how we use land through licensing and zoning, even to the point of forcing its sale through expropriation. Landowners also have an obligation to use their land in a way that does not interfere with their neighbours' enjoyment of their land. This is called a private nuisance and the neighbour can sue in tort as was discussed in Chapter 2.

Fee simple estate equivalent to ownership today

Governments have power to control or acquire land

Note obligation not to interfere with neighbours

In some circumstances the fee simple estate in land is split. A beneficiary in a will, such as a spouse, may be given a **life estate** in a particular property to ensure that person is cared for during his or her remaining life. The estate will go to other heirs when that person dies. During their lifetime the beneficiaries are said

Life estate lasts for life and then reverts

TABLE 8.4 Limitations on Fee Simple Ownership

- Extends only to reasonably useable distance above the surface
- Extends only to reasonably useable subsurface
- Mineral rights usually withheld
- Restrictions (covenants, building schemes)
- Government powers (building permits, taxation, expropriation)

FIGURE 8.1 Life Estate

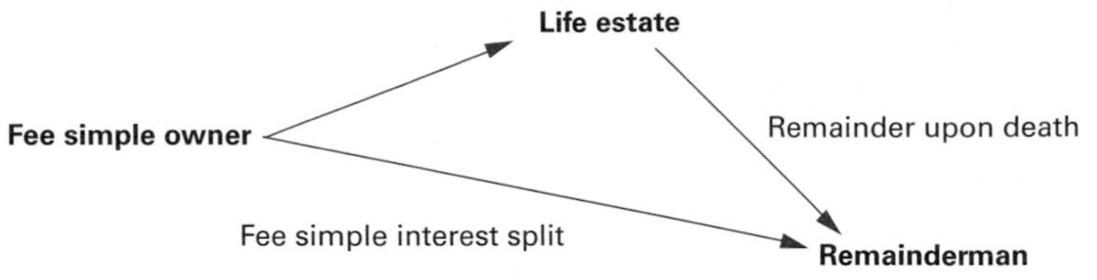

to have a life estate in the property and the other heirs have a **remainder** interest, or a **reversion**, if the interest goes back to the estate as opposed to a specified individual (see Figure 8.1). Note that there is a restriction on the holder of the life estate not to do anything to hurt the property that might decrease its value, for example, having a forested property logged.

LEASEHOLD ESTATE

Leasehold estates are for specified time but may also be periodic

Here the tenant is given exclusive possession and right to use the land for a specified period. Lease arrangements are common to both commercial and residential properties. Most last for just a few years, although 99-year leases are not uncommon. It is also common for a lease to be periodic in nature, meaning it is from month to month, or year to year. In effect, it is for only that one month but is renewed automatically, unless notice is given by either party to end it. The landlord–tenant relationship will be discussed in more detail below.

LESSER INTERESTS IN LAND

Easement gives others the right to use the land

Right of way is a type of easement, giving someone the right to cross property

It is sometimes necessary to allow a power line, water, or sewer line to permanently cross over or under one property in order to service another or to allow one building to permanently overhang another. When this is done, the legal arrangement made with the property owner is called an **easement**. When the intrusion is not permanent, but is simply the right for a vehicle or individual to cross over one property to get to another, it is called a **right of way**. Such easements are also an interest in the land, and the formalities associated with having an interest in land should be complied with.

Restrictive covenants must be negative and restrict how property can be used

Restrictive covenants bind future owners

Another right often incorporated into land transactions is a **restrictive covenant** (see Figure 8.2). When land is sold, the seller might put some sort of restriction on what the land can be used for or what can be built on it. For example, where a person subdivides her lot she might be concerned that the portion separated not be used for commercial purposes, or she might want to preserve her view by restricting the size of any building that is erected on that property to no more than two stories or no larger than 5000 square feet. The thing to remember with such restrictive covenants is that they must be negative in nature to bind future owners. If the contract of sale required the purchaser to build a house on the land within six months and the purchaser sold the property to someone else, this would not bind the subsequent owner because of the principle of privity of contract. The new owners cannot be affected by the original contract of sale, because they were not a party to it. Restrictive covenants that are negative in nature, like other interests in land, are said to "run with the land," binding all subsequent owners.

FIGURE 8.2 Restrictive Covenants

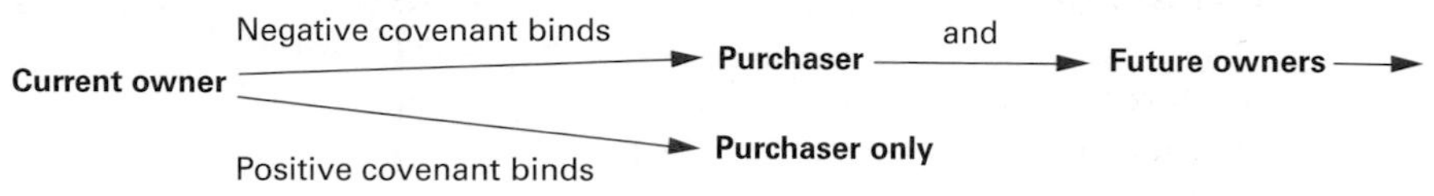

A **building scheme** is very similar. In this case all of the properties in a particular development have the same restrictions put on them: All houses must be no more than three stories; or no style can be erected except Tudor; or no other roof can be used except shake or tile. (Note that by wording the requirement as a restriction, all builders are forced to build to certain specifications.) Restrictive covenants will have one property that benefits (the dominant tenement) and one property that is restricted (the servient tenement). But with a building scheme all properties are benefited, and all are restricted. A building scheme accomplishes similar outcomes as municipal zoning, except that it is done privately by the developer.

Building schemes are like restrictive covenants but bind whole subdivisions

CASE SUMMARY 8.3

Beechwood II Homes Association Inc. v. Breadner[5]

Restrictive Covenants Must Be Negative to Bind Future Owners

A levy was placed on the residences in two separate developments to pay for a common recreational facility. Ten years later one of these developments was sold and the new owner refused to pay the levy. In this action the other owners are attempting to enforce the covenant containing the levy against the new owners. The problem was that the requirement to pay the levy, while properly registered against the property, was worded in a positive way as an obligation rather than as a restriction. The court held that since this covenant was worded in a positive way it could not run with the land, and only bound the original owner. The new owner was free of the obligation. Any restrictive covenant must be negative in order to bind future owners of the property, requiring them not to do something, rather than positive such as requiring a regular payment.

Sometimes people are given the right to use or access property for some particular purpose. This is a **licence**, not an interest, in land. It is simply a contractual right to use the land for some limited purpose. Thus when you rent a hotel or motel room, you are not given the exclusive right to use it. Others will come in and clean it, and you can be required to move to another room if necessary. Another example would be leaving a car at a parking lot. It is a bailment if con-

A licence does not convey an interest in land

5. Loker, D.J., Ont. S.C.C., January 10, 1995, as reported in *Lawyers Weekly Consolidated Digest*, Vol. 15

trol is surrendered to a parking lot attendant, as with valet parking, or where the keys are given to the attendant. But where the car is simply parked in a given slot, locked, and a fee paid upon leaving, control has not been surrendered and the use of the property is by licence. A similar right called a ***profit à prendre*** gives a right to remove something such as gravel or trees from the land.

OWNING PROPERTY TOGETHER

When people wish to share the ownership of property, there are two main ways this can be accomplished. The **joint tenancy** arrangement is often used by family, especially spouses, to get around inheritance taxes and probate fees. Here, both tenants own the whole property, but neither can point to any portion of it as exclusively theirs. When one dies, the other still owns all of the property, only now he or she owns it exclusively. That person has taken complete title of the property by survivorship. The important point is that the property did not go through the estate. The survivor owned it all, together with the other joint tenant, and after death continued to own it all. Note that it is not only real property that can be owned in joint tenancy. Bank accounts, cars, boats, and other assets are often held jointly for the same reason.

Joint tenancy includes right of survivorship

The other way to own property together is by tenancy in common. Here both parties have an undivided interest in the property. Again, neither party can point to any part of the property as his or hers alone. They both own an interest in every part of it, equal to their designated portion. But in this case, if one dies, the other still only owns his or her part interest. Either party can sell his or her portion of the property, use it as security, or otherwise deal with it during his or her lifetime. Or upon death, the deceased person's interest will go to his or her heirs. Note that if people own property as joint tenants, and they don't want to continue as joint tenants, that joint tenancy can be severed. When that is done, the result is a tenancy in common. When one party sells or attempts to sell his or her interest, that will sever the joint tenancy. Or an application can be made to the court to have the joint tenancy partitioned, accomplishing the same result. It is important to understand that this severance cannot be accomplished in a will. The will takes effect after death, and the right of survivorship in a joint tenancy will take effect with death. Hence, there is no interest left to will to your heirs, as the right of survivorship has already operated to give the survivor the whole interest in the land.

Tenancy in common does not include the right of survivorship

A joint tenancy can be changed to a tenancy-in-common severance

CASE SUMMARY 8.4

Kish v. Tompkins; Tompkins Estate v. Tompkins[6]

Negotiation of Severance Does Not Sever Joint Tenancy

Mr. and Mrs. Tompkins owned their home in joint tenancy, but they had separated and were negotiating the division of their property, including the severance of the joint tenancy, when he died. There were even letters between their lawyers with the

(continued)

6. (1993), 99 D.L.R. (4th) 193 (B.C.C.A.).

understanding that the home was to be sold with each getting a share, but these were all headed "Without Prejudice." The question for the court was whether the joint tenancy gave Mrs. Tompkins full claim to the house as survivor or whether it had been severed before death, creating a tenancy in common. The court decided that although they had anticipated and talked about severing the joint tenancy, it had never actually taken place and that Mrs. Tompkins was entitled to the house. The case illustrates the difference between a joint tenancy and tenancy in common, and how important that difference can be.

STRATA TITLES The growth of high density housing in cities has led to a unique statutory development in common ownership called the **condominium**. These allow people to own property that is separated vertically as well as horizontally. Condominium owners have a fee simple interest in their individual unit and share an interest in the common elements of the development. The units can be sold, mortgaged, or otherwise dealt with as any fee simple property. The sale or mortgage of the unit doesn't affect the other units in any way.

Statutes now allow fee simple to be separated vertically and horizontally: condominiums

The unique aspect of condominium ownership is the shared ownership attached to each unit with respect to common property such as hallways, foyers, and elevators as well as fitness and recreational facilities, pools, lawns and gardens, and parking lots. The owners of each unit must pay a maintenance fee for the operation and upkeep of these common areas, including insurance on the common areas and the building as a whole. Those fees, as well as other rules and restrictions applicable to the use of the property—even including what can take place within each unit—are set by the **condominium corporation** (sometimes called the **strata corporation**). Each unit owner has a vote and can participate in elections to a condominium council that sets the fees, makes the rules, and otherwise makes decisions with respect to the condominium as a whole. One of the dangers of such condominium ownership is that the owner of each unit is at the mercy of the others as far as fees and restrictions on what they can do. Normally, the fees set are reasonable, but when things go wrong, those fees can become excessive. Unlike normal ownership, condo owners are responsible to cover major expenses that occur with respect to the whole building or complex. Normal maintenance can be built into the regular fees and, if the condominium council shows wisdom, a contingency fee for unusual expenses. But there can be large unexpected expenses for such things as a leaky building, plumbing or electrical problems, a new roof, or the replacement of elevators. When such problems arise, a special levy will be ordered, and each individual owner may be required to pay thousands of dollars per unit for the unexpected expense. Owners can be forced to sell if their fees are unpaid or they have sufficient violations of the rules. These potential expenses and unwanted rules and restrictions often discourage some people from condominium ownership.

Condominiums involve shared property and rules

Special levy for unusual expenses

Older buildings are often converted to condominium ownership, and this poses another problem for potential owners. It may be a new unit to them, but if the building is 50 years old, it likely has a limited life expectancy. Certainly the maintenance and repair costs will be higher than with a new building. Also, the return on investment will likely be less than what could be expected from property where a considerable portion of the value is in the land the unit is built on.

The affordability of purchasing condominiums and the lifestyle associated with them make them very attractive to many, but the potential problems and conflicts persuade others to avoid this form of property ownership.

Option to purchase holds offer to sell open for specified time

There are still other kinds of interests in land to consider. Sometimes when property is to be sold, an **option to purchase** the land will be arranged. As you will recall from the discussion of offer and acceptance in Chapter 3, an option is a subsidiary contract where for a fee the offeror commits to hold his offer open for a given period of time. Thus, the offeror is bound by its terms and can't revoke the offer during that period. But the purchaser has no obligation beyond paying the normally small option price. Developers will often use this arrangement when they are trying to assemble a block of properties from several different owners. They will acquire an option on each property, usually for a small fee. When they have options on all of the properties they need, they exercise the options and purchase the properties. If they can't persuade some key property owners to sell for a reasonable price, they can walk away from the transaction, losing only what they paid for the option agreements.

Options often used by developers and speculators

Speculators will also use options on properties to flip the property and get a significant profit on a minimal investment. For example, the speculator might learn of a house on the market for $250 000, and he knows its market value is $275 000. After some bargaining he might persuade the owner to sell him a 30-day option to purchase the property for, say, $240 000. The option may only cost $100. The speculator would then find a purchaser willing to pay $260 000 and simply sell the option to her for $20 000, making a sizable profit on his investment over a very short period of time. Or he might sell the property to the purchaser for the $260 000 knowing that he has a right to purchase it for $240 000. If he can't find a buyer, he can walk away from the deal and lose only the $100 he paid for the option. This form of speculation is not restricted to land transactions. Whether dealing with land or personal property, options must be registered to protect their value. If the seller of the property, after entering into such an option arrangement, sells the property to another, the option holder would lose any claim to the property, unless it was registered as a charge against the property.

Mortgages on property used to secure loan

The common method of financing the purchase of property is through a **mortgage**. Here the purchaser conveys the title to the creditor (usually a bank or other financial institution), and the bank holds onto the title as security until the final payment is made. The bank then conveys title to the debtor. While the debt is outstanding, the creditor has title as security. If there is a default, the creditor can take steps to reclaim the property, but mortgages must be registered in order to be effective against third parties. Mortgages will be discussed in more detail below.

REQUIREMENT OF REGISTRATION

Registration protects creditor's security against third party

Land registry depository of documents

As indicated in the discussion above, it is important to register any of these interests in land for protection against outsiders who might deal with the property in question and otherwise defeat the unregistered interest. The problem is that any business people dealing in property might have their position weakened by other competing claims for the property of which they are unaware. The registration systems were developed to ensure that does not happen. There are two different systems of land registry in place in Canada. The traditional **land registry** involves the creation of a depository or registry to keep copies of documents that affect the title of land (see Figure 8.3). The purchaser or lender has the assurance that only those documents registered in the land registry will affect them, but they have to search the documents themselves to determine just who the rightful

FIGURE 8.3 Land Registry

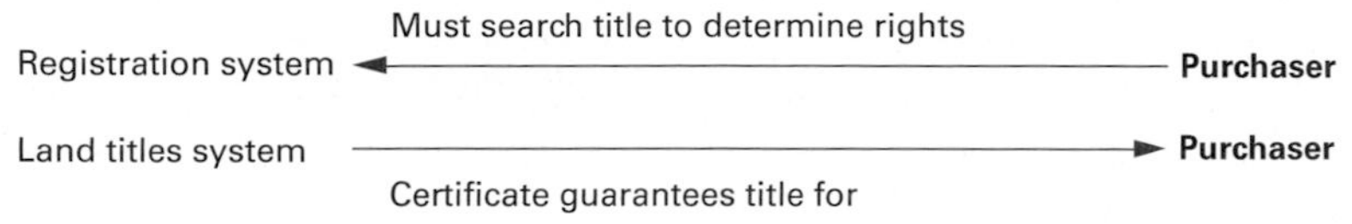

owner is and what claims there are against the property. If you purchase a house, for example, one of the first things your lawyer will do is to go through those documents, checking the chain of ownership to make sure that the seller has the right to sell the house and that there are no other undisclosed interests such as judgments, easements, or mortgages registered against the property. Hence the expression "searching the title." Most unregistered claims will have no effect on subsequent purchasers.

The other system of land registry used in Canada is the **land titles system**, first adopted in British Columbia and now used in several other provinces and districts. It has the singular advantage of guaranteeing title. When property is transferred, a form is filed with the land titles office which generates a new "certificate of indefeasible title," certifying the purchaser as the registered owner of the property. The key to understanding the difference between the two systems is that the certificate of indefeasible title is guaranteed and is conclusive evidence of who has title to the property in any court. Note that any mortgages, liens, judgments, or other interest such as an easement or right of way are noted on the certificate form as charges against the title. No other claims can affect subsequent purchasers. Sometimes this can lead to problems when mistakes are made or titles are changed by fraud. However, there is an insurance fund created to compensate people who are injured because of such problems.

In land titles jurisdictions title is guaranteed by certificate

CASE SUMMARY 8.5

Hermanson v. Martin et al.[7]

Forged Documents Transfer Property

The Hermansons owned property as joint tenants. Mr. Hermanson forged his wife's name on the sale of the property to Mr. Martin. Mrs. Hermanson had no knowledge of this fraud until her husband died and she tried to sell the property. She thought she had title to the whole property as survivor of a joint tenancy, but Mr. Martin claimed that he owned the property. She asked the court to declare the sale to Mr. Martin void. But because he did not know of the fraud, Mr. Martin also was an innocent party. Since this was a land titles jurisdiction, his certificate of title guaranteed his ownership of the property. Mr. Martin had also arranged a mortgage on the property

(continued)

7. (1982), 140 D.L.R. (3d) 512 (Sask. Q.B.).

with Co-operative Trust that was valid and binding. Mrs. Hermanson's only recourse was against her dead husband, which was useless, or against the registrar of titles and the fund provided for such cases. Note that she was successful, but only for the amount that she actually lost. Since the fraud had taken place before the death of her husband, that fraud caused her to lose only the half interest that she had in the property at the time. Normally, fraud such as this would void a transaction, but the essential nature of the land titles system requires that the title be guaranteed.

TRANSFERRING LAND

Transfer by deed in land registry jurisdiction

Form submitted to transfer title in land titles jurisdiction

Criminal offence to falsify or conceal title documents

The traditional method of transferring land involves the use of a grant, often called a **deed of conveyance**. Initially, a contract in the form of an **agreement of purchase and sale** is concluded between the parties. This may contain conditions that have to be met before the deal is finalized. At the closing date a deed of conveyance under seal is executed, which accomplishes the actual transfer. Of course, the documents are then deposited in the registry to ensure protection against subsequent claimants. In a land titles jurisdiction a similar purchase and sale agreement is concluded, which establishes the rights of the parties, but the actual transfer is accomplished by completing and filing the appropriate transfer form with the land titles office. That office then generates a new certificate of indefeasible title. The importance of preserving the authenticity of these documents is emphasized in the *Criminal Code*, which makes it a criminal offence punishable by up to 10 years' imprisonment to destroy, cancel, conceal, or obliterate the title to goods or land (section 340a). And more specifically, in section 385 it is a criminal offence for someone in possession of documents that affect title, when asked to produce them, to conceal them, or to falsify the pedigree on which title depends (an indictable offence punishable up to two years). This is primarily designed for offences that take place in a land registry jurisdiction. Section 386, which makes it an indictable offence to make a false representation or suppress or conceal anything material to the registry, applies more to a land titles jurisdiction.

Right to land may be obtained by adverse possession or prescription in land registry jurisdiction . . .

- but not in a land titles jurisdiction

In the past rights to property were sometimes acquired through use alone. If a person openly occupies a house or land for a period in excess of 20 years and the owner of the property takes no steps to remove him or her, after 20 years it is too late to try to recover the property. We often refer to this as *squatter's rights*, but more correctly this is acquiring land though **adverse possession**. Similarly, if people regularly cross a portion of land and the owner does nothing to stop them, after 20 years they would acquire a right to cross that land without interference by **prescription**. It is not unusual at apartment buildings, ports, rail yards, and other locations where there are private roadways used by the public to see the owners of the property close off access for a period of time. They are exercising control so that no one can later claim the users of the roadway have acquired a right to the property through use. Acquiring rights to property in this way is still possible in those jurisdictions using the traditional land registry system. But in a land titles jurisdiction, acquiring rights to land through adverse possession or prescription would be completely inconsistent with the idea of a certificate of indefeasible title. This is specifically prohibited by statute.[8]

8. *Land Title Act*, R.S.B.C. 1996, c. 250, s. 24; and *Limitation Act*, R.S.B.C. 1996, c. 266, s. 12.

It should also be noted that a major advancement that has taken place in the field of registration of interests in land is the adaptation to technological change. Not only have most land registries changed to the digital storage and retrieval of registered data both in registration and land titles jurisdictions, but also most now allow the actual electronic registration of important documents.

CASE SUMMARY 8.6

Wells v. Wells[9]

Unauthorized Use of Land Creates Right of Way

A neighbour had been using a right of way over property to access his own property for 40 years. Because it ran diagonally across that property, making it unusable, the property owner changed the access to the side of his property so he could build a house on it. But the neighbour who had been using the right of way objected and demanded that it stay the way it was. The court found that the driveway had been created out of necessity and openly used for 40 years. A right of way by prescription had been created, and the property owner had no right to change it. The court awarded $2000 against the property owner for trespass. This case shows how a right to property can be obtained in some provinces simply by open use over a long period of time. This would not be the case in land titles jurisdictions where title is guaranteed.

MORTGAGES

Most real property transactions involve financing, with the mortgage the most common form of security taken. In the following discussion, since the mortgage is a form of security given by the debtor, that debtor is called the **mortgagor**. The creditor or person in receipt of the security is called the **mortgagee**.

Mortgage involves transfer of title to creditor as security

When land is used to secure debt, the title is transferred as security, but possession remains with the debtor. Since the title is returned upon repayment of the loan it is a dead transfer, or a *mort gage*. Originally, if there was a default, the transfer of title allowed the creditor to take possession of the property as well, but in addition the debt was still owed by the debtor. This was unfair to the debtor and the Courts of Chancery intervened. They recognized that the transaction was primarily the loan of money and that the transfer of property was only incidental as security. The court recognized a right in the debtor to redeem his or her property from the creditor even after default by paying what was owed. This **equity of redemption**, as it has become known, has a distinct value and is of central importance in today's law of mortgages (see Figure 8.4). If the property was worth $500 and the debt secured by the mortgage was $200, the value of the equity of redemption would be $300. This term has been shortened to **equity** and is used commonly in all our financial dealings to describe the value of the interest we have in a possession after the amount owing on it has been deducted.

Equity of redemption allows debtor to regain property even after default

This was unfair to the creditor, who could face the possibility of the debtor redeeming the property even years after the default, and so the Courts of

9. (1994), 116 D.L.R. (4th) 524 (N.S.S.C.).

Chancery, at the request of the creditor, put a time limit on the exercise of that equity of redemption. After the expiration of that time limit, the debtor/mortgagor was forever foreclosed from exercising that equity of redemption. This describes the origin and the nature of the **foreclosure** process. The mortgage represents security by the transfer of title, and if the debt is paid, the title is retransferred. If there is a default, the foreclosure process takes place in two stages. First, the creditor/mortgagee asks the court to put a time limit on the exercise of the equity of redemption, for example, six months. After that period expires and payment is not made the creditor/mortgagee returns to the court and asks that the foreclosure be made absolute. During that redemption period efforts are usually made by the mortgagor to refinance or to sell the property.

Foreclosure puts a time limit on debtor's right to redeem

Final order ends equity of redemption

Since the equity of redemption has value, it too can be transferred to a creditor as security. This is known as a second mortgage, but there is more risk to the second mortgagee. If there is a default, the foreclosure process is aimed at stopping that right to redeem, and so the second mortgagee has to be prepared to pay off the first mortgage to protect his or her position (see Figure 8.5). Hence, a higher interest rate is charged because of the higher risk. It is also possible to have a third or fourth mortgage, but these are rare because of the even higher risk for these creditors.

Equity of redemption can be used to secure further debt

Second mortgagee must be prepared to pay out first

In the provinces using the land registry system, the process takes place as described above with the title actually transferring to the creditor. The second and subsequent mortgages are then referred to as *equitable mortgages*, because it is the equity of redemption that is being used as security rather than the legal title to the property. In provinces using the land titles system, the mortgagor remains the registered owner on the certificate of title and the second and subsequent mortgages, and other claims are simply listed as charges on that title document, with the priority among them established by the order of registration. The rights existing among the parties are essentially the same in both systems.

Mortgage doesn't actually transfer title in land titles jurisdiction

The possibility of foreclosure puts the second and subsequent mortgagees as well as any other creditors that might have a claim against the property at considerable risk. Consequently, during that redemption period these parties are given the right by the court to try to sell the property. This is referred to as an order for **judicial sale** or an exercise of the **power of sale**, depending on the jurisdiction. In British Columbia, for instance, an application is brought before the court and the judge orders the property to be sold (a judicial sale). In Ontario the court simply endorses the exercise of the provision contained in the mortgage agreement to sell in the event of default (the power of sale), but the result is essentially the same. During that six-month period, referred to as the *redemption period*, these par-

FIGURE 8.4 Nature of Equity of Redemption

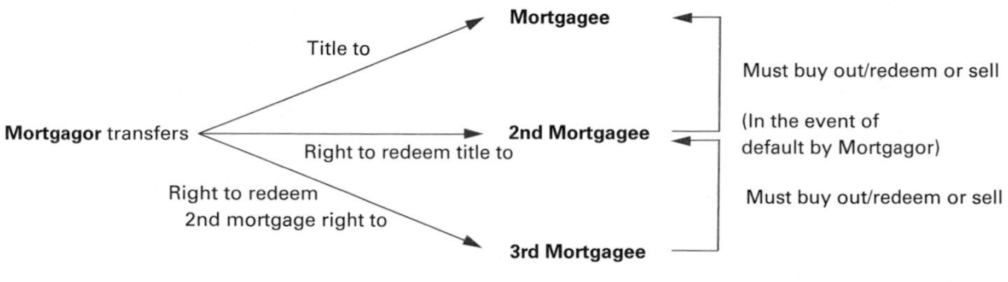

FIGURE 8.5 When Mortgagor Defaults

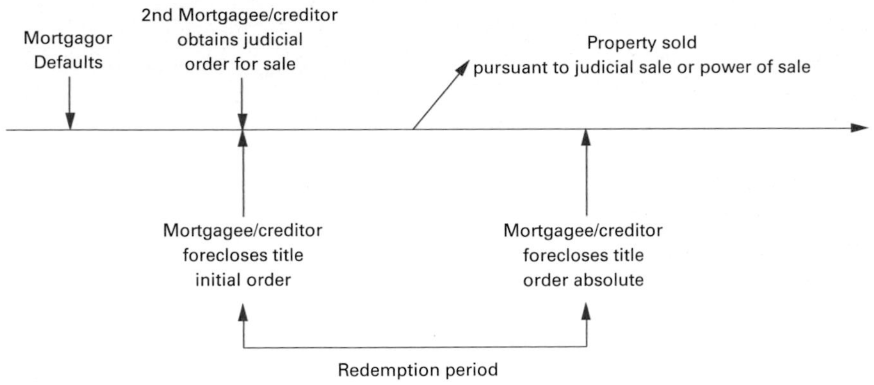

ties are given the right to find a buyer and sell the property. The mortgagor/debtor often fails to understand this. They think they have six months to solve their problems, when in fact their home might be sold to satisfy the debt in the next week. The immediate sale of the property may seem harsh, but given the value and amounts owed, there is often very little likelihood that there would be anything left for the mortgagor. Because of interest and costs, every delay increases the amounts owed, reducing the likelihood of recovery for the mortgagor, the second mortgagee, or any other claimants.

The exercise of the power of sale/judicial sale shortens the redemption period

If the property is sold pursuant to a court order and there is not enough to pay off the second mortgage and other claimants completely, the debtor may still be required to pay the shortfall, depending on the jurisdiction. If a property sells for $160 000, a first mortgage claim of $125 000 might become $140 000 because of the added interest and legal costs. Similarly, a second mortgage of $20 000 might become $30 000 with the result that after the first mortgage claim is paid, there is only $20 000 left to pay off the second mortgage. Not only is there nothing left for the mortgagor but that debtor will still owe $10 000 to the unpaid second mortgagee. This is not an uncommon scenario, especially when the economy declines, causing people to lose their jobs, which also often leads to a decline in the housing market. Typically, a mortgage agreement will also give the mortgagee the right to take possession of the property in the event of a default, but this is seldom pursued unless the property has been abandoned.

A less common remedy involves taking possession of the property

CASE SUMMARY 8.7

Bank of Nova Scotia v. Dorval et al.[10]

Obtaining Property through Foreclosure Eliminates Right to Deficit upon Resale

The Dorvals borrowed money from the bank, giving a mortgage on their property as security. Upon default, the bank went through the foreclosure process—obtaining a

(continued)

10. (1979), 104 D.L.R. (3d) 121 (Ont. C.A.).

final order, obtaining the title to the property through foreclosure, and then selling the property. The amount obtained from the sale was less than what was owed, and they sued the Dorvals for the shortfall. The court held that the nature of a foreclosure was that they had taken title to the house as their remedy and were not entitled to anything else. If they had obtained more than owed in the sale, the creditor would have been entitled to keep it and so they cannot complain if they received less. Had the bank asked for a judicial sale supervised by the court before the final foreclosure order, their claim for the deficit would have been enforced. This case shows the difference between a judicial sale and a sale after foreclosure, and the importance of making the right choices.

CASE SUMMARY 8.7 Bank of Nova Scotia v. Dorval et al.

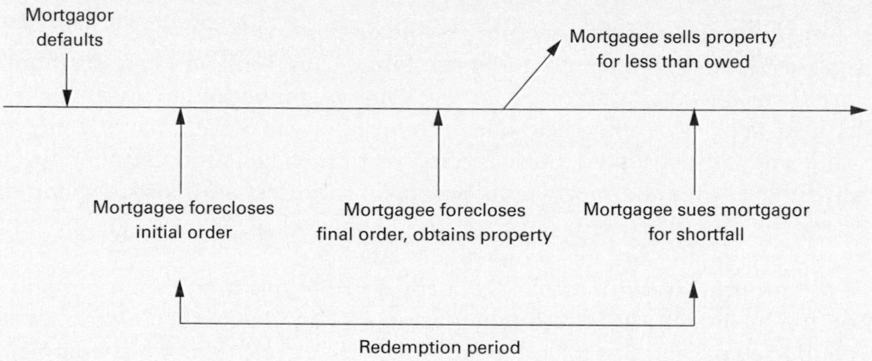

LEASEHOLD ESTATES

A lease conveys possession of property for a specified period

Periodic leases involve automatic renewal until notice

A leasehold estate provides the tenant with a right to exclusive possession and use of the premises for a specified period of time. Such leases may be of short duration such as a month or for much longer periods, even 99 years. **Periodic leases** are also common where the lease is only for one month but then is automatically renewed every month until notice is given to terminate. Any period may be specified, but month-to-month is the most common with week-to-week and year-to-year also used. This discussion must distinguish between commercial lease and residential lease arrangements. Both may be governed by statute, but the commercial tenancy acts normally allow the parties much more scope to alter their rights and obligations by agreement in the lease itself. Residential tenancy acts (or their equivalent in place in all provinces) are more like a form of consumer protection legislation imposing many obligations on the parties, which cannot be modified by agreement. The following general discussion relates primarily to commercial tenancies. Remember, however, that the principles discussed here also apply to residential tenancies, except where they have been changed by statute. These statutory modifications for residential tenancies will be discussed separately below.

COMMERCIAL TENANCIES

One of the requirements of the ***Statute of Frauds*** is that any interest in land, including a lease, must be evidenced in writing to be enforceable. Most jurisdictions modify this, so leases, whether residential or commercial for less than three years, are still enforceable even without writing. The doctrine of frustration does not apply to leases under common law. So if leased premises were to burn down through no fault of either party, the tenant would still have to pay rent unless, of course, the parties have specified otherwise in the lease agreement. In some jurisdictions, such as Ontario, the doctrine of **frustration** is made applicable to leases by statute, with the result that the tenant's obligation to pay rent would be ended if the premises were destroyed by fire that was not the tenant's fault.[11] Even where frustration has not been imposed by statute, if the lease relates to an office in a high rise and the building is destroyed, the obligation to pay rent would likely end, since you can't lease something that doesn't exist. Because a lease is an interest in land, even though it is created by contract, the leasehold interest will **run with the land**. Suppose Jones leased his home to Smith for five years and then sold that home to Green. Because the interest is attached to the land, if it was properly registered Green would be bound by the terms of that lease, even though he was not party to the contract that created it.

Statute of Frauds **require longer leases to be evidenced in writing**

Frustration applies to leases in some jurisdictions by statute

Leases are binding on a subsequent purchaser if registered

CASE SUMMARY 8.8

Fitkid (York) Inc. v. 1277633 Ontario Ltd.[12]

Accepting Rent Overrides Notice to Vacate

The commercial lease was to run to 2006, but in 1999 a disagreement arose between the landlord and the tenant, Fitkid, over the amount of rent to be paid and repairs to the roof. For several months Fitkid withheld rent and then paid after a default notice. When a rent increase came into effect, the tenant paid rent at the lower rate, not the increased one. Finally, in April 1999 after again accepting rent at the lower rate, the landlord changed the locks and evicted the tenant. Fitkid could not find other premises and went out of business. In this action Fitkid is seeking damages from the landlord for wrongful termination of the lease. The court held that the failure to pay the proper rent would have been grounds for evicting the tenant, but when the landlord took the lower payment in April before changing the locks, he reinstated the lease and lost the right to evict. Accepting the rent payment was inconsistent with the termination of the landlord and tenant relationship. As a result, Fitkid was awarded $198 201 in damages. Note that seizing the tenant's property before termination has the same effect, and landlords should seek legal advice before resorting to such action.

Although the lease agreements can modify these obligations between the parties, there are some basic obligations that are normally in place in all tenancies.

Agreement determines obligations in commercial lease

11. *Tenant Protection Act, 1997*, S.O., c. 24; or *Frustrated Contracts Act* in various jurisdictions.
12. 2002 CanLII 9520 (Ont. S.C.J.).

Landlord must deliver vacant possession and quiet enjoyment

For example, the landlord has an obligation to deliver **vacant possession** of the property. This means that he has to make sure that any prior tenants are gone before the scheduled time for the new tenants to occupy the premises. The landlord also has to provide **quiet enjoyment**, which means the tenant has to be able to use the premises for the purpose for which they were let. If there is blasting going on nearby that interferes with the tenant's work or sleep, or no stairs to the suite, or even a major leak so that the premises are no longer fit for human habitation, all of these things are breaches of the tenant's right to quiet enjoyment.

Responsibility for repairs is subject to agreement

The question of who has the obligation to make repairs is normally an obligation that is specified in a commercial agreement. Usually neither party has an obligation to make repairs where normal wear and tear is involved. The tenant takes the premises in the condition let and returns them in the same condition, except for normal wear and tear. If the tenant causes damage beyond normal wear and tear, either wilfully or through neglect, he or she will be responsible to repair it. Sometimes the tenant causes more damage than expected by using the premises in a way different from what was intended when it was originally let. For example, if the premises were let as an office but were used for heavy manufacturing, the tenant would be responsible for any excess damage caused by this non-approved use. As mentioned above, if there is unusual damage that causes the premises to be unusable such as a major leak or fire that interferes with the tenant's right to quiet enjoyment, the landlord has an obligation to make the repairs.

Tenant must use premises as agreed

A problem often arises with respect to the termination of the tenancy. Of course, if the lease is for a set time, such as two years, the tenant will have to be out at the expiration of that term. Sometimes the tenant, either with or without the agreement of the landlord, stays after the expiration of the lease. If the landlord wants the tenant out, he can take steps to have the tenant removed and the landlord is entitled to compensation from the over-holding tenant. But if rent is paid and accepted, normally a month-to-month periodic tenancy is created. Where a periodic tenancy is involved, it can be terminated by either party giving one clear rental period notice. Thus, in a month-to-month tenancy where the tenant wants to move at the end of May, that tenant must give notice at the end of April to be effective at the end of May. If the rent is due on the first day of the month, the notice must be given the day before (April 30 in this case) to be effective the last day of the next month (May 31). Unsophisticated landlords and tenants often make the mistake of giving notice on the same day the rent is paid, expecting it to be effective at the end of that month. This is improper notice and will be ineffective, unless the other party agrees to accept it. The amount of notice required is usually one of the changes imposed in residential tenancy legislation.

Commercial lease terminated at end of specified lease period

Where a periodic lease is involved, one clear rental period notice is required

The obligations of the tenant consist of paying rent, using the property only as agreed, and otherwise living up to the terms of the lease agreement, which may include other obligations such as paying taxes, insurance, and utilities. If the tenant fails to pay rent, the landlord must make a choice. In a commercial tenancy he can terminate the tenancy by removing the tenant, or he can distrain for rent. Terminating the tenancy, even by simply changing the locks, is called **forfeiture** and no court order is needed. Note that an important right of the tenant in these circumstances is to ask the court to order **relief against forfeiture**, which will allow the tenant to reinstate the lease by paying the back rent due. **Distraint** involves seizing the tenant's goods for the rent owing. This is inconsistent with termination of the tenancy, since the rent is being paid by the seized property. Since there is no longer a breach of the lease, tenancy continues. Where the tenant abandons the premises before the lease period is up, the landlord can sue for

Tenant must comply with agreement and may be required to pay utilities and taxes

In the event of default, the landlord can evict tenant

In the event of default, landlord can seize tenant's goods

the rent for the remaining term of the lease. The landlord is not required to find another tenant or otherwise mitigate his losses. But if he does take over the premises or leases them to someone else, the landlord has accepted the tenant's surrender of the premises, and the tenant's only obligation would to be to pay any arrears in rent. Other remedies such as monetary compensation (damages) for damage to the premises or an injunction to stop certain practices inconsistent with the lease terms may also be available. The tenant may also have an action for damages or obtain an injunction where the landlord has breached important terms of the lease.

If tenant defaults, landlord can sue for rent for remaining term

Landlord has no obligation to mitigate

Injured party can seek damages or injunction

Neither the landlord nor tenant will be required to repair normal wear and tear unless specified in the lease. Where major repairs are needed, the tenant must notify the landlord of the problem. If the landlord then fails to make appropriate repairs as required in the lease, the tenant can seek a court order whereby he will be allowed to pay less rent (**abatement**), using the excess to make the required repairs. Other terms often included in commercial leases are a right for the tenant to renew the lease and an option for the tenant to purchase the property at the expiration of the lease period. These terms must be specific and clearly state the amounts to be paid, or how the funds involved can be calculated in order to be binding on the parties. The tenant is also generally permitted to sublease the premises or to assign them to someone else, although in both situations they remain primarily responsible on the lease. This right is usually restricted in the lease agreement, which normally requires the landlord's consent before the assignment or sublease can take place. Note that the landlord cannot unreasonably withhold this consent.

Normally neither party is required to pay for normal wear and tear

Court may authorize tenant to pay less rent to pay for repairs

Lease also may provide right for tenant to renew, to sublease, or assign

Another problem regarding just what they can take with them often arises when tenants leave. A fixture is something that has been permanently attached to the property, such as a building or foundation, and it becomes part of the real property. But tenants often attach items onto the property to use in their business that they have no intention of leaving with the property. The general rule is that tenants can detach such items and take them with them, providing they do no serious harm to the property by removing them. Tools in a workshop often have to be attached to the floors or walls in order to operate, and these would normally be tenant's fixtures that they could take with them at the end of the lease period.

Tenant's fixtures can be taken with them when they go, if they've caused no damage

There are commercial tenancy acts in place in some jurisdictions, but even in those only minor changes are made to the common law. The parties are allowed to make whatever kind of arrangement they want by setting it out in the lease agreement. The same is not true for residential tenancies. Here important statutes are in place that impose obligations on both parties and make substantial changes to the common law.

Commercial tenancy statutes normally allow parties to determine lease obligations

RESIDENTIAL TENANCIES

Under the common law there is very little distinction made between commercial and residential tenancies. But all jurisdictions have passed legislation that considerably modifies the common law and essentially creates a consumer protection scheme, designed primarily to protect tenants. There are considerable differences among jurisdictions, and so no comprehensive attempt will be made to cover the subject. In the discussion below we will look at the main areas where changes have been made by the various residential tenancy acts. These areas of change deal primarily with rent increases, security deposits, termination requirements, repairs, privacy, and services.

Legislation creates protection for residential tenants

Standard form leases often required

Several jurisdictions require the tenancy agreement creating the lease to follow a standard form, and all require a copy to be in writing and delivered to the tenant within a few weeks of its creation. Most permit some terms to be added if they are reasonable, but acceleration clauses, requiring all payments to become due if any default, are generally prohibited.

Landlord obligated to make general and emergency repairs

Consistent across jurisdictions is an obligation on the landlord to make general and emergency repairs to the premises and to maintain minimum health standards. That means that the premises must be reasonably fit for human habitation, satisfying the local municipal bylaws with respect to health and sanitation. There is a corresponding obligation placed on the tenant to maintain the premises to a minimum standard of cleanliness. The tenant is also responsible for any damage caused by his or her own wilful or negligent conduct or that of a guest. But the tenant is not responsible for the normal wear and tear that takes place on the premises, nor is the landlord, unless it expands into other damage that interferes with the tenant's use and enjoyment of the premises. Thus, if a leak developed in the roof and the landlord didn't bother to repair it, that leak could expand, eventually destroying that part of the roof and making the premises uninhabitable.

Tenants are obligated to pay for damages they cause

Neither party required to repair normal wear and tear

Landlord restricted from entering premises

One consistent provision in all of these statutes is a restriction placed on the landlord from entering into the premises once rented. In general, the landlord has a right to inspect or to enter to make repairs, but only upon giving the tenant notice and only during the day. This right expands slightly once notice of termination has been given and it becomes necessary to show the premises to potential tenants. In the same vein, neither the landlord nor the tenant can change the locks or re-key them without the agreement of the other party. Tenants also generally have the right to sublet or assign the leased premises. This means they can find someone to replace them for a portion or the duration of the lease. But they have to obtain permission from the landlord to do this, and the statutes state that such permission shall not be unreasonably withheld.

Tenant can sublease or assign with landlord's permission

Amount and purpose of security deposits restricted and must be returned with interest

In most jurisdictions the practice has developed of landlords taking a security deposit to cover any damage done or rent not paid. This practice is controlled in all provinces with most restricting the amount to one month or one-half of one month's rent. In most provinces the security deposit is to cover damages to the premises, but with the agreement of the tenant it can also be used to help cover the last month's rent. But Ontario allows one month's rent to be taken as security deposit, which can only be used against unpaid rent, not damage. In all cases the landlord is required to hold the funds in trust and to pay the tenant a specified rate of interest on those funds within a short time after termination.

Rent increases normally limited to one per year with substantial notice

Most jurisdictions limit how often the rent can be increased (usually once per year) and some limit the amount it can be increased or require the landlord to justify the increase. Notice of the increase must be given to the tenant several months in advance (at least 90 days in Ontario).

Notice period for landlord to terminate lease is extended

There are also special rules with respect to the termination of the tenancy. Notice must be given at least one clear month before termination of a month-to-month tenancy under common law, but most jurisdictions have expanded this with respect to notice to terminate by the landlord. In Ontario, 60 days' notice of termination must be given and this even applies where the lease is for a fixed term. Even more notice may be required where the premises are to be converted to ownership units or are to be used by the landlord's family. The tenant is only required to give one month's notice, and in several jurisdictions this is even shorter, to allow the tenant to give notice of termination on the same day he or she pays rent.

Tenant can give notice when rent is paid in some jurisdictions

In addition to these specific requirements, landlords are generally prohibited from making changes or charging more for the services provided. For example, where parking is included or laundry facilities are provided, withdrawing the service or charging a higher fee for them would be an indirect rent increase and so is prohibited.

Landlord must maintain services

Where the lease is breached by the tenant, as where rent is not paid or the unit is used for an inappropriate purpose, the landlord may be able to give the tenant reduced notice to vacate. Usually the landlord will turn to a tribunal where disputes can be arbitrated or the officer can make an order requiring the breach to stop or even requiring the tenant to vacate the premises. If the order is not obeyed, there is normally provision for an application to the court to enforce the order. In most jurisdictions the remedy of distress, where the landlord seizes the tenant's property for failure to pay rent, has been abolished with respect to residential tenancies. Also when the tenant abandons the premises, the landlord is now required to mitigate the damages by re-renting the premises to another tenant. The tenant can also bring complaints to the tribunal. The officers have considerable power to award remedies that will overcome the problem, ranging from ordering the landlord to stay out of the premises, to reducing the rent to pay for repairs or in recognition of reduced services, to even ordering the landlord to restore services that have been discontinued. It should also be noted that the doctrine of frustration does apply to residential tenancies.

Landlord may give reduced notice where tenant is in default

Landlord cannot seize tenant's property and must mitigate loses

Statutes establish tribunals to hear complaints

Frustration applies to residential tenancies

The statutes also usually contain special provision for dealing with unique situations such as mobile homes. In that case only the pad is rented, but it is extremely difficult for the tenant to vacate, which would involve moving the mobile home. Some acts, including Ontario's, contain provisions with respect to special care homes for disabled tenants.

The *Criminal Code* defines several forms of immoral conduct as crimes, but in some cases it goes further. All businesses should be aware that when premises are used for unauthorized gambling, as a common bawdy house (premises used for prostitution), or for underage sexual activity, it is not only the operator that has committed a crime, but it is also an offence to knowingly be the owner, landlord, lessor, tenant, manager, agent, or occupier of such property. Note that the penalties for most of these offences range from simple summary conviction to up to two years for an indictable offence. Note that in the case of a common bawdy house, when a person is convicted of such an offence, a notice is sent to the landlord or lessor, who then has a duty to evict the tenants. If the landlord cannot show that reasonable steps were taken to do so, he or she will also be guilty of any subsequent offences.

Property owners and occupiers responsible for immoral acts on property

Even an immoral theatre production is prohibited, with all those who participate in its production or promotion, including the actors, owners, manager, lessee, agent, etc. subject to criminal prosecution. The Code also provides for the seizure and forfeiture of property used for terrorist purposes. Of course, arson, even of your own property, is also a criminal offence, as is an occupant damaging a building or interfering with a marked property boundary line.

Insurance

Insurance involves paying a premium to spread the risk

The main principle involved with insurance is the spreading of risk. Each participant pays a relatively small sum called a **premium** to cover a specified type of risk such as fire damage or lost property, and since only a few will have to be compensated, the risk of loss is thus spread amongst the many premium payers. In fact, huge sums are involved and large companies provide the insurance service, covering most of the various types of risk that may be encountered personally or in business. These companies will then often turn to even larger companies to insure themselves against unusual losses caused by unexpected circumstances such as the ice storm in Ontario and Quebec or the forest fires in British Columbia. This practice is called **reinsurance**. Because of the potential for abuse these companies are highly regulated, as are the **insurance agents** who sell the insurance coverage to businesses and the general public. Note that sometimes this insurance is obtained through an insurance **broker** rather than through an agent. The difference is that the broker represents the insured and arranges insurance for him or her with the companies, whereas the agent represents the insurance company itself, either as an employee or an independent agent (see Figure 8.6).

Insurance companies will often reinsure to cover their risk

Insurance agents represent the company whereas insurance brokers represent the insured

The contracts involved called **insurance policies** usually take the form of a standard form contract dictated by regulation, and often a **rider**, which provides added coverage related to the unique needs of the particular customer, will be attached. The policies may be renewed each year with the premium changing to reflect changes in the market, higher costs of meeting the risks, or changes to the circumstances of the insured. When modifications to an existing policy are needed, an **endorsement** outlining the specific change is added.

Insurance policies may include riders or endorsements that modify or add to the original terms

A major area of insurance coverage deals with damage or loss of property, both personal and real. It is traditional in the insurance field to acquire specific coverage for different types of risk. Losses through fire, flood, accident, and theft must be specified. It is vital, therefore, that you exercise great care in determining the extent of the insurance coverage obtained. What is covered in the policy will vary from company to company and what looks like a more reasonable rate may only be lower because the coverage is less.

Take care to read the contract, especially the fine print

There is a great similarity between insurance and a wager. A fee is paid and, if certain events take place, a large sum of money is returned. What makes insurance different is that when the event takes place, the insured doesn't "win" but is simply compensated for the loss. No windfall is experienced. Thus, to obtain insurance, the insured must have an **insurable interest** in the thing covered. If my neighbours took out insurance on my house and it burned down, they would not be able to collect since they have no insurable interest in my house and have,

An insured must have an insurable interest in order to recover for a loss

FIGURE 8.6 Insurance

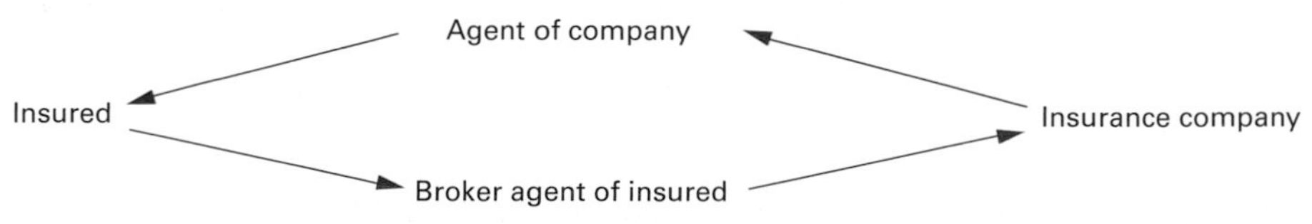

therefore, lost nothing. But if I were to take out insurance on my house and it burned down, I would be compensated for my loss to the extent of my interest. Until recently it was thought that because a corporation is a separate legal entity, the shareholders had no insurable interest in the assets of the corporation. When a company was newly incorporated and assets were transferred to the corporation, any insurance policies also had to be transferred to the corporation. But a recent Supreme Court of Canada decision has made it clear that shareholders do have a sufficient, although indirect, interest in the assets of a corporation to take out insurance on them and receive compensation if they are damaged or destroyed. [13]

Shareholders now have an insurable interest in a company's assets

CASE SUMMARY 8.9

Assaad v. The Economical Mutual Group[14]

No Insurable Interest in Stolen Car

Mr. Assaad had a client who owed him $10 000 for financial services he had provided. That client sold him his car, valued at $30 000, for a payment of only $16 000 plus the cancellation of the $10 000 debt. Assaad insured the vehicle and, when it was stolen, made a claim. The insurance company investigated and determined that the car had been previously stolen with the result that Mr. Assaad was not the rightful owner. Since the car was stolen, the client didn't have title to it or any right to transfer it to Mr. Assaad. The insurance company refused to pay the claim on the basis that Assaad, not being the lawful owner, had no insurable interest in the vehicle. At the Court of Appeal level the court agreed with the insurance company. The court held that because of the prior theft, Assaad had no right to the vehicle. Further, because he had no insurable interest, he had no right to claim. He had lost nothing because he had no right to the car in the first place. His only recourse was against the client who sold him the car, but he had left the country. This result may seem harsh, but it dramatically illustrates the nature of the requirement of an insurable interest in order to insure such assets.

Note also that any claim is limited to the extent of the insurable interest in the property. It would do no good to take out $500 000 insurance on a house only worth $400 000. The insurance company will take the higher premium for the $500 000 amount but will only pay for the actual loss suffered, in this case no more than $400 000. On the other hand, there may be a temptation to underinsure a house to pay lower premiums covering only $200 000. This is also a problem. If there is a total loss there will only be partial coverage ($200 000 of the $400 000 loss), but even where the loss is less, because of **co-insurance** clauses in most policies, the insurance company will only pay a percentage of the loss. These clauses usually require that 80 percent coverage be maintained, so in this example, if the actual loss was only $50 000 and premiums paid were for $200 000 coverage, instead of the $320 000 required (80 percent of $400 000), the insur-

Be careful not to overinsure

Be careful not to underinsure

13. *Kosmopoulos v. Constitution Insurance Co. of Canada Ltd.*, [1987] 1 S.C.R. 2 (S.C.C.).

14. (2002), 214 D.L.R. (4th) 655 (Ont. C.A.).

ance company would pay only 200/320 of $50 000 = $31 250. Thus, you can readily see how important it is to maintain insurance approximately equal to the value of the property insured. In addition, insurance policies covering loss or damage to property usually require the insured to pay a deductible. For example, if a claim is determined to be $20 000 and there is a $1000 deductible, the insured will only receive $19 000 from the insurance company. As the deductible amount increases, the premium required will usually decrease. These principles apply whether real property such as buildings or personal property in the form of chattels are involved. The insurance company usually maintains the right to either repair the damage or replace the property insured. In either case they also retain the right to **salvage** whatever value they can from the replaced parts. Similarly, the insurance company will be **subrogated** to the rights of the insured. This means that once they have paid, they take over the rights of the insured to sue whoever caused the loss in the first place.

Insurer has the right to salvage what he or she can from the loss

Once paid, insurer assumes insured's right to sue

One major problem with property insurance is that it doesn't provide any compensation for the lost business opportunities caused by the delays. It is now quite common for business people to obtain **business interruption insurance**, which provides an income during this downtime.

Insurance is also available to cover business downtime

Another major area of coverage deals with personal liability to others. This is called **liability insurance** and covers such things as other people or their property being harmed by a business person's personal conduct or through the operation of the business. Examples of such injury would be people injured while on business property, in accidents involving vehicles owned by the company or driven by employees, as well as the malpractice of professionals. Normally, such liability insurance will not only provide coverage for the loss, but also will provide legal representation when the insured is being sued. This is in the insurance company's best interest, since it will ultimately have to pay if the insured is found liable for the loss or damage claimed.

Liability insurance covers injury or loss caused to others

As a rule insurance will only cover negligence in these situations, not the wilful actions of the insured or their employees. Bonding is similar to insurance and involves the business purchasing a **fidelity bond** to cover wrongful conduct by employees. If an employee steals or cheats clients, the bonding company will provide compensation, but retains the right to go after the employee to recover what they have to pay out. Sometimes a construction company will be required to put up a bond to ensure they will perform as required in a contract. This is a **surety bond** and guarantees performance of a contract rather than compensation for wrongful conduct.

Bonding is available to cover wrongful acts of employees . . .

Or failure to perform contractual obligations

CASE SUMMARY 8.10

Andrusiw v. Aetna Life Insurance[15]

False Disability Claim Costs Claimant Over a Quarter Million Dollars

Mr. Andrusiw had been receiving disability payments for several years as the result of a stroke, when the insurance company discovered he was still going into work reg-

(continued)

15. Alta. Q.B., Murray J., June 13, 2001, as reported in *Lawyers Weekly Consolidated Digest*, Vol. 21.

ularly and supervising the operation of his own business. They cut off his payments and he brought this action to have them reinstated. With testimony from employees that he came to work every day and was making all the important decisions, the court held that he had misrepresented his level of disability. He was not only cut off from further benefits but the court ordered that the benefits he had received in the past also had to be repaid. This amounted to $259 000. People are often tempted to make insurance claims that are not justified, but this case dramatically illustrates what can happen when such false claims are made.

There are many other types of insurance that are commonly available. **Life insurance**, for example, provides compensation to named beneficiaries when the insured dies. Term insurance involves a premium paid strictly to insure against the death of the insured. Whole life involves a certain investment aspect as well as the insurance coverage, so that the insured will receive a return on that investment to assist in his or her retirement. There are many different combinations of these various schemes, some of which have important income tax implications. From a business point of view, partners will often take out life insurance on their partners to sustain the business if one dies. Larger businesses will also take out life insurance on key personnel for the same reasons. Today, businesses also often supply health and disability insurance for their employees, providing extended coverage for such things as dental care and drugs over and above the basic provincial coverage provided in all jurisdictions in Canada. Disability insurance provides an income to the insured when, because of accident or sickness, they can no longer work. For those who are professionals, self-employed, or in a business where such extended coverage is not provided, it can be obtained by paying a separate premium, often at higher rates, to an insurer on an individual basis. To have a separate policy and pay a separate premium for each of these various types of risk is not only a nuisance but would very likely result in gaps in the coverage. Today it is common to obtain comprehensive policies that will provide coverage for all or most of these various forms of risk in one policy without the requirement that each type of risk covered be specified. The cost may be a little higher, but the advantages usually outweigh the disadvantages.

Life insurance pays beneficiary when insured dies

Businesses often obtain life insurance on key personnel

Health and disability insurance are also common

A comprehensive policy covering all or many risks may be the best solution

Insurance involves a good-faith relationship between the insured and the insurance provider. That means that there is an obligation on the part of the insured to provide full disclosure of any condition or circumstance that might affect the creation of the policy or the cost of the premium. For example, with real property there is an obligation to inform the insurer if the premises are to be left vacant for any extended period of time or to be used in a way that exposes them to extra risk, for instance, storing fireworks, or changing its use from an office to some other function such as furniture manufacturing. With life or disability insurance there is an obligation to inform the insurance company of any pre-existing condition or disease that would put the insured at greater risk. Where this kind of information is intentionally withheld from the insurance company, it constitutes misrepresentation and may void the policy. A good example of this is found in a Quebec case[16] where the beneficiary of a smoker was denied the

16. *Ouellet v. L'Industrielle compagnie d'assurance sur la vie*, Que. C.A., 1993, as reported in *Lawyers Weekly*, Vol. 12 No. 44 (March 26, 1993).

benefits of a life insurance policy, even though he was killed in a car accident. He had lied on his insurance application claiming he no longer smoked, and as a result he obtained insurance coverage at a reduced premium. This was sufficient for the insurance company to avoid payment of the benefit, even though the cause of death had nothing to do with his smoking. It should also be noted that this duty of good faith works both ways as illustrated by the following case.

CASE SUMMARY 8.11

Whiten v. Pilot Insurance Co.[17]

Punitive Damages Upheld for Insurance Company Abuse

The Whitens experienced a total loss of their home to fire on a winter night in 1994. The husband, wife, and daughter had to take refuge outside in sub-zero cold. Mr. Whiten suffered serious frostbite to his feet as a result. The insurance company initially made a payment of $5000 for living expenses, which only covered expenses for a few months. They then cut off payment, leaving the family in very difficult financial circumstances. The company refused to pay any more, claiming the family had set fire to their own home. This resulted in lengthy litigation and trial, with the insurance company dragging its feet and adopting a confrontational style through the whole process. Finally, at trial the lawyer for the insurance company, in face of strong evidence from the fire chief and even from their own expert witness, was compelled to admit there was no basis for the claim of arson and no basis for the refusal of payment of the benefits of the insurance policy. Madam Chief Justice McLachlin characterized this conduct as exceptionally reprehensible. It was planned and deliberate, taking place over a two-year period. It not only denied the Whitens compensation for their loss and the extra costs of finding new accommodation, but also imposed considerable unnecessary legal costs as well. An incensed jury not only awarded $345 000 for the insurance claim and $320 000 for legal costs in compensation but also $1 million in punitive damages. This was reduced on appeal but reinstated by the Supreme Court of Canada in this very important decision. This case illustrates the special relationship of trust between an insurance company and their clients. It also indicates the powerful impact of punitive damages as a method of controlling abuses of such good-faith relationships.

17. [2002] 1 S.C.R. 595, 2002 SCC 18 (S.C.C.).

QUESTIONS FOR REVIEW

1. Distinguish between real property, personal property, and intellectual property. Distinguish between a chattel and a chose in action. Explain how personal property can be used to secure a loan.

2. Explain how the expression "finders keepers" relates to property law. Explain who is entitled to goods found in the public part of a building. What if it is found by an employee of the owners of the building?
3. Explain bailment and the obligations of the bailee when it is a voluntary bailment for the benefit of the bailee. What if it is for the benefit of the bailor?
4. Explain how the obligations of the parties are determined when a bailment for value is involved. What if the bailee is an innkeeper or common carrier?
5. Explain what is meant by a fee simple estate in land and any limitation on a person's right to that land. How can personal property become real property?
6. Explain the rights of the landowner with respect to the airspace above that property and the earth beneath, including mineral rights.
7. What is the nature of a life estate? Who is entitled to the reversion and what obligations are imposed on the holder?
8. Distinguish between a leasehold estate and other interests in land. Explain what is meant by a periodic tenancy.
9. Distinguish between an easement, a right of way, a restrictive covenant, and a building scheme.
10. Explain what is meant by a licence and a *profit à prendre*. Why is an option to purchase useful to developers and speculators in land?
11. Compare a joint tenancy and a tenancy in common, and explain severance and its effect on such tenancies.
12. Explain the nature of a mortgage and how it is used to secure a loan. Identify the parties to the mortgage.
13. Distinguish between the effects of registration in a land registry as opposed to a land titles jurisdiction, and explain why registration of interests in land is important. How does a mortgage affect the title in these jurisdictions?
14. How is land transferred in a land titles as opposed to a land registry jurisdiction? Explain the effect of a certificate of title in a land titles jurisdictions.
15. Explain what is meant by adverse possession and prescription, and the role these principles play in a land titles and land registry jurisdiction.
16. Describe an equity of redemption, foreclosure, and the redemption period. Why are they important to mortgage transactions?
17. What is meant by a judicial sale, what is the effect of such a sale on the redemption period, and why it is so important to the second mortgagee?
18. Explain what is meant by a lease and distinguish the lease from other types of interests in land. What is meant by a periodic lease and how is it ended?
19. What is meant by the statement that the lease runs with the land and what is its significance with respect to subsequent purchases?

20. Summarize the landlord's and tenant's obligations with respect to commercial tenancies and the lease terms on those obligations. Indicate the amount of notice that must be given by the parties to terminate the tenancy or to increase the rent.
21. Explain the purpose of residential tenancy statutes and summarize the types of things they cover.
22. How do most residential tenancy statutes modify the obligations of the parties to make repairs to the premises? Explain how the rights of the landlord to enter residential premises have been restricted.
23. Explain the nature of a security deposit and any restrictions on how much can be taken and what it can be used for.
24. How has residential tenancy legislation affected the amount of notice that must be given for termination by landlord and tenant? For rent increases by the landlord? How often is a rent increase permitted for residential premises?
25. Explain the landlord's obligations with respect to services provided during the term of the tenancy. What can a landlord do when a tenant defaults in a residential tenancy?
26. Explain what is meant by an insurable interest, and distinguish between an insurance agent and a broker.
27. Explain the nature of the insurance policy, a rider, and an endorsement and reinsurance. Summarize the different types of insurance that are available to businesses.
28. Explain what is meant by the insurer's right to salvage and to be subrogated to the position of the insured, and explain why it is important for a person or business not to overinsure or underinsure.
29. Distinguish between liability, property, and life insurance. Explain the difference between whole life and term insurance, indicating why life insurance might be important for a business or for professionals to acquire.
30. Distinguish between a bond and insurance. Explain the difference between a fidelity bond and a surety bond.

QUESTIONS FOR FURTHER DISCUSSION

1. There is a considerable difference between the laws with respect to residential and commercial tenancies. Most of the statutory changes favour the tenant and have led to considerable complaints by landlords about the difficult position they find themselves in. Do you feel that the changes introduced by statute have unfairly interfered with what should be a relatively simple commercial relationship? Is this another instance of government imposing inappropriate regulation that unfairly restricts a landlord's right to manage his or her property? Consider this as a form of consumer protection legislation and ask what problem it was intended to solve, whether an adequate solution has been arrived at, and whether the solution creates more problems than it solves.

2. When a mortgagor defaults on a mortgage, the mortgagee usually gets a court order to foreclose the defaulting debtor's interest in the property. If the property is eventually taken and resold, the mortgagee gets to keep any profits, even where the debtor has significant equity in the property. Some jurisdictions don't allow this and require the property to be sold under the supervision of the court, with any profits after repayment of the debt and costs going to the mortgagor debtor. Should a creditor ever be allowed to foreclose and profit from the process? Consider the safeguards in place that avoid such abuse. Consider the redemption period provided (say six months) for the debtor to redeem that property. Is that good enough? What about when a second mortgagor or other creditor is involved and is given a court order to sell the property during that redemption period? In effect the debtor is liable to have the property sold immediately. Consider whether this practice is appropriate, given the vulnerable nature of the mortgagor.

3. Bailment involves one person putting his or her personal property into the care of another. The responsibility to look after that property is often limited in the contract creating that relationship. Do you think that a party agreeing to be responsible to look after another property, either in the process of repair, storage, or otherwise, ought to be able to contract out of their responsibilities with an exemption clause? This question really is much broader. This is because whenever an exemption clause is included in any contract, one party is severely disadvantaged. Should the parties to contracts, especially where the bailment of goods is involved, be able to contract out of such basic responsibilities? In your discussion consider the often unequal bargaining power of the parties, standard form contracts, and the concept of fundamental breach discussed in Chapters 4 and 5 and how it should be applied to these contracts.

4. A serious problem that often arises for an insured claiming on an insurance policy is the requirement that all information be accurate or that any changes in circumstances be communicated to the insurance company. Benefits have been denied when the loss takes place when the premises were left vacant, where the use of the premises has changed, or where the information on the application is accidentally or knowingly incorrect—even if the information has nothing to do with the event giving rise to the claim. Discuss whether such an approach is too harsh and gives too much advantage to the insurance companies and whether consumers are adequately protected from abuse.

CASES
FOR DISCUSSION

1. **SENECAL V. THE QUEEN** (1983), 3 D.L.R. (4th) 684 (F.C.T. D.).
Mr. Senecal was an employee of Air Canada, working as a loading supervisor at Dorval airport when he found a packet of money on the floor of the cafeteria and turned it over to the RCMP. It turned out to consist of $10 000 US. He was told that if it were not claimed by the rightful owner within three months, it would be returned to him. After waiting the three months, Mr. Senecal asked that he be given the money but his request was refused. Instead, the regional administrator chose to give him only $2000 and gave the rest to charity. Mr. Senecal brought this action to recover the entire $10 000 to which he felt entitled as the finder. Discuss the rights of the parties in this situation.

How would it affect your answer to learn that there was a regulation in place empowering the administrator to dispose of personal property by choosing one of the following courses of action: 1) by returning it to the finder if the finder was not an employee of the department; 2) by disposing of the property by private sale or auction; 3) by disposition to a charitable institution; or 4) by destruction? (See section 3 of the *Airport Personal Property Disposal Regulations*, C.R.C. 1978, c. 1563, made pursuant to the *Department of Transport Act*, R.S.C. 1970, c. T-5.)

2. **HEFFRON V. IMPERIAL PARKING CO. ET AL.** (1974), 46 D.L.R. (3d) 642 (Ont. C.A.).
Mr. Heffron parked his car in a parking lot operated by Imperial Parking Company and left the keys in the ignition as instructed by the attendant. When he returned at about 1:00 a.m., he found the car missing. It was eventually found with considerable damage and several personal items missing. The lot in fact closed at midnight but the practice was for the attendant to take the keys of the cars remaining and give them to an attendant at a nearby parking garage, who would then return them to the owners when they claimed their cars. Discuss the obligation of the operators of the parking lot in these circumstances.

How would it affect your answer if the ticket involved contained the words, "We are not responsible for theft or damage of car or contents, however caused." What if the driver had merely parked the car and taken the keys with him?

3. **RE PUBLIC TRUSTEE OF MANITOBA AND LECLERC** (1981), 123 D.L.R. (3d) 650 (Man. Q.B.).
Mr. and Mrs. LeClerc held their home in joint tenancy when Mr. LeClerc murdered his wife. He was first charged with murder, but the charge was later reduced to manslaughter. He was found not guilty by reason of insanity. It was, therefore, established that he was insane at the time and at the time of this action was confined in a mental institution. The problem is whether one joint tenant can take the whole property by way of survivorship when he has killed the other joint tenant. Mrs. LeClerc's parents brought this action, claiming, as their daughter's rightful heirs, her half of the proceeds of the sale of the property.

How would your answer be affected if Mr. LeClerc was not insane but murdered his wife so that he could pursue another relationship?

4. **PARAMOUNT LIFE INSURANCE CO. V. HILL ET AL.** (1986), 34 D.L.R. (4th) 150 (Alta. C.A.).
Mrs. Audrey Hill owned a house, and her husband, without her knowledge, forged her name on transfer documents to his business partner, Mr. Laidlaw. He then arranged for a mortgage on that property with Paramount in the name of the new owner, Laidlaw. Mr. Laidlaw then rented the premises back to Mr. Hill. No mortgage payments were made by Laidlaw, who thought the Hills were making them. Mr. Hill died and Mrs. Hill knew nothing about the mortgage. Paramount commenced foreclosure proceedings against the property. When Laidlaw learned what had happened, he retransferred the property to Mrs. Hill. She claimed in this action that the mortgage should be set aside because of the fraud and that full title to the home should be restored to her. There was no evidence that Mr. Laidlaw or Paramount knew anything about the forged documents or Mrs. Hill's claims. Discuss what would likely happen in a land titles jurisdiction and how this would be different in a normal land registry system.

5. **880682 ALBERTA LTD. V. MOLSON BREWERIES PROPERTIES LTD.,** [2003] 2 W.W.R. 642, [2002] Alta. Q.B. 771 (Alta. Q.B).
In 1997 Molson sold property they had in Calgary to the Canzyme Corporation. This property had been operated as a brewery, but there was a restrictive covenant included in the transfer documents, which was properly registered and permanently prevented this property from ever being used as a brewery again. Such restrictive covenants must name not only the servient lands (the property restricted) but also the dominant lands (the property gaining the benefit from the restrictive covenant). In this case the dominant lands were named as the Molson Brewery properties in Edmonton. The purchaser ran into financial difficulty, and the Calgary property was acquired by the plaintiff (880682 Alberta Ltd.) through foreclosure proceedings. The plaintiff then brought this action to have the restrictive covenant removed. Discuss the arguments that both parties would make and the likely decision of the court.

6. **KICELUK V. OLIVERIO,** 2001 ABQB 704, [2001] A.J. No. 1085.
Ms. Kiceluk was a tenant living in a property operated by the defendant landlord. She was walking down some steps when her high heel caught in a crack in the concrete step. She fell and severely broke her ankle. She sued the landlord for compensation, which both parties agreed amounted to $55 000. Note that the landlord did not live on the premises and that she had notified the landlord of the problem in the past and he had promised to repair it. What would be the basis of Ms. Kiceluk's complaint against the landlord and what arguments might he raise in his defence?

7. **SPORTSMAN'S R. V. RESORT BLIND BAY B.C. LTD. V. CAPRI INSURANCE SERVICES LTD.** 2003 BCCA 310, [2003] B.C.J. No. 1269.
Sportsman's Resort, the plaintiff, had relied on the advice of the defendant insurance agent when they took out insurance on their property. Later a fire occurred, and, when they sought compensation from the insurance company, they learned that they were underinsured. Not only did they not have replacement coverage they thought they had acquired, they also were considered a co-insurer, thus reducing their compensation even more. They then claimed that the defendant insurance agent had been negligent and given them improper advice. Do you think the insurance agent should be responsible for the fact that the plaintiff didn't purchase enough insurance through them?

CHAPTER 9

Ideas and Information

Great changes caused by computers and internet

An information revolution has taken place over the past 30 years, fuelled primarily by the use of computers. This chapter discusses the intersection between law, business, and information technology. It includes an examination of intellectual property, including copyright, patents, and trademarks, as well as a review of the legal issues associated with the internet. It also considers the problems associated with securing information and protecting personal privacy. These issues have become extremely important in recent times with the current movement of business to the internet and other forms of electric commerce. Recent high-profile cases involving the copying of music from the internet onto MP3 players and DVDs—as well as the sheer ease of copying movies, games, and music to DVDs, miniature hard drives, and other forms of mass storage—illustrate just how important these issues have become to business. Not only is technology changing so fast it is difficult to keep up, but our understanding of the social impact of these changes and the development of laws to govern them are also lagging behind technological change. In this chapter we can do no more than outline the problems and the directions in which our lawmakers seem to be going.

Intellectual Property

Intellectual property is intangible personal property

We identified the forms of property in the last chapter, dividing personal property into chattels (tangible, movable goods), and choses in action (intangible personal property). Intellectual property is a special type of intangible personal property. Copyright does not refer to a particular book, song, or painting, but to the right to control its reproduction. In the same sense patents, trademarks, and industrial designs do not refer to actual things produced, but to the protection of the idea, mark, or design associated with a product.

Intellectual property is a valuable business asset that can be stolen or damaged. Unauthorized exploitation may deprive the author of income from a copyright, or damage the goodwill associated with a trademark. Patented inventions can be misappropriated, and confidential information can be misused. Intellectual property is often underdeveloped, undervalued, and underprotected by business people. A business may be so focused on marketing that it fails to realize the potential of a production process or software that has been developed for its own purposes. If a business does sell or licence the process or software, there may be a failure to properly account for royalties.

Businesses often undervalue and fail to protect intellectual property

Intellectual property law usually requires that active steps be taken to protect an asset. The federal government has enacted legislation dealing with intellectual property, including copyrights, patents, and trademarks. Thus, most disputes dealing with intellectual property matters are heard by the Federal Court, but this is one area where federal and provincial courts have concurrent jurisdiction, and so these matters may be dealt with by provincial superior courts as well.

Federal and provincial courts often have concurrent jurisdiction with respect to intellectual property

COPYRIGHT

The federal *Copyright Act*[1] protects books, photos, music, and other artistic works. Keep in mind that it is only the expression of the idea that is protected, not the idea itself. If someone photocopies the text that you are now reading, they will be in breach of the author's copyright, but if they simply write another book expressing the same ideas in a different way, they have a right to do that. Copyright protection is extended to authors and artists for 50 years after the death of the creator of the work.[2] In effect, the owner of the copyright controls the reproduction of the work during that period, after which the work becomes part of the public domain and no longer subject to anyone's control. The idea is to give the creator of the intellectual property the exclusive right to profit from and otherwise control his or her creation for a specified period of time. This period is reduced to just 50 years when a corporation is involved, the author is not known, or the work involves such things as movies or photographs.

Copyright protects the expression of the idea, not the idea itself

Copyright lasts for the life of author plus 50 years

It is common for a publishing company to produce and market the work and for the author, artist, or composer to receive royalties from the sales. Royalties consist of a percentage payment (e.g., 10 percent), based on the net proceeds the publisher receives from each item sold. The copyright is then assigned to the publishing company. Of course, creators can publish their own material, retaining for themselves complete control over the copying, reproduction, or performance of their work.

Even where the copyright has been assigned to a publisher or some other party, the author retains some significant rights. **Moral rights** consist primarily of the author having the right to continue to have his or her name associated with the work as creator, and to have the integrity of the work preserved. This means that the work cannot be modified, distorted, or defaced without the author's permission, even after it has been sold. If an author assigned the copyright of a book to a publisher, who then decided to publish it using the name of a different author, that would violate the original author's moral rights. An example of the protection of moral rights involved a sculpture of Canadian geese in a shopping mall. A retailer decided to hang red ribbons on it for Christmas. The sculptor protested; the court agreed that the added decoration interfered with the artist's

Copyright can be assigned, but authors retain moral rights

1. *Copyright Act*, R.S.C. 1985, c. C-42.
2. Only 50 years where a corporation or a photograph is involved.

moral rights not to have his work degraded and ordered the mall to remove the ribbons.[3] It is not always the creator of the work who is entitled to copyright. Where an author is working as an employee, the work created will belong to the employer, unless the employment contract states otherwise. Also, where consultants write an instruction manual for a software producer, for example, the contract may state that copyright will be held by the software company. It is vitally important that contractors specify not only what work is to be created, but also which party will acquire copyright.

Employers entitled to copyright unless agreement otherwise

CASE SUMMARY 9.1

Hanis v. Teevan et al.; Guardian Insurance Co. of Canada et al., Third Parties[4]

An Employer Holds Copyright for Items Created While on the Job

A court found that Hanis had been wrongfully dismissed from his employment as manager of the university's computer lab. He had not been given a warning about his unacceptable behaviour nor an opportunity to change. But the court rejected his claim of copyright infringement of the computer software programs he had developed while in that position. Section 13(3) of the *Copyright Act* provides that when copyrightable materials are produced in the course of employment, the first copyright holder is the employer, not the employee. The court also rejected his claim that these rights had been assigned to him by the university and by his fellow consultants. There was no proof with respect to the university, and the consultants were also employees and had no right to the copyright in the first place. Even though the court found the conduct of the university "reprehensible" with respect to his termination, the university was still entitled to the copyright. Note that Hanis had rejected a $1 million offer to settle and only received a $158,034.54 judgment, plus costs for the wrongful dismissal.

In addition to the creative products mentioned above, there are several less obvious areas that are covered by the *Copyright Act*. Copyright can extend to "every original literary, dramatic, musical and artistic work" produced in Canada as well as a "performer's performance, sound recording, and communication signals." Past confusion about whether computer programs and software were better protected under patent or copyright legislation resulted in amendments to the *Copyright Act* to protect computer programs as literary work. Table 9.1 lists examples of what is included in these various categories. Note that there can be considerable overlap among them.

Computer software is now protected by copyright

Other nations have similar laws, and there are treaties between nations giving copyright protection in one nation to works created in another. So long as the originator is a citizen or resident of Canada, or of a country that is a signatory to the Universal Copyright Convention, the Bern Convention, the Rome Convention, or is a member of the World Trade Organization, that work has copyright protection in Canada and those other countries.

Copyright protection in Canada can give protection in other jurisdictions

3. *Snow v. Eaton Centre Ltd.* (1982), 70 C.P.R. (2d) 105 (Ont. H.C.J.).

4. (1998), 162 D.L.R. (4th) 414 (Ont. C.A.).

TABLE 9.1 The Scope of Copyright

Category	Examples
Literary works	Books, manuals, computer programs, and translations
Dramatic work	Plays, recitations, mime, movies (including the scenery)
Musical work	Musical compositions and arrangements
Artistic work	Paintings, drawings, maps, charts, plans, photographs, engravings, and sculptures
Performances	Dancing, singing, instrumentals, acrobatics, and acting
Sound recording	Tape recordings, records, computer memory, compact disks, memory cards, and DVDs
Communication signals	Radio, television, cable, and internet broadcasts

It is also important to note that no special steps need be taken in Canada to create copyright. Registration is not required, since the mere production of the work creates the copyright. Still, registration is permitted under our Act[5] and this is often done to establish when the work was created or to ensure that the work has copyright protection in other nations that require such registration. Copyright is indicated by the symbol © accompanied by the year of publication and the name of the copyright holder.

Copyright protection is automatic in Canada but registration provides additional benefits

CASE SUMMARY 9.2

CCH Canadian Ltd. v. The Law Society of Upper Canada[6]

Attention Must Be Paid to Who Owns the Copyright

CCH Canadian Ltd. published compilations consisting of court judgments and sold them to lawyers and others for a fee. The Law Society provided a library service to their members. They made single copies of these cases, which they sent out by fax. They also allowed members to make their own copies by using the Law Society's photocopier. There is a sign above the photocopier summarizing the copyright law. CCH sued, claiming the Law Society was infringing copyright. The action went to the Supreme Court of Canada, which held in favour of the Law Society. They held that the Law Society, having no control over its members, was not responsible for copies made by them on the photocopier. The court did agree with the plaintiff that, although a reproduction, there was originality in the work entitling it to copyright protection. The headnotes, indexes, and other reference material added made the work original as required under the *Copyright Act*. Still, the service provided by the

(continued)

5. *Copyright Act*, R.S.C. 1985, c. C-42, s. 54.
6. [2004] 1 S.C.R. 339 (S.C.C.).

Law Society was not an infringement of that copyright as it constituted "fair dealing" under the Act. The copy was made for research and private study, and just because the lawyers used the materials as part of their business, that didn't make it any the less research. Also, the court stated that a library could not be held to have infringed copyright by doing anything that a client was permitted to do as fair dealing, and that the services provided by the Law Society qualified as not-for-profit library services. This case shows not only what constitutes original work, but it also clarifies what is permitted as private study and research. This case also has a much broader application; it was followed in the recent federal decision finding that downloading music was not a violation of copyright.

For copyright protection work must be original and fixed in a permanent form

In order to qualify for copyright protection, the work must be original. This doesn't mean it has to satisfy some critical standard, but it must originate with the author. Facts, numbers, images, or material copied from other sources are not protected by copyright, only the part that originates with the author or artist is protected. The protected work must also be fixed in some permanent form as in the recording of a song in digital format or capturing an image on film. It could also include a written choreography, a stage play, or a manuscript stored on computer.

Limited copying is permitted

It is only when substantial portions of the work are copied that there is an infringement of the copyright. Photocopying a few pages of a textbook for personal use might not violate copyright but copying several chapters or even a few lines of a vital portion clearly would. Use of small portions of a work for research or for private study is permitted, and there is no infringement when portions of a work are reproduced for review, criticism, or news reporting. Educational institutions, as well as libraries, museums, and archives have additional rights to use portions of such works for educational and research purposes. Special exceptions are made for reproductions that are done to facilitate someone who is blind or deaf. But just because an item is available in a library or archive doesn't mean it can be freely copied without consequence.

Licences to copy can be obtained for a fee

The solution is to get a licence from CANCOPY, which is the non-profit body set up to represent authors in these matters. CANCOPY collects a fee and distributes it to the author, legitimizing a reasonable amount of photocopying. SOCAN provides the same service for musicians and composers of recorded music. The Copyright Board, a government regulatory body established under the *Copyright Act,* sets the royalty fees charged by these bodies and other matters, including the arbitration of some disputes with respect to copyright.

PATENTS

Patent protection continues for 20 years but requires disclosure

A patent is a form of monopoly that gives an inventor the exclusive right to produce and profit from his or her invention for a period of 20 years. A government regulatory body created for that purpose deals with applications. The inventor must disclose in the form of drawings, plans, and text material enough information so that someone else could reproduce the invention. Inventors are encouraged to share their invention with others who will then benefit by the knowledge and be inspired to further innovation and invention. There is no obligation to disclose this information by getting a patent, but when it is kept secret, there is the danger that someone else will independently produce the same item. In such a case the first inventor will have no protection. If the second inventor is granted a patent, the original inventor will be prohibited from using his or her own invention. The source of these rights in Canada is the federal *Patent Act*.[7]

Patent protects the idea, not the work itself

Unlike copyright, it is the idea that is protected in a patent, not the expression of the idea. Thus, if someone produces another product that is quite dissimilar to a patented invention, but incorporates the same principles or ideas, it would still be an infringement of the patent associated with that invention. The Act defines an invention as " . . . any new and useful art, process, machine, manufacture or composition of matter, or any new and useful improvement in any art, process, machine, manufacture or composition of matter." In order to be patentable the invention must be useful in the sense that it is functional or can do what it claims and contributes in some way to improving our society by making some aspect of production more efficient or our lives more enjoyable. It also must be new. A patent will not be granted to someone who simply finds some process or machine that is in use but has not been patented. A patent will be denied if the invention has been the subject of prior publication more than a year before the application. It will also not succeed if the invention is embodied in some product that has been sold prior to the application or if the nature of the invention can be discovered by examination of the product, known as reverse engineering.

Invention must be new and useful

CASE SUMMARY 9.3

Canwell Enviro-Industries Ltd. v. Baker Petrolite Corp.[8]

Patent Protection a Business Concern

Baker Petrolite developed a product to remove the offensive odour from sour gas. But its patent was challenged on the grounds that it had been disclosed to the public more than a year before the patent had been applied for. In fact, Petrolite had started to sell the product more than a year before applying for patent protection in either the United States or Canada, and the court held that this amounted to such disclosure and refused the patent. Although they didn't actually disclose how the product could be made, it was a simple matter of reverse engineering for an expert in the field to take the product, analyze it, and reproduce the effect. The patent was invalid. Note the dilemma of the manufacturer, who is often pressured to get the product to market as fast as possible but also to delay long enough to get patent protection.

Nor will a patent be granted for some improvement to an existing machine or process that would have been obvious to someone with similar knowledge and training. The Act also makes it clear that, "No patent shall be granted for any mere scientific principle or abstract theorem."[9] Thus Einstein's famous formula $E=MC^2$ could not be the subject of a patent.

No patent is granted for obvious improvement, scientific principle, or higher life form

7. R.S.C. 1985, c. P-4.

8. (2002), 23 C.P.R. (4th) 346 (F.C.C.A.).

9. *Patent Act,* R.S.C. 1985, C. P-4 s.27(8).

Also higher life forms such as modified animals are not patentable in Canada.[10] But the Supreme Court has made it clear that a modified gene can be patented. In order to protect that gene, the court will also protect the animal or plant produced by that modified gene, thus arguably accomplishing the patenting of modified animals indirectly.[11]

Special provisions are in place with respect to the production of patent medicines in Canada. These are designed to consider the interests of consumers and protect them from excessive pricing, while providing sufficient protection and income to the patent holder. Historically, Canada forced international companies to grant licences at low cost to Canadian companies so that they could produce cheaper generic drugs for this country. That was changed in 1993. Drug manufacturers gained greater patent protection with the cost of patented drugs going up as a result. This has been balanced by introducing the requirement that the prices at which patent-protected drugs are sold must be justified before a Patented Medicine Prices Review Board (PMPRB). The result has been a significant increase in the price of patent- protected drugs in this country. To make matters worse, practices such as "evergreening" have been introduced to further increase the length of patent protection. This involves developing some small change in the already successful drug so that it can be treated as a new drug with another 20-year span of patent protection.

Note that the problem is much worse for third-world countries that simply can not afford the costs of modern drugs. The World Trade Organization (WTO) now permits the creation of generic drugs, under licence, for export to third-world countries, and this has gone some way toward responding to the battle against AIDS, especially in Africa. Historically, this had to be left to the generosity of the drug producers, the patent holders, to supply such drugs for such third-world requirements. Now that licences are granted to other producers, cheaper drugs are available, but there is also a growing problem with the cheaper drugs getting back into Western countries at the lower costs.

Patent must be applied for and fee paid

Unlike copyright, patent protection does not come automatically, but must be applied for. The process of applying for a patent is complex and expensive, and is best left to the experts who are registered patent agents. They, typically, will make a search of the patent registries of Canada and other countries to see if a similar patent has been granted. Then they will submit an application in which they set out full disclosure with respect to the invention. The documentation must also describe what is new and innovative about the invention. The application must be provided in a specified form, along with accompanying documents and a fee to the patent office. The documents are examined to determine if the invention qualifies as something new. If it is indeed new, and the requisite fees are paid, the commissioner for patents grants approval for the patent. The payment of an annual maintenance fee is also required to maintain the patent protection over its 20-year life.

Where patent not used, the patent holder can be forced to grant a licence

Once a patent has been obtained, the invention must be used. Inventors can't simply sit on their invention, using their patent rights to prevent others from using them. Upon application to the patent board, an individual can require a patent holder to grant a licence to use the invention, thus ensuring that the public benefits from it.

10. *Harvard College v. Canada (Commissioner of Patents)*, [2002] 4 S.C.R. 45 (S.C.C.).

11. *Monsanto Canada Inc. v. Schmeiser*, [2004] 1 S.C.R. 902 (S.C.C.).

Although a patent granted in Canada only provides patent protection in this country, once a patent has been granted here, protection can be obtained in other countries that are signatories to applicable treaties. The general rule is that the first to apply is the one entitled to the patent. But under these treaties this priority is established with the original application in Canada, not the later date of application in another country. The reverse is also true, of course, giving patents obtained in other countries priority in Canada as well. Foreign patents are vitally important for Canadian businesses involved in significant international trade.[12]

Canadian patent establishes right to patent in other jurisdictions

As was the case with copyright, it is important to include provisions that clearly state who is entitled to any patent arising from work done under the contract or pursuant to the employment in contracts with consultants, employees, and independent contractors. As was the case with copyright, patents can be assigned to third parties and can be used as security for a corporation's financing arrangements.

Employer has right to patent unless agreement otherwise

Decisions to grant or not grant a patent or patent infringements may be challenged in the Federal Court, which has the ultimate jurisdiction with respect to the validity of such patents and the rights associated with them. Where an infringement has taken place, the *Patent Act* gives both the federal and provincial courts concurrent jurisdiction to deal with that infringement and to provide appropriate remedies.

Federal and provincial courts can hear patent infringement case

Two other acts providing similar protection are the *Industrial Design Act* and the *Integrated Circuit Topography Act.* These federal statutes are relatively unknown but can provide significant protection in the right circumstance. The *Industrial Design Act*[13] protects distinctive designs, shapes, or patterns associated with a product that have no useful function, but simply add to the appeal. The distinctive shape of a utensil, a chair, or even the unique icons found on computer screens are examples. Protection of such designs is acquired by registration lasting for 10 years with the payment of the appropriate fees. The *Integrated Circuit Topography Act*[14] is legislation intended to protect the unique design of the integrated circuits that are the heart of the modern computer revolution. The various components that make radios, televisions, computers, automobiles, watches, and most other modern products work are now miniaturized onto semi-conductor material. They form the integrated circuits protected by this Act. To obtain this protection the design must be registered, and the protection also continues for a 10-year period.

***Industrial Design Act* protects distinctive shapes**

***Integrated Circuit Topography Act* protects printed circuit design**

TRADEMARKS

Trademarks are names, symbols, logos, or other distinctive marks that are associated with a business. A valuable business asset is its good relationships with customers, suppliers, and the public. This is referred to as goodwill and is often associated with the business name or some distinctive mark such as McDonald's golden arches or the shell symbol appearing on all of Shell's service stations and other operations. The federal *Trade-marks Act*[15] provides a mechanism for trademarks to become registered and protected in a formal way. This protection gives

***Trade-marks Act* protects distinctive names and logos**

12. Over 4000 U.S. patents were issued to Canadians in 2001 alone.

13. R.S.C. 1985, c. I-9.

14. S.C. 1990, c. 37.

15. R.S.C. 1985, c. T-13.

Trademark protection is obtained by registration and lasts for 15 years

Infringement involves others using the mark to confuse the public or devalue the business

the owner of the trademark the exclusive right to use it throughout Canada with respect to the particular type of business, or similar products or services as indicated on the application. This protection lasts for a period of 15 years and is renewable, but it must be used during that time or it will be considered abandoned. A trademark registered in Canada will provide proof of ownership for registration in another country. The converse is also true; registration in another country will provide proof of ownership in Canada.

If another business uses a similar symbol so as to make their customers think they are dealing with the actual owner of the trademark, an infringement has taken place. Intentional copying of a registered trademark is not the only way an infringement can take place. Any use of a similar mark that devalues the goodwill or reputation of the business can qualify as an infringement, whether intentional or not.

CASE SUMMARY 9.4

Re Carson and Reynolds[16]

What's in a Name?

Reynolds applied to register the trademark "Here's Johnny" with respect to portable fibreglass toilets he developed to be used at construction sites and other temporary locations. Johnny Carson, the popular TV personality of the time who was always introduced by his co-host with the words "Here's Johnny," opposed the registration of the trademark. The Federal Court refused to register the trademark on the grounds that it falsely suggested, and a number of people would believe, that there was a connection between the portable toilets and Johnny Carson. Such false associations are prohibited under the *Trademarks Act*. Remember that not every clever turn of phrase can be used to identify a business.

When an infringement takes place, the owner of the trademark may seek a remedy in either the Federal Court or the superior courts of the provinces. The advantage of going to the Federal Court is that the judgment can be enforced throughout Canada.

Trademarks can be words, symbols, or both in combination

Certification marks, proposed trademarks, and distinctive shapes are also covered by the *Trade-marks Act*

Trademarks can consist of words, expressions, trade-names, symbols, logos, designs, or combinations of them. The apple logo associated with the word "Apple" on Macintosh computers is an example of such a combination. Trademarks include the specialized marks associated with quality or standards such as the CSA (Canadian Standards Association) approval found on electrical appliances. These are called certification marks and have the same protection in Canada as other forms of trademarks. It is also possible to register the distinctive shape of a product or its container such as the unique Coca-Cola bottle shape. This is called a **distinguishing guise** and registration also provides trademark protection. Under the *Trade-marks Act* an application can also be made for a **proposed trademark** where the mark has not yet been used and is not known to the public but will be used in the future.

The process of applying for and registering trademarks in Canada is a complex one, usually requiring the services of experts called *trademark agents.*

16. (1980), 115 D.L.R. (3d) 139 (F.C.T.D).

Searches of indexes and registries must be made in Canada and usually in other countries—especially the United States—to determine if the mark has already been granted or is in use here or elsewhere. Then the agent makes the application to the Registrar of Trademarks setting out a description of the mark, the wares or services it is to be used with, and the names and addresses of the agent and owner of the trademark along with the appropriate fee.

Trademark protection requires registration and the payment of a fee

There are several restrictions on what can be used as a trademark. For example, anything associated with royalty, national flags, institutions such as the Red Cross or R.C.M.P, or provincial or national coats of arms cannot be used without permission. Of course, anything obscene or illicit is also prohibited. Normally, a simple surname of a living or recently deceased individual will not be accepted. But there are exceptions if the name has already become associated with the product or business. Also, a term that is simply descriptive of the product, the nature of the service, the location, or one that is misleading in any way will be rejected. And of course, no trademark can be used that can be confused with the registered or unregistered mark of another similar business or one selling similar products or services.

Trademark must be distinctive, socially acceptable, and not associated with prohibited institutions

Disputes with respect to the registration of trademarks are handled by the Registrar of Trademarks, with appeals going to the Federal Court. It is appropriate, although not required, to indicate the presence of a trademark by the symbols ® where the trademark is registered or ™ when unregistered. Trademarks can be challenged up to five years after registration. It should also be noted that such trademarks as well as the licences associated with them can be assigned to other companies.

Trademarks can now be licensed for use by others

PASSING-OFF The *Trade-marks Act* provides statutory protection for registered trademarks, but even unregistered marks and names are protected under the common law tort of passing-off. Any people or businesses that advertise their service or product in such as way as to lead others to believe they are being supplied by or associated with another business, when they are not, is liable to be sued for the tort of passing-off. Counterfeit Rolex watches are an example. Sometimes a business will use a similar name, which might lead customers to believe they are associated with another business when they are not. This too may qualify as passing-off. For example, the B.C. Supreme Court issued an injunction restraining a newly formed real estate company from using the name Greystone Properties Ltd. on the basis that it caused the public and the customers of the already established Greystone Capital Management Inc. to be confused. Their use of the name devalued the goodwill of that company, even though the plaintiff company was based in Saskatchewan. It had no office in British Columbia, but did some business with the real estate and pension fund investment community in that province. The court found that: 1) the plaintiff had a reputation of goodwill in British Columbia that could be injured; 2) the businesses were similar enough to cause confusion by the action complained of; and 3) the value of the goodwill or reputation was injured. These are the necessary elements to establish a passing-off action.[17] In effect, the ability to bring a passing-off action prevents other businesses from trading on the reputation and goodwill of another business through intentional or accidental misrepresentation and in the process injuring the value of that reputation and goodwill. A passing-off action will be available to an injured party whether or not their trademark is registered under the *Trade-marks Act.* Table 9.2 provides a summary of the legislation protecting intellectual property in Canada.

A business that passes itself off as another may be liable

A registered trademark not required for a passing-off action

17. *Greystone Capital Management Inc. v. Greystone Properties Ltd.* (1999), 82 C.P.R. (3d) 501 (B.C.S.C.).

CASE SUMMARY 9.5

Walt Disney Productions v. Triple Five Corp.[18]

The Danger of Using Similar Names

When in 1983 the Edmonton Mall used the name "Fantasy Land" for their new amusement park, the Walt Disney Corporation, which had used that name in association with their amusement park for decades, sued them for passing-off. The court agreed that the use of the similar name would cause confusion in the minds of the public and issued an injunction against the Alberta corporation that prevented the continued use of the name. Even though Walt Disney Corporation didn't carry on business in Alberta, they did advertise there, and the goodwill developed by that promotion had been damaged. The fact that there was no intention to mislead did not take away from the damage caused, and an injunction was the appropriate remedy.

TABLE 9.2 **Intellectual Property Legislation**

Statute	What Is Protected	Requirements	Protection Period
Copyright Act	Original books, photos, music, and other artistic works (the expression)	Mere production	Death of author of work plus 50 years or in some cases only 50 years
Patent Act	Original invention or innovation (the idea)	Application and registration	20 years from filing
Industrial Design Act	A product's distinctive design, shape, or pattern	Registration	10 years from registration
Integrated Circuit Topography Act	Design of integrated circuits	Registration	10 years from filing or use
Trade-marks Act	Trade names, symbols, and logos associated with a business	Registration*	15 years renewable

*Note that some trademarks receive unregistered protection through passing-off action.

REMEDIES

The remedies available to the court when intellectual property rights are infringed are similar in all cases (see Table 9.3). Damages are available, but only at trial and after a lengthy delay. The needs of the parties in intellectual property disputes are usually urgent, requiring a more immediate remedy to prevent further losses. Often when an infringement is discovered, the offended party will make an imme-

18. (1994), 113 D.L.R. (4th) 229 (Alta. C.A.).

diate application to the court for an injunction to stop the offending practice until the court can deal with the matter at trial. An interim injunction will only be granted when the applicant can show a strong case, indicating a likelihood of success at trial and also that the **balance of convenience** is in the applicant's favour. This means that the court has to be convinced that more damage will be suffered by the applicant if the injunction is not granted than would be suffered by the offending party if the injunction were issued. Another effective interim order is an **Anton Piller order**. Here the court orders that offending products or records be seized before they can be destroyed or removed. To be effective this must be done without notice to the offending party. Such an order will only be granted where the applicant can demonstrate: 1) there is a strong *prima facie* case; 2) there is danger of considerable further damage to the applicant; and 3) it is clear that the offending party has the documents or products in its possession and is likely to destroy or otherwise dispose of them before any hearing or trial.

Interim injunction requires the balance of convenience to favour the applicant

Interim injunction common where need for remedy is urgent in intellectual property disputes

Anton Piller order provides for seizing of offending documents or products without notice

Any other remedy must wait until trial, but often, given the fast pace of intellectual property disputes, once an interim injunction is or is not granted, there is no sense in taking the matter further. If the dispute does go to trial, the object is usually to make the injunction permanent or to obtain damages. But the actual value of intellectual property involved and the damages suffered are often difficult to determine. Often, it is more appropriate to seek an order for an accounting. As explained earlier, with this remedy the court determines any improper profits made by the defendants through their offending conduct and orders these profits to be paid to the plaintiff. Of course, if there are no profits, damages are a more appropriate remedy. The court may also order that the offending product or documents be surrendered to the plaintiff, but an award of damages or an injunction are still the primary remedies when intellectual property rights are infringed.

Accounting requires improper profits to be paid to victim

In addition to the civil remedies available for copyright and patent infringement, both of these acts contain specific provisions that make some forms of infringement a criminal offence. Under the *Copyright Act* the penalties when the prosecution is by indictment can be as high as five years in jail and a million dollar fine. The penalties for a *Patent Act* infringement are considerably less, even when treated as an indictable offence. The maximum penalty for pricing offences with respect to patented medicines can be as high as $5000 ($100 000 for a corporation) and six months in jail. Note, however, that with some specific forms of infringement, each day the infringement continues can be treated as a separate offence with the penalties accumulating. When patent infringements with respect to other forms of inventions are involved, the penalties are much less.

Criminal penalties in *Copyright Act, Patent Act*, and *Criminal Code*

The *Trade-marks Act* itself contains no criminal penalties, but there are specific offences found in the *Criminal Code* relating to trademark infringement. In addition, other general remedies associated with fraud and theft—sections 406 to 412—make it an indictable offence to forge, alter, deface, conceal, or remove a trademark or even to refill a bottle with someone else's trademark in order to deceive or defraud. Also, passing-off as well as the practice of reselling goods without disclosing them to be used or reconditioned are also indictable offences. The potential punishment is two years in jail if treated as an indictable offence. Note that it is also a criminal offence to claim that the goods in question were made by someone holding a royal warrant or in the service of the royal family or some government department.

Failure to keep track of intellectual property resources and to account for licensing fees and royalties is a major problem when dealing with this type of

TABLE 9.3 Remedies for Interference with Intellectual Property

Remedies	Nature of Order	When Available
Damages	Monetary compensation and on rare occasions punitive	Only at trial
Injunction	Order to stop the offending conduct	Before trial as an interim injunction or at trial as a permanent injunction
Anton Piller Order	Order to seize documents, products, or other material before it can be destroyed or removed	Before trial without notice to other party
Accounting	Disclosure and payment to the plaintiff of improper profits made from the offending conduct	At trial only
Criminal	Imposition of fine and/or imprisonment	At trial only

asset. Where circumstances permit, businesses and individuals should take steps to keep track of and protect these resources. And when such an infringement is detected, usually speedy intervention is required to prevent significant damage.

Business and the Internet

The enormous expansion of the internet has brought about another round of significant and basic changes to our economy and society. Communication of information and ideas has never been so easy and so seamless. The internet is much broader than just a business tool. It provides education, entertainment, and social interaction. It has, to a large extent through electronic mail services, supplanted paper correspondence. It also facilitates socially irresponsible activities, including pornography, gambling, and other illegal activities.

Laws are outdated and regulation is lacking with respect to the internet

The development of the internet and electronic commerce has moved forward at an astounding rate and has created a free and open, Wild West–style online environment, which is relatively free of government regulation and legal restrictions. It is important to note that the various forms of law, including civil remedies for fraud, breach of contract, and tort, as well as most forms of criminal law and federal and provincial regulation, apply to transactions and activities conducted online. The difficulties consist primarily in determining the laws of what jurisdiction should apply and enforcement. The laws that are in place are often not readily adaptable to this new form of communication, and the courts, legislators, and regulators have been slow to respond. The lack of effective regulation may explain why some business people are still reluctant to make a move into the world of ecommerce. One of the greatest fears of the proponents of the internet and other forms of digital communication is government control that would inhibit the freedom which has been the basis of the tremendous growth and flexibility that has characterized the medium thus far. Governments, realizing that too much regulation would destroy the very nature and value of the internet, have also been reluctant to introduce regulation and control too quickly. But that is beginning to change.

JURISDICTION

An important feature of the internet is that it is not restricted to one country or state. It does not recognize borders, which gives rise to some serious present and potential problems for internet users. For example, what is legal in a jurisdiction such as Nevada, where gambling and sexually explicit material are common, might well be prohibited in another state or province, and yet material on the internet is generally available to everyone. Valid laws may apply, but from which province or state—where the product originates or where it is used? For example, in 2000 certain World War II Nazi memorabilia was offered for auction over the internet. The French government brought an action against Yahoo, the U.S. internet provider, for selling racist material in France in violation of French law. Yahoo was required to block all such advertising from being presented to French viewers. The difficulty posed by trying to make every advertisement or service conform to the local law of each nation, state, or province is overwhelming and would completely destroy the freedom of internet communication. Similar problems have arisen with gambling as well as with obscene, racist, subversive, and seditious material.

A major problem is to determine what laws apply to internet and internet transactions

Another difficulty is that it is often not clear whom to sue, or where to bring the legal action. One advantage of the internet is that a company or individual can work anywhere in the world, and the place of origin of the material will not be apparent to the users. Kazaa, for example, is a popular music downloading service on the internet. The program was developed for a company in the Netherlands, which then sold it to another company operating from a small Pacific island whose executives and principals work out of Australia. Which jurisdiction is appropriate for an action to be brought against them? Could they bring an action in the Netherlands or Australia, or are they limited to suing in that small Pacific nation where the laws likely neglect to mention such offences? Online gambling leads to a similar result. U.S. law[19] prohibits taking bets over a network, such as the internet, and this has led several significant internet gambling businesses to set up offshore, particularly in Caribbean countries, which encourage this activity. It is impossible for U.S. authorities to intercept these gambling operations, which have created a billion dollar industry with most of its customers in the United States. Some regulatory steps have been taken to overcome these difficulties, but each has the potential effect of limiting freedom of expression, movement, or association—rights the courts are bound to protect.

Another major problem is determining where an action should be brought

Regulations can compromise freedom of expression

A huge online retail business has developed as well. This has caused a considerable problem for local jurisdictions with respect to taxation. A store physically located in a province or state is required to collect sales tax from its customers, but that is easily avoided where the purchase is made over the internet. Laws have been passed in some areas requiring online retail businesses to pay local sales taxes or to levy taxes on the internet service provider, but enforcement is a continuing challenge.

19. *Federal Interstate Wire Act,* 18 U.S.C. § 1084.

The general rule is that a particular location can exercise jurisdiction if the person being sued is resident in that jurisdiction or if that is where the complained of action took place. The problem is that most offensive content does not target a particular victim in a particular state, but is directed at anyone with a computer. Many jurisdictions have passed **long-arm statutes** allowing them to take jurisdiction even when no resident is directly involved, with the result that business people providing an internet service from one area where the activity is completely legal will find themselves being sued or prosecuted in jurisdictions they were not aware of, and where they had no idea they were breaking the local law. A better approach is to allow a judicial action only where there is a close connection between the jurisdiction and the act complained of. Thus, if an internet site offers pornographic materials or gambling services, and an internet user in a particular state or province subscribes or places a bet, that would establish the jurisdiction and an action could be brought there. But even this goes too far for many.

Danger that internet providers may be subject to very different laws in place in a multiplicity of jurisdictions

CASE SUMMARY 9.6

Dow Jones v. Gutnick[20]

Unsettled Questions of Jurisdiction

In this case an article by an American company published on the internet defamed an Australian resident. The Australian court found that the harm done was in Australia, thus creating a sufficient connection between the defamation and that country for the case to be heard in an Australian court. The American company, Dow Jones, pointed out that this would require them to know and comply with the laws of every country, "from Afghanistan to Zimbabwe." In a similar case brought in Ontario,[21] an article published on the website of the *Washington Post* stated that the United Nations, after several investigations, failed to renew Mr. Bangoura's contract because of "misconduct and mismanagement." Mr. Bangoura, an Ontario resident, brought an action where he lived. The *Washington Post* brought an application to have the action dismissed, claiming that the most convenient jurisdiction was the District of Columbia in the United States. It should also be noted that the libel laws in the United States are much friendlier to media than in Canada, and require proof of actual malice when public figures are defamed. In dismissing the application by the *Washington Post* and allowing the Canadian action to proceed, the judge quoted from the Australian decision. "A publisher, particularly one carrying on the business of publishing, does not act to put matter on the Internet for it to reach a small target. It is its ubiquity which is one of the main attractions to users of it... Publishers are not obliged to publish on the Internet. If the potential reach is uncontrollable then the greater the need to exercise care in publication." Obviously anyone using the internet for such publications has to be aware that the laws of other jurisdictions may apply, and they may well face actions from "from Afghanistan to Zimbabwe."

20. [2002] H.C.A. 56 (Aust.).

21. *Bangoura v. Washington Post*, 2004 CanLII 26633 (Ont. S.C.J.).

Canadian courts are willing to find jurisdiction where there is a real and substantial connection between the act complained of and the province. But even then jurisdiction will be declined if the court can be convinced that it would be more reasonable for some other jurisdiction to deal with the matter. It is evident that there is a great potential for people doing business online to find themselves embroiled in disputes in various jurisdictions all over the world. Only if the business can demonstrate that the internet message was passive in the sense that there was no interaction in that jurisdiction, that no bets were taken, and no orders or subscriptions were sent, then there is little likelihood that an action could be brought against that business in the courts of that state or province. But it is often difficult to selectively do business in that way. It may help to state within the contract of service or goods that the law of a particular jurisdiction, such as Ontario or British Columbia, will govern the transaction. It could also be stated in the website or internet pop-up advertisement that the offer is not extended to specific provinces or states where the activity is prohibited. But even these steps are no guarantee that such a business won't find itself sued or prosecuted in another jurisdiction.

Canada requires a real and close connection for action to be brought

Passive internet messages are more likely to be exempt

Internet offer or service should state limitations of availability

Of course, when a foreign judgment is obtained against a business or individual, there is always the problem of enforcement. But that protection is often an illusion. If the business has assets in the foreign jurisdiction or there are treaties in place to allow for enforcement, a substantial threat does exist. It can be very dangerous to ignore such actions, even when commenced in some remote province or state. Also note that where criminal conduct or regulatory offences are involved, it can be difficult, if not impossible, to extradite and prosecute the accused residing in another country.

Dangerous to ignore foreign actions since judgments can be enforced in other jurisdictions

CASE SUMMARY 9.7

Beals v. Saldanha[22]

The Importance of Responding to a Notice of Court Action

An Ontario couple had incorrectly described the property they sold in Florida to the Bealses, causing them to build their new home on the wrong lot. The Bealses sued in a Florida court, claiming fraud, and the sellers (the Saldanhas) failed to defend that action. The Florida court found against the sellers and awarded substantial damages, including punitive damages, which, with interest, grew to $800 000. The original selling price of the lot was only $8000. In agreeing to enforce the Florida judgment in Ontario, the judge made clear that the merits of the case and whether the Saldanhas had a good defence was irrelevant, since they had missed their chance to make those arguments by not defending in Florida. Although this is not an internet case, it does dramatically demonstrate the dangers of ignoring actions brought in other jurisdictions.

22. (2002), 220 D.L.R. (4th) 558 (Ont. C.A.).

INTELLECTUAL PROPERTY

Intellectual property law applies to the internet as well ...

But rights may be too difficult or costly to pursue

Disputes arising with respect to intellectual property on the internet generally involve allegations of copyright or trademark infringement. Most people are familiar with the disputes that have arisen with respect to the online music industry. Services such as Napster and Kazaa that assist users to freely copy popular music and other entertainment material have collided head-on with the music and entertainment industry, which has sued successfully for copyright infringement. There are no special rules with respect to copyright law and the internet, and copyright infringement is actionable whether it takes place by print, broadcast, the internet, or some other medium. But special problems arise when copyright law is applied to the internet. As soon as businesses such as Napster are dealt with, others arise. They either use new technology or locate in remote jurisdictions, making it almost impossible to stamp out the practice. Recently, the entertainment industry targeted the actual users rather than the music providers. To discourage uploading they launched legal actions against a few individuals for illegally copying and using their music. Recently, an action was brought by BMG Canada in the Federal Court to force the internet service providers to divulge the identity of these subscribers.[23] It is usually not worth the trouble to pursue individual cases of copyright infringement, even if it is possible to detect them. But music download operations cost the entertainment industry billions of dollars, and every effort is being made to stop the practice. BMG Canada failed in this application, but it does indicate the direction that these businesses are heading. It is also interesting to note that the judge in this case found that the downloading and copying of music off the internet, for personal use only, was not a violation of copyright but was more like taking advantage of a library service.

Initially, business often failed to register domain names

Trademarks are a major area of conflict on the internet. Most businesses now find the internet to be vital to their business, either as a vehicle to advertise, to transact business with the public, or to communicate product and promotional information. Their brand names, email addresses, and the domain names associated with their websites have become extremely valuable assets. Think of the power of such names as Microsoft, General Motors, Coca-Cola, Disney, and Sony. In the early stages the process of registering domain names was on a first-come, first-served basis, causing a virtual gold rush of applications to acquire names that were the same as or similar to the trade-names associated with large businesses as well as with other potentially popular names and phrases. Many businesses did not appreciate the potential significance of the internet to take the steps necessary to protect these valuable assets by registering their business and brand names. When they eventually tried to do so, they often discovered someone else had appropriated their name or phrase by registering it first. It is not surprising, therefore, that conflicts have arisen over domain names.

Each domain name is a unique address, giving rise to considerable conflict

Such conflicts may arise legitimately because of the global nature of the internet, where two similar businesses in different locations try to register the same name, or two dissimilar businesses have similar names. The problem is that each domain address is unique and not limited to the geographical location where the business is active. Only one of them can have that domain name. Conflicts also arise when less well-intentioned individuals register the names first and then, in effect, hold the names for ransom. Sometimes similar names are registered so that visitors making slight but expected mistakes are intercepted and redirected

23. *BMG Canada Inc. v. John Doe*, [2004] F.C.J. No. 525 (F.C.T.D).

to a competing business. This is called *cybersquatting*, and even when there are methods for dealing with such practices, it is often cheaper for a business to simply purchase the address, name, or phrase from the cybersquatter who has managed to register it first.

Cybersquatters capture domain names that rightfully should go to others

Arbitration processes have been established to deal with disputes over the entitlement to domain names. The bodies responsible for the registration of domain names, for example the Canadian Internet Registration Authority (CIRA), have established a policy for the arbitration of bad-faith domain name registration disputes, which gives preference to the businesses with the more legitimate claim. In Canada, for *.ca* designation domain names, bodies such as the British Columbia International Commercial Arbitration Centre and Resolution Canada Inc. have been authorized to provide arbitration services in such disputes. The largest organization providing domain name dispute arbitration services is the **World Intellectual Property Organization (WIPO)**. Disputes involving legitimate conflicting interests can be handled through traditional trademark or passing-off litigation.

Arbitration and litigation is possible, but it is often cheaper just to buy the name

CASE SUMMARY 9.8

Bell Express Vu Limited Partnership v. Tedmonds & Co.[24]

Freedom of Expression on the Internet

Bell, the operator of a properly licensed satellite TV service under the registered trademark of "Express Vu," brought this action for trademark infringement against the defendant company, which operated a rival but unlicensed satellite TV service when they registered an internet website using the domain name of "expressvu.org." The opening page made it clear that this website was not associated with Bell, but was set up to criticize Bell's service. Bell sued for trademark infringement, but the judge considered this a non-commercial use, which was protected by the freedom of expression provisions of the *Charter*, and so he refused to grant an injunction. This was only an application for summary judgment, but it does illustrate how proprietary rights might conflict with freedom of expression.

Compare this to *Itravel2000.com Inc. (c.o.b. Itravel) v. Fagan*,[25] where a travel company had been using the name "ITravel" for several years before they tried to register it as a domain name. They discovered that another company had registered the name a month earlier, and then offered to sell it to the travel company for $75 000. There was no internet name registration dispute mechanism in place at that time, and so this action was brought. The plaintiff applied to stop the second company from using or selling the name, claiming it was a trademark violation. Neither company had registered the name as a trademark, but it was clear that the travel company had been using the name under various circumstances in Ontario for years.

(continued)

24. [2001] O.J. No. 1558 (Ont. S.C.J.).

25. [2001] O.J. No. 943 (Ont. S.C.J.).

The defendant had not used the name and had no connection to the travel industry, and so an injunction was granted. The difference in the two cases is that in the second the registration of the name was simply being used as a method of extracting funds from someone who had a superior claim.

It is important to take steps to avoid name infringement problems

As in most situations, litigation and arbitration of disputes represents an expensive business failure, even when ultimately successful. It is much better to avoid such confrontation. When a company is about to promote a new brand or launch a new name, they should take steps to register the brand name and all similar names—even misspellings as well as plural, singular, hyphenated, and non-hyphenated variants and combinations. It might also be wise to register any embarrassing variants of the brand name that might come to mind to prevent others from abusing the name.

TORTS

Internet defamation is a particular problem because of ease of widespread distribution

The most common type of tort on the internet is defamation, but the approach will likely be the same where passing-off, fraud, or other forms of tort are involved. Wide-spread distribution and uncertain jurisdiction are the factors that make internet cases unique. As with written communications, online defamation can take many different forms, ranging from a remark made in a private email message, to chat room conversations, or to an article posted on a business' website that says disparaging things about a competitor. Even newspapers and magazines run into problems when they place their material on the internet.

CASE SUMMARY 9.9

Stanley Young v. New Haven Advocate et al.[26]

Defamation on the Internet

In this case offensive material defaming a prison guard in Virginia was published in Connecticut and distributed over the internet. The Connecticut article was prompted because that state was considering sending some of their prisoners to serve time in Virginia. Young brought his action in Virginia, but the court held they didn't have jurisdiction, as the published article was only intended for local consumption. Contrast this to the *Dow Jones v. Gutnick*[27] case, discussed above, where the Australian court did have jurisdiction and the *Bangoura v. Washington Post* case (see Case Summary 9.6) where a Canadian court retained jurisdiction, despite a similar argument. Whichever approach prevails, it is clear that the wide availability of remarks made on the internet poses an ever-increasing vulnerability.

26. 315 F. 3d 256 (4th Cir. 2002).

27. *Dow Jones v. Gutnick*, [2002] H.C.A. 56 (Aust.).

As demonstrated in the cases discussed above, there are conflicting cases with respect to jurisdiction for defamation, which should emphasize the danger for businesses that are not careful about their internet and email communications. Note that not only will the person making the defamatory statement be liable, but the business that employs him or her may be liable as well, especially if company email services or websites are used to publish the offending statements. When a business provides access to their website for chat rooms or for discussion forums, there is also the danger it too could be held responsible for any defamatory, or otherwise offensive statements, that are made. It is unlikely that the actual ISP (the internet service provider) will be liable, unless it fails to remove or block the offending messages once required to do so by a court. It is likely that those providing access to the internet will also be responsible where criminal law or other government regulations are infringed, depending on the degree of control they had or should have exercised over the offending communications.

Note the danger of liability extending to employer or business providing bulletin board or chat room service

BUSINESS TRANSACTIONS OVER THE INTERNET

Whether a company is involved in direct retailing of products, software, or service to consumers over the internet or are simply contracting with other companies through email or a website, they are transacting business and creating new legal relationships. The common thread with respect to all of these internet transactions is that their legal status is determined by contract law. Written evidence of a contract, while not generally required, is a sensible thing to have. It is a permanent record that can be referred to later and constitutes evidence if any disagreement arises. In some cases, under the *Statute of Frauds* or equivalent legislation, such writing and signatures are required for the transaction to be legally enforceable. But when transacting business electronically, there are no signatures or written documents. It is true that written copies can be produced, but they are unreliable due to the ease with which they can be altered.

Electronic commerce is becoming a significant method of doing business

Traditional contract rules apply to internet transactions

Under the auspices of the federal government, a working group following international recommendations produced the *Uniform Electronic Commerce Act* (*UECA*).[28] This document has no legal standing, but it serves as a model for the design of provincial legislation so that similar statutes will be in place throughout Canada. Most provinces have enacted such statutes, although they vary considerably between jurisdictions. The object is to make electronic documents and signatures as binding on the parties as are written ones. In general, the *UECA* and provincial acts do not change the law with respect to the requirement of written documents and signatures. Rather, they recognize electronic or digitally stored documents and signatures, or their equivalent, as satisfying those requirements. A signature equivalent might be a password or some other form of encryption, which is controlled by the author of the document (and possibly verified by a trusted third party). The password or encryption would authenticate the document and give it the same status as one that was written and signed. Note that this doesn't apply in all cases and some types of documents, such as wills, still have to be in writing and signed to be valid. Note, as well, that there are important variations between provinces and that some provinces now allow many forms of government documents, including court registry and land registry transactions, to take place electronically. Many jurisdictions also allow the use of electronic documents relating to proxies, prospectuses, and other documentation related to the purchase and sale of securities.

Provinces are adopting federal *Uniform Electronic Commerce Act* guidelines

Statutes recognize electronic equivalent of written documents and signatures

28. www.chlc.ca/en/us.

Another problem that arises with respect to the formation of contracts is to determine when and where the contract was created. This can determine whether an offer was accepted within time, what law applied to the transaction, and whether a particular court had jurisdiction to hear a dispute. It might also determine whether the individuals involved were minors or adults at the time, whether transactions involving such things as pyramid selling schemes, gambling, or pornography are legal, and what consumer protection statutes apply to the transaction, all of which varies with the jurisdiction. A business will often state that the law of a particular jurisdiction will apply to the transaction, and, while this is helpful, it does not always end the dispute.

The parties can declare in the contract which jurisdiction's law will apply

CASE SUMMARY 9.10

Greenshields Inc. v. Johnston[29]

Parties Can Specify Which Law Applies

This creditor brought this action against the guarantor on a defaulted debt. Although the parties were in Alberta and the action was brought in Alberta, the creditor claimed that Ontario, rather than Alberta, law should apply. The Alberta *Guarantees Acknowledgment Act*[30] requires that all such guarantees be notarized; this was not done. But the guarantee itself stated that the law of Ontario will apply to the transaction, and there is no similar notarization requirement in that province. The court found that because of the statement in the guarantee, the Ontario law applied, meaning that there was no requirement that the guarantee be notarized. Therefore, it was valid and the defendant had to pay. Stating in the transaction that the law of a particular jurisdiction will apply can go a long way to avoid these jurisdictional problems.

Post box rule will not apply to internet transactions

In most cases a contract comes into existence when and where the acceptance is communicated to the offeror. The exception is the post box rule, which holds that where the use of the mail is appropriate, the acceptance is effective when and where it is posted. This presents several problems for internet transactions. It is now generally accepted that where such instantaneous methods of communications are involved, the post box rule should not apply. Thus, an offer will be accepted and a contract formed only when and where the offeror learns of the acceptance. This is consistent with the recommendations of the *UECA* with respect to contracts formed over the internet. Also, although internet communication involves intermediaries located in other jurisdictions, the *UECA* recommendations make the location of these intermediaries irrelevant in determining the validity of the contract and the legal obligations between the parties. Whether a contract or another form of internet communication, these provisions determine that a message is sent as soon as it is committed to the system (hitting send), and it is received as soon as it arrives on the recipient's computer, even if it is never read. As you will recall, an offer ends when a revocation is received or a counteroffer is sent, and, where implemented, these *UECA* recommendations

Location of intermediaries will not affect transaction

UECA **guidelines determine when and where communications are sent and received**

29. (1982), 131 D.L.R. (3d) 234 (Alta. C.A.).

30. R.S.A. 1970, c. 163.

determine when that takes place and can have a direct impact on that pre-contract negotiation process.

A practice in retail selling that has caused difficulty over the internet is the sellers' provision of a button on their website for the customer to activate (mouse click) indicating the placement of an order, the acceptance of warranty terms, an acceptance of licensing provisions, or other terms of the agreement. As in traditional contracts, such terms must be brought to the attention of the parties, and where they are clearly worded and there is no mistake in making the response such as choosing the wrong button, it appears that clicking does impose legal obligations on the contracting party. The *UECA* even anticipates and validates automatic contracting or ordering that takes place between computers governed only by software with no intervening human action.

Clicking a button will bind party to terms

Of course, major problems with business transacted over the internet arise when something goes wrong. This is especially true when retail sales are involved and the product is defective. Most jurisdictions have in place some form of consumer protection legislation, and these statutes apply as well to internet transactions. Again, the problem arises as to which province or state's law governs, and then where an action must be brought. In most circumstances it is not worthwhile for a purchaser to pursue a matter when they live in Toronto but have to seek redress in Los Angeles. Many legitimate retailers doing internet business provide warranty services simply to protect the goodwill they have developed, but when dealing with less established businesses, there is little protection. The problem also arises with paying for the purchase. Most sales go through without a problem, especially where large and established dealers are involved, but when problems arise, the purchaser is at the mercy of the retailer, unless he or she has paid through some third party and can stop the payment. The new Ontario *Consumer Protection Act*[31] has specific provisions in it to solve many of the unique problems that arise with respect to internet transactions.

Internet poses practical problems in enforcing consumer protection rights

Danger of paying for defective or non-existent products unless payment is through trusted third party

There are many schemes, developed by unscrupulous dealers working on the internet, to cheat and defraud. An essential part of all such schemes involves providing assurance to the unsuspecting purchasers that they are dealing with a reputable and legitimate business. Sometimes goods and software sold on the internet are counterfeit or pirated, and whether the purchaser is aware of this fact or not, there is a clear violation of copyright or trademark that victimizes the legitimate manufacturer. Of course, where a crime or regulation offence has been committed, there is the overwhelming problem of enforcement, usually with the victim in one jurisdiction and the perpetrator in another. This is especially difficult when the laws of the jurisdiction where the perpetrator resides don't make the same activity an offence. Another serious problem arises when an unauthorized retailer brings goods in from another country, infringing the rights of a legitimate importer with exclusive rights to sell those products in Canada. These are called *grey market goods*, and while the customer appears to be getting the same product for a cheaper price, usually no warranty service is available and the product itself may have significant differences that are not apparent.

There are many schemes to defraud internet users

Often there are serious warranty problems where goods come from a foreign jurisdiction

It is important to remember that when we are talking about torts, frauds, or other wrongs, there are more parties involved than just the victim and the abuser. The internet involves several intermediaries who may also be held responsible for the abuses they help perpetrate. Website operators and internet service providers (ISPs) are vulnerable because they are easily identified and are often the only

31. S.O. 2002, c. 30.

parties that are available to be sued or prosecuted. When internet content is objectionable, it will be the ISP that will be targeted to stop the service or block the offensive material. This was the case with Yahoo when the French government prosecuted them for advertising Nazi memorabilia for sale, contrary to French criminal law. Yahoo was just the internet service provider and had no role in determining the actual content of the messages. Still, they were the ones targeted because they were identifiable and the ones in control. Website operators who allow defamatory or other objectionable material to run on their site, even if they didn't originate it, are even more vulnerable since they are actively participating in the publication of the offensive material. One of the problems is that regulating these areas will limit free speech on the internet and may be used to stifle legitimate commentary. For example, if a website is set up to criticize a particular product or manufacturer, should litigation be allowed to stop it? What if the website is designed to facilitate criticism of government or social organizations? It is often difficult to determine where free speech stops and abuse begins.

Increased regulation will be directed to intermediaries such as internet service providers

Increased regulation will challenge free speech

Finally, a word should be said about spam. This is unwanted email that is sent generally as a form of advertising to most email addresses. Well over 30 percent of email messages received fall into the unwanted spam category, and it is a threat to the email system as we know it. Countermeasures have been introduced, such as filtering systems that separate out the unwanted material, but this is only partially effective and there is the risk of filtering out wanted messages as well. This is one area where regulations are being introduced aimed at the internet service providers with the objective of forcing them to cut off and block the source of spam messages. But many see this as the beginning of a regulatory environment that will destroy the internet.

Controlling spam is a major challenge

Privacy, Security, and Confidential Information

Almost all businesses have some sort of confidential information that they want to keep away from competitors, customers, shareholders, or the public. This might be in the form of trade secrets, customer lists, or negative information about the company, the executives, or other key employees. Much of the intellectual property of a company is stored in databases that summarize such information as its customers and their buying habits, future production plans, or even in secret strategies, processes, or techniques. The common thread is that the information is not generally known, and its disclosure will cause harm to the business. When secret processes, recipes, or formulas are involved, they are known as trade secrets and are often not protected by patent, copyright, or trademark. While not property in the strict sense, so long as it remains confidential, such information constitutes a valuable asset of the business and must be safeguarded.

Confidential information and trade secrets require protection

There are no federal or provincial statutes designed to protect such confidential information, but as a rule, employees, suppliers, and contractors have a common law obligation not to disclose this information to others. This may be based on a fiduciary relationship of trust or simply as part of the contractual obligations between the parties. A **fiduciary duty** arises where one party places trust in another and is vulnerable to harm if that trust is abused. Examples of such fiduciaries are partners, senior employees, and agents. This duty can best be described as an obligation to act in the best interest of the party to whom the fiduciary duty is owed. An important aspect of that duty is the obligation to keep confidences. Even without a fiduciary duty, there can be a legal obligation not to disclose such information or to use it for your own purposes where the information was given in confidence.

Common law requires confidential information not to be disclosed or used by the confidant

Such an obligation can also be imposed by contract, either expressed or implied. When businesses work together, or when a consultant or contractor does work for a business, it is common to include a non-disclosure provision in the contract. An employer will often include a restrictive covenant in the initial employment contract, requiring an employee not to work in the same industry or for a competitor while employed and for a specified period after that employment ends. This protects the employer, not only from having customers follow the terminated employee, but it also prevents that employee from disclosing customer lists, production plans, and even manufacturing methods to a competitor. Even without such a contract, the courts have no hesitation in finding that employees have breached an important obligation when they solicit clients in the last few days of their employment with the idea of taking them with them when they leave. But even an honest employee can be guilty of disclosing confidential information, if he or she doesn't know that it is confidential. It is, therefore, vital to make sure employees understand what is confidential and what is not.

It is a good policy to include non-disclosure provisions in employment and consulting contracts

Important to inform employees of what is confidential

The most common remedies associated with abuse of confidential information are the award of damages, injunction, and in some cases where improper profits have been made, an accounting. Damages, as well as an accounting, are only obtained after the loss has been suffered. Often the most effective weapon to keep the confidential information from being disclosed is to obtain an interim injunction where the employee, contractor, etc. is ordered not to work for the competitor or not to disclose the information. Sometimes a competing employer will attempt to hire away a key employee, primarily to get access to this kind of confidential information or better access to the competitor's customers. Where the competitor has encouraged the employee to leave and to breach his or her duty of confidentiality or contract of employment, it may be possible to seek redress from that competitor in the form of damages for inducing a breach of contract. This would also be an appropriate situation for the remedy of an accounting, which requires the competitor to disclose any profits earned by his or her abuse and to surrender them to the injured employer.

Injunction is often more effective as a remedy than damages or accounting

Inducing breach of contract can sometimes be claimed when an employee moves to a competitor

CASE SUMMARY 9.11

Polyresins Ltd. v. Stein-Hall, Ltd. et al.[32]

Obligations That Go Beyond Termination

Three employees who were aware of the secret formulas used by Polyresins Ltd. to develop acrylic thickeners quit that company and were hired by a competitor, which shortly thereafter began to develop similar products. This interlocutory application was brought by Polyresins for an injunction to prevent those former employees from disclosing the secrets and to prevent the production and sale of the products developed from such improper disclosures. Because this was an interim order, Polyresins only had to establish a strong *prima facie* case. The judge found that without the injunction Polyresins would suffer irreparable harm, so that the balance of conven-

(continued)

32. (1972), 25 D.L.R. (3d) 152, [1972] 2 O.R. 188 (Ont. H.C.J.).

ience favoured Polyresins. The injunction was granted. The court decided the obligation not to disclose secrets followed the employees to their new employment, and since Polyresins would be more harmed if the injunction were not granted than the new employer would be if it was, the interim order was made.

PRIVACY

Several provinces have made breach of privacy an actionable tort

Closely related to confidential information is the topic of privacy. There is no separate privacy protection under common law. In most provinces it is only where the conduct constitutes some other tort, such as defamation or trespass, or where a contract or fiduciary duty has been breached that it will be actionable under common law. Several provinces have statutes making breaches of privacy actionable torts.[33] These acts leave it to the court to determine what constitutes a violation of privacy, but they also state that privacy may be violated by eavesdropping, surveillance, or by the unauthorized use of a name or portrait. The technological advances in data compilation and email communications have led to a number of statutes, both at the federal and provincial levels, being enacted to protect personal information. The federal government, in response to international pressure and the threat of lost business, enacted two statutes. The *Privacy Act*[34] protects personal information in the hands of federal government institutions, limits its collection, and provides for limited access where appropriate. It also establishes the office of the Privacy Commissioner. It is the second Act that is more important for business. This Act, referred to as the *Personal Information Protection and Electronic Documents Act* (*PIPEDA*),[35] is unique in that it is declared to be the law in areas of federal jurisdiction and in all provinces unless a province enacts a "substantially similar" act. Several provinces including Quebec, Ontario, and British Columbia have enacted their own legislation, but it is yet to be seen whether all of these statutes qualify as "substantially similar."

Federal *Privacy Act* protects personal information in federal government institutions

Federal *PIPEDA* applies in all provinces that don't have substantially similar statute

Other provinces have simply adopted the federal act by not passing a similar statute. These acts are meant to control the collection, use, and disclosure of personal information. The federal act came into force in three stages, but as of January 1, 2004, it applies to all organizations in Canada involved in the collection, use, and disclosure of personal information in connection with a commercial activity. The only exceptions are companies already subject to "substantially similar" provincial legislation. Note that this applies to both health and non-health information such as medical conditions, prescriptions and other medical services, customer lists, consumer purchasing habits, credit and entertainment information, information gathered from websites as well as subscriptions to magazines and internet services by an individual, or any other personal information that a company has in its possession that relates to identifiable individuals. It applies not only to the personal information of customers and clients but also to anyone about whom the business compiles personal information, including—to a limited extent—their employees. The provincial acts impose much more strin-

These acts impose restrictions and obligations on all companies that have personal information in their control

33. For example, *Privacy Act* R.S.B.C. 1996, c. 373; and *Privacy Act*, R.S.N.L. 1990, c. P-22.

34. R.S.C. 1985, c. P-21.

35. S.C. 2000, c. 5.

gent standards with respect to an employer's compilation, use, and disclosure of personal information, especially the health information of employees.

The federal act requires the business or organization to develop a privacy policy that will protect such private information from being disclosed to others. A model policy is included in Schedule 1 of the *PIPEDA* (adopted from a prior model policy developed by the Canadian Standards Association when voluntary compliance was hoped for). Each organization is required to develop and implement policies and procedures to protect personal information, to handle complaints and inquiries, and to train staff about the policies developed. Each business must develop its own policies and procedures, but they must satisfy the following:

Businesses must develop policies and procedures:

- The organization must be accountable for the information collected.
- Consent must be obtained from those whose information is used (although in some circumstances this can be implied).
- Reasonable limits must be placed on the collection, use, retention, and disclosure of the information.
- Provisions must be in place for maintaining the accuracy and safeguarding of personal information, including safeguarding from abuses by the employees of that organization.
- Individuals must have access to the collected information in order to determine its accuracy and challenge the information collected where appropriate.

- To make business accountable for information

- To place limits on information use, retention, and disclosure

- To ensure accuracy and safeguard information

- To provide access and a process for challenging the information's accuracy

An individual in the organization should be identified who will be responsible for implementing these policies and for the organization's compliance, even when that information is conveyed to third parties.

The obligations associated with a company's collection and use of such personal information have become a significant aspect of doing business; something as commonplace as selling a customer or subscription list can run afoul of these statutes. While current enforcement of these provisions may be somewhat haphazard, the intense concern about the misuse of personal information compiled in various databases associated with the internet and the ease of accessing that information make it likely that this will be an area of intense regulation in the future. All businesses must develop policies and procedures to protect the private and personal information in their possession in compliance with protection of privacy statutes.

All businesses must develop policies and procedures to protect private information

The *PIPEDA* also contains serious penalties for infractions. Failure to provide requested information, obstructing the process or an employer, or dismissing or otherwise disciplining an employee for acting as required under the Act constitutes an indictable offence, punishable by fine up to $100 000.

There is also a prohibition against "invasion of privacy" that can be effective in curtailing interference with the internet and other forms of electronic data communication and storage. Section 184 makes it an indictable offence to wilfully intercept a private communication using electronic or other means. Section 184 of the *Criminal Code* makes it punishable by up to five years' imprisonment with the unusual additional remedy of up to $5000 in punitive damages which can be awarded to the victim.

SECURITY

Whether a business is concerned with protecting the private information of others or their own confidential information, keeping such information secure has become a great concern. The problems associated with security relate to preserving information, protecting it from corruption, and preventing its interception and disclosure to others. These are not areas where government regulation will likely be of much help.

Keeping information secure requires action by business

When information was stored on paper, filing vast quantities of it posed a considerable problem. Today, whole libraries can be stored on one small disc, and while this eliminates one problem, it raises another. Discs are easily lost, stolen, or destroyed. The decision to dispose of information may be made consciously, but when it is erased unintentionally, the results can be disastrous. For example, a large amount of valuable raw data collected by Statistics Canada was deleted from a permanent collection because of unclear guidelines.[36] Even the crash of a hard drive or the loss or destruction of a CD or DVD can cause the loss of volumes of irreplaceable information.

Digital storage makes information subject to easy loss, whether intentional or inadvertent

The solution, of course, is to make regular backups of all important information and to store them in a different location. But it is surprising how many individuals and businesses fail to follow such a fundamental requirement. It is certain that the days of great paper archives of information and libraries full of books and collections of periodicals and government publications are ending. Paper archives are being replaced by digital storage, but mechanisms must be in place to preserve the information so that it is accessible even by different technologies in the future. We must protect such information from inadvertent or intentional destruction.

Importance of backups stored in different locations can't be overemphasized

An equally important problem for business is to protect confidential information from interception or accidental disclosure. Email communication is not secure; it's more like a postcard than a sealed letter. It is now common for email communications to be systematically scanned by hackers or even government agencies that use sophisticated programs to look for key words and phrases. But the information can also be misdirected inadvertently simply by typing in the wrong email address or by returning a message to a group rather than an individual. The best way to ensure the privacy of electronic communications is through encryption. Email has been judicially recognized as not secure and a business may soon be required to use encryption of email communication and other stored personal information to meet their obligations under the federal *PIPEDA* or equivalent provincial privacy legislation discussed above.

Encryption is important to keep information secure, especially for electronic communications

Passwords go some way to protect information, but many of us either don't change our passwords often enough, or we make them too simple to provide protection. Encryption is a much better way of ensuring that sensitive information won't be intercepted. There are software programs available that provide different levels of encryption. As the name suggests, encryption basically puts the information needing protection into code. The more complex the code, the more difficult it is to intercept the information. But no level of encryption is perfect. Someone with adequate resources, determination, and access will likely be able to intercept all but the most sophisticated encrypted information. Still, for most purposes, a high level of encryption, combined with restricted access to the data storage devices, will provide the greatest protection possible for most businesses. Information that is no longer needed, but still sensitive, should be removed from the system. However, simply deleting email messages or the files from a computer's hard drive will not erase them. This process only allows the computer to write over the confidential data. It is relatively easy to recover most deleted information. Emails are also easily recovered. Further steps have to be taken to ensure removal. Again, encryption should help.

Even encrypted communications are not completely secure

Simply deleting computer files does not remove them

The threat to a business' computer system is not always associated with the internet or the direct accessing of a company's computers on their premises. When a business uses a wireless network, communications can be accessed by

36. Claridge, Thomas, "Disappearing digital info a hot topic at CALL," *Lawyers Weekly*, Vol. 22 No. 4 (May 24, 2002).

computers outside or in another part of the building. There are security programs available to protect businesses from this kind of violation. Security concerns of individuals and businesses must extend much further than their computer resources. For example, electronic banking abuses such as credit and debit card fraud are now commonplace. The signature requirement on credit card transactions is a limited safeguard against misuse. When a card has been stolen or the number copied and misused, banks will usually not charge the rightful owner for the loss unless there has been some negligence involved. But the problem is more difficult with debit cards. The key is to guard the personal identification number (PIN) at all costs. There are schemes ranging from false fronts on automatic banking machines to double striking debit cards to get access to your accounts. But in all cases the culprit must obtain your PIN as well. Sometimes there is a false security camera or someone may be looking over your shoulder, but in all cases there must be someone watching the victim enter his or her PIN to get access to it. One incident at a bank ATM involved the use of an almost invisible pinhole camera.

Wireless networks can be easily compromised

Credit card and debit card fraud becoming a big problem

Steps must be taken to ensure that PINs are protected

Any business allowing payment by debit card must take great care to protect their customers' privacy. Rather than the retailer swiping the card, the customer should do it, and a handheld unit on a cord should be provided. And, of course, the units themselves, and the employees operating them, should be regularly monitored to make sure they are not part of a fraudulent scheme.

Employees and the machines should be regularly monitored to ensure that there is no misuse

Dishonest or careless employees can pose a greater threat to a business than dishonest customers. Aside from theft, fraud, and other forms of white-collar crime, employees may cause harm through inadvertent conduct. They may disclose confidential information unwittingly or cause damage and loss though misuse of the business computer and communication system. Beyond simple waste of resources, where the computers are used for personal purposes such as playing games or using the internet for personal entertainment, employees may expose the company to embarrassment and liability when they use company equipment or company email accounts for illegal or otherwise inappropriate purposes. This may include accessing a customer or client's private information; downloading inappropriate material such as child pornography; gambling; or distributing defamatory, sexually explicit, harassing, or hateful material. The remedy is for the company to have mechanisms in place to monitor the employees' use of the computers and other company resources. If this is done surreptitiously, however, it may violate the employees' right to privacy and subject the business to fines or other punishment. The best option is to inform employees at the outset that their phone calls, computer use, and other employment-related activities are subject to monitoring. This not only avoids the problem of being accused of violating employees' privacy, it also informs them of what they can and cannot do with respect to company resources.

Employers may be liable for employees' abuses

Solution is to monitor employees' use of computers and other resources

Important to inform employees of surveillance

Of course, there is always the danger of an employee being persuaded by a competitor to convey confidential information or trade secrets such as the company's new line of products to a competitor. It is difficult to prevent this problem other than by being extremely careful when hiring. But the risk may be contained to some extent by making sure that this kind of confidential information is only given to those that require it as part of their jobs. Passwords to computers should only be given to those that need them. Different levels of password protection can be arranged so that even on the same computer, information is only given out according to the level of the password used. Blocking software can also be used to prevent employees from accessing inappropriate websites. In all cases the best protection against improper conduct of employees is the development and communication in writing of clear policies and procedures with respect to the use of

Confidential information should be contained, and employees should be told what information is confidential

Careful hiring practices are the best safeguard

company resources; careful hiring practices, including criminal and credit record checks; thorough training; and appropriate accountability, including surveillance and monitoring.

As can be seen from this discussion, while there has been some attempt to regulate the internet, criminal law and other forms of federal and provincial regulatory statutes have thus far been largely ineffectual. In addition to the general provisions relating to fraud, gambling, obscene material, and the like, the *Criminal Code* contains specific provisions relating to computer and internet offences. Section 184 makes it an indictable offence to intercept private communications and is punishable with up to five years in prison. Section 342.1 specifically prohibits the fraudulent obtaining of computer and internet services, whether directly or indirectly, including the possession of passwords and various forms of equipment to accomplish that purpose. This is an indictable offence, punishable with up to 10 years in prison. Section 430 prohibits the commission of mischief and includes a special section prohibiting the destruction or interference with computer data or with someone's authorized use of that data. This would cover hackers as well as computer viruses that wreak havoc on computer information and operations. Mischief, with respect to data, can also be treated as an indictable offence, punishable with up to five years in prison.

Computer viruses and the conduct of hackers in all forms have become known as cyber-crimes and the effect can be devastating. The above sections of the *Criminal Code* can be effective, but often hackers and virus creators are underage and are subject to the less rigorous penalties included in the *Youth Criminal Justice Act*. For example, the infamous "Mafia Boy" from Montreal who interfered with eBay, Amazon.com, and CNN was only 15 years old at the time of the offence. It is generally accepted that only the amateurs get caught. Most sophisticated hackers are also effective in covering their tracks. Hackers often consider themselves to be crusaders fighting big business domination of the internet and computers generally, and some claim to be advocates of reforming computer services. Many, however, are simply mercenaries profiting from the information they manage to steal or the destruction they cause. Whatever the motivation, the effects are extremely costly to business.

The only sure way for businesses to protect themselves is to take their own defensive measures. Like the ongoing battle between the creators of viruses and virus protection programs, a business must take steps to protect itself from the threats posed by the internet.

QUESTIONS FOR REVIEW

1. Distinguish between intellectual property and other kinds of property, and explain which courts have jurisdiction with respect to intellectual property disputes.
2. What is protected under copyright law? How is that protection obtained and how long does it last?
3. Who is entitled to patent and copyright protection when an employee or consultant develops the material?

4. What federal statute protects computer software?
5. What qualifications must be met in order for a work to qualify for copyright protection?
6. Explain what a patent protects, how patent protection is obtained, and how long that patent protection lasts.
7. What qualifications must an invention meet in order to qualify for patent protection? What will not qualify?
8. What is protected by the *Industrial Design Act* and the *Integrated Circuit Topography Act*?
9. Distinguish between a certification mark, a trademark, and a distinguishing guise.
10. Explain the distinction between a trademark infringement action and a passing-off action, and indicate when one would be chosen over the other.
11. Explain what is protected by the *Trade-marks Act*, how that protection is obtained, and how long it lasts.
12. What harm does a trademark infringement cause a business?
13. What will cause an application for trademark to be refused?
14. Distinguish between an injunction, an Anton Piller order, damages, and an accounting. Explain where one would be preferred over the others.
15. Explain what problems have been raised by the internet with respect to jurisdiction and what steps a company can take to avoid them.
16. What must be demonstrated for a Canadian court to take jurisdiction in a dispute arising from the internet?
17. What is the danger of ignoring an action brought in a foreign jurisdiction?
18. Explain the problems that arise when applying trademark and passing-off rules to the internet. How does this encourage cybersquatting and what mechanisms are now in place to solve these disputes?
19. Explain why internet defamation has become a greater potential problem compared to ordinary written or spoken defamation.
20. Explain the unique problems associated with the formation of contracts over the internet and how they have been resolved with the help of federal and provincial statutes.
21. Explain the role played by the federal *Uniform Electronic Commerce Act* and how it relates to provincial legislation.
22. Explain how the problem of payment is resolved and why very few consumer protection actions are brought with respect to defective products purchased over the internet.
23. Explain the common law obligations with respect to people who are given confidential information.
24. What steps should be taken by a business to ensure their employees don't divulge confidential information?

25. Explain the importance of provincial privacy acts, the federal *Privacy Act* and the federal *Personal Information Protection and Electronic Documents Act* and how they interrelate.
26. Explain why the *Personal Information Protection and Electronic Documents Act* is in force in some provinces and not in others.
27. What must be included when a business develops policies and procedures under this Act?
28. Explain why digitally stored information is particularly vulnerable to loss or disclosure. How can that information best be secured from intentional or inadvertent loss?
29. How can a business best protect their communicated information from inadvertent disclosure or intentional interception?
30. Explain how a business can ensure that their employees are not involved in any illegal or other inappropriate activity with respect to computers, the internet, and voice mail.
31. What steps should be taken to ensure that the employees don't become involved in such inappropriate activities in the first place?

QUESTIONS FOR FURTHER DISCUSSION

1. There are two ways of looking at the problems associated with intellectual property. As with any form of property law, the rules restrict and protect that property for the use of one individual or group and exclude others. But intellectual property is the vehicle for commercial and economic progress and is not restricted by international boundaries. Also, because it is intangible, the use by one group does not deny it to others as would be the case with a stolen car, for example. Third World countries, even emerging economic giants like China and India, often look at such intellectual property laws as a way to restrict their advancement and further the profits of Western capitalistic nations and corporations at their expense. The same kind of debate happens at home between those who copy music over the internet and those large record companies and artists that feel that such activities are akin to theft. Consider these positions and discuss the relative merits of both sides. Is there any way to accommodate these conflicting interests?
2. One of the great advantages of the internet, and one of the reasons for its tremendous growth in recent years, has been its freedom from controls and regulation. It has been a little like the Wild West with entrepreneurs, artists, and anyone with a desire to communicate free to do so, and only limited by his or her imagination. This has led to invention and creativity, but also to abuses. The debate today relates to control and regulation of the internet and the question for discussion is whether you think that this beast should be tamed. Consider the arguments pro and con, and discuss the various ways that such controls could be imposed. Look at the jurisdictional problems, but consider also how to maintain the freewheeling nature of the internet that has contributed to so much creativity.
3. The AIDS epidemic is just one of the catastrophic health problems that illustrate the disparity between medical advances and the costs that make them inaccessible to

those who need them. Today, steps are being taken to provide low-cost drugs to Third World countries, but the general problem remains, and it surrounds the patent protection provided to the companies that develop the drugs. Consider the balance now struck between guaranteeing profits of pharmaceutical giants that developed these drugs and the need of inexpensive variants in those countries and ours to preserve life. Discuss the negative impact of our patent protection policies in these areas and consider what can be done to overcome the problem.

4. Consider the recent introduction of privacy laws at both the federal and provincial levels and the restrictions and controls this imposes on business. Does this place an unreasonable burden on business? How would you suggest that these provisions be expanded, reduced, or otherwise altered?

CASES
FOR DISCUSSION

1. **BOUDREAU V. LIN ET AL.** (1997), 150 D.L.R. (4th) 324 (Ont. Gen. Div.); **AUBRY V. DUCLOS ET AL.; CANADIAN BROADCASTING CORP., INTERVENER** (1997), 157 D.L.R. (4th) 577 (S.C.C.).
Boudreau was an MBA student attending university under the supervision of the defendant Lin. As part of part of the requirements, he prepared a paper and submitted it to Lin. Lin later published it with only minor revisions and without acknowledging the role Boudreau played in its preparation. The paper was later included in a casebook, which was used in other classes at the university. When Boudreau discovered his paper, he brought this action against both the university and Profession Lin. Explain the arguments available to both parties and the likely outcome.

2. **WOLDA V. TECHFORM PRODUCTS LTD. ET AL.** (2001), 206 D.L.R. (4th) 171 (Ont. C.A).
Wolda had been employed by Techform for a number of years when he retired and was given a contract to consult on special projects. The contract was for one year, was renewable, and could be terminated on 60 days' notice; there was no provision with respect to patents or ownership of intellectual property. During this period of consultancy, he designed a special hinge, and the employer presented him with an Employee Technology Agreement (ETA) to sign, which surrendered all claims to this and other inventions that he might develop while employed by the company. He signed reluctantly, fearing he would be terminated if he did not. He also put a question mark beside the word employee, showing that he doubted that it applied to him as a consultant. Subsequently, he designed another unique hinge and applied for the patent. Note that company employees assisted him in the development and a company patent attorney assisted in preparing the application. He tried to charge a fee for the design and for assigning it to the company. As a result he was terminated, and he brought this action for a declaration that he was entitled to the patents for these special hinges. The company brought a similar application. Explain the arguments that Wolda and the company could use to support their position, and indicate the likely outcome of the action.

3. **PRO-C LTD. V. COMPUTER CITY, INC.** (2001), 205 D.L.R. (4th) 568 (Ont. C.A.).
Pro-C was a small Ontario company providing services to Ontario computer software developers under the name WINGEN. They had a website under that name at *www.wingen.com*, and had registered the WINGEN trademark. Computer City was a large American company involved in retail sales of computers all over the United States, but not in Canada. One of their computer lines was given the name WINGEN and heavily promoted on their Computer City website. Although they did no business in Canada and did not promote or advertise their products in Canada, their customers inundated the *www.wingen.com* website address to the extent that Pro-C's business was seriously disrupted. Pro-C brought this action, claiming infringement of their trademark. Explain the arguments available to both sides and the likely outcome.

4. **MOTEL 6, INC.V. NO. 6 MOTEL LTD. ET AL.** (1981), 127 D.L.R. (3d) 267 (F.C.T.D.).
Motel 6, Inc. is an American firm operating motels all over the United States, but not in Canada. They do, however, take bookings from Canada and advertise in Canada. The Canadian defendant operated three motels in British Columbia under the Motel 6 name and had registered the Motel 6 trademark in this country. They also used a logo that was very similar to the U.S. company's logo. The American firm brought this action. What is the nature of their complaint? What remedies do you think would be appropriate for the American firm to ask for? Indicate any arguments that can be used by the Canadian firm in its defence.

5. **LAC MINERALS LTD. V. INTERNATIONAL CORONA RESOURCES LTD.** (1989), 61 D.L.R. (4th) 14 (S.C.C.).
Lac Mineral owned certain valuable mining claims in Ontario and was looking for a partner to help develop them. Corona was invited to participate, and their representative came out and visited the site. While there, they were informed that Lac didn't own the claims surrounding this property, but were hoping to acquire them. The partnership deal did not materialize, but Corona, without informing Lac, managed to acquire the surrounding claims and the two companies developed the adjoining properties. Lac brought this action, claiming that Corona had violated their obligations to Lac when they acquired these properties. Explain what obligations were violated and what defences Corona could raise. What is the likely outcome?

6. **BRAINTECH, INC. V. KOSTIUK** (1999), 171 D.L.R. (4th) 46 (B.C.C.A.).
Kostiuk was accused of publishing defamatory information about the defendant on a website bulletin board in 1996. Kostiuk was a B.C. resident and Braintech was a company incorporated in Nevada, but domiciled in British Columbia and doing business all over the United States, including some business in Texas. This defamation action was brought in Texas; a judgment was obtained and Braintech asked the B.C. courts to enforce the Texas judgment. Do you think that this kind of foreign judgment ought to be enforced in Canada? What are your reasons?

7. **BANGOURA V. WASHINGTON POST ET AL.** (2003), 235 D.L.R. (4th) 564 (Ont. S.C.J.).
Consider an Ontario case where Bangoura, a former United Nations employee living in Ontario, was defamed by the *Washington Post*. The paper published the defamatory statement on their website which was read in Canada as well as other jurisdictions. Mr.

Bangoura brought this defamation action in Ontario and the court had to determine whether they had the appropriate jurisdiction to hear the case. What do you think?

8. **AUBRY V. DUCLOS ET AL.; CANADIAN BROADCASTING CORP., INTERVENER** (1997), 157 D.L.R. (4th) 577 (S.C.C.).
   In this case a photographer took a photograph of a Montreal woman without her knowledge or permission and allowed it to be published in an artistic magazine without charge. The woman claimed that she was embarrassed and that her friends laughed at her. She sued the photographer and the publisher of the magazine. Explain the arguments available to all. Consider the different legislation in place in different provinces. Compare this case to the Ontario case below involving an internationally known, professional waterskier.

9. **ATHANS V.ADVENTURE CAMPS LTD. ET AL.** (1977), 80 D.L.R. (3d) 583 (Ont. H.C.J.).
   The waterskier, Athans, had a promotional photograph taken that was well known, as it had been used on various brochures and for other commercial purposes. The public relations firm associated with Canadian Adventure Camps (a summer camp program for children) took that photograph, made a line drawing of it, and used it on the camp's promotional material. It is clear that they didn't intend any harm but just wanted to have a waterskiing photo on their brochure. Athans sued. Explain the nature of his complaint and his likelihood of success.

CHAPTER 10

The Regulatory Environment of Canadian Business

It is interesting that when we live in a village or small town there is little need for a complex body of rules to live by. Simplicity is possible because there are fewer things that can go wrong. But as we become involved in a complex urban environment, more forms of social interaction and misbehaviour have to be anticipated and we end up with a lengthy list of rules that we must follow. As our society has become more complex, so too have the mechanisms necessary to govern it. Government consists of the elected law-making bodies, including Parliament and the provincial legislatures (**legislative branch**); the courts at all levels (**judicial branch**); and the bureaucracy, including the prime minister, cabinet, and all government departments (**executive branch**). It is in this latter area that growth in government has taken place at a tremendous rate. Even given recent attempts to downsize government bureaucracy and the rules and regulations it has spawned, the regulatory environment has become an overwhelming component of doing business in this country. Government interacts with its citizens on many different levels. It collects direct and indirect taxes in various forms; it regulates trade, commerce, and the various other activities of its citizens; and it provides many services, both directly through government agencies and departments, and indirectly by providing funding to individuals, businesses, and other institutions.

Complex society leads to more rules

Executive branch regulates

Government controls can be indirect

In this chapter we will concentrate on the government regulation of business in Canada. The following material is in no way a comprehensive examination of government regulation. Rather the first goal is to help the reader appreciate the extent of that regulation. The second is to familiarize you with the body of rules called administrative law, which sets out our rights when dealing with government regulatory bodies. In the latter part of the chapter we will examine two selected areas in a little more depth, as examples of how businesses are affected by such government regulation.

Areas of Government Regulation

We are all touched by government regulations and the bureaucrats who enforce them. We pay income tax, GST, sales tax, and property taxes. We face security checks, examination of our purchases, and pay duties when we cross a border. As homeowners we must get permits to build or modify our homes, submit to building and other inspectors, pay fees for such things as garbage collection and water. We are told not only what we can and cannot do on our property, but there are even rules about what we must wear in certain situations or how much noise we can make at certain times. As drivers, of course, we must comply with all of the regulations associated with operating a motor vehicle. We are even restricted as to where we can park our vehicles.

Government regulation touches all of us

A business trying to comply with federal and provincial government regulations is faced with immense challenges and additional costs. All businesses must pay federal, provincial, and local taxes, and must keep appropriate records available for inspection. They must obtain the appropriate federal, provincial, or municipal licences and permits to carry on their business and face regulations when importing or exporting goods. Other regulation controls securities transactions such as selling shares or otherwise organizing the financial affairs of a business. Businesses face regulations when transporting goods by sea, rail, air, or on the highways, and they face even more control when their products or the production processes are dangerous or damage the environment. They face restrictions on what businesses they can purchase and operate; how much they can charge for products; what kind of arrangements they can make with suppliers, customers, and competitors; and what methods they can use to compete in the marketplace.

Business is extensively regulated

One of the most important areas of regulation for business is in the area of employment. Employment standards statutes and labour relations boards set out what wages must be paid, the amount of vacation pay and statutory holidays entitlement, overtime, leaves from work, notice and severance pay upon termination, whether deductions can be made for uniforms, and what records and statements have to be maintained by the employer. Labour relations boards or their equivalents in the various jurisdictions have the power to hear complaints, inspect records and premises, and enforce these provisions by making orders and imposing fines. And there is a whole body of rules providing for the unionization of employees and governing how the relationship between those unionized employees and the employers are to be conducted, including rules over the collective bargaining process, mediation, strikes, lockouts, and the enforcement of any agreement concluded. Any disputes must be heard by arbitrators or the labour relations board and comply with the statutes and regulations in place. Note that an employer who fires, refuses to hire, or otherwise discriminates against an employee because of his or her trade union activity commits an offence under the *Criminal Code* punishable by fine and imprisonment. Employment insurance premiums must be paid by both the employer and employee. There is a significant government organization set up under the employment insurance statute with which the unemployed must contend in order to collect employment insurance benefits.

Employment is especially regulated

A major area of concern and compliance for a business is in the field of workers' compensation. Complicated rules of safety and health for businesses, plants, and job sites have been established under workers' compensation and occupa-

Workers' compensation boards play an important role . . .

tional health and safety statutes in all jurisdictions. Under that legislation regulations are in place that must be complied with. Inspectors are empowered to enforce those regulations, even to the point of imposing fines or closing down the job site when they determine there is significant non-compliance. Employers are required to pay premiums which vary, depending on the nature of the job and their past history of infractions or claims, as determined by compensation board officials. Employees must apply to the board for compensation when they suffer a job-related injury or health problems. Again, compensation board officials will determine whether the claim is valid, and the amount to be paid in compensation. Violations of the provisions of the statute can result in a fine or even imprisonment. Disputes over any of these matters, either by the employee with respect to coverage or the employers with respect to premiums, fines, etc., will be heard at various levels within that workers' compensation board structure.

- As do human rights boards

Human rights boards are government agencies that have their greatest impact on business in the field of employment. Employees or would-be employees who feel they have been discriminated against in their employment, such as being denied promotion or even employment in the first place on the basis of the various areas of discrimination designated in the legislation, can lay a complaint against the employer. These areas vary with the jurisdiction, but usually include race, religion, ethnic origin, colour, and gender. Sexual preference has been implied into the provincial statutes by the Supreme Court of Canada even when not specifically included, but age discrimination is only prohibited in some jurisdictions. Human rights officials have great power to investigate, inspect, seize records, hold hearings, and impose very serious fines and other penalties. The employer can even be held responsible for not providing a harassment-free work environment. Thus, where an employee of colour is taunted by other employees, or where a female employee is offended by sexually explicit photos displayed on lockers or in the workroom, the employer can be held responsible.

In addition, there are a myriad of other regulations that target specific types of businesses. Professionals such as doctors, dentists, lawyers, and accountants must comply with the regulations of their professional organizations, and although these are not government regulators in the sense that they are actually arms of the government, professional bodies such as law societies and the various accounting organizations are established under provincial statute, which gives them their regulatory power. This is only a brief and incomplete summary of the regulatory regimes that must be met by most people doing business in Canada.

RESTRICTIONS ON REGULATORY POWER

Positive incentives normally cannot be challenged

It is important to emphasize at the outset that these government regulatory powers are not always applied directly. Often there are benefits that are available for voluntary compliance. Persuasion and positive reinforcement are often used, such as giving funding advantages as a way to encourage a business to adopt a particular course of action. The Canadian Medicare regulations are an example. The provinces have authority to deal with health care matters under the *Constitution Act (1867)*. The federal government has no specific power in this area, and yet it is federal legislation that governs. The reason is that the federal government simply provides funding that it is not required to supply. The threat of the withdrawal of that federal funding is usually enough to make the provinces comply with the federal statute. So it is with government incentives at the local level. When government regulators make decisions that must be complied with, there are limits and controls within which they must function. The following discussion is an overview of those controls often referred to as the principles of administrative law.

The government regulatory bodies to be dealt with here are of two types. The first hears disputes between competing parties, usually in response to a complaint. Labour relations boards, human rights boards, and professional bodies such as the Law Society are examples. The second kind of body is charged with enforcing a government department policy. Organizations charged with the regulation of environmental pollution, transportation of dangerous goods, broadcast and telephone transmissions, competition, or responsibility for the various tax and licensing regimes are examples. In both cases an individual or business that wishes to challenge the way a policy has been applied to them has certain rights, whether the decision was made by an individual official or by a committee or board. The term **administrative tribunal** is usually used when referring to such decision-making bodies, and applies whether the decision in question is made by a single official or by an appointed board.

Administrative tribunal may adjudicate between complainants . . .

or impose government regulations

RULE OF LAW Decision-makers are limited by the statutory authority that is the basis for that decision. This is an application of the *rule of law* discussed in Chapter 1. Simply put, no government official can impose a decision, restriction, or other control or obligation on a business or individual unless it is authorized by statute. There can be no decision made on the basis of policy, merits, or even fairness and justice that is not supported by legislation that authorizes the making of the decision.

All regulators are limited by statutory authority

CASE SUMMARY 10. 1

Laba v. Manitoba Dental Association[1]

Tribunals Must Have Statutory Authority for Decisions

Dr. Laba was a dentist whose licence to practise was suspended for four months after an inquiry alleging professional misconduct. After taking the remedial training required at the inquiry, the registrar still refused to reinstate him, requiring more testing and training. He challenged those additional requirements, and the court agreed, finding that the dental board and the inquiry decision had exceeded the statutory authority given. The board had not been given the authority to order remedial training in the *Dental Association Act.* No statutory body can do anything unless supported by statute or regulation. This is a basic application of the rule of law.

The first task then, when faced with an unfair or unreasonable decision by a government official or board, is to determine whether the decision-maker was authorized by valid legislation, including the statute itself and any regulations passed under that statute. These regulations must go no further than is authorized under the statute and must be approved by the cabinet (Governor General in Council). When properly passed, regulations have the same status as properly enacted statutes. Often statutes contain definition sections to clarify meaning. Separate interpretation statutes and general rules of statutory interpretation also assist in the interpretation process. For example, there is a general rule of statu-

Regulation must follow statute

Regulator may obtain power from statute or regulation

1. (1990), 70 D.L.R. (4th) 154 (Man. C.A.).

Definitions, interpretation statutes, and rules of interpretation clarify meaning

tory interpretation that any word or phase used should be given its ordinary grammatical meaning, unless it is clear from the rest of the statute that a different meaning was intended. In that case, the meaning consistent with the rest of the statute should be applied. In determining whether the decision was authorized by the legislation, the complainant must look to both the regulations and the statute relied on. If the decision falls within the authority given the official under the regulation or statute, then the validity of the statute itself must be tested.

Did statute or regulations authorize decision?

JURISDICTIONAL AUTHORITY First, the statute must comply with the division of powers under the *Constitution Act (1867)*. If it is federal legislation it must be authorized under one of the heads of power set out in section 91. If it is provincial it must comply with section 92 of the *Constitution Act (1867)*. Watch for **colourable legislation** here. Sometimes a level of government will enact statutes that look like one class of legislation, when upon closer examination their true nature is something completely different. For example, a town or municipality might try to control a bar that allows nude dancing or a video outlet that rents pornographic material by charging an exorbitant licence fee or by zoning it out of business. The true purpose of such a bylaw has nothing to do with zoning or licensing; rather, it is an attempt to restrict or prohibit activities the municipality considers immoral. Laws designed to curb immoral activity are characterized as criminal. The power to pass criminal law legislation is given to the federal government under section 91, hence, the bylaws would be *ultra vires* (beyond the power of) the body that passed them and of no effect.

Statute must be valid under *Constitution Act (1867)*

Must look at the true nature of statute

***CHARTER* RIGHTS** The second way that the statutory or regulatory provision relied on can be challenged is under the Canadian *Charter of Rights and Freedoms*. This even applies to the conduct of the government official involved. The *Charter* sets out rights when dealing with government and its agents at any level, and thus all statutes, regulations, and actions of anyone representing government must comply with the provisions of the *Charter*. If the conduct of the official—even if authorized by statute—is discriminatory, restricts freedom of expression or association, or prohibits the complainant from earning a living, that behaviour may be used as a basis to challenge the decision in court. Section 24 of the *Charter* gives the judge the power to impose any remedy that is just in the circumstances.

Is the action of the decision-maker consistent with the *Charter*?

If the statute itself has some provision, such as a reverse onus clause which is inconsistent with the *Charter*, then that provision can also be challenged. A **reverse onus** requires a person charged with an offence to prove that he or she didn't do it, rather than being presumed innocent as set out in section 11(d) of the *Charter*. But remember that section 1 of the *Charter* allows some of those *Charter* rights to be overridden if it is deemed to be a "reasonable limit" on those rights "demonstrably justified in a free and democratic society." Most of the cases coming before the courts today deal with whether this exception applies or not. A reverse onus clause in criminal matters clearly violates the *Charter* and cannot be justified under section 1. But the courts have shown a willingness to allow such reverse onus clauses where the prohibition involved is regulatory rather than criminal. Basically, this requires that the potential penalty is only a fine, not imprisonment, and that the objective of the legislation is to accomplish some regulatory purpose such as ensuring proper competition in the marketplace rather than controlling immoral behaviour. In these regulatory offences the burden can be shifted to the accused, who then must show he exercised due diligence to avoid the problem. This was established in a *Competition Act* case where the decision that the accused was required to show due diligence to avoid being found

Is the provision of the statute or regulation relied on consistent with the *Charter*?

If the statute or conduct infringes the *Charter*, is it justified under section 1?

guilty of misleading advertising was upheld by the Supreme Court of Canada.[2] In the future when regulatory offences containing reverse onus clauses come before the courts, they will have to look at each individual provision to determine whether it is an appropriate exception under section 1 of the *Charter*.

PRINCIPLES OF FUNDAMENTAL JUSTICE Section 7 of the *Charter* gives everyone the "right to life, liberty and security of the person and the right not to be deprived thereof except in accordance with the principles of fundamental justice." These **principles of fundamental justice** are essentially the same as due process, procedural fairness, and the rules of natural justice. As a result of this requirement, the principles of fundamental justice may override statutory provisions where government officials make decisions that interfere with individuals and businesses. But even in those situations not caught by section 7, there is a general obligation for the decision-maker to follow the fundamental rules of natural justice. As a result it is only in rare cases, where there is clear statutory direction otherwise, that a government official can get away with not following these basic and important procedural rules. See Table 10.1 for a checklist for validity of authority.

If a matter of life, liberty, or security of person is interfered with, the principles of fundamental justice must be applied

In most situations the decision-maker must follow the rules of natural justice

CASE SUMMARY 10.2

R. v. Mainstream Transportation Services Inc.[3]

Truck Driver Has Right to Presumption of Innocence

Mainstream was charged under the *Highway Traffic Act* when a wheel fell off a truck they were operating. When they were not permitted to use the defence of due diligence, they asked the court to review the decision on the grounds that it violated their right to procedural fairness as guaranteed under section 7 of the *Charter of Rights and Freedoms*. The court rejected that argument since the process didn't fall within the category of life, liberty, or the security of person. They did find for Mainstream, however, under section 11 of the *Charter*, which required them to be presumed innocent until proven guilty of the offence. The court determined that the large fines, moral taint, and other negative consequences of a conviction under the Act were so serious that it required that innocence be presumed. The statutory provision was not saved by section 1 of the *Charter* and so the conviction was overturned.

TABLE 10.1 Checklist for Validity of Authority

- Is the conduct of the decision-maker authorized by statute or regulations?
- Are the regulations consistent with and properly passed under the statute?
- Is the statute valid under the division of powers in the *Constitution Act (1867)*?
- Is the conduct of the decision-maker and are the provisions and regulations of the statute consistent with the *Charter of Rights and Freedoms*?

2. *R. v. Wholesale Travel Group Inc.* (1991), 84 D.L.R. (4th) 161, [1991] 3 S.C.R. 154 (S.C.C.).
3. Ont. S.C.J., 2001, as reported in *Lawyers Weekly Consolidated Digest*, Vol. 21.

RULES OF NATURAL JUSTICE

Even before we look at the requirements of procedural fairness, it should be noted that in all cases where boards and government officials are exercising statutory power, they must adhere to the procedures set out in the statute itself. Often a hearing is required. How it is to be constituted and what procedures have to be followed—before, during, and after—may be specified in the statute and any deviation can make the decision subject to challenge. Thus, if the statute required 30 days' notice to be given in writing of a hearing, anything less would not be sufficient. Even if the person being affected was told personally in an interview 40 days before the scheduled hearing, the lack of written notice would invalidate the hearing.

Decision-maker must comply with procedures specified in statute or regulations

Basic to the rules of natural justice is the requirement of a fair hearing. People affected by that decision have to be given an opportunity to speak to it before the decision is made. Implicit in the concept of a fair hearing is the requirement that the parties to be affected by the decision be given proper notice of the hearing. Such notice must not only indicate when and where the hearing is to take place, but must contain sufficient detail so that the respondent will have sufficient time and information to respond. To illustrate, in an Ontario case[4] a chief of police was asked to appear before the police commission to discuss the administration of the force. He was not informed that the board was considering his own competency, and as a result of the hearing his employment was terminated. He challenged the decision on the basis that the board's failure to let him know that his job was at risk was a failure to give proper notice, making the hearing unfair. The court agreed and, consequently, quashed the decision.

Natural justice requires notice of any hearing

Notice must include details of case to be answered and sufficient time to prepare

The hearing itself need not always be a gathering where the parties involved have an opportunity to present their evidence and make their arguments in person. Depending on the nature of the decision and the impact on the parties, it may be enough to allow the affected party simply to make a written submission. What constitutes procedural fairness is "flexible and variable and depends on an appreciation of the particular statute and the rights affected."[5] The operative word is *fairness*, and what is fair in any situation depends on the context and the application of a little common sense. Keep in mind this flexibility as we discuss what must be present for a hearing to be fair.

Fairness may not require an actual formal hearing

CASE SUMMARY 10.3

Hill v. University College of Cape Breton[6]

University President Entitled to Fair Hearing

The president of a university brought this application, asking the court to review a decision to terminate his position even though he was only partly through his six-year term. He had been told that some members of the executive committee were

(continued)

4. *Sinkovich v. Strathroy (Town) Commissioners of Police* (1998), 51 D.L.R. (4th) 750 (Ont. Div. Ct).
5. *Baker v. Canada (Minister of Citizenship & Immigration),* [1999] S.C.R. 817 (S.C.C.).
6. (1991), 81 D.L.R. (4th) 300 (N.S.T.D.).

not happy with his performance, but when notice of an inquiry was given, there was no indication of its purpose. Before the meeting several board members were sent letters asking them to comment on what they thought of his performance, and a subcommittee held a private meeting to obtain its opinions. At the inquiry the president was required to respond to these complaints immediately, and the names of those complaining were omitted. He was then prevented from attending the meeting of the full executive committee, which followed immediately afterwards, where they decided to terminate his employment. He brought this application before the Nova Scotia Supreme Court to have that decision overturned. The court agreed, and issued an order of *certiorari,* which quashed the decision of the board. They found that the board was a public body exercising statutory authority with a duty to treat the president fairly, and this they did not do. They failed to give adequate notice of the special meeting; the Act required five days' notice. They failed to state in the notice the purpose of the meeting as required. They acted unfairly in conducting private interviews and in not disclosing the full case to which Hill had to respond, and they did not give him a proper opportunity to make that response. He wasn't given a fair hearing, and he never was made fully aware of the case he had to answer to and the evidence against him. All of these things showed that the university board failed to act fairly towards him.

DECIDER MUST HEAR EVIDENCE Fundamental to a fair hearing is the principle that the decision must be made by the person who hears the evidence. It's not good enough for someone else to listen to the presentation of the evidence and then make recommendations to the actual decision-maker, or for the actual decision-maker to hear the matter and then ask others who have not heard the evidence to make a recommendation. Of course, the official is entitled to take legal advice, but if he is the one charged with making the decision, then he is the person who must hear the evidence and decide. If part way through a hearing it is necessary to change one of the committee members, the committee has to start all over or continue on, short the member who left. The new member cannot simply take the seat vacated by the member who left because that new member will not have been present to hear all of the evidence. Even if the new member doesn't participate in the actual decision, her sitting on the board gives the impression that she may have influenced the decision. This happened in the City of Langley, British Columbia where the municipal council was holding a hearing that was adjourned for local elections. When it resumed there were both original and newly elected council members participating in the decision making. The court quashed the decision on the basis that it was made by members who had not heard all of the evidence.[7]

Natural justice requires the decision to be made by the person hearing the evidence

In the same vein the board must actually give the party affected by the decision an opportunity to present his or her side. In *Re Ladney and Moore (Township),*[8] Ladney appeared before the Ontario Municipal Board proposing an amendment

Natural justice requires an opportunity to state your side

7. *Bailey v. Langley (Township) Local Board of Health* (1982), 32 B.C.L.R. 298 (B.C.S.C.).

8. (1984), 10 D.L.R. (4th) 612 (Ont. Div. Ct.).

to the official plan of the Township of Moore. The board heard from one expert witness and then adjourned, making their decision without hearing evidence from Ladney or submissions from his lawyers. Because one side was not given the opportunity to be heard, and the decision was made without having all of the evidence presented, the decision was quashed. Also, the tribunal must base their decision only on the evidence presented at the hearing. If the decision-maker hears certain evidence at the hearing and then upon deliberation also looks at other matters—such as past complaints with respect to other departments or previous applications made to the board—without giving the parties affected an opportunity to speak to these matters, the decision can be challenged. The parties must be given the opportunity to present their side and to refute all of the evidence against them.

Only the evidence at the hearing can be considered in making the decision

WITHOUT BIAS There are several other ways that a hearing can be tainted. Sometimes the decision-maker may be biased or appear to be biased. Impartiality is essential to fairness in such hearings, and if it can be shown that one or all of the decision-makers was biased, that will invalidate the decision. Since it is very difficult to determine the presence of actual bias in a decision-making process, the principles of natural justice only require that there be a reasonable apprehension of bias to invalidate the decision. If it looks bad, that's enough. Any conflict of interest on the part of the decision-maker, such as having a monetary interest in the outcome, a family member or friend involved, or a past history of hostility towards the person being affected by the decision, will be enough to establish a reasonable apprehension of bias. In *Bennett v. British Columbia (Superintendent of Brokers)*[9] the former premier of British Columbia was charged with insider trading along with Herb Doman, the president of a large forest company operating in the province. One of the board members who would be making the decision in the matter was a director of another forest company. This was enough to create a reasonable apprehension of bias and he was required to step down. The idea was that if Doman were convicted, he would no longer be allowed to manage his company, and this would benefit the other forest companies, thus creating the conflict of interest. There was no suggestion that any decision would actually be biased, only that there was the appearance and that was enough. In some cases bias is intentionally built into such boards by statute. For example, labour relations panels typically have one representative from labour and one from management with a third mutually chosen member as the chairman. The idea is that the bias on both sides will create balance and lead to a just decision.

Natural justice requires the decision-maker to be free of even the appearance of bias

Conflict of interest is an established reasonable apprehension of bias

Bias, when balanced, is sometimes allowed

CASE SUMMARY 10.4

Haight-Smith v. Kamloops School District No. 34[10]

Reasonable Apprehension of Bias Leads to Overturned Decision

A teacher was temporarily suspended for striking a student; a hearing followed. At that hearing the superintendent, who had investigated the original complaint and

(continued)

9. (1993), 109 D.L.R. (4th) 717 (B.C.C.A.).

10. (1998), 51 D.L.R. (4th) 608 (B.C.C.A.).

made the determination to suspend the teacher, made a revised submission and recommended continuation of the suspension. The teacher and her counsel attended that hearing, responded to the complaints, and denied the allegations. The board and superintendent then held a private meeting, deciding that the suspension should stand. That decision was challenged and the court found an appearance of bias since the superintendent was, in effect, both accuser and prosecutor. Although the superintendent claimed to have made no submissions during the *incamera* meeting, his presence gave rise to a reasonable apprehension of bias, causing a denial of natural justice and the board's decision was quashed.

ACTING BEYOND AUTHORITY Another problem may arise when decision-makers act beyond the powers given to them. It is one thing for the matter to fall within the authority of the official or board, as discussed above, but the board must also properly exercise the powers they have been given. If a statute requires that a board make the decision, a decision of a subcommittee of the board will not be good enough. Another example would be where the decision-maker imposes a decision beyond his or her power, as where an arbitrator in a wrongful dismissal action orders reinstatement or a five-day suspension when he or she was only authorized to decide whether the termination was justified or not. Even the decision to hear the matter in the first place might create a jurisdictional error. A labour arbitrator might be authorized to hear a payment dispute between a unionized employee and the employer but step outside his or her authority when hearing a similar dispute between that employer and an independent contractor.

Decision-makers must act within their powers

RIGHT TO REPRESENTATION Whether the parties to such a hearing have the right to be represented by a lawyer or to cross-examine the witnesses will depend on the circumstances of the case. You only have the right to be represented by a lawyer where criminal charges might flow from the decision, or where it has been authorized by statute or permitted by the tribunal itself. Only in a few situations will criminal consequences be likely or a statute will authorize such representation. You normally can't be sure that you can bring a lawyer to the hearings and should inquire ahead of time. The right to cross-examine will only be present if that is the only way to determine the facts. If one student accused another of copying from her exam, the accused student would likely have the right to challenge his accuser. But if the allegation was one of plagiarism on an essay, this could likely be independently verified by examining the paper; it would not be necessary to cross-examine or even reveal the identity of the accuser.

No automatic right to be represented by a lawyer

Right to cross-examine only if necessary to ensure fairness

RULES OF EVIDENCE NOT NECESSARY There is no general obligation that a board must follow the strict rules of evidence at a hearing or that written reasons be provided for the decision, although this might be required by the particular statute or regulation involved. Only some statutes impose an obligation on the decision-maker to give reasons for the decision reached, but if such a record is produced, the courts will also overturn that decision where a substantial error of law has been made on that record. The record involves the written decision itself, any reasons given, plus all supporting documentation. The courts are exercising a supervisory role when they review these decisions and they won't tolerate a decision that is based on an incorrect interpretation or application of the law as determined by the court.

No obligation to follow rules of evidence

The courts will review errors of law on the face of the record

TABLE 10.2 Checklist for Procedural Fairness

- Did decision-maker follow statutory procedure and act within his or her powers?
- Was notice of hearing given with sufficient detail and time?
- Was there a sufficient opportunity to be heard and state your side?
- Was the opportunity to be represented provided?
- Was there an opportunity to cross-examine?
- Was there an appearance of bias on the part of the decision-maker?
- Was the decision made only on the evidence presented as heard by the decision-maker?
- Did the decision involve an error of law?

Note that this obligation to follow the standards of procedural fairness applies not only to criminal and regulatory prosecutions and to the activities of government and government agencies but also to social and professional organizations. Social clubs, professional organizations, and even religious bodies have been required to follow these rules of procedural fairness when disciplining their members. Even employers owe a duty of good faith to their employees and, according to procedural fairjness, must give the employee an opportunity to be heard before they can be terminated. See Table 10.2 for a checklist for procedural fairness.

Procedural fairness is required in situations where a duty of good faith is owed

Judicial Review

Where the tribunal has made an error of law, acted beyond its jurisdiction, or failed to meet the requirements of procedural fairness, the decision of that tribunal can be challenged. Historically, there has been considerable conflict between these administrative tribunals and the courts, which jealously guarded their exclusive right to adjudicate disputes. In more recent times, with the expansion of government and the pressure on the court system, there is more acceptance of the advantages and the positive role played by these tribunals and boards. Today, it is only with reluctance that the decisions of such boards will be interfered with by the courts. The Supreme Court of Canada has declared that, "So long as the administrative decision-maker has acted within the authority granted and any discretion has been exercised in a fair and honest way so that the decision can be said to be reasonable, the decision should stand."[11] And so it can be seen that the courts will not interfere lightly with the decision of such government officials. Only if the decision is unauthorized or can be characterized as patently unreasonable will the courts review the decisions of a properly constituted administrative tribunal.

Courts now reluctant to overturn administrative tribunals' decisions

Courts will review where decision is patently unreasonably or unauthorized

This process is not an appeal; rather, it is referred to as judicial review and any avenue of normal appeal provided for in legislation must be exhausted before judicial review can be sought. Judicial review involves the court exercising its supervisory jurisdiction over all adjudicatory bodies to ensure that they function properly. The process involves the use of ancient prerogative writs, a holdover from the writ system, which dominated the early development of the common law. This is now supplemented by statute (*Judicial Review Procedure Act*),

Judicial review is not an appeal

11. *Canada (Director of Investigation & Research) v. Southam Inc.*, [1997] 1 S.C.R. 748 (S.C.C.).

but an understanding of these prerogative writs is helpful. These are orders by the court to correct problems that have developed with respect to the administration of justice. Most people are aware of the writ of *habeas corpus,* which ensures that a person is not imprisoned against his or her will. This writ requires the warden or keeper of the prisoner to appear before the court and show cause why the prisoner should not be released.

***Judicial Review Procedure Act* replaces prerogative writs**

PREROGATIVE WRITS

For our purposes the important writs involved are the writs of prohibition, *certiorari,* and *mandamus.* A **writ of prohibition** involves an order by the court to a decision-maker not to proceed with the hearing. For example, when someone receives notice of a hearing, or learns of it some other way and believes that the board or official involved is stepping beyond his or her statutory authority, that person could bring an application for an order of **prohibition** to the court. If the court agreed, it would issue the order prohibiting the hearing from taking place. An ***order of certiorari*** is similar but takes effect after the decision has been reached. Here, a party who believes the decision was made without authority or violated the rules of procedural fairness could bring an application to the court for an order of *certiorari* to have the decision quashed. If the court agreed, the order would be made and the decision of the board or official would then have no legal effect. An ***order of mandamus*** is quit different. Sometimes a board or official will delay making a decision to obtain some other objective such as putting pressure on the parties, or simply because they haven't gotten around to it yet. Often such delay can cause serious problems for the parties involved, and so they can apply to the court for an order of *mandamus* to force the decision-maker to decide. Such an order will only be given where the official or board has a duty under the statute to render a decision, but not where there is a discretion to decide. The court normally will not order that a particular decision be made unless it is the only one possible. But usually once a decision has been made, favourable or not, there are then other avenues of recourse the parties can pursue.

Prohibition stops decision from being made

***Certiorari* overturns decision**

***Mandamus* forces decision to be made**

CASE SUMMARY 10.5

Re District of North Vancouver et al. and National Harbours Board et al.[12]

National Harbours Board Subject to *Mandamus*

A number of houseboats were moored without permission in the North Vancouver waterfront, but when complaints were made to the National Harbours Board, nothing was done. An application was made to the Federal Court for an order of *mandamus* requiring the board to clear the unwanted obstructions from the harbour as required under the *National Harbours Board Act.* The court found that it had the authority and the duty to do this under the statute and that it failed in that duty. Consequently, the court issued the order. The National Harbours Board had some discretion in the way it performed its duties, but it could not escape that duty altogether. This case shows that *mandamus* can be a very effective remedy in the right circumstances.

12. (1978), 89 D.L.R. (3d) 704 (F.C.T.D.).

TABLE 10.3 List of Available Remedies

- Court may order prohibition. Decision-maker will be ordered not to proceed.
- Court may order *certiorari.* Decision will be overturned.
- Court may order *mandamus.* Decision-maker will be ordered to decide.
- Court may declare the law. Court will state the correct law applicable.
- Court may issue injunction. Court will order offending conduct to stop.
- Court may award damages. Court will award monetary compensation.
- Court may make another order under section 24 of the *Charter,* where appropriate.

Court may declare the law, issue injunctions, and award damages

Other remedies are also available to the court in these situations. Sometimes the court will simply make a **declaratory judgment**, declaring the correct interpretation of the law as it applies to the matters being considered in the hearing. This, combined with other remedies such as an injunction or damages, can provide an effective remedy. Injunctions are often effective to prevent actions being taken that flow from such inappropriate decisions. And when actual injury or loss has taken place, damages are the appropriate remedy. For example, where a city manager ordered a non-conforming fence to be removed, an order of *certiorari* to quash the decision would be effective if the fence had not yet been removed. Once removed, however, only damages would compensate the injured party for the loss of that fence. Remember that if the applicant's *Charter* rights have been infringed in the process, section 24(1) of the *Charter* allows the judge to provide any remedy that he or she considers "appropriate and just in the circumstances."

***Judicial Review Procedure Act* provides a simplified procedure**

The effect of the *Judicial Review Procedure Act,*[13] or its equivalent which is in place in most jurisdictions, is to greatly simplify the complicated procedure involved when these prerogative writs are applied for. The Act provides that any application for one of these writs or remedies will be taken to be an application for judicial review under the Act, and as such must proceed by way of petition, a common process. It also allows the court to treat an application for any one remedy as a request for judicial review and to grant relief in the form of any of them (prohibition, *certiorari, mandamus,* a declaratory judgment, or an injunction.)

Local remedies must be exhausted before judicial review application

Most statutes that give boards and officials the power to make these decisions also provide a process to appeal the decision. It must be emphasized that before this process of judicial review can be taken, all local remedies must be exhausted. This means that if a method is provided to deal with the complaint under the statute, no court will grant a request for judicial review until that process has been completed as far as it can go. See Table 10.3 for a list of available remedies, and Table 10.4 for a checklist for action.

PRIVITIVE CLAUSES

The statutes that establish these boards and give officials power to make decisions also often incorporate a **privitive clause** designed to insulate that decision from review by the court. Such a clause will typically state that no order of the official is reviewable in any court of law and that no order of prohibition, *certiorari, mandamus,* declaratory judgment, or injunction can be applied to the decision or the process used to reach it. The idea is to make it very clear that the decision of the

13. R.S.O. 1990, c. J.1.

TABLE 10.4 Checklist for Action

Ask the following questions to determine if a complaint should be made:

- Is the decision authorized by properly enacted statutes and regulations?
- Has the decision-maker acted within his power?
- Have the statutory procedures been followed?
- Have the rules of natural justice or procedural fairness been complied with?
- Is there any benefit in seeking a court to review the decision?
- What is the appropriate remedy to ask for?

administrative tribunal, not the court, is to prevail. But such clauses should not be taken at face value. Over the years the courts have shown great reluctance to follow such provisions, avoiding application where possible through careful interpretation. Certainly the courts will ignore such privitive clauses when the challenge relates to its constitutionality or the authority of the official to make the decision. And in other situations the court may well find ways to avoid the privitive clause through careful examination of the language used. But remember that the courts usually respect the decisions, especially of specialized boards, and only review them where there is a clear and pressing reason to do so.

Courts will carefully interpret privitive clause

CHALLENGES ARE COSTLY

Finally, it must be emphasized that this discussion of rights should not be taken as encouragement to enforce them. In most cases the costs of seeking these remedies are exorbitant, requiring the employment of specialists at prodigious rates. The government bodies involved usually have deep pockets (lots of money) and find it worth the cost of fighting the action to the highest level to avoid the embarrassment of being found wrong. Even with a successful challenge, the results may be unsatisfying. Where a board has made an error and an order to set aside the decision is obtained, it will usually only cause the board to go back and hold another hearing, this time being careful to make no mistakes and then come to the same decision. The aim is to provide the reader with information that will be useful in negotiating other options when dealing with these officials and boards. Officials are often quite prepared to consider alternatives, especially when they know they have made a mistake. Thus, a little knowledge can be powerful and encourage discussion. Often other avenues will open up such as further negotiation, mediation, or arbitration of the dispute.

Make sure it is worth it before challenging a decision

The Regulation of Canadian Business

As examples of the regulatory environment, we will take a closer look at two areas where the activities of business are strongly influenced by government regulation. These deal with the regulation of the environment under various statutes and with unacceptable business practices under the federal *Competition Act*.

REGULATION OF THE ENVIRONMENT

Environmental protection has become an increasingly important concern of the public and governments at all levels. There has always been the recognition of an individual's right to protect his or her immediate environment from pollution and degradation by others under the common law. The large-scale expansion of mining, forestry, coal, oil, hydro-electric, and nuclear generating plants as well as other large undertakings, has put an increasing strain on the environment. There has been a general recognition of the deterioration of the environment and the need for greater controls, not only to prevent further damage, but also to correct the damage that has already occurred. Statutory intervention at the federal, provincial, territorial, and municipal levels has become an important consideration in doing business, especially when a new venture is undertaken.

Increasing environmental regulation has become important concern of business

THE COMMON LAW The main area where common law provides protection is with riparian rights, which give people living on a river or stream (except for normal domestic depletion) the right to have the water continue to flow to them with undiminished quantity or quality. This basic right continues but is often overridden by a government's statutory power when it issues water-use permits to industries and municipalities. Thus, if the government grants a permit to a pulp mill to dump pollutants into a river, the downstream users can't complain, as their riparian rights have been overridden by the exercise of a statutory power.

Riparian rights are the right to continued quality and quantity of water flow

Riparian rights are often overridden by statute

The tort of private nuisance can be used to seek a remedy when a neighbour interferes with a person's enjoyment of his or her property, through the escape of water, noise, smoke, odours, etc. The injured party can bring an action seeking damages or an injunction. Even negligence or the principle of strict liability as discussed in Chapter 2 can be relied on when dangerous things escape from one property, causing damage or injury to those on a neighboring property. In rare circumstances, where there is actual physical interference with a property, the law of trespass can be used to obtain a remedy. But all of these common law provisions have one thing in common. They require an individual to go to the expense and take the time to sue. The polluting activity is treated as a private matter between the person injured and the offender. Someone who is not directly injured has no right to bring an action. There is no community right to action, and except in the most serious of cases, most individuals won't go to the trouble or expense to sue. These factors make the common law an ineffective tool to control pollution or protect the environment in any comprehensive way.

Nuisance can be used to stop pollution

Common law is not efficient in protecting the environment

CASE SUMMARY 10.6

Scarborough Golf & Country Club v. Scarborough (City)[14]

Golf Course Has Riparian Rights

As the City of Scarborourgh expanded, more and more rain runoff was diverted into a particular stream, eventually causing considerable damage to a golf course. The golf course sued the city, claiming nuisance and a violation of their riparian rights (the right to have water continue to flow in undiminished quantity and quality). The city had the right to natural drainage through the stream, but they had diverted water into it, causing the damage. The court determined that this infringed the riparian rights of the golf course and the city had to pay compensation. The court also based the award of damages on private nuisance.

14. (1988), 54 D.L.R. (4th) 1 (Ont. C.A.).

FEDERAL LEGISLATION

This is an area where both the federal (including territorial) and provincial governments have the power to pass legislation. A business may find itself dealing with provincial or federal regulatory bodies, and sometimes both, depending on the nature of their business. The federal jurisdiction applies to all areas where a business is involved in a matter given specifically to the federal government under the *Constitution Act (1867)*. This includes such areas as navigable waters, fish-bearing waterways, inter-provincial or international undertakings, railways, ferry services, banks, broadcasting, and air transportation. Note that almost every stream and river is fish-bearing, giving the federal government power to regulate in almost all areas involving natural resources, or where there is some discharge of polluting material in a water course. Beyond this, the federal regulations can also apply to all businesses providing services to the federal government, federal agencies, or federally supported activities, including all projects that receive federal funding. This creates considerable overlap and businesses often find themselves dealing with federal, provincial, territorial, and even municipal environmental regulations, especially on larger projects.

Environmental regulation comes from all levels of government

Federal environmental regulation may apply even to local projects

CASE SUMMARY 10.7

Friends of the Old Man River Society v. Canada (Minister of Transport)[15]

Provincial Project Subject to Federal Regulations

Alberta was involved in a project to dam the Old Man River but had to get a permit from the federal Minister of Transportation to do so. The federal *Fisheries Act* and the *Navigable Waters Act* gave the federal government jurisdiction, even though this was a provincial project. The minister was required to follow certain guidelines in granting that permit, including holding a public hearing and doing an environmental impact assessment. When a group opposing the project discovered that had not been done, they brought this application to have the project stopped. The court found that the permit had been improperly obtained and ordered the approval overturned. The case went to the Supreme Court of Canada, which upheld this decision. The case not only shows how important and far reaching the decisions of the federal environment ministry can be, but how the regulations must be carefully complied with, and how even provincial projects can be subject to these federal regulations.

CANADIAN ENVIRONMENTAL PROTECTION ACT The main federal statute in this area is the *Canadian Environmental Protection Act*.[16] This legislation provides for the establishment of a government department charged with preventing pollution and protecting the environment and human health while contributing to sustainable development. In brief, the Act provides for research—the gathering, compilation, storage, evaluation, and publication of information and data; the setting

15. (1992), 88 D.L.R. (4th) 1 (S.C.C.).

16. S.C. 1999, c. 33.

Statute authorizes government department

of standards, guidelines, and codes of conduct; monitoring and inspection; the identification of prohibited and controlled activities; and the enforcement, remediation, and imposition of penalties when offences and violations take place.

Cooperation is encouraged

An advisory committee encourages cooperation between provinces and aboriginal groups. The Act allows for equivalent provincial legislation to replace the federal system where such an agreement has been negotiated.

Controls imposed and whistle blowers protected

Under the Act, where environmentally sensitive activities are involved, an individual or business can be required to develop and implement pollution prevention plans. Lists of toxic substances are specified, and their importation, export, and use in Canada are prohibited or controlled. Individuals are required to report the escape of such materials, and employees who do so (whistle blowers) are protected from reprisals.[17]

Businesses can be required to provide information

There are restrictions on the disposal of waste at sea without special permits and on the use of unregulated fuels in Canada. The authority to establish vehicle emission standards and restrictions on the movement of hazardous waste and recycling materials is granted under the Act. Where the activity involves a federal work or undertaking, or takes place on aboriginal land, more extensive control is imposed. Those involved in activities on these lands can be required to supply detailed information to the government about that activity. This can amount to a very onerous requirement.

Enforcement officers given significant powers of inspection and enforcement

Enforcement officers have significant power under the Act. They can enter and inspect premises, stop and inspect conveyances to take samples, detain vehicles and material to make tests, and examine records and computers. They can issue environmental compliance orders, which may involve, among other things, the requirement that a person refrain from or stop doing something in contravention of the Act. Finally, they can charge individuals with offences where violations do occur. Note that these orders can be appealed to review officers and then to the Federal Court, if necessary.

Spills must be reported and remedied

If a company fails to act, costs can be imposed on the violator

Significant penalties are imposed on company and its directors

In most cases due diligence is available as a defence

When an unauthorized release of toxic substances or pollution does take place, there is an obligation on the property owner or business person to take immediate steps to remedy the situation, to report the release to the appropriate agency, and to warn the public of any danger. Where they fail to act, the enforcement officer can take the necessary action to remedy the situation and charge the costs back to the violator. The penalties for offences committed under the Act are substantial, providing for up to three years in jail and up to $1 million in fines where they are treated as an indictable offence. This can be raised to five years where the perpetrator causes an environmental disaster or shows reckless disregard for the lives of others. Judges can also make other orders that they deem appropriate in the circumstances. Directors, managers, and agents can be held directly responsible where the offences are committed by a corporation. In most cases, if the individuals can show due diligence, they will have a defence. Due diligence requires the officer to show that they have set up systems to ensure that the Act will be followed, including training employees and establishing policies to ensure compliance.

---

17. *Canadian Environmental Protection Act,* S.C. 1999, c. 33, s.16(4).

CASE SUMMARY 10.8

R. v. MacMillan Bloedel Ltd.[18]

The Nature of the Due Diligence Defence

The defendant's underground pipeline leaked into a watercourse, and the company was charged under the federal *Fisheries Act.* The company and a government inspector had recently inspected the pipeline and found no indication of trouble. It was discovered that the leak was caused by microbiological corrosion, something no one could have anticipated. At trial the company's due diligence defence was rejected, but the case went all the way to the Supreme Court of Canada, which accepted its right to claim that due diligence had been exercised. The company could not be held responsible for something it could not reasonably have foreseen. It also could not be held liable when it had taken all reasonable steps to prevent any hazard that they could foresee. This illustrates the two ways that due diligence may be established.

Some offences can be designated as ticket offences, where the officer gives a ticket for a violation and the offender can simply plead guilty and pay a designated fine. For some lesser offences it is also possible to negotiate alternate measures where agreements are negotiated to help the business or industry comply with the regulations. If the agreement to stop the infraction or repair the damage is honoured, the charges will be dismissed. If the accused shows a "wanton or reckless disregard for the lives or safety of other persons and thereby causes death or bodily harm to another person," they can be prosecuted for criminal negligence under the *Criminal Code.* Recent amendments to the *Criminal Code* make it easier to prosecute organizations such as corporations and individuals for environmental offences.

Act provides ticket offences and alternate measures

Charges of criminal negligence can also be laid

The *Canadian Environmental Protection Act* also provides for civil remedies. Where someone is injured, or their property threatened or damaged by the prohibited activity, that person can bring an action for an injunction to stop the activity and for damages to compensate for any injury suffered. The Act also provides a very limited right, where a complaint is made and the government fails to take action, for the complainant to bring an environmental protection action on his or her own.

Limited civil remedies are provided

This brief summary of the Act just touches the surface, and we haven't looked at the great volume of regulations authorized under the Act to accomplish its objectives.

CANADIAN ENVIRONMENTAL ASSESSMENT ACT Another important federal act is the *Canadian Environmental Assessment Act.*[19] This Act requires all projects that the federal government has control over from granting permits, licences, and funding, etc. to go though an environmental assessment process. This assessment process can take several different forms, depending on the potential risks involved and the size of the project. Relatively small projects usually just go

18. (2002), 220 D.L.R. (4th) 173 (B.C.C.A.).

19. S.C. 1992, c. 37.

Screening process involves simplified environmental assessment process

through a **screening process** where a company provides documentation to a designated government official who reviews it and submits a screening report. On the basis of this and any other information available, a determination is made whether adequate steps have been taken to ensure the environmental impact has been minimized. If the responsible authority is satisfied, the project can go ahead. More complicated projects go through a **comprehensive environmental assessment process**; these require more extensive documentation, research, public input, and reporting. In both cases, if the responsible authority or minister is not satisfied, modifications can be recommended, and if necessary, mediation or a review panel can be ordered. The review panel conducts public hearings and submits a report containing recommendations to the minister. This environmental assessment process can be costly, time-consuming, and one of the most serious obstacles for a business trying to embark on an environmentally sensitive activity.

Comprehensive assessment involves a more involved process, including public input

Public hearings can be ordered

There are also a number of other federal statutes that impact the environment. Examples include the *Fisheries Act,* [20] as discussed above in the *Friends of the Old Man River Society* case and the *MacMillan Bloedel* case, the *Hazardous Products Act,*[21] the *Canada Shipping Act, 2001,*[22] and the *Transportation of Dangerous Goods Act, 1992.*[23]

PROVINCIAL LEGISLATION

All provinces have legislation similar to *Canadian Environmental Protection Act*

While the legislation in place varies considerably from province to province and the territories, all have acts similar to the *Canadian Environmental Protection Act* designed to create general standards and monitoring and enforcement mechanism to deal with environmental concerns in the areas of provincial jurisdiction. With the federal statutes as the examples, no attempt will be made here to do any kind of comprehensive review, but a few points should be noted. These statutes regulate the transport and disposal of waste, the use and transportation of hazardous materials, the cleanup of contaminated sites, the treatment of sewage, motor vehicle emission discharges, and the disposal of byproducts from manufacturing mining and other activities. The statutes also control what happens at specific locations by limiting industrial, commercial, and residential uses. Most provinces, like the federal government, have an environmental review process that must be complied with before environmentally sensitive projects can go forward.

Provinces also require environmental assessment process

Government departments have been created to implement these policies. They establish codes of conduct and regulations that must be adhered to. To keep degradation of the environment to a minimum, government departments grant permits with restrictions and requirements, and supervise the discharging and storing of waste. There is an enforcement arm that is charged with enforcing those standards through inspection, investigation, the holding of hearings, and the levying of fines and other penalties. In fact, most of the litigation involving environmental matters takes place at the provincial level and involves provincial legislation. Often alternative remedies are provided that allow for negotiation, mediation, and agreements that facilitate working with the business to help them obtain compliance.

Provincial departments enforce environmental protection provisions

20. R.S.C. 1985, c. F-4.
21. R.S.C. 1985, c. H-3.
22. S.C. 2001, c. 26.
23. S.C. 1992, c. 45.

CASE SUMMARY 10.9

R. v. Consolidated Maybrun Mines Ltd.[24]

The Danger of Ignoring Regulations

After considerable negotiation the company was ordered by an Ontario Ministry of the Environment official to clean their abandoned mine. It ignored the order and the ministry did the clean up and charged the company and its "directing mind" with failing to uphold the order. The company had had several opportunities to make submissions and to appeal the decision, which they failed to take advantage of. After their conviction at trial, they appealed, claiming the original order was unreasonable, but the appeal court wasn't interested. The company had a chance to challenge the order, and the failure to respond was its own fault. The appeal court was only interested in whether there had been a failure to uphold the order, not the reasonableness of the order itself. Business people may well be frustrated with such interference, but this case shows how dangerous it is to ignore government officials and their directions, especially when it comes to environmental concerns.

There is a tendency to increase penalties, and in Ontario, for instance, the maximum fine that can be imposed for violation of its *Environmental Protection Act* has been increased to $6 million per day for every day the offence continues. For a second conviction the penalty may be imprisonment up to five years less a day.[25]

Provincial penalties can be very severe

All jurisdictions have removed the protection offered by the incorporation process, so that both managers and directors of the corporations can be held personally responsible for violations. The reverse is also true, so that the corporation can be held liable for the actions of their employees and agents under the principle of vicarious liability. Like the federal provisions, most provincial offences are strict liability offences, meaning that the individual or the corporation charged can defend by showing that due diligence was exercised to avoid the offence from happening and ensuring that the Act was complied with. This usually requires evidence that reasonable steps were taken to comply with the Act. The corporation can show due diligence if the directing mind (the appropriate manager or director) developed and implemented a reasonable policy to comply with the Act, and that employees were properly trained to implement that policy. An effective follow-up and monitoring system would also have to be in place. Very few offences are absolute liability offences where, once the violation has been established, the parties are liable no matter how careful they are. These are sometimes referred to as **absolute liability offences** where administrative penalties and any fines imposed are usually considerably less.

Managers can be held liable for corporation's wrongdoing

Due diligence normally available as a defence

Due diligence not available where absolute liability offences involved

One of the major problems involved is to determine who is responsible for the cleanup of a contaminated site. Usually those that cause the pollution are held responsible for the damage suffered, but sometimes that cost can be imposed on others. For example, in some jurisdictions the obligation to clean up pollution will fall on the owner of the property, even though it may have gone

24. (1998), 158 D.L.R. (4th) 193 (S.C.C.).

25. *Environmental Protection Act*, R.S.O. 1990, c. E.19, s. 187(8)(a).

Owner may be liable to pay, even though they didn't cause the pollution

through several different owners since the contamination took place, and the new owner may not even be aware of the problem. This can also affect the position of a creditor who has taken a claim against the property as security. The costs can sometimes be exorbitant and great care should be taken, including arranging for an environmental audit and insurance, before purchasing or obtaining interest in a property that may be contaminated in this way.

Municipalities also have power to impose controls on business

It is important to understand that even municipalities have extensive powers to deal with the environment. A business will often have to comply with municipal bylaws with respect to where a business is to locate. Nuisance, noise, odours, vibration, illumination and dust emanating from the business, the discharge of sewage, and what can be discharged into the municipal drain system are also municipal concerns. This illustrates the major problem of overlap and duplication of environmental regulation at the various levels of government, especially where the granting of permits is concerned. For example, a permit under the provincial regulations may be granted for a pollution-causing activity, and yet it may still be in violation of federal statutes and punishable. Several provinces have taken steps to reform their environmental regulatory regime to make them more business friendly and eliminate red tape. For example, Nova Scotia has amalgamated several enactments into one statute. But the problem of complying with these various regulatory requirements at all levels of government remains and presents a serious problem for business.

Overlap of regulation poses a serious problem for business

Important amendments to the *Criminal Code* have made it much easier to convict corporations and other organizations of environmental offences. These provisions were inspired by the Westray mine disaster. As explained in Chapter 7, in the past a company could only be convicted of a criminal offence where it could be shown that the person committing the crime was the directing or controlling mind of the corporation. This was not normally the case, especially where large corporations were involved. But now, under section 22.1 of the *Criminal Code,* an organization such as a corporation can be more easily convicted of a criminal offence. It requires that negligence committed by representatives such as directors, partners, employees, members, agents, and contractors who are acting within their authority be demonstrated. A responsible senior official can be convicted where it can be shown that he or she departed "markedly from the standard of care that, in the circumstances, could reasonably be expected"[26] to prevent the representative from committing the offence. Another important change provides that the corporation itself can be held liable for the intentional acts of representatives that are committed by a senior officer, under the direction of a senior officer, or where a senior officer knowing that an offence is about to be committed by such a representative fails to take all reasonable steps to stop it. This makes corporations much more exposed to prosecution for criminal negligence and other existing criminal offences.

Another amendment inspired by the Westray mine disaster (section 217.1) imposes a legal duty on anyone having the authority to direct workers, or anyone doing a particular task, to take reasonable steps to avoid bodily harm to that person or others arising from that work. This, combined with offence sections (220 and 221), makes someone who fails in such a duty liable to conviction for criminal negligence. Where there is bodily harm, the potential penalty is up to 10 years' imprisonment; where a death results, the penalty is up to life imprison-

26. *Criminal Code,* R.S.C. 1985, c. C-46. s. 22.1(6).

ment. When environmental offences are committed that qualify under these sections, both individuals and the organization risk prosecution.

The Federal *Competition Act*

A free market system is considered vital to our economy. Businesses compete with each other, and this forces each to find the most cost-effective way of doing business so that they can charge lower prices and sell more than a competitor. This benefits us all, as competition leads to the most efficient production of goods and services provided at the lowest prices. But the underlying driving factor in a business is to make as much money as possible, which creates an incentive not only to reduce costs but to keep prices high. This results in pressure on the businesses to interfere with that free market system if they can, reducing competition so they can extract higher prices from customers. The federal *Competition Act* is designed to counter this pressure and to eliminate any such market manipulation. The stated purpose of the Act "is to maintain and encourage competition in Canada."[27] This anti–free market conduct can range from secret arrangements between businesses to aggressive tactics to hurt competitors, to directly misleading customers. Some of the offences under the Act are prosecuted using a criminal model, while others adopt a non-criminal or administrative approach to enforcement. Note that there is considerable overlap so that several types of prohibited conduct can be treated either way at the option of the competition commissioner. These offences have been categorized as follows.

Competition is vital, but businesses try to reduce competition

Object of the Act is to preserve competitive environment

OFFENCES AGAINST COMPETITION

Conspiracies that unduly lessen competition are prohibited. Note that not all such agreements are prohibited, only those that have the effect of unduly lessening competition. That qualification applies to most of the controls discussed here and should be kept in mind in the following discussion. A conspiracy involves businesses getting together, and through agreement, trying to control the market and prices. The basic principle here is that any agreement or arrangement between businesses that has the effect of unduly restricting competition constitutes an offence. Where merchants agree together not to sell a product below a certain price, or agree not to open a store or compete in a given area, their conduct is prohibited if it unduly restricts competition. Where these agreements restrict production, transport, storage, supply, or increase the price of insurance with the object of increasing the price, the businesses have committed an indictable offence. There are also similar provisions with respect to professional sports with important exceptions. Any attempt at bid rigging is also an indictable offence. This involves competitors conspiring together to control the bids on a particular project so that they can control the winning bid and charge a higher price. Even directors, officers, and other employees of banks and other federal financial institutions are sometimes caught; any agreement to fix rates of interest and prices charged for services also constitutes an indictable offence punishable with fines up to $10 million and up to five years' imprisonment. See Table 10.5 on p. 296 for a summary of offences against competition.

Competition offences include:

- Agreements to restrict production, transport, storage, or supply

- Agreements to increase price of insurance

- Bid rigging

- Banks and financial institutions agreeing to set prices for service charges and interest rates

27. *Competition Act*, R.S.C. 1985, c. C-34.

CASE SUMMARY 10.10

R. v. Lorne Wilson Transportation Ltd. and Travelways School Transit Ltd.[28]

The Offence of Bid Rigging

In this case several companies bidding on providing school bus services got together to control the price. Such bid rigging was prohibited under the *Combines Investigations Act* and charges were laid. The accused argued that no offence is committed when the other party knows of the cooperation between the bidders, but this was rejected since the fact that identical bids were submitted was not notice to the school board. It was evidence of the conspiracy. They also argued that there was no *mens rea* (the requirement of intention needed for a criminal conviction). This was also rejected because it was clear that the parties intended to do the very thing prohibited in the Act. Thus, they were convicted of the offence of bid rigging. Note that the results would be similar today under the current federal *Competition Act*. Bid rigging is just one of the prohibited conspiracies that businesses often are tempted to try in order to control the market and maintain prices.

- Giving one purchaser a lower rate

- False and misleading representations

- Double ticketing

When a supplier discriminates between purchasers by refusing to sell to one or by selling to another at a lower rate, giving a discount or rebate, or providing some other advantage not available to another purchaser, they have committed an illegal trade practice. Any false or misleading representation to promote a product or other business interest is specifically prohibited. The practice of double ticketing is also prohibited. This involves the merchant placing two price tags on an item and charging the higher price.

Telemarketers must disclose all pertinent information

Where telemarketing is involved, the telemarketer commits an offence when there is a failure to disclose the identity of the seller, the nature of the product or business being promoted, the price, and any other terms and restrictions applicable to the sale and delivery of the product. False and misleading representations are specifically prohibited, as is the use of any contest or game where obtaining the prize is dependent on prior payment, or proper disclosure of the value of the prize and the chances of winning have not been made. Where the sale of one product is tied to the sale or gift of another, there must be full disclosure of the fair market values of both and of any restrictions associated with the sale.

Multilevel schemes must also make full disclosure

There are also controls imposed with respect to multilevel marketing schemes. These are businesses where a person at a higher level will earn a given percentage income from the sales of someone at a lower level that they have brought into the organization. Thus, the person at the highest level earns a substantial income by taking a percentage from all persons making sales at a lower level than themselves. Any representation with respect to earnings must be fair and all relevant information affecting those earnings with respect to the actual sales and expected sales must be disclosed. They must also disclose whether the person offering the plan is a sole proprietor, a partner, or a corporation. Pyramid selling, where people pay a fee to participate in the multilevel organization which

28. (1982), 138 D.L.R. (3d) 690 (Ont. C.A.).

is not based on the sale of a product, is an offence with substantial fines and jail terms. Under the *Competition Act* (section 55.1) the fine is at the discretion of the court and up to five years' imprisonment. Under the *Criminal Code* (section 206(1)e) such schemes constitute a summary conviction offence.

Pyramid selling is prohibited

CASE SUMMARY 10.11

R. v. CLP Canmarket Lifestyle Products Corp.[29]

Pyramid Marketing Schemes Are Also Prohibited under the *Competition Act*

The defendant established a multilevel marketing scheme where new distributors, who had to pay a $30 registration fee to participate, were recruited by other distributors. The defendant company was charged under the *Combines Investigation Act* with creating an illegal pyramid scheme. (Note that the current federal *Competition Act* has a similar provision.) The accused argued that this covered the expense of a "career kit" needed to sell its products, but the court agreed with the prosecution that this amounted to a fee charged to participate, and it didn't matter what the fee was used for. Even though the amount could be legitimately justified, it still constituted a fee charged for participating and thus created an illegal pyramid. The problem with pyramid schemes is this: Where the sale of a product is not involved, the higher levels in such a scheme can simply skim funds from the lower levels, cheating them out of their money. Multilevel marketing schemes must be careful not to cross the line and become an illegal pyramid. The question does arise in this case whether we have gone too far and are simply interfering with an effective method of doing business.

A business also commits an offence when it manipulates the market through threats or inducements, tries to force the prices up by refusing to supply products to retailers who sell at low prices, or sells below a suggested retail price. A business can state a suggested retail price in their advertising but must make it clear that retailers are free to charge less. It is also an offence to manipulate the price by favouring one business over another through the control of credit, credit cards, patents, copyright, and trademarks.

Offences include manipulating the market through the control of the resell price or credit

The *Competition Act* also sets out a number of offences that are related to the enforcement of the Act. Conduct that amounts to obstruction with respect to an inquiry or examination under the Act, the failure to supply information when ordered, and the destruction or alteration of documents and records are serious offences. Employers are also prohibited from disciplining any employee who informs or otherwise assists in the process (whistle blowing). A criminal model is used to prosecute these offences. They are treated as either indictable or summary conviction offences and are prosecuted in the Federal Court or the regular provincial court system.

Offences include obstructing the investigation or enforcement process

Whistle blowers are also protected

29. Man. Q.B., 1989, as reported in *Lawyers Weekly Consolidated Digest,* Vol. 8.

TABLE 10.5 Offences against Competition

- Conspiracies
- Restricting supply, production, storage, and transportation
- Controlling through credit or credit cards
- Bid rigging
- Banks controlling interest rates and service charges
- Aggressive tactics with competitors
- Giving one customer, but not others, a better rate, discount, or advantage
- Suppliers controlling the resale price to consumers (retail)
- False and misleading representations
- Double ticketing
- Telemarketers not disclosing required information or misleading the consumer
- Multilevel schemes not disclosing required information
- Pyramid selling schemes
- Obstructing investigation or enforcement
- Retaliation against whistle blowers

Reviewable matters include:

- False and misleading representations

- Warranty or performance claims not supported by tests

- Unsupported tests and testimonials

- Bargain prices not supported by goods sold at regular prices

- Bait and switch tactics

DECEPTIVE MARKETING PRACTICES Table 10.6 provides a list of deceptive marketing practices. The following are designated as reviewable matters. They are not classified as offences in a criminal sense, but significant "Administrative Remedies," as they are called in the heading for section 74.09 of the *Competition Act*, are provided for prohibited conduct. These prohibitions against deceptive and misleading practices are designed to protect the consumer. Any false or misleading representation made to the public with respect to the promotion of a product is reviewable. Any claim with respect to life expectancy or performance that is not based on proper testing, and any misleading warranty promises that are not likely to be carried out constitute reviewable conduct. Testimonials or tests used to promote a product must only be used where such a test or testimonial has been published and permission has been given to use it. When goods are being sold at a "bargain" price and a regular price is referred to as the one normally offered by that particular retailer or others, they must be able to show that a reasonable volume of the product was sold at that higher price. The *Sears* case[30] discussed in Chapter 5 is a good example. The retail chain sold tires at "45% off" when, in fact, they sold only 2 percent of those tires at the regular price. It is reviewable conduct to advertise at a given price and charge a higher price upon delivery. The practice of **bait and switch** is also prohibited. This is where a product is advertised at one price, but not enough are supplied so that the customer can be persuaded to buy a higher priced alternative.

30. *Commissioner of Competition v. Sears Canada Inc.* Comp. Trib., No. CT-2002-004.

CASE SUMMARY 10.12

Mead Johnson Canada v. Ross Pediatrics[31]

An Injunction Granted for False and Misleading Advertising

In this case one baby food producer claimed in promotional material that a scientific breakthrough had been made, that their product was better than that produced by their rival, that it was similar to breast milk, and that it strengthened the baby's immune system. Mead Johnson asked the court for an interlocutory injunction to stop the distribution of this promotional material on the grounds that it was false and misleading and was prohibited under the *Competition Act*. The plaintiff also claimed that it constituted an injurious falsehood resulting in unlawful interference with the economic relations of the company. The court found that the claims made were clearly not supported by the guarded language used in the report relied on. The plaintiff had a good case involving a serious matter and the balance of convenience favoured the plaintiff. This meant that the plaintiff would suffer more harm if the injunction were not granted than the defendant would if it were. The court granted the interim injunction until the matter could be finally determined at trial. This case illustrates what constitutes false and misleading representations and also the effectiveness of the interlocutory injunction, under what circumstances it will be granted, and the devastating effect it can have on the activities of a business.

Where a contest or game is used to promote a product, there must be full disclosure of the number and value of the prizes as well as the chances of winning. There must be no undue delay in distributing the prizes and any winner must be chosen at random or on the basis of skill. You can't arrange it so a friend or family member will win the prize. Where products or other activities are promoted through prizes, games, or contests, the award of the prize can't be subject to a payment, not even to cover costs. Where there are attempts to manipulate the market using "deceit, falsehood, or other fraudulent means," such actions are indictable offences under the *Criminal Code* with a potential penalty of up to 10 years' imprisonment.

Full disclosure required for contests and winners must be chosen at random or on skill

TABLE 10.6 Deceptive Marketing Practices

- False and misleading representations
- Warranty or performance claims not supported by tests
- Unsupported tests and testimonials
- Bargain prices not supported by goods sold at regular prices
- Selling at a higher price than advertised
- Bait-and-switch selling
- Failure to disclose chances and value of prizes in a contest
- Failure to base contestants on skill or at random

31. (1996), 70 C.P.R. (3d) 417 (Ont. Gen. Div.).

MATTERS REVIEWABLE BY THE COMPETITION TRIBUNAL

These matters can also be treated in a non-criminal way with the questionable conduct being reviewed by the Competition Tribunal rather than identified as an offence. In each case the tribunal is given power to review the arrangement or transaction, to reverse it, or to do what is necessary to overcome the infringement of competition. For example, where the tribunal finds that a retailer can't get supplies from a particular supplier because of one of these factors, it can order the supplier to sell to that retailer on the same terms as other customers.

Controlling prices through consignment is reviewable by tribunal

A tactic sometimes used to control the selling price of an item is for a supplier to sell it to a retailer on consignment rather than through the normal retail process. This matter is reviewable by the tribunal. The tribunal can also intervene where a major supplier has **exclusive dealing** arrangements or some other **marketing restriction** with a particular retailer. Thus if Sony had such an arrangement with one particular chain of electronics stores to the detriment of other retailers the tribunal could order the practice to cease. Note that this doesn't prohibit all such arrangements; it just gives the tribunal the power to act on complaints that competition has been lessened to a serious extent. Another example is **tied selling**, where the sale of one product is tied to another so that a merchant can only acquire one product form a supplier if he or she takes both.

Schemes that tie the sale of products to others or restrict who can buy are reviewable by tribunal

Tribunal can review abuses of power such as:

- Squeezing of prices by a vertically integrated business

- Buying up a supplier's business or supplies to deny a competitor

- Changing specifications to defeat competitors

Merchants who abuse their dominant position in the market may have those practices reviewed. An example of such abuse is the practice of squeezing. This consists of a vertically integrated supplier with its associated customers increasing the price of the supplied goods to all customers with the effect of making the business of a competitor or customer less profitable. For the integrated business, the increased price reduces profits at the customer level, but this is balanced by an increase of profits at the supplier end. A similar unacceptable tactic relates to increasing freight charges when the supplier of transportation owns one of its customers. Another abuse happens where a large customer acquires a supplier in order to deny those supplies to a competitor. A similar abuse involves a business buying or otherwise tying up scarce supplies, facilities, or products to deny them to a competitor and thus driving up prices. A more unique prohibited practice is for the supplier to change specifications on their product to make products supplied by other competitors incompatible with them. Microsoft was accused of doing this with their Windows product, which resulted in an antitrust action against them. When faced with these anti-competitive acts, the tribunal can order the company to cease the offensive conduct and to make other orders designed to overcome the damage. These tribunal orders can include the imposition of significant monetary penalties as well as the requirement that the company divest its assets or sell its shares.

Tribunal can order changes and impose penalties

Predatory pricing also reviewable by tribunal

Sometimes one business will simply sell a product below cost at an unreasonably low price or at a price lower in one part of Canada than another with the object of driving their competition out of business. Or they will temporarily introduce a fighting brand for the same purpose. This is called predatory pricing and is reviewable by the tribunal.

The goal is to balance the loss of competition against increased efficiency

There is a growing trend today towards mergers and acquisitions. This can lead to less competition on the one hand but can also, through economies of scale, create a more efficient business. The *Competition Act* provisions attempt to balance these considerations. Where businesses of any size have merged through the acquisition of assets or the purchase of shares so that competition is lessened, the Competition Tribunal has the power to review the acquisition and order, among other things, the dissolution of the resulting corporation. A **vertical merger** is one where a supplier buys out a customer, or the reverse, often resulting in the supplier favouring the now integrated customer over others and in the process lessening competition. **Horizontal mergers** involve one company purchasing a competitor with the obvious reduction in competition. These types of mergers are most likely to be interfered with by the tribunal, whereas **conglomerate mergers** of companies in unrelated industries and not in competition are not likely be reviewed. It is important to remember that these mergers are only prohibited where competition is unduly reduced. Factors for consideration would be if the business were more efficient as a result and if there were other businesses that remained to compete. The tribunal would also ask whether the merger was in the public interest. Table 10.7 provides a summary of matters reviewable by the Competition Tribunal.

Tribunal can review mergers and acquisitions

Not all mergers that reduce competition are prohibited

CASE SUMMARY 10.13

Canada (Commissioner of Competition) v. Superior Propane Inc.[32]

Increased Efficiency Overrides Lessening of Competition

Two propane companies decided to merge, and the matter was brought before the Competition Tribunal by the Competition Commissioner. It was determined that the merger would significantly lessen competition in the field, but also that the merger would greatly increase efficiency; consequently, the merger was permitted to go ahead.

The greater efficiencies derived from the merger outweighed the significant reduction in competition. At first, the tribunal only considered production of propane and costs, but on the application of the commissioner, the Federal Court ordered the Competition Tribunal to look at social considerations as well. They reconsidered the matter, looked at all factors, and reached the same decision. Again, the case was appealed, but this time the Federal Court upheld the decision of the tribunal allowing the merger. The case illustrates how increased efficiency can be more important than reduced competition in allowing mergers. The case also dramatizes the role of the Competition Commissioner in relation to the Competition Tribunal. The commissioner acts like a prosecutor bringing matters before the tribunal for their determination, and then, if not satisfied, he or she can further appeal to the Federal Court.

32. (2003), 223 D.L.R. (4th) 55 (F.C.C.A.).

TABLE 10.7 Matters Reviewable by the Competition Tribunal

- Prices controlled through consignment selling
- Suppliers only selling goods to some retailers
- Selling of one product tied to the sale of another
- Abuses of power
    - Squeezing of competitors by integrated supplier
    - Buying a supplier or supplies to deny access to a competitor
    - Changing specifications to defeat a competitor
    - Selling products below cost to defeat a competitor
- Mergers and acquisitions that affect competition

NOTIFIABLE TRANSACTIONS

Permission must be obtained first for significant mergers

A separate part of the Act lists transactions where such acquisitions and mergers must first obtain permission from the Competition Tribunal. Where mergers are proposed involving large sums ($35 to $400 million depending on whether share value, gross revenue, or aggregate value of the corporation is being considered), the tribunal must first be notified of the proposed merger and permission must be obtained from the Competition Tribunal before it can proceed. That permission will be granted or withheld depending on several factors, including the degree of monopolization, the increase of efficiency that will result, the impact on competition generally, and any negative impact on the public interest.

ADMINISTRATION AND ENFORCEMENT

Competition Tribunal is like a court

Considerable power under the Act is given to the Competition Tribunal, but that tribunal is set up under another statute. The *Competition Tribunal Act*[33] sets up a tribunal consisting of six federal court judges, one of whom is designated as chairperson, and up to eight additional lay members. It authorizes the tribunal to hear matters assigned to it under various sections of the *Competition Act.* The tribunal is also designated as a court of record and is given the same powers as a superior court with respect to calling witnesses, producing and inspecting documents, and enforcing orders. An important function of the tribunal is to approve settlements in the form of consent orders negotiated by the Competition Commissioner. Some minor applications can be heard before just one of the judges, but normally there will be a panel of three to five members. Appeals go to the Federal Court of Appeal. Decisions of the Competition Tribunal can be accessed at its website: **http://www.ct-tc.gc.ca**.

The federal *Competition Act* provides for the appointment of a Commissioner of Competition and deputies, as required, who have the power to conduct inquiries in response to information about a contravention of the Act, a request from the minister, or a complaint made by at least six Canadian residents. The commissioner and deputies have the power to obtain a search warrant from an appropriate judge, to inspect premises to obtain information, data, and records (including computer records), and also to apply to a judge for an order that a

33. R.S.C. 1985, c. 19 (2nd Supp.).

person submit to a personal oral examination or submit reports or other documents. At any stage in the inquiry, the matter may be referred to the Attorney General for prosecution.

The role of the commissioner and his or her staff, known collectively as the Competition Bureau, is to administer and enforce the *Competition Act*[34] as well as the *Consumer Packaging and Labelling Act*[35], the *Precious Metals Marking Act*[36], and the *Textile Labelling Act*[37]. Much like a police force, they have extensive powers of investigation and prosecution. Powers of enforcement are exercised under the direction of the courts or the Competition Tribunal. The role of the Competition Tribunal is to investigate complaints and to review conduct that may or may not be restricting competition. The criminal prosecution model is used where the commission of a serious offence is involved.

Competition Bureau functions like police and prosecutor

The remedies that can be imposed include fines and penalties normally from $5000 to $200 000, depending on the offence. However, when an indictable offence is involved, fines can be up to $10 million. In some cases the fine is simply said to be "at the discretion of the court" (section 51.1 of the *Competition Act*). A jail term of up to two years (up to five years for some indictable offences) can also be imposed. Other potential remedies include orders that a company stop the offending conduct, divest its assets, sell its shares, or sell—or not sell—products to customers. In special circumstances the tribunal or judge can order that customs duties be reduced or removed, that the terms of an agreement or arrangement not be performed or be declared void, and that a patent, copyright, or trademark, etc. be revoked. An appropriate court can order an interim injunction to stop or prevent the commission of an offence at the request of the Attorney General of Canada or the provincial or territorial equivalent. Where anyone suffers damage because of an offence committed or due to a failure to obey a proper order under the Act, he or she may sue for damages and costs in an appropriate court. Like other similar legislation, it is also possible, except where serious offences are involved, for the offending party to negotiate arrangements and agreements that will avoid these processes and provide for a mutually acceptable alternative. The criminal prosecution model is used where serious offences such as bid rigging, conspiracy to fix prices, and other overt attempts to limit competition are involved. For the less serious or more questionable matters, referred to as reviewable conduct under the Act, the Competition Commissioner investigates and then applies for an order from the tribunal. The matter is usually resolved at this level by negotiating some sort of solution acceptable to both sides. There are also a few offences that may or may not be seriously misleading and deceptive where the commissioner has the choice of handling it himself or herself or handing it over to the Attorney General for prosecution. When a corporation is involved, the fines and penalties are generally higher. And there is specific provision where the directors and officers of the corporation that make the decisions can be directly charged for the offence. In most cases these are due diligence offences, and the corporation or officer charged can defend by showing that they took reasonable steps, including developing policies and training employees, to ensure compliance with the provisions of the Act.

Substantial fines and penalties can be imposed

Orders can be made to stop, correct, or remedy the offending conduct

Persons injured can sue to recover compensation

Other arrangements are usually available through negotiation

Reviewable conduct involves less serious matters

The company as well as directors can be liable, but usually due diligence is a defence

34. R.S.C. 1985, c. C-34.

35. R.S.C. 1985, c. C-38.

36. R.S.C. 1985, c. P-19.

37. R.S.C. 1985, c. T-10.

CASE SUMMARY 10.14

R. v. Multitech Warehouse Direct Inc.[38]

Due Diligence Defence Raised against Misleading Advertising Charge

Multitech placed an ad in the newspaper leading people to believe they would get a free vacation, including accommodation, if they purchased a particular product. A manager discovered the mistake and quickly corrected it in the next edition. Proper information and explanations of the promotion were available at every store. After a complaint by a competitor, Multitech was charged with misleading advertising. The court looked at the immediate correction—the availability of correct information—and concluded this was simply a mistake. There was no intention to mislead, and Multitech had done all it reasonably could to avoid any misdirection, including asking officials of the Department of Consumer and Corporate Affairs for advice with respect to the ads. It had exercised due diligence to avoid the problem and correct it when it arose, and so the charges were dismissed. This case shows how a charge of misleading advertising can be prosecuted in the courts and that the object is to pursue intentional wrongdoing, not a reasonable error where due diligence has been exercised by the parties.

In this chapter we have looked at the regulation of the environment and competition as it relates to business, but these are only two examples of many different areas of federal, provincial, and municipal regulation that create a regulatory environment of Canadian business that is both onerous and costly. These regulations may seem an unreasonable interference in the operation of business, but in most cases, some regulation is necessary to preserve our quality of life and to ensure that the abuses in which businesses often feel pressured to participate are controlled. Attempts are being made at all levels to rationalize the overlapping and repetitive regulatory regimes in place, but there is still a long way to go.

38. (1993), 330 A.P.R. 52 (N.S. Prov. Ct.).

QUESTIONS FOR REVIEW

1. Explain what is meant by the rule of law.
2. What should be examined to determine whether a decision-maker has acted within his or her authority?
3. When will a person have the right to a hearing under the *Charter of Rights and Freedoms*?

4. Explain what is meant by the rules of natural justice, and explain the requirements of procedural fairness.
5. Explain what must be included for the requirements of notice to be satisfied.
6. What must be included for a fair hearing to take place?
7. Explain what the rules of natural justice require with respect to the presentation and hearing of evidence.
8. Explain what is meant by a reasonable apprehension of bias and how that relates to the rules of natural justice.
9. Distinguish between an order of prohibition, *certiorari,* and *mandamus.*
10. What other remedies can a court use in reviewing the decision of an administrative tribunal?
11. What is a privitive clause, and what effect does that have on a court's power to review the decision of an administrative tribunal?
12. Explain why it may not be a good idea to challenge the decision of an administrative tribunal, even though clearly wrong.
13. Explain the nature of riparian rights and the disadvantages of relying on the common law to regulate and preserve the environment.
14. Why does federal legislation with respect to the environment become important for local projects?
15. Explain the role of the *Canadian Environmental Protection Act* and how its objectives are realized.
16. Explain the role of enforcement officers appointed under the *Canadian Environmental Protection Act* and how they can interact with business.
17. Distinguish between offences, ticket offences, and alternate measures. Explain what kind of penalties can be imposed in each case.
18. Explain the nature of the due diligence defence, and explain when it will or will not be available.
19. Who can be charged with an offence under the *Canadian Environmental Protection Act*?
20. Distinguish between screening and the comprehensive process of environmental assessment under the *Canadian Environmental Assessment Act.*
21. How can a business avoid liability risks with respect to pollution when purchasing property or advancing credit?
22. Explain the purpose of the federal *Competition Act.*
23. List and explain five offences against competition.
24. Explain what is meant by bid rigging, double ticketing, and predatory pricing.
25. Distinguish between multilevel marketing schemes and pyramid selling. Explain what controls are put on multilevel schemes.

26. List and explain five deceptive marketing practices, and explain how they are treated differently from offences against competition.
27. What kind of matters are reviewable by the Competition Tribunal? What is the purpose of such a review?
28. Indicate several ways that a business can abuse their power in the marketplace.
29. Explain how mergers and acquisitions are handled before the Competition Tribunal.
30. Distinguish between the role of the Competition Commissioner and the Competition Tribunal. Indicate the nature of penalties and other remedies that may be employed by them or the courts in enforcing the provisions of the *Competition Act.*

QUESTIONS FOR FURTHER DISCUSSION

1. Many government bodies, called administrative tribunals, have been created that make decisions affecting individuals and companies. Many of these take the place of courts or exclude courts from reviewing their decisions. Consider the advantages of such bodies, whether they have been given too much power, and whether enough safeguards are in place to prevent government abuse.
2. The basic requirement of natural justice is that whenever a decision is being made that affects someone, that person should have an opportunity to state his or her side and answer the case against him or her. Historically, a distinction was drawn between quasi-judicial decisions, where a hearing was required, and administrative decisions involving normal bureaucratic processes, where there was no such requirement. But this has broken down, extending the situations where fairness must be followed. Consider various circumstances from discipline in employment or membership in clubs and organizations to dealings with government officials or boards. Where should we draw the line? Do you think you ought to have the right to procedural fairness in all of these situations? What about application for membership in a social club? What would this requirement do to the general efficiency of government? How far should such a right be taken?
3. The purpose of the *Competition Act* is to restrict the activities of businesses so that free competition and an open market can be maintained. Mergers and other business practices that tend to lessen competition are controlled, as are business abuses that take advantage of consumers, such as bait-and-switch retail tactics and misleading advertising. Is the goal appropriate and reachable, or does it simply interfere with the free operation of the market rather than protect it? Would businesses be better off if they were freed from this great weight of regulatory control and allowed to simply exercise their commercial skills as their business interests dictate? Consider the different areas of control. What would you maintain? What would you change?
4. In most jurisdictions there is a movement to cut government red tape. This means to streamline the regulatory process, usually letting up on the regulation of various businesses and reducing the government bureaucracies currently in place to enforce them.

Environment is a prime example where in many jurisdictions the departments and enforcement arms have been gutted, often accompanied by the practice of making the industries self-regulating. Discuss the wisdom of such an approach. Consider the balance between control and policing these areas, compared to removing those controls in order to encourage industry and save tax dollars. Consider the wisdom of such self-regulation. Can it work? Are there any other approaches that could be used that would work better than the traditional regulation, investigation, and penalty model?

CASES
FOR DISCUSSION

1. **IDOWU V. YORK CONDOMINIUM CORP. NO. 128,** [2002] O.J. No. 2102 (Ont. S.C.J.).
Idowu was involved in a dispute with his condominium association. The bylaws required that such disputes be put to arbitration. The matter was put to the Condominium Dispute Resolution Centre and the assigned lawyer held a hearing and decided against Mr. Idowu. Later, Idowu found out that the Condominium Dispute Resolution Centre was owned and run by members of the same law firm of which the lawyer acting for the condominium association was a member. In fact, the lawyer that actually arbitrated the dispute wasn't a member of that law firm, but did have a mutually beneficial contract with the centre. Does he have a complaint in these circumstances, and if so, what is the nature of that complaint? What is the appropriate course of action?

2. **HANIS V. TEEVAN** (1998), 162 D.L.R. (4th) 414 (Ont. C.A.).
Hanis had been working for the university for a number of years as the director of their computer department when his employment was terminated. Allegedly, this was for using the university's computer equipment for his own use. In such cases, the university procedures required that the employee be given a warning, and in serious cases, that an interview be conducted. These procedures did not happen and Hanis was dismissed without being given an opportunity to defend himself or answer the charges against him. Explain the nature of his complaint, whether it should apply in these circumstances, and the likely outcome to his wrongful dismissal action.

3. **GILBERT V. ONTARIO PROVINCIAL POLICE FORCE (COMMISSIONER)** (2000), 193 D.L.R. (4th) 151 (Ont. C.A.).
Gilbert was a police officer charged criminally with sexual assault. The alleged assault took place seven years prior to the charges, due to the fact that the complainant claimed a loss of memory. When Gilbert obtained the right to access the records of the complainant's therapist with respect to the regaining of her memory, she refused to testify. The charges were dismissed. Still, Gilbert was charged with discreditable conduct under the *Police Act*. At the disciplinary hearing, even though the complainant continued to refuse to testify, the adjudicator allowed a transcript of her testimony at the preliminary hearing to be entered into the proceedings. Explain the nature of Officer Gilbert's complaint in these circumstances and his appropriate course of action as well as the likelihood of success.

4. **R. V. PETRO-CANADA** (2002), 222 D.L.R. (4th) 601 (Ont. C.A.).
Petro-Canada was charged with "discharging a containment into the environment," an offence under the Ontario *Environmental Protection Act*. In fact, a pipe had failed and leaked gasoline, but Petro-Canada responded quickly. It was also established that there were a number of safety systems and procedures in place. Petro-Canada claimed due diligence as a defence. Explain what must be established to succeed in a due diligence defence and on which side the onus of proof resides. How would it affect your deliberations to know they had used piping "not up to industry standards?"

5. **CANADIAN NATIONAL RAILWAY CO. V. ONTARIO (DIRECTOR, ENVIRONMENTAL PROTECTION ACT)** (1992), 87 D.L.R. (4th) 603 (Ont. C.A.).
The owners of certain lands located within the boundaries of a national harbour leased that land to a lessee that operated a creosote wood preserving operation. The lease was then assigned to the respondent, and the Ontario director under the *Environmental Protection Act* initiated procedures directed at requiring the owner and current lessee to clean up the land. Initially, they were ordered to develop a plan of compliance. Note that a national harbour falls under the jurisdiction of the federal government. Explain what arguments could be raised by both the owner of the land and the lessee with respect to this process.

6. **R. V. ROYAL LEPAGE REAL ESTATE SERVICES LTD.** (1993), 105 D.L.R. (4th) 556 (Alta. Q.B.).
In this case a group of real estate brokers came together and attempted to influence the price charged for their real estate services by keeping them higher. They discriminated against other real estate companies by refusing to provide services to them because of their low pricing policy. The *Competition Act* restricts private actions from influencing upward or discouraging the reduction of prices either by agreement, threat, or promise, "or any like means." The real estate brokers claimed this was too vague. They also claimed that the prohibition against them agreeing, promising, or threatening interfered with their freedom of expression as guaranteed under section 2(b) of the *Charter of Rights and Freedoms*. How do you think the court responded to these arguments?

7. **R. V. CLARKE TRANSPORT CANADA INC.** (1995), 130 D.L.R. (4th) 500 (Ont. Gen. Div.).
A group of five companies provided freight forwarding services through container shipments in the Toronto area. They would take orders from customers, charge on the basis of weight, fill a container with those orders, and transport the goods by rail. All five agreed to control prices. They exchanged information and promised not to undercut each other's prices. Explain how their conduct would be viewed under the *Competition Act*. What arguments might they raise in their defence?

The *Constitution Act, 1867* (formerly the *British North America Act*)

Sections 91 and 92
VI. Distribution of Legislative Powers

POWERS OF THE PARLIAMENT

Legislative authority of Parliament of Canada

91. It shall be lawful for the Queen, by and with the Advice and Consent of the Senate and House of Commons, to make Laws for the Peace, Order, and Good Government of Canada, in relation to all Matters not coming within the Classes of Subjects by this Act assigned exclusively to the Legislatures of the Provinces; and for greater Certainty, but not so as to restrict the Generality of the foregoing Terms of this Section, it is hereby declared that (notwithstanding anything in this Act) the exclusive Legislative Authority of the Parliament of Canada extends to all Matters coming within the Classes of Subjects next herein-after enumerated; that is to say,

1. (Repealed)

1A. The Public Debt and Property

2. The Regulation of Trade and Commerce

2A. Unemployment insurance

3. The raising of Money by any Mode or System of Taxation

4. The borrowing of Money on the Public Credit

5. Postal Service

6. The Census and Statistics

7. Militia, Military and Naval Service, and Defence

8. The fixing of and providing for the Salaries and Allowances of Civil and other Officers of the Government of Canada

9. Beacons, Buoys, Lighthouses, and Sable Island

10. Navigation and Shipping
11. Quarantine and the Establishment and Maintenance of Marine Hospitals
12. Sea Coast and Inland Fisheries
13. Ferries between a Province and any British or Foreign Country or between Two Provinces
14. Currency and Coinage
15. Banking, Incorporation of Banks, and the Issue of Paper Money
16. Savings Banks
17. Weights and Measures
18. Bills of Exchange and Promissory Notes
19. Interest
20. Legal Tender
21. Bankruptcy and Insolvency
22. Patents of Invention and Discovery
23. Copyrights
24. Indians, and Lands reserved for the Indians
25. Naturalization and Aliens
26. Marriage and Divorce
27. The Criminal Law, except the Constitution of Courts of Criminal Jurisdiction, but including the Procedure in Criminal Matters
28. The Establishment, Maintenance, and Management of Penitentiaries
29. Such Classes of Subjects as are expressly excepted in the Enumeration of the Classes of Subjects by this Act assigned exclusively to the Legislatures of the Provinces

And any Matter coming within any of the Classes of Subjects enumerated in this Section shall not be deemed to come within the Class of Matters of a local or private Nature comprised in the Enumeration of the Classes of Subjects by this Act assigned exclusively to the Legislatures of the Provinces.

EXCLUSIVE POWERS OF PROVINCIAL LEGISLATURES

92. In each Province, the Legislature may exclusively make Laws in relation to Matters coming within the Classes of Subject next herein-after enumerated; that is to say,

1. (Repealed)

Subjects of exclusive provincial legislation

2. Direct Taxation within the Province in order to the raising of a Revenue for Provincial Purposes
3. The borrowing of Money on the sole Credit of the Province

4. The Establishment and Tenure of Provincial Offices and the Appointment and Payment of Provincial Officers

5. The Management and Sale of the Public Lands belonging to the Province and of the Timber and Wood thereon

6. The Establishment, Maintenance, and Management of Public and Reformatory Prisons in and for the Province

7. The Establishment, Maintenance, and Management of Hospitals, Asylums, Charities, and Eleemosynary Institutions in and for the Province, other than Marine Hospitals

8. Municipal Institutions in the Province

9. Shop, Saloon, Tavern, Auctioneer, and other Licences in order to the raising of a Revenue for Provincial, Local, or Municipal Purposes

10. Local Works and Undertakings other than such as are of the following Classes:

    (a) Lines of Steam or other Ships, Railways, Canals, Telegraphs, and other Works and Undertakings connecting the Province with any other or others of the Provinces, or extending beyond the Limits of the Province;

    (b) Lines of Steam Ships between the Province and any British or Foreign Country;

    (c) Such Works as, although wholly situated within the Province, are before or after their Execution declared by the Parliament of Canada to be for the general Advantage of Canada or for the Advantage of Two or more of the Provinces.

11. The Incorporation of Companies with Provincial Objects

12. The Solemnization of Marriage in the Province

13. Property and Civil Rights in the Province

14. The Administration of Justice in the Province, including the Constitution, Maintenance, and Organization of Provincial Courts, both of Civil and of Criminal Jurisdiction, and including Procedure in Civil Matters in those Courts

15. The Imposition of Punishment by Fine, Penalty, or Imprisonment for enforcing any Law of the Province made in relation to any Matter coming within any of the Classes of Subjects enumerated in this Section

16. Generally all Matters of a merely local or private Nature in the Province

The *Constitution Act, 1982*

Charter of Rights and Freedoms
Schedule B
Constitution Act, 1982

Part I: Canadian Charter of Rights and Freedoms

Whereas Canada is founded upon principles that recognize the supremacy of God and the rule of law:

Rights and freedoms in Canada

GUARANTEE OF RIGHTS AND FREEDOMS

1. The *Canadian Charter of Rights and Freedoms* guarantees the rights and freedoms set out in it subject only to such reasonable limits prescribed by law as can be demonstrably justified in a free and democratic society.

Fundamental freedoms

FUNDAMENTAL FREEDOMS

2. Everyone has the following fundamental freedoms:
   (a) freedom of conscience and religion;
   (b) freedom of thought, belief, opinion and expression, including freedom of the press and other media of communications;
   (c) freedom of peaceful assembly; and
   (d) freedom of association.

DEMOCRATIC RIGHTS

3. Every citizen of Canada has the right to vote in an election of members of the House of Commons or of a legislative assembly and to be qualified for membership therein. **Democratic rights of citizens**

4. (1) No House of Commons and no legislative assembly shall continue for longer than five years from the date fixed for the return of the writs at a general election of its members. **Maximum duration of legislative bodies**

   (2) In time of real or apprehended war, invasion or insurrection, a House of Commons may be continued by Parliament and a legislative assembly may be continued by the legislature beyond five years if such continuation is not opposed by the votes of more than one-third of the members of the House of Commons or the legislative assembly, as the case may be. **Continuation in special circumstances**

5. There shall be a sitting of Parliament and of each legislature at least once every 12 months. **Annual sitting of legislative bodies**

MOBILITY RIGHTS

6. (1) Every citizen of Canada has the right to enter, remain in, and leave Canada. **Mobility of citizens**

   (2) Every citizen of Canada and every person who has the status of a permanent resident of Canada has the right **Rights to move and gain livelihood**

   (a) to move to and take up residence in any province; and

   (b) to pursue the gaining of a livelihood in any province.

   (3) The rights specified in subsection (2) are subject to **Limitation**

   (a) any laws or practices of general application in force in a province other than those that discriminate among persons primarily on the basis of province of present or previous residence; and

   (b) any laws providing for reasonable residency requirements as a qualification for the receipt of publicly provided social services.

   (4) Subsections (2) and (3) do not preclude any law, program, or activity that has as its object the amelioration in a province of conditions of individuals in that province who are socially or economically disadvantaged if the rate of employment in that province is below the rate of employment in Canada. **Affirmative action programs**

LEGAL RIGHTS

7. Everyone has the right to life, liberty, and security of the person and the right not to be deprived thereof except in accordance with the principles of fundamental justice. **Life, liberty, and security of person**

8. Everyone has the right to be secure against unreasonable search or seizure. **Search and seizure**

9. Everyone has the right not to be arbitrarily detained or imprisoned. **Detention or imprisonment**

Arrest or detention

10. Everyone has the right on arrest or detention
    (a) to be informed promptly of the reasons therefor;
    (b) to retain and instruct counsel without delay and to be informed of that right; and
    (c) to have the validity of the detention determined by way of *habeas corpus* and to be released if the detention is not lawful.

Proceedings in criminal and penal matters

11. Any person charged with an offence has the right
    (a) to be informed without unreasonable delay of the specific offence;
    (b) to be tried within a reasonable time;
    (c) not to be compelled to be a witness in proceedings against that person in respect of the offence;
    (d) to be presumed innocent until proven guilty according to law in a fair and public hearing by an independent and impartial tribunal;
    (e) not to be denied reasonable bail without just cause;
    (f) except in the case of an offence under military law tried before a military tribunal, to the benefit of trial by jury where the maximum punishment for the offence is imprisonment for five years or a more severe punishment;
    (g) not to be found guilty on account of any act or omission unless, at the time of the act or omission, it constituted an offence under Canadian or international law or was criminal according to the general principles or law recognized by the community of nations;
    (h) if finally acquitted of the offence, not to be tried for it again and, if finally found guilty and punished for the offence, not to be tried or punished for it again; and
    (i) if found guilty of the offence and if the punishment for the offence has been varied between the time of commission and the time of sentencing, to the benefit of the lesser punishment.

Treatment or punishment

12. Everyone has the right not to be subjected to any cruel and unusual treatment or punishment.

Self-incrimination

13. A witness who testifies in any proceedings has the right not to have any incriminating evidence so given used to incriminate that witness in any other proceedings, except in a prosecution for perjury or for the giving of contradictory evidence.

Interpreter

14. A party or witness in any proceedings who does not understand or speak the language in which the proceedings are conducted or who is deaf has the right to the assistance of an interpreter.

EQUALITY RIGHTS

Equality before and under law and equal protection and benefit of law

15. (1) Every individual is equal before and under the law and has the right to the equal protection and equal benefit of the law without discrimination and, in particular, without discrimination based on race, national, or ethnic origin, colour, religion, sex, age or mental or physical disability.

Affirmative action programs

(2) Subsection (1) does not preclude any law, program, or activity that has as its object the amelioration of conditions of disadvantaged individuals or

groups including those that are disadvantaged because of race, national, or ethnic origin, colour, religion, sex, age or mental or physical disability.

OFFICIAL LANGUAGES OF CANADA

Official languages of Canada

16. (1) English and French are the official languages of Canada and have equality of status and equal rights and privileges as to their use in all institutions of the Parliament and government of Canada.

Official languages of New Brunswick

(2) English and French are the official languages of New Brunswick and have equality of status and equal rights and privileges as to their use in all institutions of the legislature and government of New Brunswick.

Advancement of status and use

(3) Nothing in this Charter limits the authority of Parliament or a legislature to advance the equality of status or use of English and French.

English and French linguistic communities in New Brunswick

16.1 (1) The English linguistic community and the French linguistic community in New Brunswick have equality of status and equal rights and privilages, including the right to distinct educational institutions and such distinct cultural institutions as are necessary for the preservation and promotion of those communities.

Role of legislature and government in New Brunswick

(2) The role of the legislature and government of New Brunswick to preserve and promote the status, rights and privileges referred to in subsection (1) is affirmed.

Proceedings of Parliament

17. (1) Everyone has the right to use English or French in any debates and other proceedings of Parliament.

Proceedings of New Brunswick legislature

(2) Everyone has the right to use English and French in any debates and other proceedings of the legislature of New Brunswick.

Parliamentary statutes and records

18. (1) The statutes, records and journals of Parliament shall be printed and published in English and French and both language versions are equally authoritative.

New Brunswick statutes and records

(2) The statutes, records and journals of the legislature of New Brunswick shall be printed and published in English and French and both language versions are equally authoritative.

Proceedings in court established by Parliament

19. (1) Either English or French may be used by any person in, or in any pleading in or process issuing from, any court established by Parliament.

Proceedings in New Brunswick courts

(2) Either English or French may be used by any person in, or in any pleading in or process issuing from, any court in New Brunswick.

Communications by public with federal institutions

20. (1) Any member of the public in Canada has the right to communicate with, and to receive available services from, any head or central office of an institution of the Parliament or government of Canada in English or French, and has the same right with respect to any such institution where

(a) there is a significant demand for communications with and services from that office in such language; or

(b) due to the nature of the office, it is reasonable that communications with services from that office be available in both English and French.

Communications by public with New Brunswick institutions

(2) Any member of the public in New Brunswick has the right to communicate with, and to receive available services from, any office of an institution of the legislature or government of New Brunswick in English or French.

Continuation of existing constitutional provisions

21. Nothing in sections 16 to 20 abrogates or derogates from any right, privilege or obligation with respect to the English and French languages, or either of them, that exists or is continued by virtue of any other provision of the Constitution of Canada.

Rights and privileges preserved

22. Nothing in sections 16 to 20 abrogates or derogates from any legal or customary right or privilege acquired or enjoyed either before or after the coming into force of this Charter with respect to any language that is not French or English.

MINORITY LANGUAGE EDUCATIONAL RIGHTS

Language of instruction

23. (1) Citizens of Canada
   (a) whose first language learned and still understood is that of the English and French linguistic minority population of the province in which they reside, or
   (b) who have received their primary school instruction in Canada in English or French and reside in a province where the language in which they received that instruction is the language of the English or French linguistic minority population of the province, have the right to have their children receive primary and secondary school instruction in that language in that province.

Continuity of language instruction

(2) Citizens of Canada of whom any child has received or is receiving primary or secondary school instruction in English or French in Canada, have the right to have all their children receive primary and secondary school instruction in the same language.

Application where numbers warrant

(3) The right of citizens of Canada under subsections (1) and (2) to have their children receive primary and secondary school instruction in the language of the English or French linguistic minority population of a province
   (a) applies wherever in the province the number of children of citizens who have such a right is sufficient to warrant the provision to them out of public funds of minority language instruction; and
   (b) includes, where the number of those children so warrants, the right to have them receive that instruction in minority language educational facilities provided out of public funds.

ENFORCEMENT

Enforcement of guaranteed rights and freedoms

24. (1) Anyone whose right or freedoms, as guaranteed by this Charter, have been infringed or denied may apply to a court of competent jurisdiction to obtain such remedy as the court considers appropriate and just in the circumstances.

Exclusion of evidence bringing administration of justice into disrepute

(2) Where, in proceedings under subsection (1), a court concludes that evidence was obtained in a manner that infringed or denied any rights or

freedoms guaranteed by this Charter, the evidence shall be excluded if it is established that, having regard to all the circumstances, the admission of it in the proceedings would bring the administration of justice into disrepute.

GENERAL

25. The guarantee in this Charter of certain rights and freedoms shall not be construed so as to abrogate or derogate from any aboriginal, treaty or other rights and freedoms that pertain to the aboriginal peoples of Canada including **Aboriginal rights and freedoms not affected by *Charter***
    (a) any rights or freedoms that have been recognized by the Royal Proclamation of October 7, 1763; and
    (b) any rights or freedoms that may be acquired by the aboriginal peoples of Canada by way of land claims settlement.

26. The guarantee in this Charter of certain rights and freedoms shall not be construed as denying the existence of any other rights or freedoms that exist in Canada. **Other rights and freedoms not affected by *Charter***

27. This Charter shall be interpreted in a manner consistent with the preservation and enhancement of the multicultural heritage of Canadians. **Multicultural heritage**

28. Notwithstanding anything in this Charter, the rights and freedoms referred to in it are guaranteed equally to male and female persons. **Rights guaranteed equally to both sexes**

29. Nothing in this Charter abrogates or derogates from any rights or privileges guaranteed by or under the Constitution of Canada in respect of denominational, separate, or dissentient schools. **Rights respecting certain schools preserved**

30. A reference in this Charter to a province or to the legislative assembly or legislature of a province shall be deemed to include a reference to the Yukon Territory and Northwest Territories, or to the appropriate legislative authority thereof, as the case may be. **Applications to territories and territorial authorities**

31. Nothing in this Charter extends the legislative powers of any body or authority. **Legislative powers not extended**

APPLICATION OF CHARTER

32. (1) This Charter applies **Application of *Charter***
    (a) to the Parliament and government of Canada in respect of all matters within the authority of Parliament including all matters relating to the Yukon Territory and Northwest Territories; and
    (b) to the legislature and government of each province in respect of all matters within the authority of the legislature of each province.

    (2) Notwithstanding subsection (1), section 15 shall not have effect until three years after this section comes into force. **Exception**

33. (1) Parliament or the legislature of a province may expressly declare in an Act of Parliament or of the legislature, as the case may be, that the Act or a provision thereof shall operate notwithstanding a provision included in section 2 or sections 7 to 15 of this Charter. **Exception where express declaration**

Operation of exception

(2) An Act or a provision of an Act in respect of which a declaration made under this section is in effect shall have such operation as it would have but for the provision of this Charter referred to in the declaration.

Five-year limitation

(3) A declaration made under subsection (1) shall cease to have effect five years after it comes into force or on such earlier date as may be specified in the declaration.

Re-enactment

(4) Parliament or the legislature of a province may re-enact a declaration made under subsection (1).

Five-year limitation

(5) Subsection (3) applies in respect of a re-enactment made under subsection (4).

CITATION

Citation

34. This Part may be cited as the *Canadian Charter of Rights and Freedoms.*

. . .

Part VII: General

Primacy of Constitution of Canada

52. (1) The Constitution of Canada is the supreme law of Canada, and any law that is inconsistent with the provisions of the Constitution is, to the extent of the inconsistency, of no force or effect.

GLOSSARY

A

abatement a court order to reduce the rent to be paid to compensate for breach of lease by landlord

absolute liability offences where liability is imposed once the offence has been proven, regardless of care exercised by the accused.

absolute privilege exemption from liability for defamatory statements made in some settings (such as legislatures and courts), without reference to the speaker's motives or the truth of the statement

accounting court-ordered remedy where any profits made from wrongdoing must be paid over to victim. Also, where court orders agent to pay to the principal any money or property collected on behalf of that principal

actual authority authority given to agent expressly or by implication

actus reus the physical action that constitutes the offence. For example, taking money or striking another

administrative tribunal government decision-makers (committees, commissions, tribunals, or individuals) who act as judges or referees

adverse possession a right to actual possession can be acquired by non-contested use of the land over a long period of time

agency the service an agent performs on behalf of a principal

agreement of purchase and sale a contract between parties for the purchase of reall property.

anticipatory breach repudiation of contract before performance is due

Anton Piller order court order to seize offending material before trial

apparent authority conduct of principal suggests to third party that agent has authority to act on his behalf

appearance document filed by the defendant indicating that the action will be disputed.

appearance notice document issued by police officer requiring offender to appear before a judge.

arrest warrant document issued by judicial official authorizing police to arrest offender

articles of association sets out the procedures for governing a corporation in Nova Scotia and must be filed along with memorandum to incorporate

articles of incorporation the constitution of a corporation that must be filed as part of the process of incorporation in most jurisdictions in Canada

assault an action that makes a person think he or she is about to be struck

assignment in bankruptcy a voluntary transfer of assets to a trustee in bankruptcy

attachment under the *Personal Property Security Act* where value has been given pursuant to contract and the creditor now has a claim against assets used as security

B

bailee person acquiring possession of a chattel in a bailment

bailment when one person takes temporary possession of chattels owned by another

bailment for value where possession of a chattel is temporarily transferred to another with the exchange of some consideration

bailor the owner giving up possession of the chattel in a bailment

bait and switch where a product is advertised at a low price and the purchaser is persuaded to purchase a higher priced product when the lower priced one is not available

balance of convenience the test used by the court in an injunction application to determine which party will be most harmed by the issuance of the injunction

bankruptcy process by which an insolvent person voluntarily or involuntarily transfers assets to a trustee for distribution to creditors

bankruptcy offence punishable wrongdoing associated with bankruptcy such as withholding information or wrongfully transferring assets

battery actual physical contact

bills of exchange negotiable instrument where drawer directs the drawee to pay out money to a payee; drawee need not be a bank, and the instrument may be made payable in the future

bills of lading a receipt for goods in the care of the shipper

bonds a share interest in the indebtedness of a corporation

broadly-held a corporation that has many shareholders and is usually publicly traded on the stock market; also called a distributing corporation in some jurisdictions

broker agent retained by the insured to ascertain their insurance needs and secure the necessary coverage

building scheme restrictions placed on all the properties in a large development

business interruption insurance a form of insurance to protect the insured if business is interrupted

C

cause of action the legally recognized wrong that forms the basis for the right to sue

certification (1) a process whereby a bank commits to honour a cheque drawn on that institution, (2) government authorization of a union to bargain collectively with an employer

certiorari judicial order overturning the decision of a body or individual usually exercising statutory authority

charge or encumbrance an interest in property giving a creditor a prior claim to that property, often called a lien

chattel mortgages where title to a chattel is transferred to a creditor as security for a debt

check-off employees agree to have employer deduct union dues from payroll

cheques negotiable instruments; a special form of bill of exchange drawn on a bank, payable on demand

choses in action the thing or benefit that is transferred in an assignment; intangible personal property, such as a claim or the right to sue

CIF a contract term placing the responsibility for arranging and paying for the insurance and freight for goods being transported from seller to purchaser

Civil Code the legal system used in most of Europe based on a central code, which is a list of rules stated as broad principles of law that judges apply to the cases that come before them

closed shop only workers who are already members of the union can be hired

closely-held a corporation in which there are relatively few shareholders with restrictions on the transferability of their shares; referred to as "non-distributing corporations" in some jurisdictions

COD a contractual term where goods that are sold are paid for upon receipt

co-insurance an arrangement where the insured pays for only partial insurance coverage, and thus is only partially compensated for any loss that takes place

colourable legislation one level of government enacts legislation beyond its power by making it look like another class of legislation under section 91 or 92 of the *Constitution Act (1867)*

common law the legal system developed in Great Britain based on the practice of judges following precedent embodied in prior judicial decisions

common shares shares in a company to which no special rights or privileges attach

comprehensive environmental assessment process a required process subjecting a project to public input and research before receiving government approval to proceed

condition precedent conditions under which the contractual obligations will begin; also called "subject to" clauses

condition subsequent conditions under which the contractual obligations will end

conditional discharge a bankrupt is discharged but still required to pay a specified amount to creditors, as opposed to an absolute discharge where no such conditions are imposed.

conditional sales the seller provides credit to the purchaser, holding title until the goods are paid for

conditions major terms of a contract

condominium an arrangement for owning real property separated vertically, as with an apartment in a high rise development

condominium corporation a vehicle for operating a condominium development, to charge fees and administer common areas controlled by individual condominium owners

conglomerate mergers merger of companies not in direct competition

consent a defence to an assault charge; can be expressed or implied

consumer an individual purchasing goods or services not for resale or to be used in a business

consumer protection legislation designed to ensure that consumers are treated fairly in the marketplace

control test employment relationship determined by employer's power to give instructions to employee of how to do the job

conversion a tort where a person takes property belonging to another and uses it as his/her own (corresponds to theft in criminal law)

counterclaim a statement of claim by the defendant alleging that the plaintiff is responsible for the losses suffered and claiming for those losses

counteroffer a response to an offer that suggests different terms and causes the original offer to end

cross-examination the practice of one party putting questions to a witness produced by the other party to a litigation. Generally more latitude is allowed in such questioning.

cumulative rights the obligation to make up for unpaid dividends owed to preferred shareholders before paying any dividends to other shareholders

D

damages an amount of money that the court orders one party to pay the other in civil litigation paid by the defendant; damages usually compensate the injured party but may be punitive as well

debentures a share interest in the indebtedness of a corporation similar to bonds

declaratory judgment the power of the court to declare what the law is in any matter brought before it

deed of conveyance document transferring an interest in property

defamation a published false statement to a person's detriment

democratic rights rights set out in sections 3–5 of the *Charter of Rights and Freedoms* protecting rights to vote, hold elections, and run in those elections

deposit money prepaid with the provision that the funds are to be forfeited in the event of a breach

description where goods are purchased on the basis of a description set out in an advertisement or on packaged material

direct examination the practice of a party to litigation putting questions to a witness they have produced. Generally less latitude is allowed in such questioning compared to cross-examination

directors officers voted in by shareholders to control a corporation

discharge by agreement agreement by parties that a contract has ended

discharge by performance where a party is relieved of further obligations by properly performing their contractual obligations

discharge through frustration where an outside, unforeseen and interfering event renders further performance of a contract impractical

dissent the right of a shareholder in some jurisdictions to have their shares purchased where decisions are made that negatively affect their position

distinguishing cases the process judges use to decide which case is the binding precedent

distinguishing guise the unique shape of a product which can also be registered under the *Trade-marks Act*

distraint a landlord's right to seize the property of tenant for failure to pay rent

dividends payments to shareholders out of company profits

Division One proposal an alternative to bankruptcy under the *Bankruptcy and Insolvency Act* giving corporations and debtors with significant debt the right to make a proposal to creditors, which if accepted and performed, will avoid bankruptcy

Division Two proposal an alternative to bankruptcy under the *Bankruptcy and Insolvency Act* giving individual debtors involving lesser indebtedness the right to make a proposal to creditors which if accepted and performed will avoid bankruptcy

down payment an initial payment under a contract that must be returned to the purchaser in the event of a breach

due diligence doing everything reasonable to avoid the problem leading to legal liability

duress force or pressure to enter into a contract

duty of care an obligation to take steps to avoid foreseeable harm; an essential element for establishing liability in the tort of negligence

duty of good faith a fiduciary duty where an agent has a duty to act in the best interests of a principal

E

easement the right of a person other than the owner to use a portion of private property

employee a person working for another who is told what to do and how to do it

employment insurance a government-sponsored program designed to provide a limited number of payments to an individual after his or her employment has ended

Employment Standards Act legislation in place in most jurisdictions setting out a number of standards and obligations that employers must provide for their employees

encumbrance or charge an interest in property giving a creditor a prior claim to that property, often called a lien

endorsement the signature on the back of a cheque of the person assuming the obligation to pay if the drawee or maker defaults

equality rights are among the basic rights provisions in the *Canadian Charter of Rights and Freedoms*; include the right not to be discriminated against on the grounds of gender, age, religion, race, or colour, and the guarantee of equality before the law

equitable remedies remedies developed by the Courts of Chancery, including the right to an accounting, injunction and specific performance

equity legal principles developed in Courts of Chancery to relieve the harshness of the common law; value left in an asset after subtracting what the owner owes

equity of redemption mortgagor retains an interest in land even after default

exclusive dealing arrangements limiting products from a supplier to a particular customer often controlled under the *Competition Act*

executive branch part of government comprised of the Queen acting through the prime minister, cabinet, deputy ministers and government departments and officials; also known as the Crown

executory contracts when an agreement has been made, but before there has been any performance

F

fair comment defence available when defamatory statements are made about public figures or work put before the public

false imprisonment holding people against their will and without lawful authority

fidelity bond insurance against an employee's wrongful conduct

fiduciary duty a duty to act in the best interests of others such as partners, principals, and in some circumstances employers

fitness and quality a requirement of the *Sale of Goods Act* imposing an obligation on the seller to ensure a certain standard of fitness and quality on the goods they sell

FOB (Free on Board) a term designating the point that title and responsibility for goods sold transfers to the purchaser

foreclosure court process ending the mortgagor's right to redeem

forfeiture when lease is breached the landlord may terminate the lease and require the tenant to vacate the property

franchise arrangements based on contracts where a smaller party (usually a corporation) exclusively agrees to provide goods or services supplied by a larger corporation to consumers

fraud or deceit intentional misrepresentation where one party gains an advantage over another

frustration some outside, unforeseen event makes the performance of the contract impossible

fundamental freedoms the basic rights in the *Canadian Charter of Rights and Freedoms* including freedom of conscience and religion, of thought and belief, of opinion and expression, and of assembly and association

G

good title an obligation on the seller under the *Sale of Goods Act* to convey ownership in the goods being sold.

goods tangible, movable personal property that can be measured and weighed; also known as chattels

guarantee a written commitment whereby a guarantor agrees to pay a debt if the debtor doesn't

H

holdback person owing funds under a construction contract must retain a specified percentage to be paid at a later time

holder in due course an innocent third party entitled to collect on a negotiable instrument in spite of any claims of the original parties

horizontal mergers one competitor buys out another

human rights legislation provincial and federal statutes designed to protect people from racism, sexism, and similar wrongs committed by others

hybrid offences criminal offences where the prosecutor has the choice to treat them as indictable offences or summary conviction offences

I

independent contractor a person working for himself who contracts to provide specific services to another

indictable offence serious criminal offence with a more involved procedure and more serious penalties

inducing breach of contract encouraging someone to break his or her contract with another

information document sworn before justice or other judicial official by police or complainant setting out the nature of the alleged wrongdoing

injunction court order to stop offending conduct

injurious falsehood or product defamation defamation with respect to another's product or business; also known as *product defamation* and *trade slander*

innuendo an implied statement that is detrimental to another

Insolvency and Bankruptcy Act federal legislation creating bankruptcy process and alternatives to it

insolvent where a person is unable to pay his or her debts as they become due

insurable interest a real and substantial interest in specific property

insurance agents the agents for insurance companies who sell policies to customers

insurance policies contracts with insurers to provide compensation for covered losses

intellectual property personal property in the form of ideas and creative work

interest dispute disagreement about the terms to be included in a new collective agreement

invitations to treat invitations (often advertisement) to engage in the bargaining process leading to a contract

involuntary bailment where someone acquires possession of the property of another unintentionally as where it is left on their property or is found

J

joint tenancy shared ownership with right of survivorship

joint ventures two or more corporations joining together to accomplish a major project

judgment creditor the winner of an award of damages in a civil action

judgment debtor the loser in a civil action who has been ordered to pay an award of damages

judicial branch part of government comprised of courts and officers of the court

judicial sale court ordered and supervised sale of real property, usually resulting from default

jurisdictional dispute a disagreement over who has authority; in the labour context, a dispute between two unions over which one should represent a group of employees, or over which union members ought to do a particular job

just cause valid reason to dismiss an employee without notice

justification defence to a defamation action based on the truth or the substantial truth of the offending statement.

L

land registry a system requiring all documents affecting the title of real property be kept in a land registry office available for the inspection of interested parties

land titles system registration system that guarantees title to real property

legal rights among the basic rights provisions in the *Canadian Charter of Rights and Freedoms* (sections 7–14); includes rights such as the right to life, liberty, and security of the person and security against unreasonable search and seizure and arbitrary imprisonment and detention

legislative branch part of government comprised of Parliament and legislatures

letters patent method of incorporating granted by government when company is set up in some jurisdictions in Canada

liability insurance provides coverage for wrongs committed by self or employees

libel the written form of a defamatory statement

licence a non-exclusive right to use property; permission to use another's land that can be revoked

life estate an interest in land ending at death

life insurance coverage providing compensation upon the death of the insured party

liquidated damages a contractual provision requiring party responsible for a breach to pay a stated amount

lockout employer prevents employees from working

long-arm statutes where a jurisdiction has passed legislation giving them the right to take action against offending conduct taking place outside of that state or province

M

mandamus a judicial order requiring a body or individual exercising statutory authority to make a decision

manufacturer's warranty a term of the sales contract limiting a seller's or manufacturer's obligations with respect to a product beyond what they would otherwise be under the *Sale of Goods Act*

marketing restriction where a supplier tries to place controls or other limitations on the retailers it supplies, usually to maintain price control or market share

memorandum of association constitution of a corporation in a registration jurisdiction which is filed as part of the incorporation process

mens rea the mental element of a crime; the intention to do the evil act

minority language education rights the right to have English or French, as the case may be, taught in the schools or made available to speakers of those languages set out in the *Charter of Rights and Freedoms*

mistake a misunderstanding about the nature or subject matter of an agreement that destroys consensus

misunderstandings when two parties to a contract have a different understanding as to the meaning of a specific provision.

mitigation victims of a breach must make an effort to lessen the loss

mobility rights the right of all citizens of Canada to reside in or work in all parts of Canada as guaranteed by section 6 of the *Charter of Rights and Freedoms*

moral rights author's right to prohibit the copyright owner from changing or degrading the original work

mortgage means of securing loans; title of property is held by the money-lender as security in some jurisdictions; in other jurisdictions, a mortgage is simply a charge against title

mortgagee the creditor who takes the title to the property as security

mortgagor the debtor who grants the mortgage on his property as security for a loan

N

negotiable instruments substitutes for money or instruments of credit that bestow unique benefits; vehicles for conveniently transferring funds or advancing credit

no par value shares shares created in the incorporation process that have no advanced value set for the share; value is determined by market

notice where one party is required to indicate to the other that they are exercising an option that will affect them, as where a tenant gives a landlord notice to terminate, where a defendant is given notice of a hearing, or a union gives an employer notice of a strike

novation when a new contract is created by substituting a new party for one of the original parties to the original contract

O

offer a tentative promise to do something if another party fulfils what the first party requests

offer and acceptance the process by which consensus is reached creating a contract between parties

offer to settle where one of the parties to civil litigation makes an offer to settle the matter before trial; if accepted this forms a binding contract between the parties and ends any right to litigation

one-sided mistake where only one of the parties makes a mistake with respect to the nature or effect of a contract; without misrepresentation, the contract will normally continue to be binding

oppression action against the directors who have offended the rights of creditors or minority shareholders

option to purchase a subsidiary contract where some additional consideration is given to hold an offer open for later acceptance

organization test determines whether employment exists on the basis of the extent of a person's involvement in the employer's organization

P

par value a share given a stated value at the time of issuance (most shares are now no-par-value)

paramountcy when a matter is covered by both federal and provincial legislation and there is a conflict, the federal legislation takes precedence

parliamentary supremacy the primary law-making body is Parliament or the provincial legislatures in their respective jurisdictions, and statutes take priority over the common law

passing-off a tort action available to prevent someone from misleading the public into thinking it is dealing with some other business or product when it is not

past consideration some benefit conveyed before an agreement is made; it is not valid consideration

payment into court the defendant estimates the true value of the claim and deposits it with the court; if the decision is for less than the deposit the plaintiff will be penalized through payment of additional costs

perfection registering a security or taking possession of the collateral used to secure a debt under the *Personal Property Security Act*

performance of the obligations when each party has completed its obligations under the terms of a contract

periodic leases automatically renewing tenancy; usually monthly with no specific termination date

personal property also known as personalty, chattels (tangible, movable things), and intangible rights called *choses in action*

picketing job action during a legal strike when employees circulate at the periphery of the jobsite to persuade people not to deal with that employer

plaintiff the party who initiates a civil action

plea-bargaining the process whereby the accused and prosecutor negotiate, usually resulting in a lesser charge being imposed in exchange for a guilty plea avoiding a trial

pleadings the exchange of documents (statement of claim, statement of defence, counterclaim) between plaintiff and defendant at the early stage of a civil action

post box rule the rule that an acceptance is effective when posted when that method of response is appropriate

power of attorney written authority by a principal giving an agent power to act on his behalf

power of sale a normal term in a mortgage agreement giving the creditor/mortgagee the power to have the property sold in the event of a default

precedent a prior decision made by a court of higher jurisdiction that a lower court must follow in our common law system.

preemptive rights a right given to a shareholder ensuring that in the event of a new offering of shares that shareholder will be given first refusal on enough of those shares to maintain his portion of control of the corporation

preferred creditors creditors that are secured so that they have a priority with respect to their claims against the debtor

preferred shares special shares structured to give the preferred shareholder a claim to a specified dividend each year. Normally they cannot vote unless that dividend is not paid.

premium an amount paid by the insured to secure insurance coverage

prescription a right to access property acquired by non-contested use of the land over a long period of time

presumption a condition or set of facts assumed to be true in the absence of any evidence to the contrary

principles of fundamental justice principles set by tradition and convention that protect the right to a fair hearing such as the requirement of notice and the right to have a decision made free of bias

private law the rules that govern our personal, social, and business relations, which are enforced by one person suing another in a private or civil action

private nuisance a tort action protecting against the use of property in such a way that it interferes with a neighbour's enjoyment of theirs

privative clause terms in a statute that attempt to restrict the right of judicial review

privity of contract contract terms apply only to the actual parties to the contract

procedural law determines how the substantive laws will be enforced; the rules governing arrest and criminal investigation, pre-trial and court processes in both criminal and civil cases are examples; law can also be distinguished by its public or private function

product defamation false statement with respect to another's product or business; also known as *injurious falsehood* and *trade slander*

professional liability a person who puts himself forward as an expert must live up to the standard expected of a reasonable expert

profit à prendre contracts to take resources off the land

prohibition an order that the decision-maker not proceed with a hearing or a decision

promissory estoppel when a gratuitous promise to do something in the future causes a person to incur an expense, the promissor may be prevented from acting in a way inconsistent with that promise; also known as *equitable estoppel*

promissory notes a type of negotiable instrument where a maker promises to pay the amount stated on the instrument to a payee

proposed trademark the *Trade-marks Act* permits an application to register a trademark that has not been used yet but will be in the future

proxy where one shareholder gives authority to someone else to vote that share on their behalf

published the communication of a defamatory statement to someone other than the plaintiff

punitive damages a monetary payment in excess of compensation for the plaintiff's actual or estimated losses intended to punish the wrongdoer for outrageous or extreme behaviour; also known as *exemplary damages*

Q

qualified privilege exemption from liability for defamatory statements made pursuant to a duty or special interest, so long as the statement was made honestly, without malice, and circulated only to those having a right to know

quantum meruit (as much as is deserved) reasonable price paid for requested services where there is no actual contractual obligation; sometimes called a *quasi-contract*

quasi-criminal offences offences under provincial legislation or federal regulatory statutes that impose penalties but do not qualify as criminal law

quiet enjoyment landlord must ensure that nothing interferes with tenant's normal use of the property

quiet possession goods must be usable by the purchaser in the way normally intended

R

Rand Formula option in collective agreement enabling employees to retain the right not to join the union, but they are still required to pay union dues

ratification majority agrees with terms of collective bargain; principal confirms a contract entered into by his agent

real property land, buildings, and fixtures attached to land or buildings

reasonable foreseeability test what a prudent and careful person would be expected to anticipate in the same circumstances as the defendant

reasonable notice the amount of notice that must be given in terminating an employment contract, taking into consideration the position of the employee and time served

reasonable person test the standard of conduct that would be expected of a careful and prudent person in the same circumstances as the defendant in a negligence action; standard to determine the existence of apparent authority

reasonable time when an offer would be expected to end if there is no acceptance considering the nature of the goods and other circumstances of the transaction

receiver a person or organization appointed to take over the management of a corporation defaulting on its obligations to a creditor

receivership proceeding in which a receiver is appointed for a corporation or partnership which has defaulted on its obligations to a creditor in order to protect its assets for the creditors

receiving order court ordering the transfer of debtor's assets to a trustee as part of the bankruptcy process

recognition dispute dispute arising between unions and employers while union is being organized

rectify court corrects the written wording of a shared mistake in the contract

registration a legislated requirement for incorporating a company in some jurisdictions in Canada; also the process of filing a form in order to perfect a security under the *Personal Property Security Act*

regulations supplementary rules passed under the authority of a statute and having the status of law

reinsurance where an insurance company takes out insurance with another company to cover the risk they face if they are called upon to pay out on the insurance coverage they have issued.

relief against forfeiture when a landlord retakes a property for failure to pay rent prior to the end of the lease term, the tenant can pay the arrears and apply in the court to have the lease reinstated

remainder third party with the right to the title of real property (fee simple) after the death of a life tenant

remote determining whether the damages were too far removed from the original negligent act; in contract, a breaching party is only responsible for reasonably expected losses

representative action the right of shareholders to sue the directors on behalf of an injured corporation; sometimes called a *derivative action*

repudiation one party indicates to the other that they will not perform their contractual obligations (expression can be expressed or implied)

rescission returning the parties to the position they were in before the contract

restrictive covenant seller imposes restrictions on what the purchaser can use the land for; in employment law, it is a commitment not to work in a certain industry or geographical area for a designated period of time

reverse onus a legislated term requiring an offender to prove that they did not engage in the offending conduct (as opposed to the normal requirement where the prosecution must prove the accused did it)

reversion upon death of life tenant, the title to real property reverts to original owner

revocation withdrawal of an offer before acceptance (must be communicated to the offeree)

rider a term added to a standard form insurance contract usually arranging for extra or specialized coverage

right of way type of easement that allows the crossing of another's land

rights dispute disagreement about the meaning of a term or the enforcement of a collective agreement

rule of law the requirement that everyone in Canada is subject to the law and must obey it; government officials must be able to point to some law authorizing them to make the decision they have made affecting the rights of others

run with the land obligations with respect to land can bind future owners even though they are not one of the original parties to the agreement.

S

Sale of Goods Act provincial statute controlling the sale of personal property in the form of chattels imposing certain rights and obligations on the seller and purchaser

salvage that portion of goods or property which has been saved or remains after a casualty such as fire or other loss

sample a chattel used to indicate to a purchaser the nature of similar goods usually to be delivered in the future; those goods must match the sample

screening process a process to ensure that proper steps have been taken to ensure that environmental impact is minimized on minor projects under the *Canadian Environmental Assessment Act*

seal formal mark on a document (usually an impression or wafer in contract law), which eliminates the need for consideration

secured creditors creditors who have taken steps to ensure that they will be paid, usually by acquiring first claim to some property that ensures payment over other creditors

secured transactions collateral right to debt giving the creditor the right to take back the goods or intercept the debt owing used as security in the event of a default

self-defence a person can respond to an assault with as much force as is reasonable in the circumstances

shared mistake both parties make the same mistake, sometimes called *common mistake*

slander spoken defamation

specific performance court orders a breaching party to live up to the terms of the agreement

specific time an unaccepted offer will end at the occurrence of a time specified by the offeror

standard of care the test used to determine whether a person has exercised sufficient care in dealings with others to avoid being liable for the tort of negligence. The degree of care required is usually that of a reasonable person in the circumstances

stare decisis a principle by which judges are required to follow the decision made in a similar case in a higher court

statement of claim the document setting out the nature of the complaint and alleged facts, which form the basis of the action served on the defendant at the beginning of the litigation process

statement of defence response to a statement of claim by the defendant setting out the alleged facts by the plaintiff and the contrary facts alleged by the defendant

Statute of Frauds Old English statute, a version of which is in place in most common law jurisdictions setting out the types of agreements that must be in writing to be enforceable

statutory assignment an assignment of contractual rights and benefits that meets certain specified qualifications; assignee can enforce a claim directly without involving the assignor

stoppage in transitu seller retains the right to stop the shipment in event of default

strata corporation a vehicle for operating a strata title development, to charge fees and administer common areas controlled by individual strata owners (usually takes the form of condominium developments)

strict liability offences regulatory offences at the provincial or federal level where the accused can be found liable even though no fault is demonstrated

strike unionized employees withdrawing their services from the employer

subrogated the right of insurer, upon payment, to take over the rights of the insured in relation to whoever caused the injury

substantial performance the parties have performed all but a minor aspect of the contract

substantive law establishes both the rights individuals have in society and also the limits on their conduct

summary conviction offences minor criminal offences involving a simplified procedure with less significant penalties imposed as compared to indictable offences

summons to appear a document served on a person accused of a criminal offence requiring them to appear before a judge at a specific time and place

surety bond a commitment by a third party, such as an insurance company, to pay compensation if the company or individual on whose behalf the bond is issued fails to properly perform their contractual obligations

T

tender of performance one of parties attempts to perform their contractual obligations, and where they are prevented by the other party, they are considered to have properly performed

tied selling the practice of a supplier of products providing a product to a merchant only if he takes another along with it, a practice prohibited under the *Competition Act*

trespass to chattels direct intentional interference causing damage to the goods of another

trespass to land entering upon another's land without permission or authority

trustee in bankruptcy licensed professionals who, for a fee, assist the debtor and creditors in the bankruptcy process, holding and otherwise dealing with that bankrupt's property for the benefit of the creditors

U

unconscionability when one of the parties to a transaction is under extreme disadvantage; merchants take advantage of disadvantaged customers

undue influence a special relationship that induces a person to enter a contract to his disadvantage

unenforceable a binding contract or other obligation that the courts will not enforce, such as a contract that does not satisfy the *Statute of Frauds*

unfair labour practices practices by management or by employees in the collective bargaining process that are prohibited, such as intimidation or firing employees for their union activity

unilateral one-sided contract where only one party makes a mistake with respect to the terms or nature of a contract; also the term used to describe a contract that is accepted by performance of the act required as consideration

union shop new employees must join the union

unsecured creditors (or *general creditors*); there is only a contract requiring a debt to be repaid, but no collateral contract giving that creditor priority with respect to some property in the event of default

V

vacant possession owner has obligation to provide premises that are empty and ready for occupancy

vertical merger merger of a supplier and a retailer

vicarious liability employer is liable for the injuries caused by employees during the course of their employment

void not a legally binding agreement because an essential ingredient is missing; there is no contract

voidable there is a contract but one of the parties has the option to end it

voluntary bailment for the benefit of the bailee an individual (the bailee) borrows another's property for their own use without giving consideration

voluntary bailment for the benefit of the bailor an individual (the bailee) voluntarily looks after another's goods

W

warranties minor terms of a contract

workers' compensation a government system set up to provide monetary compensation for someone who becomes sick or injured because of their employment

World Intellectual Property Organization (WIPO) an international organization set up to arbitrate disputes over the use of domain names on the internet

writ of prohibition a court order that a decision-making process, such as a hearing by a board or other statutory body, cannot proceed

writ of summons the written order endorsed by the court by which civil actions are commenced in many jurisdictions

TABLE OF STATUTES

Note: The page numbers given in parentheses at the end of each entry refer to pages in this book.

TABLE OF CASES

Note: The page numbers given in parentheses at the end of each entry refer to pages in this book. Numbered companies are alphabetized under the first number: e.g., 880682 Alberta Ltd. appears under "Eight."

INDEX

Key terms and the pages on which they are defined appear in ***boldface.***